Heaven's Messages for The Family

Volume I

How to become the family God wants you to be.

by Janie Garza

Published by St. Dominic Media
Herndon, Virginia

DECLARATIONS

Since the abolitions of Canons 1399 and 2318 of the former Code of Canon Law by Pope Paul VI in AAS 58 (1966), p. 1186, publications about new apparitions, revelations, prophecies, miracles, etc., have been allowed to be distributed and read by the faithful without the express permission of the Church, providing that they contain nothing that contravenes faith and morals. This means no imprimatur is necessary. However, it is welcome!

In Chapter II, No. 12 of the Second Vatican Council's *Lumen Gentium*, we read

"The Holy Spirit... distributes special gifts among the faithful of every rank... Such gifts of grace, whether they are of special enlightenment or whether they are spread more simply and generally, must be accepted with gratefulness and consolation, as they are specially suited to, and useful for, the needs of the Church... Judgment as to their genuineness and their correct use lies with those who lead the Church and those whose special task is not indeed to extinguish the spirit but to examine everything and keep that which is good." (confer 1 Thess. 5: 19-21)

"That private revelations occur in all times is evident as appears from the testimony of the Sacred Scripture and tradition. To stamp these testimonies as untruths gives scandal and bears witness to impiety."

              Cardinal Bona

Published by ST. DOMINIC MEDIA
P.O. Box 345, Herndon, Virginia 20172-0345

Phone 703-327-2277 / Fax 703-327-2888

www.sign.org

Copyrighted © 1998 Signs of the Times Apostolate, Inc.

ALL RIGHTS RESERVED
No portion of this book may be transmitted or copied, by any means whatsoever, without the written approval of the publisher.

Library of Congress Catalog Card Number: 98-85939
ISBN: 1-892165-04-X

Cover design by Tina B. Isom

ACKNOWLEDGMENTS

No words in my heart could ever express my deep gratitude to my dear Spiritual Director, Fr. Henry Bordeaux, O.C.D., who encouraged me and gave me hope when my spirit lagged and whose prayers and sufferings gave me strength, and to Kathie Caspary, whose tireless dedication and perseverance brought to completion this book. I would also like to thank my past Spiritual Directors who helped me and guided me in a loving way, and my Parish Pastor, Rev. Msgr. Lonnie Reyes who said 'yes' to Our Lady. Thanks also to his staff, especially Flo Tenorio and Guadalupe Martinez.

I extend my gratitude to the prayer group of Our Mother of Compassion and Love for all their love, prayers and support. I wish I could name each one of you, but God knows who you are. I love you all. My special thanks goes to L.L. (thank you also for all your help on the book), J.B., M.W. and Dana Peaks. I am deeply grateful for your love, dedication and perseverance. Thanks also to Kathie Caspary and Kathy Bue for their hard work on the mailing list, to Linda Broz and Maria Dawson who head up our prayer line, and to Tonie Gil, T.B., J.A., M.D., C.P., Nellie Tellez and others for their hard work at special events. My thanks to Henry Montalvo and Ann Lassiter for videotaping important events.

I would like to thank Glenn Galbraith for being my dear spiritual brother, and Lillian Timma for her sweet friendship. My special thanks to P.L., B.B., Glenn and Kathie Caspary, H. and M. G., G. and M. D., Enereo(deceased) and Cruz Aguilera, Mr. and Mrs. Vogel and Mr. Don Ralph, for their love and their unique contributions. Special thanks also to Donna (Sam) Proctor, Kathie Caspary, and Laly Cardenas for traveling with me to minister to God's people. I would like to thank Mrs. Juanita Farren for the beautiful painting of Our Mother of Compassion and Love, and Mrs. Ann Urban for the beautiful chalk of St. Joseph.

Most of all, I extend my deepest gratitude to My Lord and Savior for His immense love, and to my Dear Blessed Mother who came from Heaven to love me and my family. To my beloved St. Joseph, I thank you for your love, guidance and strength, and to the Three Archangels, St. Michael, St. Gabriel and St. Raphael, I love and honor you.

Janie Garza (left) of Austin, Texas shown with Vicka, the visionary from Medjugorje

DEDICATION

This book is dedicated
to the Holy Family,
who during these past nine years
have helped me to love and embrace my family,
to our beloved Pope, John Paul II,
to the Holy Trinity,
to my husband Marcelino,
my sons, Jesse, Mitchell, Armando and
Marcelino Jr.,
and to my precious grandchildren,
Robert, Marissa, Veronica,
Jessica, Maria, Monica, Jesse Jr.
and Alex.

Table of Contents

Preface by Robert L. Fastiggi, Ph.D......................................VI
Introduction by Rev. Henry Bordeaux, O.C.D......................X
Addition to the Introduction by Rev. Henry Bordeaux, O.C.D....... XII
Expanded Autobiography of Janie Garza.......................XIII

VOLUME I –
Our Lady and Our Lord's Messages

Chapter One: Mary and the Rosary, *1989*............................3
Chapter Two: Lessons on prayer of the heart, *1990*...................13
Chapter Three: Lessons on conversion, *1991*.......................35
Chapter Four: Abandoning everything to Jesus and Mary, *1992*........47
Chapter Five: Your role in God's plan, *1993*.........................71
Chapter Six: Purity and holiness of heart, *1994*....................125
Chapter Seven: Become Eucharistic, *1995* 199
Chapter Eight: The Holy Spirit and Divine Union, *1996*..............373
Chapter Nine: Trust, and the Safe Refuge of the Two Hearts, *1997*....411

Appendix

A Compilation of beautiful prayers:............................435
Letter from Vicka:..445
In Memoriam: The loss of a dear prayer group member.............446
Additional Information:..447

PREFACE

"The future of humanity passes by way of the family." These words of Pope John Paul II, given in his 1981 Apostolic Exhortation on The Role of the Christian Family in the Modern World (Familiaris consortio), provide a fitting context for this book of beautiful messages given to Janie Garza between the years of 1989 and 1998.

We all know that the family in under attack by the forces of evil. The rise in divorce, spousal violence and child abuse - all point to a situation which makes supernatural intervention both appropriate and credible. It also seems providential that a book like this should be published in 1994 (the first edition), the International Year of the Family. His Holiness, Pope John Paul II, has highlighted the importance of the family in the recent beatification of Elizabeth Canori Mora and Gianna Beretta Molla - two devout women who, like Janie Garza, pursued holiness as wives and mothers, even in the midst of much pain and struggle.

"Blessed are the pure in heart, for they will see God (Matthew 5:8)." This Scripture seems to be the guiding light of these messages. Mary, speaking under the title of **Mother of Compassion and Love**, tells Janie: *"Be loving, be prayerful, be obedient. Pray for purity of heart, for when you pray with a pure heart, God answers your prayers. He loves purity* (August 15, 1992)." Prayer and purity of heart emerge as two of the most important themes in these messages along with a special emphasis on the need for family prayer as the remedy for the problems which exist in all too many households. By praying together family members draw closer to each other and to God. Praying the Rosary is especially recommended since it provides a powerful protection against the assaults of Satan who is intent on destroying as many families as he can. All this confirms the teachings of the recent Popes who have recommended the family Rosary "with particular solicitude and insistence (Familiaris consortio, 61)."

While it is not my role to provide official ecclesiastical approval of the supernatural character of these messages, I think it is fair to say that they present a series of exhortations and recommendations which are in perfect harmony with the Scriptures and the Catholic faith.

The themes that are repeatedly stressed - **prayer, purity of heart, conversion, fasting, compassion, forgiveness, mercy, detachment, trust in God, patient endurance and abandonment to the Immaculate**

Heart of Mary and the Sacred Heart of Jesus - resonate not only with approved Marian apparitions (e.g. Fatima) but also with the spirituality of many great saints and mystics (e.g. St. Theresa of Avila, St. John Eudes, Jean-Pierre de Caussade and St. Therese of Lisieux). In terms of human faith, I find it quite credible that Janie Garza, a woman whose heart has been purified through much suffering, would be the type of humble soul that God would choose to grace with interior visions and locutions containing messages of particular importance for our time.

One of the extraordinary qualities of this book is the way it links the domestic Church of the home with the universal Church. This is manifested by the geographic movement of the messages from their origin in the simplicity of Janie's home in Austin, Texas to their eventual reception in places like New Orleans, Detroit, Mexico, Lourdes, Lisbon, Rome, Prague and Red Square in Moscow. This incredible odyssey, guided it seems by supernatural Providence, eventually returns to the home. The lesson is that Mary's "prayer warriors," gathered together on a pilgrimage to the ends of the earth, must return to their individual families to build up the reign of peace in the domestic Church of the home. Prayer in each family is the spiritual precondition for world peace and the renewal of the universal Church.

Another extraordinary quality of this book is the way the prayer life of the family on earth is supported by the supernatural guidance of the Holy Family of Jesus, Mary and Joseph (since Janie receives messages from all three). The involvement of angels and the exhortations to pray for the souls in Purgatory highlight the importance of linking the individual family to the larger family of the Mystical Body of Christ which includes the faithful on earth, the souls in Purgatory and the angels and saints in Heaven.

A number of themes are also stressed which seem to resonate with other reported messages of this age. Jesus speaks to Janie from His Eucharistic Heart, and the importance of Eucharistic devotion is highlighted. Prayers for priests are urged by Mary because many priests have grown weak in their faith and are resisting the authority of the Pope.

Fidelity to the Holy Father is stressed by Mary, and she refers to the Pontiff as "my beloved Pope." Several references are made to the urgency of the present times, the activity of Satan in the world and the need to prepare for the tribulation. Although the dangers of too much television, materialism and sexual immorality are noted, abortion seems to be singled out as the "horrible evil" of this age.

While a sense of urgency is present in these messages, there is also a pervasive exhortation to trust God and not to worry or be anxious. While Mary does identify herself to Janie as the **Mother of Sorrows** on some occasions, she most frequently appears as the **Mother of Compassion and Love** who urges her children to seek refuge in the warmth of her Immaculate Heart and the mercy of her Son's Sacred Heart. When Jesus speaks, there is an ever-present sense of love and tenderness and He makes clear to Janie: *"I am here for you always. I have given you My Precious Body and Blood so you would be redeemed. Take My Body and be nourished. Take My Blood and do not thirst. I am your strength. I am your hope. I am your teacher* (October 22, 1991).*"*

Beginning in 1993, messages from St. Joseph become more frequent, and the great saint gives special instructions for husbands to be chaste, prayerful, pure, gentle, loving, obedient and humble. St. Joseph also urges wives to pray for the virtues of purity, obedience and humility. He counsels children to be pure and chaste, obedient to their parents and prayerful in their choice of friends and careers. A beautiful prayer to St. Joseph is given to Janie, along with other inspired prayers given for family consecrations to the Holy Spirit, the Immaculate Heart of Mary and the Sacred Heart of Jesus. Prayers to St. Michael the Archangel and the Holy Spirit are given special encouragement, along with daily recitation of the Rosary and the wearing of the Scapular.

It is clear from these messages, that prayer and purity of heart are central to the renewal of the family, the priesthood and the Church. The attacks of Satan against the sanctity of the family and the priesthood give these messages a special urgency and a special credibility.

While the assaults of the evil one appear to be on the increase, the **Mother of Compassion and Love** tells us: *"Do not have the smallest worry or fear, for I, your heavenly Mother, am with each one of you. I protect all my children through my motherly mantle. Take refuge in my Son's Sacred Heart and in my Most Immaculate Heart, for in the Two United Hearts you will find your safety. Everyday, consecrate your lives to the Two United Hearts and no harm will come to you as a family* (July 20, 1993).*"*

There is a beautiful simplicity to the messages of this book, a simplicity which is at once direct and profound. The essence of these messages can only be appreciated by those willing to accept the way of spiritual childhood - those who are willing to become like little children in order to enter the Kingdom of Heaven (Matthew 18:3).

While it is not within my competence to confirm these messages as supernatural in character, I do feel confident to recommend this book for spiritual inspiration and prayerful reflection. The pure and humble quality of Janie Garza's soul breathes through every page of this book. However, as Janie would be the first to admit, our focus should not be on her, but on the Immaculate Heart of Mary and the Sacred Heart of Jesus united as a secure refuge of mercy and compassion in a world crying out for love.

Robert L. Fastiggi, Ph.D.
Associate Professor of Religious Studies
St. Edward's Catholic University
Austin, Texas - January 28, 1998

INTRODUCTION

"Give evidence of your deeds of old, fulfill the prophecies spoken in your name, reward those who have hoped in you, and let your prophets be proven true. Hear the prayer of your servants, for you are ever gracious to your people, thus it will be known to the very ends of the earth that you are the eternal God (Sirach 36:14-17)."

This selection of an Old Testament prayer finds an echo in the souls of numerous Christian families today, as they experience the fierce tugging of the world and the evil one. Indeed, the family is being assaulted today as never before. The mentality of the world has seeped into families bringing with it divorce, fighting, lack of discipline and forgiveness - driving out family prayer and a humble spirit which seeks wisdom not from the world but from the infallible Word of God and the sure teachings of His Church.

Many are the prophets whom the Holy Spirit has raised up today to teach us the true and divine plan for the family. The chief prophet in the Church today is John Paul II, our saintly and courageous Pope, who speaks so clearly with divine wisdom about our families and what is God's Will for them.

Mrs. Janie Garza of Austin, Texas, wife and mother, was chosen by the Lord to be a vessel of simple and holy messages for the family of today. These messages are given by the Holy Family - Jesus, Mary and Joseph. Messengers like St. Michael the Archangel are also mentioned. Janie has been receiving messages since February 15, 1989.

I can testify that since I became her Spiritual Director nearly five years ago, I have seen immense growth in virtue in her, in her husband and in her sons, two of whom are teenagers. The purpose of these messages is no doubt to help Christian families to become holy families. Thus, Our Lady teaches us from her own experience as wife and mother, being of course full of grace.

The great St. Joseph gives us sublime teachings on the family, coming from his own experience as husband and foster father of the Divine Infant. His soul, so full of love for his Divine Foster Child and his wife, and so full of God's wisdom, makes his teachings fresh and absorbing for husbands and wives, fathers and mothers and for the young, too.

As Janie Garza's Spiritual Director, I have never found anything in all the messages which in any way goes against any teaching of our Holy Catholic Church. I have seen the profound effects these messages have had in others when they read them or have heard Janie speak. So, together with her two previous Spiritual Directors, I have, after years of prayer for discernment and wisdom, affirmed that these messages are of heavenly origin. I wish, however, to quickly add that I, together with Janie and Marcelino, her husband, submit our judgment to our Holy Catholic Church.

Particular points raised by Our Lady are family prayer, the great power of the Rosary, the sacraments of Penance and Eucharist, a return to God and devotion to her Immaculate Heart and her Son's Sacred Heart. She always speaks as a tender Mother, but warns us of the dangers of the present age and the supreme importance of living her messages. Let the reader partake of this rich fare. Each particular family, each parish family, the family of the Church and the family of man also, can greatly profit from these enlightening instructions.

The Garza family and I thank the Holy Family for the greatness of their love and compassion. May our Mother of Compassion and Love, who appears to Janie under this title, accept our love and gratitude and through the powerful prayers of her husband, St. Joseph, lead us to complete unity with Jesus Christ, who is Lord of lords and King of kings. Amen.

Reverend Henry Bordeaux, OCD,
October, 1994
Dallas, Texas

ADDITION TO THE INTRODUCTION

Four years have passed since the messages of Jesus, Mary and Joseph to Janie Garza were first published. The title of the book was I Am Your Mother Come From Heaven to Love You. Published in 1994, they have all sold out. The title of the new edition of this work has been changed, to Heaven's Messages For The Family - Volume 1 to express better the fact that Our Lord, St. Joseph and the Archangels are also giving instructions.

This new edition contains all the public messages given by the Holy Family to the families of the Church and the world from February 1989 to December 31, 1997. Volume II to be published by Fall of 1998, will contain messages from St. Joseph and the Archangels.

Since May 1, 1996, St. Philomena has been coming on a daily basis to Janie with important messages. These messages are being prepared for publication as of this writing. St. Philomena's last message was given to Janie on May 1, 1998, although she will continue to visit with Janie on a daily basis.

As of May, 1998, the three Archangels are coming to Janie daily, praying with her for the intentions which they indicate to her. The sufferings of the present time cry out to God for extra help. He's giving it.

The regularly scheduled visits of Jesus, Mary and Joseph ceased by the end of the year 1995. Beginning in January, 1996, one or more members of the Holy Family come to Janie on special days such as a feast day dedicated to one person of the Holy Family, on Janie's birthday, on a day of intense suffering, or as she prepares to leave Austin to give a talk.

I wish to say again that Janie and I submit entirely and happily to our Holy Mother, the Roman Catholic Church, for Its final discernment of these messages. At the end of our lives, each of us, together with our family and dear friends, will want to say with St. Theresa of Jesus, "I die a daughter/son of the Catholic Church."

We firmly hope in the Holy Spirit as His year, 1998, progresses and in our dear Heavenly Father as His year, 1999, arrives. Then, the Triumph of the Immaculate Heart of Mary will become the great joy of God's holy people as the great Jubilee year 2000 arrives.

St. Joseph, Protector of the Family, pray for us.

Rev. Henry Bordeaux, OCD,
Marylake Monastery
Little Rock, Arkansas
May 13, 1998
Anniversary of the first apparitions at Fatima

Expanded Autobiography of Janie Garza

My name is Janie Garza and I have lived in Austin, Texas all of my life. I am married, and my husband Marcelino and I have been blessed with four sons, three grandsons and five granddaughters. I was raised a Catholic, but I had no devotion to the Virgin Mary or the Saints. As a child I used to see my mother praying before her altar and lighting candles to all her statues. It seemed to me that she had every statue in the world! I used to resent her devotion, and seeing her praying to all the statues used to make me angry. I believed that she should pray only to God and stop wasting her time praying to statues! I was very young and I didn't understand about devotions. My mother was uneducated and did not know how to explain to me about devotional love. She was a simple woman.

As I grew older, I learned to pray the Rosary all by myself, because Jesus was mentioned in these prayers. I had also read somewhere that the Rosary was a powerful prayer and this appealed to me as a child. I came from a family of nine children and my mother was the sole provider. We were very poor. I had a stepfather that stayed drunk all the time and who was verbally abusive to the whole family. I couldn't understand why my mother stayed in this relationship.

I never knew my father, as my parents separated before I was born. I remember how much my mother hated my father and how angry she was with him, so she kept me from ever meeting my father. Because of my mother's anger towards my father, she was very abusive to me. She used to tell me that I looked exactly like my father. Quite frequently she would tell me that I was adopted and that's why I was very homely looking. This hurt me terribly and it made me angry.

As a child I remember suffering much and feeling very lonely. As I grew older it seemed to me my mother resented me more and more. I share this about being an abused child, because I know that many of you who read this book, you, too, have been victims of some sort of abuse. I remember that I loved my mother no matter how she treated me. In my own way I knew that she needed healing.

My mother never understood the importance of education, so she hardly saw to my education. I attended first grade in a Catholic school. During this time the nuns taught me about Jesus in the Blessed Sacrament. I remember that after school and whenever I could sneak into the church, I used to sit in front of the Blessed Sacrament, waiting for Jesus to come out. I know that He knew I was watching for Him. He never came out, but I never gave up on going and sitting before the Blessed Sacrament.

I didn't get to finish first grade because my mother took me out of school and she never told me why. I didn't get to make my first Communion and I didn't understand the concept of not being able to receive Jesus until I made my first Communion. I felt such love for Jesus and I walked to the church everyday to attend Mass. I received Holy Communion because I didn't know that I had to make my first Communion to receive Him. I didn't make my first Communion until I was sixteen years old, but I used to attend Mass daily to receive Jesus. To me He was my first real love. I feel in my heart that God forgave me for my ignorance.

As I grew up, I remember promising myself that I would never hurt anyone because I didn't want anyone to suffer like I had, but that was the promise of a child. As I continued to mature in my life I became very controlling of all the people in my life. I was very liberated in my morals and values. When I married I became worse. I wanted to wear the pants in my family and I took charge of making all the decisions concerning our family. I didn't have the love or respect for my husband that I should have so our marriage suffered. I wanted equal rights, and many times I thought of divorce if things didn't go my way.

It was at this point that God in His love and mercy sent Most Holy Mary into my life. God wanted to teach me to embrace my vocation as a wife and mother. On February 15, 1989, Our Lady came to me. It was about five in the evening or so. I was praying my Rosary while driving on my way to St. Edward's University. I saw a bright light that was right above where I was driving. I looked to each side, but the bright light was only in front of me.

Now being the big mouth that I was and although I was praying the Rosary, I said out loud, "What the hell!" Before I could say anything else, there in the light I saw an outline of a person. Quickly, the outline became very clear and it was a very young girl between 14-17 years of age maybe. She was dressed in all white with a long white dress and a long white cape. I learned later that this cape is called a mantle. She had long black wavy hair and large beautiful blue eyes. This young girl was brighter than the sun, but I could look at her without it hurting my eyes. She did not speak. She motioned to me to join her in praying the Rosary. She had a beautiful white Rosary that shined as she moved her slender little fingers from one bead of the Rosary to the next.

I was so absorbed in this experience that I do not remember driving. The distance between the place where Our Lady came to me and the university was about four miles. I was absorbed by a peace I had not known before except in prayer. The next thing I remember was when the car gently tapped the parking curb in front of the college. I went to class but could not think. I could not bring myself to share this with anyone, for I thought this to be perhaps an hallucination. Each time I prayed the Rosary I would see her. I thought perhaps if I closed my eyes I would not see her, but even with my eyes closed I could see her!

I stopped praying the Rosary for about a week hoping that maybe these hallucinations would go away. When I resumed praying the Rosary, she came again and on February 26, believing in the power of holy water, I placed a bowl of holy water at my side as I knelt down, leaning back on my feet. I slowly stuck my hand in the holy water and threw it at her rebuking her in the name of Jesus. She smiled at me very gently.

I asked her who she was and she responded, **"I am your Mother come from Heaven to love you."** *I asked her if she had a name and she responded,* **"To you I come as the Lady of the Rosary. I charge you and your family to make living Rosaries for my Son, Jesus."** *I did not understand what she meant. She said,* **"I, your heavenly Mother, will teach you on the virtue of obedience. I shall teach you how to be a loving wife and mother. I shall teach you how to be submissive to your husband."** *At this point I thought to myself, this isn't from God because God knows that I am not a submissive person. I submit to no one!*

Our Lady continued speaking, **"Do not share with your family or others this special time that you spend with your heavenly Mother. I will tell you when to share with your family. Pray and fast for your family, so that their hearts will be prepared."** *When Our Lady asked me not to share with anyone that she was visiting me I was glad and relieved, because I was having a hard time believing all this, and I* *thought perhaps it was my defense mechanisms that were coming to my rescue to keep me from losing my mind.*

You have to remember, here, that I was working at the adolescent psychiatric hospital as a psychiatric social worker, so I was used to dealing with people that heard voices and had visions. I really thought I was losing my mind. I began spending much time being quiet, checking all my senses to make sure that I wasn't having a nervous breakdown. Although I was experiencing all this, I had peace in my heart like never before, and I really felt that someone was looking out for me. I kept all this to myself as requested by Our Lady.

For five months Our Lady came to me everyday. Everyday she would speak to me on how to love my husband. She was teaching me the importance of praying for my family and how to embrace my vocation as a wife and mother. All that she asked of me I held dear to my heart.

I've always had a devotion to Perpetual Adoration. I went to spend time with Jesus in the last few days of February of 1989. I asked Jesus to please help me to remain sane through all this and to understand it if it was God's Holy Will. I told Him that I just came to be with Him. I then heard an audible voice say to me, **"My humble servant have no worry. You are not going insane. It is My heavenly Mother who is coming to you. Her visits to you are truly happening. My Father has sent her to help you and your family, that you in turn may help other families."**

Then, before me stood Our Lord. He wore an off white tunic all the way to His feet. This tunic had long big sleeves. I could see His wounds on His hands and feet. He had the most beautiful and most gentle blue eyes.

He had hair that came to His shoulders. He had dark hair and it was wavy. He had a beard and mustache. The sound of His voice made me feel like I should be prostrated before Him, but all I could do was look at Him. He shared that He, too, would come to me, sometimes with His Mother and other times alone. He said that He would share much with me concerning His Bride and all of her afflictions. He said that He would take me into a journey of self-knowledge.

This is how my heavenly visitations began, first with Our Lady and then Our Lord. Together they began to teach me about the importance of prayer, love and forgiveness in the family. They soon invited me to a life of prayer and suffering. By this time I had been asked by Our Lady to share my heavenly visitations with my family.

Jesus and Mary asked that I offer myself as victim for the suffering of the Church, for the unborn and the conversion of the family. *I shared this invitation of Jesus and Mary with my husband, although we did not quite understand this invitation. When my husband asked me what this meant, I said I didn't know but that I thought they were offering me a job. My husband asked me if I wanted it and I said 'yes'. I told my husband that we should perhaps go to the church.*

This was a Saturday when I was given this invitation, and this same Saturday as my husband and I knelt before the Blessed Sacrament, my husband spoke out loud to the Lord saying, **"Lord, I give you my wife to do with as you will. I know you will take care of her."** *We finished our prayers and returned home. God honored my husband's decision and God was pleased that I did not make this decision without sharing this with my husband and having my husband's blessing and permission.*

God came to us through His Most Holy Mother to help our family. Salvation came into our hearts. We have all agreed to respond to God's call to live as God's family, one day at a time. With all our struggles and daily crosses, we put our trust in the Lord Our God and in Our Lady. In times of family crises, together as a family we storm Heaven through our prayers, and God comes to our aid. The tools given to us for having victory over Satan are **frequent Confession, daily Mass as possible, Adoration as frequently as possible, praying the Rosary as a family (this is our daily weapon), and reading the Bible daily.**

We suffer like any family suffers, but we know that God is with us. Our entire family has made their consecration to the Sacred Heart of Jesus and the Immaculate Heart of Mary. Our home is enthroned to the Sacred Heart of Jesus. We honor first Fridays and first Saturdays. This is how we protect ourselves as a family, accepting one another like God accepts us. We also have strong devotion to St. Joseph.

No matter what problems we may encounter as a family, the love of God always triumphs over anything, because we put our trust in Him. When a member of the family becomes weak, the stronger members help and encourage one another. I have learned to embrace my family one day at a time. Our Lady taught me not to dwell on things of my past, not to worry about tomorrow, but to embrace God in the present moment. She taught me that the best medicine to heal wounded hearts, to forgive, to convert and to love your family and others around you is prayer. Our Lady is the perfect model of prayer. Through prayer you will discover God and when you discover Him you will know His peace.

For the past nine years, God has blessed our family with guidance from Our Lord, Our Holy Mother, beloved St. Joseph, St. Philomena and the three Archangels. May you and your family allow the love of the Holy Family to dwell in your homes and in your hearts. I pray that all that I share with whomever reads this book will help to draw you closer to God. Remember also to have devotion to the Holy Angels and to trust in your Guardian Angel everyday. God bless you.

Heaven's Messages for The Family

VOLUME ONE

*Our Lord
and
Our Lady's
Messages to Families*

> *"My child, in just a short while your book with the teachings on the family will be published. This book will have a divine effect on all who read it with open hearts. Through this book many families will come to God as a family. The teachings in the messages given to you are teachings from Heaven, for God is calling all families to be reconciled to Him through being a holy family. It is important that you pray to the Holy Spirit to prepare the hearts of the many families that will read your book."*
>
> —*Message from Our Lord To Janie*

Chapter One

MARY AND THE ROSARY
1989

What I tell you in the dark, utter in the light; and what you hear whispered, proclaim upon the housetops. And do not fear those who kill the body but cannot kill the soul; rather fear him who can destroy both soul and body in hell.

Matthew 10:27-28

Editor's Note: For an account of how Janie's visitations first began please refer to her expanded autobiography.

February 26, 1989 *I am your Mother; bring living Rosaries*

Janie: *I saw Our Lady during my prayer, and I asked,* Who are you?
Our Lady: I am your Mother come from Heaven to love you.
Janie: Do you have a name?
Our Lady: To you, my child, I come as The Lady of the Rosary, and I charge you and your family with this mission: to go out and bring living Rosaries for my Son, Jesus.
Janie: *I did not understand this message. I thought my family and I were to make Rosaries. I prayed for enlightenment.*

February 27, 1989 *Be submissive*

Our Lady: My child, I come to teach you how to be a loving wife and to help you to be submissive to your husband.
Janie: *I rebuked these words just in case it may have been the devil lying to me. I felt that God knew that I had never been submissive to anyone!*
Our Lady: My child, your husband is very special to God. He is gentle, kind and loving. He is a good provider and a good father. He has a gentle heart.
Janie: Blessed Mother, are we talking about the same man I married?
Our Lady: *She smiled.* Yes, my child, yes. My child, when you submit to your husband, you help him to submit to God. Trust me, my child, and allow me to teach you all about being a prayerful and loving family - the kind of family that God intended for you to be.

February 27, 1989 *Pray your Rosary*

Our Lady: My child, whenever Satan is disturbing you, pray your Rosary. When your family is undergoing much suffering, pray your Rosary. Whenever you want to lead others to God, pray your Rosary. Through praying the Rosary those souls that you are praying for will begin to change.

Through the Rosary they will come closer to God, and they will have a desire to want to convert; but you must pray very hard. **My child, there is much healing through praying the Rosary, and I am always present when my children pray their Rosaries.**

February 27, 1989 *Be patient*

Our Lady: My child, be patient with your husband and pray for him. Offer all your own struggles and sufferings for his conversion. Accept your family with unconditional love. Teach them about the love of God and help them to pray with you. Do not become discouraged when your family refuses to pray with you. Be gentle, patient and loving with them. My child, you will suffer much for your family's conversion. As you suffer for them, your own heart will begin to convert. Pray, pray, pray.

February 28, 1989 *I believe, I adore, I hope and I love You*

Our Lady: My child, I will teach you how to pray your Rosary with love in your heart. Through your devotion to praying your Rosary, you will help others in your family to convert. My child, I ask that you add this prayer when you begin your Rosary: **My God, I believe, I adore, I hope and I love You. I beg pardon of You, for those who do not believe, do not adore, do not hope and do not love You.** My child, do not worry about your family; through your prayers they are drawing closer to my Son. Continue to pray for your family and pray and fast for these intentions.

March 17, 1989 *Be forgiving*

Jesus: My dear child, I, your Jesus of Love and Mercy speak to your heart. Do not be concerned about your husband. Be loving and patient with him and be gentle. Be forgiving, for he is trying to understand more about being prayerful. Give him to Me and allow Me to help you both. Remain loving and obedient, and through your attitude your family will pray more. You will suffer much for much is being asked of you by My Father in Heaven, for you have found much favor with My Father.

March 18, 1989 *Listen to My Mother*

Jesus: My child, listen to My beloved Mother and do all that she is asking of you. Through your obedience to her and to Me your prayers will convert many families. My child, you have such a great love for the Rosary. Pray everyday!

March 20, 1989 *The conversion of Russia*

Our Lady: My child, continue praying your Rosary for peace in your heart and for peace in your family. Pray for peace in the world and for the conversion of my daughter, Russia, for she is in need of much conversion. Offer your prayers for the most distant souls and for the Holy Souls in Purgatory. Pray for conversion throughout the world.

My child, when you pray with your family, offer up your prayers for my special intention. When the faithful pray with faith in their hearts, they will begin to see changes in their hearts and in their families. Sinners will convert, wars will cease, and my Son will begin to live in many new hearts. Teach your family how to pray with faith and love in their hearts.

March 23, 1989 *The fruits of your prayers*

Our Lady: My child, continue to pray with your family, for soon you will see their hearts change. **Healing of woundedness of heart will be one of the results, the fruits of your prayers.**

March 24, 1989 *I am praying with you*

Our Lady: My child, I am praying with you, and I am blessing your family in a special way. Your son is on his way to recovery, continue to pray for him.
Janie: *Later on that day, my son told me that he felt the love of Our Lady. My family was unaware that Our Lady is visiting me!*

April 5, 1989 *Trust in Me*

Janie: *I was praying about some concerns that I had.*
Jesus: My child, fear nothing, put your trust in Me.

April 5, 1989 *Be not afraid*

Our Lady: My child, why are you troubled? Why are you afraid? Haven't I told you that I am with you?
Janie: *I began to cry to hear her say this to me.*
Our Lady: My child, why the tears? Believe in your heart that I am with you. I called you here, so that I could console your heart and to tell you that your prayers have been heard. My little child, I know you are suffering. Do not be afraid. You have the protection and guidance of my Son and the enlightenment of my Spouse, the Holy Spirit. Your Guardian Angel is also with you at all times. He is protecting you.

My child, I know that you want to be healed from what you are going through. In just a short time you will be healed, but not now. Know that through your suffering you are being purified, for God Himself is calling you to purity. Offer up your suffering in reparation for your own conversion and for your family's conversion. Be at peace, my child, and dry your tears. Go out and enjoy this beautiful day with your husband.

April 8, 1989 *I will teach you*

Janie: *Today, I had not prayed my Rosary.*
Our Lady: My child, what is wrong? Why haven't you prayed your Rosary today? Don't you know how important it is to pray the Rosary daily? My child, I want your prayers, so that through your prayers you can help souls to convert.
Janie: *I apologized to her and prayed my Rosary.*
Our Lady: My child, I will guide you as you pray for your family. I will teach you about intercessory prayer. I will teach you about the angels and saints and how they can help you. I will lead you and your family closer to my Son.
Janie: *Since Our Lady began to visit me, I have much more peace. I am calm. I have a joy I've never known before. For this I am grateful to God.*

April 14, 1989 *Believe in your heart*

Janie: *I was doubting my experiences of Our Lady speaking to my heart.*
Our Lady: My child, believe in your heart that I, your heavenly Mother, have chosen to speak to you interiorly. I speak to your heart. I speak to my children in many ways. Some hear my voice, others see me and hear my voice. Others only hear my voice as an interior voice. This is the way that I speak to you. Be at peace, and do not be overcome with doubt.
Janie: *I saw Our Lady exteriorly when she first came. I stopped praying, so that she wouldn't come in case I was crazy. Then, when I prayed my Rosary I decided to close my eyes so that I wouldn't see her, but I saw her even with my eyes closed.*

April 15, 1989 *Share this devotion with your family*

Janie: *During prayer I was telling Our Lady how happy I was, because I had her as my Mother. I was thanking her for loving me.*
Our Lady: My child, yes, I do love you, but you also love me and I, your heavenly Mother, responded to your love. My child, you have

been devoted to praying your Rosary, and through praying your Rosary you demonstrated your love to me. Please share this beautiful devotion with your family. Share with your family that conversion is obtained through praying the Rosary. My children (your family) will be blessed and healings will take place in their hearts. Pray your Rosary everyday for conversion in your own life.

May 1, 1989 *Preparing to tell my family*

Janie: *I spent the month of May praying and preparing for a priest whom Our Lady asked me to pray for. This month was also the month in which I was to talk to my family concerning Our Lady speaking to my heart. I was very nervous and afraid of my family's reaction.*

In a way I was hoping that this moment would never come. All that Mary had told me, I was praying about. I prayed about everything. Jesus and Our Lady were being so gentle with me.

June 1, 1989 *Our Lady gave me the priest*

Janie: *Today, Our Lady gave me the priest that I am to talk to concerning my visitations. I am growing more and more nervous. I called to make an appointment for Monday at 3:00 p.m. Tomorrow I'll go to San Antonio, Texas for a private retreat. My friend invited me. I guess this is how Our Lady will prepare me.*

I met with my family in the last part of May to share with them about my visitations. I think they believed me. I don't know, but they sure were being nice to me. Maybe they thought I'd lost it! Our Lady will begin to teach us as a family now. So far she's been teaching me about submission and obedience.

June 4, 1989 *A soul without prayer*

Janie: *Tonight I wanted to tear up everything and cancel the appointment with Father. I wanted to stop praying and forget everything. Our Lady came to me, and she showed me a green meadow. Then before my eyes it turned brown; then it was all dark and burnt.*
Our Lady: This is how your own soul will become if you stop praying.

June 5, 1989 *Father believed*

Janie: *Today, I met with Father. I was so scared, but Our Lady helped* me. *Father said that he believed that what I was receiving were divine messages from Jesus and Mary. He asked me to leave everything that I have written with him. I am so nervous!*

June 18, 1989 *Of Divine origin*

Janie: *I received everything back today from Father. He said it was of divine origin. I can't believe it. He agreed to be my Spiritual Director and to see me once a week or more, as I need to see him.*

June 21, 1989 *God is calling you*

Our Lady: My child, your prayers and efforts are good, but you have not been focused on your commitment to help your family with their prayers. You have not been praying as much, and you have been impatient with your family. My child, you must have a loving attitude when helping your family. You have allowed your anger to dominate you.

My child, I know that you are suffering (*I have a physical problem*), but I will help you through this rough period. Offer all your pain for conversion in your family. Have a loving attitude and pray with faith in your heart. Through your prayers, fasting and sufferings, many others than your family will be converted.

Do not worry about anything, but write everything I tell you. God has many blessings for your family. **He is calling you to bring other families to Him through praying your Rosary. Teach others the importance of praying the Rosary as a family.** My child, I will come and visit with you again soon.

July 28, 1989 *Pray the Rosary before Mass*

Our Lady: My child, I invite you to pray the Rosary before Holy Mass. In this way, you will be an example to others.

I invite my children to spend fifteen minutes praying their Rosary, to help them to prepare for Holy Mass. **If my children respond to my request, God will heal their wounded hearts. Conversion will be easy for those who want to convert. When my children pray the Rosary together, they begin to heal as a community.** God's peace begins to flow as my children pray the Rosary.

August 30, 1989 *The family Rosary*

Our Lady: My dear children, I, your heavenly Mother, invite you to be filled with God's peace. You have my gratitude for praying your Rosary together as a family. My children, do not forget the importance of family prayer, especially the family Rosary. When you pray as a family, you grow as a family. Do not be afraid to convert, but convert! I will help you and lead you, as a family, closer to my Son, Jesus.

Open your hearts to my Son's Most Sacred Heart and to my Most Immaculate Heart, and decide for conversion. Pray for world peace, for there is so much pain, suffering and corruption due to lack of faith. Be open to my Son's love and mercy and share His love and mercy with others by reaching to the unconverted souls. Pray, my children, pray.

August 31, 1989 *My garment of grace*

Our Lady: My child, continue to pray and do all that my Son invites you to do. Do not be concerned with anything. You are protected by the Two United Hearts. My child, do not be without your Scapular, for it is my garment of grace, and you are under my protection. Never be without it!

August 31, 1989 *I spend hours alone*

Jesus: My child, welcome to My Eucharistic Heart. I have missed your visits. Thank you for coming to spend time with Me. Today, My child, I want to share My sadness with you. My children do not come to visit with Me. I spend hours alone, and very few come. Sometimes no one comes.

My child, I turn to you and ask you to invite others to come to visit Me. I will refresh their souls, I will heal their wounded hearts. I will renew their hearts, and they will be filled with My peace. I have so much love to give My children. Invite them to come and spend time with the One Who loves them more than anyone else. Thank you, My child, for all your prayers.

September 2, 1989 *The power of wearing the Scapular*

Janie: *Today, I had a question concerning taking my Scapular off while I was showering, since Our Lady asked me to wear the Scapular and never be without it. I prayed, and then Our Lady came. I did not see* *her dressed in white. She came in brown and cream. She came with a crown on her head and a Child in her arms. I asked her what her name was under this title.*

Then, before my eyes, I saw her in different attires. I didn't recognize all of them, only a few. Our Lady of Guadalupe, the Immaculate Conception, Our Lady of the Rosary, and Our Lady of San Juan were the only titles I recognized.

After this, I again saw Our Lady in brown and cream with a crown on her head and the Christ Child in her arms. I understood that she was appearing to me under the title of Our Lady of Mount Carmel.

Our Lady: My child, I have allowed you to see me in many different titles, but I am the same Mother of God and Mother of All Creation. I come to my children in the titles that they can relate to me as their heavenly Mother. Continue praying for the conversion of your family. Your commitment to your prayers brings so much joy to my Immaculate Heart. My child, regarding wearing your Scapular, wear it always, for through wearing your Scapular you are protected from many evils during the day.

September 10, 1989 *Pray together as a family*

Our Lady: My children, you bring joy to my Immaculate Heart as you pray your family Rosary. **Pray together as a family, and you will be strong during trials and tribulations.** My children, some of you are suffering and have wounded hearts. Do not worry, I am here to protect you and to lead you closer to my Son, Jesus.

November 30, 1989 *The Rosary is your weapon*

Our Lady: My dear children, I invite you to open your hearts to my Son Who loves you. Do not reject His love, but turn to Him and accept His love. Be converted, be converted! Love one another and continue to pray together as a family. Know, my children, that you are special to me, and I hold you all to my motherly bosom. I invite you to trust in my motherly intercession, so that I may lead you all to purity of heart. Take refuge in my Most Immaculate Heart, and I will help you to remain strong during hard times.

My children, continue to pray together, and remember, the Rosary is your weapon. Pray, pray, pray! When you are under Satan's attack and you cannot pray your Rosary, pray one Hail Mary; this sends Satan running. He hates prayer.

December 7, 1989 *Give the gift of love for Christmas*

Our Lady: Tonight, I say thank you all for praying together as a family. My children, some of you are hurting. You are worried about Christmas, and you have no money to give gifts. Give the gift of love that comes from your heart. Prepare your hearts for the birth of my Son and allow Him to be born in your own heart.

Do not be sad my children. God wants to bless you. Dry your tears and be open to God's love. It saddens my heart to see you sad. Pray with your heavenly Mother, and you will receive God's peace.

My children, tonight, I invite you to trust in my intercession especially in this Holy Season, so that I may help you to prepare your hearts for the birth of my Son.

December 14, 1989 *Allow me to help you*

Our Lady: My children, tonight, I thank you for coming together for prayer. I invite you to trust God with all your family concerns. Again, I invite you to allow me to help you during this Holy Season. Do not be concerned with all the distractions concerning gifts, but offer your love to one another; this is the best gift of all.

Continue to pray and have no worry, but rejoice. **My children, you are seeking answers to prayers, and some of you are becoming discouraged. Open your hearts and abandon yourselves to God. Give Him all your burdens. God is listening to all your prayers. Do not give up but continue to pray, for prayer is your strength.**

Janie: *Tonight Our Lady said we were receiving special healing of our hearts. During this time, my family and I had been coming together to pray the Rosary with Our Lady. We extended this invitation to others in our neighborhood and shared with them that Our Lady was coming. This began our neighborhood family Rosary hour.*

Chapter Two

LESSONS ON PRAYER OF THE HEART 1990

All these with one accord devoted themselves to prayer, together with the women and Mary the mother of Jesus, and with his brethren.

Acts 1:14

January 4, 1990 *Abandon yourselves to my Immaculate Heart*

Our Lady: My children, tonight, there are some of you who are suffering, and your hearts are sad. I, your heavenly Mother, invite you to pray and meditate on the Glorious Mysteries with joy in your hearts. **My children, many of you are worried about your own children, and some of you have children who are not praying. Pray for them and trust in your prayers. Leave all your worries and sadness at God's disposal. If you do this, all will go well with your children.**

I welcome all my children who are here, and I invite you to open your hearts to your heavenly Mother. Know, my children, that I have called each one of you to be here and to pray your Rosary together. My children, do not give up hope when you are suffering, but turn to my Immaculate Heart. I want to protect you all; that is why I ask that you trust your heavenly Mother. I do not want you to be sad when you are overcome by failure, but continue to pray for God's strength. Never give up, my children, but pray unceasingly!

My children, I invite you to accept me as your heavenly Mother and to accept my love. I know that it is difficult to live a good life; that is why I invite you to abandon yourselves to my Immaculate Heart. I will help you to endure your crosses with love. My children, I invite you to commit every morning to make a sacrifice to pray more for your family. **Prayer will be your strength. Begin and end each day with prayer, for prayer brings you peace.**

My children, if you only understood how much you are loved by God, you would open your hearts. You must become totally dependent on God for everything; in this way you will be able to accept all your trials and sufferings with joy. God will see to all your needs. Trust Him.

January 11, 1990 *Open your hearts and pray*

Janie: *Our Lady came as Queen of Mercy, a title I didn't recognize.*
Our Lady: My children, tonight, I come to console each one of you. My heart is sorrowful for many of you who are suffering and have stopped praying. Some of you are doubting in the blessings that you are receiving.
Janie: What would make you happy My Lady?
Our Lady: My children, open your hearts and pray. This will bring joy to my heart. My child, pray to the Holy Spirit, and He will open the door to your heart.

Janie: *I saw myself at her feet. She placed both hands on my head. Dear Lady, I do not want you to be sad.*
Our Lady: Pray, my child, pray. My children, pray the Rosary with joy. Tonight I bless each one present and I bless all your intentions.
Janie: *All the families gathered tonight felt the presence of Our Lady.*

January 18, 1990 *Pray with faith in your hearts*

Our Lady: My children, tonight, I invite you to prepare your hearts before you pray your Rosary.
Janie: *She wanted us to be silent instead of visiting before praying the Rosary.*
Our Lady: My children, pray your Rosary with love and faith in your hearts. Tonight, many of you are afflicted with illness and viruses. I ask that you offer up all your suffering for peace in your family. My children, I am aware that many of you are ill. Continue praying and know that I am praying with you. Love one another and open the doors to your hearts from within.
Janie: *She meant that our hearts are not open to receive one anothers love.*
Our Lady: My children, pray for all your neighbors and for the needs of the world. **Pray especially for the youth; they are in great need of prayer! Be strong, my children, and arm yourselves through prayer, for Satan will destroy you if you are not praying.**

Do not be afraid, for I am protecting you. I am teaching you about praying as a family and the importance of loving one another. **Pray your Rosary everyday. Some of you are feeling overcome by your crosses and tribulations, especially in your family. My children, the reason that you are feeling this way is because you are praying without faith in your hearts. Pray, my children, pray.**

January 22, 1990 *How can I help you if you do not pray*

Our Lady: My children, tonight, I invite you to pray, so that through your prayers others will come to God. My children, I call you to prayer of the heart, where you abandon all totally to God. **Satan is busy trying to destroy you, but through prayer you will conquer everything.**

My children, I, your heavenly Mother, have come to teach you how to love with God's love. Open your hearts, open your hearts. How can I help you if you do not pray? Ask the Lord for the grace to be strong through your prayers. I bless you all, my children, and I extend my love to each one. You have struggled to come together for prayer, but you remain committed, and I thank you.

January 25, 1990 *Keep your eyes on my Son, Jesus*

Our Lady: My children, tonight, I, your heavenly Mother, thank you all for coming to pray together as a family. My children, I bring you peace. Do not be concerned about your troubles, for I, your Mother, am with you. Do not be afraid. Little children, there are many needs here tonight. Through prayer and fasting you will receive the answers to your prayers and the answers that you are seeking. Open your hearts, for I have come to bring you peace.

My children, some of you are worried about finances. Do not worry; God has heard your prayers. Some of you are doubting; do not doubt. Keep your eyes on my Son, Jesus. He will help you not to become discouraged.

My children, I am happy, for many of my young people are being committed to prayer. To you, I invite you to pray your Rosary everyday. My children, do not get upset with others who do not pray or have faith. Pray for them and invite them to come to pray.

February 8, 1990 *You are all beautiful flowers*

Our Lady: My children, tonight, I bless each one of you. Do not have any doubt, but open your hearts to your heavenly Mother. I have much to teach you about love. I am here to help and protect you. I am so happy that you remain committed to praying the Rosary. You are all beautiful flowers that send the aroma of love to others through your prayer. My children, I ask you to prepare through prayer when you gather together, for this is your time with me.
Janie: *She did not want us to be visiting with each other. Tonight we were loud.*
Our Lady: Some of you have concerns about your family, and some of you are having problems in your marriages. Trust God with your problems and have faith. My children, some of you have been suffering, for you are not in a prayerful spirit. Do not be distracted with this, but pray.

Prepare for the Passion of my Son (Lent), through the guidance of the Holy Spirit. The Holy Spirit will enlighten you and lead you through these forty days. Tonight, I come to prepare your hearts to enter into a time of much prayer and fasting. Be receptive to my invitation.

February 15, 1990 *One year Anniversary with Our Lady*

Janie: *We had a family celebration with only a few friends. No message was given. Our Lady was here to bless us and to thank us for everything.*

February 22, 1990 *I call you to be my witnesses*

Our Lady: My children, tonight, I invite you to open your hearts totally to the Lord. Some of you are struggling with the spirit of doubt.

My children, I am here to help you, and I hold you close to my Immaculate Heart. Do not be afraid, but abandon yourselves with open hearts to God. Be strong and live in the light of truth.

My children, I am calling you to be my witnesses and to take my love to all your families. **Pray and fast, my children; some of you have stopped fasting. Through prayer and fasting you obtain answers to your prayers. Do not become distracted with the world around you, but trust in my Son and keep your eyes on Him, Who gave His life for love of you. Pray for the grace of obedience to do all that is required of you as children of God.**

February 28, 1990 *Pray for the gift of discernment*

Our Lady: My children, tonight, I bless you all. I invite you to pray for the gift of discernment to know the Will of God. I invite all the youth to be witnesses to other young people. Spread the Good News and bring others to my Son, Jesus. I bless you all, my children. Have no fear or doubt, but trust God. Offer up all your suffering in reparation for peace and conversion throughout the world.

March 7, 1990 *Live in total abandonment*

Our Lady: My children, tonight, I invite you to live in total abandonment to God and to my Most Immaculate Heart. My children, I will teach you how to pray and fast. All I ask is that you open your hearts to my teachings.

April 11, 1990 *Live in My love*

Jesus: My dear child, I, your Jesus of Love and Mercy, thank you deeply with deep gratitude for all the suffering that you endured so lovingly and patiently. Know, My little flower, that many souls were redeemed through your long and painful suffering. Again, I thank you.

My little one, you have been united to My Cross and I am here to tell you that you endured all your suffering without complaining. You embraced your cross with great love, for you were not thinking of your own pain. You were courageous in your suffering as you suffered for others. Every prayer that you prayed to the Father was received by My Father, and your prayers had the fragrance of brotherly love and love for all of mankind as you recommended the conversion of the whole world to My Father. Again, I thank you.
Janie: Jesus, I didn't make it to any of the Easter Celebration. How can I say You are welcome? My Jesus, my 'yes' to You is a total yes from my heart and soul. I did only what was expected of me as a humble servant in my Father's Kingdom. Let me instead, give praise to the Almighty Father forever and ever for all the blessings that I have received throughout my life. To Him alone all glory be. Hosanna to God in the Highest, blessed be He that comes in the Name of the Lord. Hosanna in the Highest forever and ever. Amen. Alleluia.
Jesus: You have responded with your heart, and your praise of thanksgiving only continues to give glory to My Father. You are blessed, oh how you are blessed! Now, My little one, I say to you, My peace I give you, My peace be with you. As My Father has sent Me, so I send you to go out and share this peace with all the places in the world that My Father calls you to. Forgive everyone and God will forgive you.

Now, I speak to all My children all over the world. As I appeared to all My disciples, so I come to you, to give you My peace and My love. I, your risen Jesus, ask that you love one another as I have loved you, share My peace and live in this peace. Take courage and live in faith, for I, your risen Jesus, have overcome the world. Live together and pray together, harvesting the Kingdom of My Father.

To My beloved priests, to you I say have faith and do not be the doubting Thomas who had to see Me to believe that I had risen. I am with each one of you My beloved brothers, and to you I ask, do you love Me? Then feed My lambs, and take care of My sheep and be ready to suffer for them and with them. Open your hearts and be prepared to attend and guide the flock entrusted into your care.

Lessons on prayer of the heart

My beloved brothers, pick up your cross everyday and follow Me, your Jesus and your brother. As I appeared to all My disciples, My beloved priests, I am with you each day in the celebration of Holy Mass. Be made pure and allow yourselves to be transformed by My Precious Blood. Many of you have abandoned Me as Simon Peter did. To you, I, your Master say, come back to Me and I will make you whole. In Me you will be healed from all your woundedness.

Do not be afraid of anything around you, not your suffering nor your persecution; fear nothing. I, your Jesus of Mercy, hold you, all My beloved, in the palm of My hand. Your names are inscribed in My Heart. I am with each one of you, My beloved, until the end of time. Live in harmony, in love, in peace. Bring unity to My Body. I love you, My beloved. Be obedient, be made pure through this love of Mine.

To all families in the world, to you, I, your Jesus say, live in My love and My peace, loving one another. Live and put into practice My Father's Ten Commandments and teach your children all that I am teaching you. Live as a holy family. Pray together, grow together, share God's blessings with others. Fear nothing around you, but prepare your hearts and work together in My Father's Kingdom, harvesting and cultivating one anothers hearts through your prayers and sacrifices.

Now, I give My blessings to all the world, and as I bless you, know that special blessings and graces are being poured out upon the Church and to all souls all over the world. This special blessing will help you in your walk with Me, your risen Christ. My peace I give to you, not as the world gives, but as I, your Jesus of Love and Mercy give. I love you all My beloved ones. Peace, peace, peace!

Janie: Thank You My Jesus, thank You!
Jesus: You are most welcome.
Janie: I love You.

April 23, 1990 *During suffering*

Janie: *Our Lord's words during my illness.*

Jesus: My child, offer all your suffering for your family's conversion and for all who are distant from My Heart.

April 24, 1990 *Unite your heart with Mine*

Janie: *I was asking Jesus how I could serve Him without failing. I felt*

that I wasn't doing enough, praying enough. I was having problems with anger and in being patient with others at work and at home.
Jesus: My child, do not be concerned with small details. It pleases Me that you are aware of your shortcomings with others. The fact that you worry about displeasing Me demonstrates your love for Me. As you abandon yourself totally to Me, the evil one will attempt to bring more difficulties your way. I ask that you trust Me in everything. Keep your heart united with Mine.

April 25, 1990 *Fast as a family*

Our Lady: My children, you please your heavenly Mother that you are trying hard to draw closer to my Son and to please Him. Through my intercession and teachings you are coming to know my Son more and more. When you fast as a family, offer your prayers and fasting for all my beloved priests and for the Holy Souls in Purgatory. Pray for world peace and trust in my Immaculate Heart.

April 25, 1990 *You are children of the light*

Jesus: My child, do not be afraid when you are being distracted by Satan and all his lies. Remember, he is the father of lies, and he will tell you lies to destroy you. He will work on your weak points to discourage you. My child, remember, you and your family are the sons and daughters of the Eternal Father, therefore, you are children of the light.

Through My Death and Resurrection you received My power and authority to defend yourself through prayer when the evil one attacks you with his lies. My child, meditate on these Scriptures: Luke 10: 1-12 and Luke 10: 17-20.

Remember that your name and many others who live as children of the light - these souls' names are written in the Book of Life. Allow faith and love to be your strength.

April 25, 1990 *Prayer nurtures the soul*

Janie: *I was sad over some family matters, and I was hurting in my heart.*
Jesus: My child, you are upset that your family is much occupied with television. Pray for them. It hurts Me also, when My children don't think about Me.
Janie: What can I do?

Jesus: Offer this suffering for your own conversion and for theirs as well. Conversion is a process, and much prayer is needed to nurture the soul. Tomorrow, My child, fast on bread and water. It will be difficult for you, for the evil one will be strong in distracting you. As you suffer, your loved ones will draw closer to Me. Prepare well in the morning through prayer, and meditate on this Scripture, John 20: 24-29.

April 26, 1990 *Love never gives up*

Janie: *Today, I had family problems. I was upset because my relatives never visit me or act like my family. I was telling Jesus all this when I asked Him:* Jesus, during Your Passion and all during Your ministry, when You were healing and performing all Your miracles and people were mistreating you, did You feel like You wanted to stop doing everything for our sake?
Jesus: No, My child, for love never gives up. I understand your deep pain. My child, you are experiencing some of My painful Passion of rejection. My own people rejected Me and called Me 'mad'. They uttered unpleasant things about Me, but I loved them even more, and you must love them too, even in your deepest suffering. Through your suffering conversion will be born in their hearts.

April 30, 1990 *Accept His love*

Janie: *While we were praying our family Rosary, during the third Mystery Our Lady was with us. She had Baby Jesus in her arms.*
Our Lady: My children, tonight I come with the Child Jesus.
Janie: *She extended her arms and handed Jesus to us.*
Our Lady: Take Him. He is the gift of love to the world. Accept His love and be converted.

May 3, 1990 *Pray, pray, pray*

Janie: *Tonight, Our Lord and Our Lady were very present during the Rosary. Many family members came to pray with us. Tonight marks one year of Holy Hour prayer, of praying the Rosary. My family smelled sweet roses and myrrh for the first time.*
Our Lady: My child, remember when I first called you and charged you and your family with praying the Rosary and leading others to prayer?
Janie: Yes, My Lady.
Our Lady: Listen, my child to how beautiful they sound as they pray their Rosary and how strong their prayer is.

Janie: *I looked at my family. They looked beautiful. I have heard angels praying, but my family sounded beautiful. Our Lady then gave this message.*
Our Lady: My children, pray, pray, for only in this way will your hearts be converted!

May 4, 1990 *Return back to the Sacraments*

Our Lady: My child, tomorrow, many of my children will come to honor me and my heart is joyful.
Janie: *She was referring to the May Crowning.* My Lady, Sister wants me to give a speech about the Rosary and devotion to you. Should I write down anything?
Our Lady: I will speak to your heart, and these are my words: My little children, I, your heavenly Mother, love you all.

I invite you to return back to the Sacraments and to pray for one another. Live the Gospel, my children, and pray your Rosary everyday.

May 6, 1990 *Make reparation*

Jesus: My child, you have been making reparation and cultivating souls and talking to many about My Kingdom. This pleases Me. You are concerned about the salvation of others, and you are generous in your prayers for others. You, My child, spend much time praying for the needs of the entire world. You cover every area of the world as the Holy Spirit enlightens you. Continue praying and making reparation for the needs of the world. Bring Me all your concerns, and I will attend to them.
Janie: My Adorable Jesus, teach me how to suffer and give me this grace. I don't know how to accept my suffering and my crosses in my daily walk with You. Please Jesus, teach me. *Jesus reassured me that He would help me.*
Our Lady: My dear child, how much you please your heavenly Mother by asking my Son for the grace to suffer. Do not be concerned; my Son and I will teach you. God is pleased with your work and all your dedication in bringing others to my Son.

May 10, 1990 *I am the Way*

Jesus: My child, thank you for coming and for greeting Me as your Adorable Savior. This title is pleasing to Me. Leave Me all your concerns. I don't want you to have any worries, only trust Me and love Me.

Janie: *During Mass, I had a vision of a road and a vision of the Eucharist. Later I asked Jesus to explain it to me. I saw a road going from one heart to another heart.*
Jesus: My child, the road that you saw is the road that leads to Heaven.
Janie: Adorable Savior, please explain the Two Hearts.
Jesus: My child, the heart coming from below was your heart. The road is the path to Heaven, and the other heart that was in the Heavens was My Father's Heart. The vision of the Eucharist along the road: that is Me. I am The Way to the Father.

Only through repentance and eating of My Body and drinking My Blood will redemption take place in sinful hearts. Share this with others, as it is important that they learn about salvation through attending daily Mass and feeding on the Holy Eucharist as their daily food.

May 11, 1990 *Peace must reign in your hearts*

Our Lady: My dear children, tonight, I invite you to pray with open hearts. Be converted, be converted! Again I say, open your hearts, for I cannot help you if your hearts are closed! Pray for conversion, before it's too late! Please, dear children, help me, help me by trusting in my motherly intercession. Peace must reign in your hearts!

May 12, 1990 *Drive out fear through prayer*

Jesus: My child, do not be afraid, but pray. Prayer brings you to perfection and to peace. When fear fills your heart, drive fear out through praying. Know that I, your Jesus, am with you.

May 26, 1990 *Pray unceasingly*

Our Lady: My dear children, pray unceasingly, for prayer is your strength and prayer brings you peace.

May 27, 1990 *Dry spells help you to grow in faith*

Janie: *I was praying to Jesus to help me, for my heart felt dry.*
Jesus: My dear child, whenever you experience dry spells in your heart, it is not because I am not with you, for I will never abandon you. These dry spells help you to grow in faith. You see, My child, once the soul comes to know Me, that soul suffers when it feels abandoned by Me. It is during this time that I am the strongest, for when you are weak then I become strong in you. Your suffering also helps you to become

stronger in prayer and in trusting in Me, your Source of eternal life.

May 27, 1990 *Pray for My beloved brothers*

Jesus: My child, pray for My beloved brothers (the priests), for they are becoming fewer and fewer in numbers. Make reparation for their suffering and persecutions, for there is much suffering among My brothers. I love them so, I love them so. Pray for them.

May 28, 1990 *If you only understood the importance of prayer*

Janie: *Tonight, Our Lady told me that I would go to Medjugorje, although she knew I had a fear of flying. Her message was given in Blanco, Texas. My family and I were visiting there.*
Our Lady: Dear children, pray unceasingly! If you only understood the importance of prayer, you would pray with love in your hearts. Pray together as a family, attend Mass together, visit my Son often. There is so much suffering in the world because of lack of prayer. Please do not close your hearts, for when you stop praying my Immaculate and Sorrowful Heart suffers for you. I cannot help you if you do not pray. Pray, pray, pray!

June 5, 1990 *Obedience: a first class virtue*

Janie: *I was having problems and struggles with my family.*
Our Lady: My dear child, have no concern in your heart, for you have been helping your family draw closer to my Son. You have taught your family the importance of prayer. Your own prayers have helped you to grow in wisdom and discernment. You have brought joy to your Mother's Heart. My child, know that when you take care of your family out of love and obedience, you are also at prayer.
Janie: *Sometimes I got irritated when I had to stop praying to attend to my family. No one knew this except Jesus and Mary.*
Our Lady: This, my child, pleases God. My little one, you have been trying so very hard to be obedient in doing all that is asked of you as a wife and mother. You are growing in the virtue of obedience as well. Remember, obedience is a first class virtue. You obtain sanctity and purity through obedience.

June 5, 1990 *I am always interceding for you*

Our Lady: Dear children, tonight, I invite you to continue to pray. My children, you are so beautiful when you are in prayer. The fragrance of your prayer pleases me so, for it is prayer of the heart. Continue to pray your Rosary. Dear children, know that I am with you when you are in prayer. You have prayed so beautifully as a family. You have made me very happy. Know, my little ones, that I am always interceding for you and asking God to bless you. Continue to pray as a family, and you will receive blessings, blessings, blessings!

June 11, 1990 *Visit Me often in the Blessed Sacrament*

Janie: Greetings, my Beloved Savior. I came to visit with You. What can I do for You?
Jesus: My child, welcome to My Eucharistic Heart and thank you for coming to spend time with Me. My little one, you ask Me what you can do for Me. I, your Jesus, ask you to take Me to your family and to others and share My love with them. Tell them all how much I love them. Invite them to come and visit with Me. I will give them joy and peace. I will heal their wounded hearts. In Me they will find rest, and I will relieve them of their burdens, for I am gentle of Heart and My yoke is light. I desire that you do this for Me, and that you continue your visits with Me, your Beloved Savior.
Janie: What can I do for you, My Lady?
Our Lady: My daughter, my desire is the same as my Son. I, too, ask that you take me to share my love with others. Tell my children how much I love them. I desire that you come and visit with my Son, every day. Through these visits you will learn much about Our love for you. Your faith will grow and little by little you will believe that God has found favor in you.
Janie: I do believe in what you say My Lady, and I want to come to visit your Son, but I don't know my schedule. Please give me the grace I need to be obedient to your request.
Our Lady: My child, your request will be granted because of your honest heart. Go in my Son's peace.

June 21, 1990 *Read Holy Scripture every day*

Our Lady: My dear children, tonight, I invite you to be witnesses of the Gospel and to live in God's peace. I invite you to read Holy Scripture every day, and God will bless you. God will bless you!

June 24, 1990 *You will suffer rejection*

Janie: *I went on a retreat out of town with two friends and a priest. This was a very special time, as these two friends were receiving visita-*

tions from Our Lady. It was Our Lady's request that I go and stay with them for five days. I received this message from Jesus while visiting Him in the Blessed Sacrament.

Jesus: My child, I brought you here to give you a special blessing through My son, the priest. Know, My child, that your suffering will come through many of My beloved brother priests. They will reject everything you have been receiving on teachings of the family. Your bishop will come to know about you when the time comes for you to be known. Your messages will be made public.

My child, you will suffer when My brother priests reject you as they reject Me. Remain calm through all this when the time comes, for you will endure all the suffering and rejection. Your own family members (distant relatives) will doubt, and some of your friends will become jealous of all the blessings and wisdom that you receive. Do not fear, My child, for just as many of My brother priests reject you, many of My other brother priests will believe in what you are receiving to be divine. These are My brother priests whose hearts are open to My Mother's Immaculate Heart. These are My brother priests that love My Mother.

Many of My brother priests will come to you for advice and prayers. Do not worry when this time comes, for the Holy Spirit will enlighten you on what to say. Many of My brother priests will love and respect you. They will help you and defend you. Remember, My child, My special blessing will help you in times of persecution from the Church. Keep your eyes on Me, and you will embrace all your persecution with joy.

July 25, 1990 *Do not be afraid during trials and sufferings*

Our Lady: Dear children, do not be afraid during trials and sufferings. Pray and have an open heart. There is much suffering within the family, and the suffering will increase. Pray for those who are having a hard time converting. Reach out to them with love. Pray for all who are suffering. Take my Son to all whom you meet and tell them how my Son loves them. Pray your Rosary with your family and be converted!

July 26, 1990 *Do not allow pride to distract you*

Jesus: My child, never allow anyone or anything to separate you from My love. Do not allow pride to distract you from My love. Trust Me in everything and never take your eyes off of Me, your Jesus of Love and Mercy.

July 27, 1990 *Inspired prayers*

*Editor's Note: On this day, the feast of the Precious Blood, Janie was inspired by the Holy Spirit to write a prayer. This prayer and other beautiful prayers are located in the prayer section at the back of this book.

July 28, 1990 *Be at peace*

Jesus: My child, I want to thank you for coming to spend time with Me. My child, I know that it was hard for you to leave your family. Do not worry about your family, I am with them as I am also with you. Trust Me while you are here and allow the Holy Spirit to enlighten your heart.

During your retreat I will speak to you of many things, and you will hold all that I tell you dear to your heart. My Mother will help you in the areas that you need her assistance. Be at peace My child, be at peace while you are away from your family. My child, take My love to your family and share with them everything I tell you, for it will help them too.

July 28, 1990 *Do all that my Son commands*

Our Lady: My sweet angel, do all that my Son commands you to do. Know, my child, that my Son and I will help you in everything. Be open to Our teaching and guidance while you are here.

August 15, 1990 *Feast of the Assumption*

Our Lady: Dear children, you have brought me much joy through your love in honoring me on this my feast day. Know, my dear children, that when you come together for prayer, your prayers are answered.

August 19, 1990 *You belong to Me*

Jesus: My dear child, it was I, your Jesus of Love and Mercy, who called you to come and spend time with Me, for I know that you are suffering. My child, you have many thoughts running through your mind. **Satan is trying hard to overpower your mind, but he cannot do it! You belong to Me! You have received blessings and graces through your prayers. Never forget this. You are protected, and you protect your family through your prayers.**

I know, My child, that you feel sad when you cannot attend Mass. I know how much it hurts you when your family does not want to join you in prayer. Continue to pray for your family. Offer all your suffering for their and all other families' conversions. Know, My child, that right this minute I have given your family peace through your intercession for them. Love your family as I love you. Be patient with them and entrust them to Me, your Jesus of Love and Mercy.

August 19, 1990 *In the Two United Hearts lies your protection*

Our Lady: My precious angel, do not be concerned about your family, but do as my Son tells you and offer your suffering for your family and for peace in the world.

Remember, my precious child, take refuge in the Sacred Heart of my Son and my Most Immaculate Heart, for in the Two United Hearts lies your protection. Return to your prayers and do not worry about your family. They, too, are under Our protection.

August 21, 1990 *You will feel my presence*

Janie: Dear Lady, I am concerned about this trip. Are you really calling me to go to Medjugorje?
Our Lady: I am inviting you to go and visit this holy area. When you go you will experience a tremendous amount of grace like never before. I have chosen this place for the conversion of many. Do not be concerned about this trip, but trust in my intercession and continue to pray.
Janie: Will my visitation with you come to an end? Is this why you are calling me to go visit this place?
Our Lady: The day will come when I will no longer visit with you in the way that I am doing now.
Janie: Blessed Mother, please don't tell me just now. I can't take it. *I began to cry.*
Our Lady: Be strong, my angel, for I will always be with you, especially in times of difficulties. You will know that I am with you. On your birthday, I will be with you in a special way. You will feel my presence on special feast days.

August 23, 1990 *I will always live in your heart*

Janie: *I had been sad since Our Lady had told me that the day would come when she would stop visiting me. This never occurred to me since I knew nothing of Mary and that such visits could take place. I had*

asked Jesus to let me suffer and to let me feel my sadness for my own conversion.
Our Lady: My dear angel, I know that you are very sad and it saddens my Immaculate Heart to see you so sad. My child, I will never abandon you. I will always live in your heart. Please allow your heavenly Mother to console you. Do not shut me out, I love you my precious angel, I love you. Let me help you in your sorrow.

Janie: *I prayed with her and suddenly my heart was full of joy. I knew that she would always love me and be with me. I knew this, oh, how I knew it in my heart. I was so thankful to God for Our Lady's love for all her children.*

August 23, 1990 *Offer all your suffering*

Jesus: Dear child, I, your Jesus, thank you for coming to spend time with Me. My precious one, I know that you are sad and that you are suffering. **Offer all your suffering and pain for the poor souls that are having a difficult time converting. Pray and fast for these souls whom Satan keeps in bondage through their sins.**
Janie: *He meant that these souls refuse to be reconciled back to God, therefore, they remain in sin.*
Jesus: Pray and be strong in your suffering. Remember, I am always with you. I will never abandon you. Remember all the blessings that My Heavenly Father has blessed you with. Cling to these blessings. Be at peace, My child.

August 23, 1990 *Many souls are going astray*

Our Lady: Dear children, you bring joy to my Heart when you pray together as a family. Pray, dear children, for many souls are going astray. They live in darkness because of lack of prayer. Pray and fast, for through prayer and fasting many who want to convert are able to do so.

My children, I am here to help you, for I know that there is much suffering in your families. Do not be afraid when you look at your situation, rather rejoice and offer everything to God Who knows your hearts. Know that I love you all dearly and your refuge is my Most Immaculate Heart. I invite you, dear children, to help your heavenly Mother with your prayers. Be reconciled back to God and be converted! Time is short! Pray, children, and be converted, be converted!

September 10, 1990 A *messenger from Heaven*

Janie: *I received this visit while I was in prayer. I had been struggling with believing if all my visitations were of divine origin. Although my Spiritual Director said the visits were divine, I still struggled. I believe this was the reason for this visit. She greeted me and said Our Lady had sent her to talk with me and to help me. She wore a dazzling white dress and had flowers in her hair. Then the messenger began speaking to me.*

The Messenger: As you know, Most Holy Mary has been appearing to six children in Medjugorje and has been teaching the world through them. You have also been chosen by God and you must be obedient to doing the Will of God. The Queen of Heaven has come to you and your family to teach you about family love. You must do all that she tells you.

Janie: *I thought to myself, nobody will believe this.*

The Messenger: It is not important that anyone else believes, but that you yourself believe in your heart. You have been given a mission, a mission of cultivating the hearts of the families through your prayers and sacrifices. Much responsibility has been entrusted to you, and you must be obedient and trust God with this mission. You must never grow tired of doing what Most Holy Mary is asking of you. Your faith is your strength, and you must live with the kind of faith that only exists in Heaven.

Janie: *I guess she means to pray for strong faith, so that I may accomplish all that God is calling me to accomplish.*

The Messenger: Live Heaven on earth, doing only holy deeds. Serve God in all that you do. Love everyone always.

Janie: *I had lost a Rosary, so I asked her if she would ask Our Lady about my Rosary.*

The Messenger: Most Holy Mary will help you to find your Rosary. Remember, do everything that Most Holy Mary is asking of you. Offer all your prayers and sacrifices with love. Love God in everything. Farewell, my friend, farewell. Remember my words!

September 10, 1990 *Heaven has chosen you*

Our Lady: My angel, do not be concerned about this visit, but believe with your heart. My angel, Heaven has chosen you.

You have been entrusted with much responsibility. You will help to bring many families to God through your prayers and sacrifices. Do not be concerned about the trip to Medjugorje. I am preparing everything for you and your husband.

Janie: My Lady, I am sorry for not finishing all my prayers.
Our Lady: Do not be concerned. I know you will get all your prayers prayed. I must go, my angel, be at peace.

September 13, 1990 *Console me through your prayers*

Our Lady: My children, I, your heavenly Mother, invite you to continue to pray as a family. Know, my little ones, that Satan is active, trying to destroy you. Love one another and know that through your love you will obtain many blessings from God. My children, I turn to you to console your heavenly Mother through your prayers. Pray for all my children throughout the world. Love one another, love one another.

October 5, 1990 *Why do you worry and suffer in vain*

Our Lady: My dear angel, why do you worry so and suffer in vain?
Janie: Please, Dear Lady, what do you mean, suffer in vain?
Our Lady: My dear one, you suffer needlessly. It is the evil one who puts all these thoughts in your mind about me. My angel, I have been with you for almost two years now, and I will remain with you a short while longer after you make your trip to Medjugorje. I want you to use this time wisely and to come to me whenever you need to. Bring me all your concerns, for I have come to help you and teach you about my Son and His love and mercy. Do not be sad because I told you that my time is short, but be happy and show your gratitude to God for allowing me to be with you and your family. Share my Son's love with everyone you meet, especially with your family.

October 13, 1990 *A prophetic dream about the Gulf War*

Janie: *I had awakened from a most disturbing dream, and I asked Our Lady to come and explain this dream to me. In my dream I had seen violence, fighting, bombing, buildings being destroyed, people getting hurt, and some were killed.* My Lady, could you please explain my dream; it was very frightening. Is there going to be a war?
Our Lady: Yes, my angel, a war will break out soon. Fear will come among many. The economy will suffer where this war breaks out. Many will be homeless and they will have no jobs. Many innocent victims will be wounded, and others will die.
Janie: Am I to share this?
Our Lady: Yes, for much prayer will be needed to bring this war to an end. Its duration will be short, but many will suffer. Share this with your Spiritual Director right away, so that he will begin to offer the Holy

Mass and prayers for this intention. Many will begin to pray again during this time. The churches will be filled, for many will be praying for their loved ones.

Janie: Blessed Mother, what if my Spiritual Director doesn't believe me?

Our Lady: My dear angel, just do as I ask you. Your Spiritual Director will believe you, for I have prepared his heart for this time. Call him and share this message with him.

Janie: *I was afraid to call my Spiritual Director and share this message, because I didn't know how he would react. I prayed to the Holy Spirit to help me, then I called him. He believed me right away and agreed to do what Our Lady asked him to do. He even thanked me for being obedient to Our Lady and sharing this message with him.*

October 20, 1990 *Through prayer and fasting you obtain answers*

Jesus: My little flower, pray and fast in reparation for the sins of the world. Through prayer and fasting you obtain answers to your prayers. Share this with others.

October 22, 1990 *Thank you for your obedience*

Our Lady: My dear angel, thank you for being obedient in doing all that I am asking of you. God will bless you, God will bless you! Know that I am with you always.

November 1, 1990 *Dallas, Texas* *Begin forming prayer cenacles*

Our Lady: My dear angel, I invite you and your family to begin forming prayer cenacles in your community. Go to your priest and ask his blessing in this effort. Share this with your Spiritual Director and get his approval first. The Holy Spirit will enlighten you as you help other families to begin praying together in their homes.

As the family cenacles grow, then you can begin to move to the church. In this way, all families can join together. Blessings will come upon those who respond to my invitation. Later, you will help guide the youth to form cenacles and pray the Rosary. **God will bless all your prayers and efforts, and through your family's prayers God will bless many families. Much conversion in the family will be the fruits of your obedience.**

November 29, 1990 *Medjugorje, Yugoslavia* *Be a witness*

Our Lady: My child, I invite you to be a witness of living my messages when you return to your home in America. Commit to coming together once a week and praying the Rosary with my children who have joined you in this journey. Share my message with all people you meet. I have brought you here to bless you in a special way, to help you in the work that you will do in the future.

Janie: My Dear Lady, I will do as you ask, and I will live your messages. I will pray for my own conversion and for the conversion of the world. I will start a Rosary group, and we will meet once a week.

Heaven's Messages for The Family

Chapter Three

LESSONS
ON CONVERSION
1991

From the fig tree learn its lesson: as soon as its branch becomes tender and puts forth its leaves, you know that summer is near. So also, when you see all these things, you know that He is near, at the very gates.

Matthew 24:32-33

February 19, 1991 *Be strong my children*

Janie: *Our Lady asked us to form a prayer group while we were in Medjugorje. This was her first message to the prayer group.*
Our Lady: Dear children, do not be afraid, but go forth and serve God with joy. Be strong my children, be strong and do not fear. Be loving, my children, and let love be your strength. Thank you for listening to my message.

February 28, 1991 *I will teach you prayer of the heart*

Our Lady: Dear children, you are so dear to me, and I thank you for coming together for prayer. Through your prayer you will draw closer to my Son. You will grow through prayer. Know, my children, that as you come together for prayer, I, your heavenly Mother, will be with you. I will teach you about love and prayer in your family. I will guide you in your prayers. I will teach you prayer of the heart. My children, I will help you to live my messages and to share my messages with your family. I ask, little children, that you prepare your hearts for my motherly teaching and guidance. Thank you for listening to my message.

March 7, 1991 *Forgive from the heart*

Our Lady: Dear children, love and peace. I thank you for all of your hard work in living my messages and sharing them with others. Today, I invite you to be a loving family and to forgive one another. Only through love and forgiveness will you achieve peace in your family. Learn to forgive from the heart. Abandon all grudges and you will obtain God's peace. Thank you for listening to my message.

March 12, 1991 *I pray with you and for you*

Our Lady: Dear children, I bring you my motherly love, and I ask you to trust in my intercession. Be loving to one another and do not allow anything to keep you from doing God's Will. My children, I am praying with you and for you. Thank you for listening to my message.

March 18, 1991 *Learn to love*

Our Lady: Dear children, today, I invite you to live in God's peace and to extend His peace to others. My children, learn to love with your hearts and be at peace with one another. Pray together as a family and know that I am praying with you when you gather for family prayer.

Thank you for listening to my message

March 28, 1991 *Decide for conversion*

Our Lady: Dear children, today, I invite you to continue to pray and to trust God with all your prayers. Do not be discouraged in your suffering, but endure your crosses with joy. Abandon yourselves to my Immaculate Heart and allow me to help you to be pure and holy. Pray and fast, my children, and decide for conversion. Live my messages and pray, pray, pray! Thank you for listening to my message.

April 2, 1991 *I have come to help you*

Our Lady: Dear children, know that I love you very much. I have come from Heaven to help you to know and love my Son. I am with you each step of the way. Pray, children, pray! Thank you for listening to my message.

April 16, 1991 *Pray hard, time is running out*

Our Lady: Dear children, love and pray for one another. You know, dear children, that I have come to love and help you. Pray, and pray very hard for time is running out. You, dear children, must pray so that all souls will be converted, especially those most distant from my Son's Heart.

April 22, 1991 *So many have stopped praying*

Our Lady: Dear children, my heart is so sad, because so many of my children have stopped praying. Please, dear children, I need your help.

Pray, dear children, pray, for there is so much suffering in this world. Be converted, dear children, be converted!

April 29, 1991 *Believe in my Son's love for you*

Our Lady: Dear children, thank you for all the work and prayers that you are doing. Dear children, pray and do not be afraid. Believe in the love that my Son has for you and continue in your prayers and in loving one another. Pray your Rosaries every day, dear children, and pray with your hearts, pray with your hearts.

May 9, 1991 *Ascension Thursday - Love, pray and listen*

Jesus: My brothers and sisters, I have ascended that you may have eternal life. Love and pray for one another and listen to My Mother. My brothers and sisters, I have come, because I am pleased with these prayer gatherings. My Mother and I are pleased with these prayer gatherings. My Mother and I are pleased to be here on this special day. Pray always to the Holy Spirit, because when you pray to the Holy Spirit, you speak directly to My Father's Heart.

May 9, 1991 *Take my messages seriously*

Our Lady: Dear children, know that I am with you. I have come to take you to Heaven with me. Dear children, I am here to help you to be clean. Please, dear children, help me. Let your prayer be prayer of the heart, where you will find peace and love. Live my messages, dear children, and take my messages seriously. Live my messages everyday!

May 22, 1991 *Open your hearts in prayer*

Our Lady: Dear children, pray and trust, dear children, pray and trust. You, dear children, do not know how to open your hearts to the Holy Spirit. Do not be afraid, for I am here to help you.

Prayer is the answer to all your suffering. Learn to pray, dear children, and allow your hearts to open up in prayer. Take refuge in my Immaculate Heart and be converted from the heart. Dear children, I love you and I am here to help you. Trust, dear children, trust and pray, and suffer for the love of others. Pray the Rosary, pray the Rosary, pray the Rosary!

May 28, 1991 *Pray the complete Rosary*

Our Lady: Dear children, I am here to take you to Heaven with me. You, dear children, must pray so that you can have a pure heart. Do not be afraid, dear children, but be converted! Dear children, you are so precious to the Lord. If you only knew how great the love of God is for you. Please, dear children, pray! Pray all the time! Find time for prayer, for through your prayer many souls can be converted. Time is running out, dear children, so be obedient and pray, fast, and be converted, be converted!

Peace, dear children, peace. I love you, dear children. I desire that peace will reign in all my children. I desire, dear children, that you pray the complete Rosary. Pray for love, peace, conversion within the Church. Pray for your families, yourselves, and do not forget the Poor Souls in Purgatory or the unborn.

May 28, 1991 *My Sacred Heart*

Janie: *Jesus came to visit. From His Heart were shining colors of red and golden yellow, and there were brilliant flames. The light from His Heart was indescribable.*
Jesus: This is My love and mercy. Take it, take it unto others. Obey My Mother. Love and honor her. Look at My Sacred Heart. It bleeds for all the sinfulness of this world. Come and take refuge in My Sacred Heart.

May 28, 1991 *Prayers and offerings*

Our Lady: My dear children, my heart is so joyful, because through your obedience some of my children are returning back to my Son.

Your prayers and your offerings are so important. Please, I beg you dear children, pray, pray, pray!

June 25, 1991 *Do not be afraid, but pray*

Our Lady: Dear children, pray as a family, for Satan is so active, and he wants to destroy you. Pray, dear children, pray and be strong. Do not be afraid of anything, but pray!

July 10, 1991 *My Heart is pierced with sadness*

Our Lady: *My child, today, I, your heavenly Mother, ask that you join your prayers to mine. Open your heart to what I am about to tell you concerning the world. Write what I tell you. My Heart is pierced with sadness, for my children continue to ignore my messages. They continue to live in sin, and in doing this they lead others to sin. If my children continue to ignore my messages, much suffering will take place, and many innocent victims will suffer and die because of hard and obstinate hearts.*

A war has begun in Yugoslavia. This situation will get worse. Many will suffer and die. Many will be left homeless. Innocent families will suffer. I ask much prayer of all my children for this war. There will be wars in different parts of the world where many will die. Earthquakes will destroy many souls. Drought will destroy crops, and my children who are farmers will suffer immensely. There will be much famine, and all these disasters will cause the economy to suffer. Some of these disasters are taking place now, but it will become much worse.

The Church will suffer more and more. Priests will leave the priesthood. Many of my priests will go against the teaching of my Son's Vicar on earth. Division will grow more and more through lack of obedience. My beloved Pope will suffer in a physical way.

Much prayer is needed for my priests who continue to live in a time of great apostasy. Many do not acknowledge the true meaning of my Son's True Presence in the Most Holy Eucharist. This pierces my Heart.

The family will suffer from violence, child abuse, rebellious sons and daughters, and the divorce rate will increase. Love and prayer will not be in existence in homes. Much division will separate the family.

The youth will turn against their parents, many causing violence to their parents even to the point of killing their parents. Drug abuse will take many lives. Abortion will increase tremendously among the youth. They will bring fear to those around them, and they will cause much destruction to society. My child, if my children do not listen and live my messages, it will be too late for them. Pray and fast, so that many will decide for conversion.

The whole world is in need of much conversion, but I am deeply concerned about your country whose sins keep increasing with each moment that goes by. My child, it is for the sake of all my children that I have remained in this world for so long. If my children do not pray, I cannot help them. If they do not pray, they cannot come to know God. It is only through prayer and fasting that conversion will take place. Soon, my time in the world will come to an end. Pray, my child, pray, so that hearts will be converted before it's too late.

July 22, 1991 *Pray for one another*

Our Lady: Dear children, pray your Rosaries and return back to the Sacraments, before it's too late! Pray with your hearts, dear children, and trust in your prayer. Love one another and pray for one another.

August 1, 1991 *Many of you do not ask me for help*

Our Lady: Dear children, pray and fast, pray and fast. Be reconciled and be converted! Dear children, I come as the Queen of Peace. Therefore, I ask you to live in peace and to practice peace. Do not be afraid to ask me for help. Many of you do not ask me for help, because you do not believe I am here. Open your hearts, for I only wish to lead you to Heaven.

August 6, 1991 *Love one another*

Our Lady: Dear children, know the importance of family prayer. Love one another. Again, I say, love one another. My heart is sad, little children, because there is no love in the family. Be converted, be converted! I love you all, little children, and I am here to help you. Love one another and pray together as a family. Little children, I have given this message many times. Know that if it was not important, I would not insist that you pray as a family.

August 15, 1991 *Feast of the Assumption - Your guide to holiness*

Our Lady: Dear children, rejoice and thank your heavenly Father for allowing me to come down from Heaven to help and guide you in your way to holiness. Dear children, please trust in my intercession, for I am your heavenly Mother who loves you. Pray, dear children, and be converted. Only through prayer and conversion will you be able to attain pure hearts.

August 22, 1991 *Queenship of Mary - You have much to learn*

Our Lady: Dear children, I am calling you to holiness. Do not be afraid, for nothing can harm you. Love one another and live the joy that God has placed in your hearts. Do not be afraid, my little ones, for I am with you each step of the way. You have much to learn, little children.

September 2, 1991 *I am depending on you*

Our Lady: Dear children, pray for obedience. For you, dear children, do not know how to be obedient. God has granted me this time to be with you. Dear children, the conversion of the world is so important. I am depending on each one of you to do what God requires of you. My time is short, so please listen to me dear children, listen to me and be converted. Pray and fast.

September 12, 1991 *Listen to and live my messages*

Our Lady: Dear children, today is a day of great rejoicing! Prepare your hearts through prayer and fasting, so that you may be able to do God's Will. Dear children, you are so special to my Heart, and I pray so for all my children. Rejoice, and live as children of the light. I am your heavenly Mother, and I have come to bring peace back into this world that continues to walk in darkness. Dear children, please listen to all my messages and live them for each one is of great importance. Please believe in my messages and now, I say, peace, little children, peace.

September 17, 1991 *Offer your fasting for unbelievers*

Our Lady: Dear children, pray your Rosaries from the heart, for these are very important times. Pray with your families and love one another. Dear children, do not get tired of serving God. Come, rather, and put all your trust in Him and decide for Him. When you fast, dear children, offer it for all the unbelievers who are walking in darkness.

September 22, 1991 *Heaven is rejoicing*

Our Lady: Dear children, how pleased you've made me with all your prayers and offerings. Heaven is rejoicing. Heaven is rejoicing! I love you all so dearly, my little children. With your many prayers and offerings you have decorated so many souls with the seed of conversion. So many hearts have bloomed just like fresh flowers. I thank you all, dear children. Keep living my messages with your eyes fixed on Heaven.

October 3, 1991 *You can make a difference*

Our Lady: Dear children, today, again, I call you all to decide for God. Satan is very busy and active trying to destroy souls. You, dear children, can make a difference in the world with your prayers, fasting and offerings. Do not get discouraged, but grow in goodness and purity. Continue praying, for these are hard times, and there is much suffering, so much suffering. Pray, dear children, pray.

October 8, 1991 *I am the Lady of Grace*

Our Lady: Dear children, repent and be converted! Accept your little crosses that God sends your way. I am the Lady of Grace. Many graces are bestowed upon the faithful through my intercession. Therefore, trust in my intercession and love my Immaculate Heart. I love you so dearly, I love you so dearly. Trust in my intercession.

October 14, 1991 *I am the Mother of All Creation*

Janie: *I saw Our Lady standing over a globe, and rays were streaming down from her hands illuminating all areas of the world. She was wearing a white dress, blue mantle, and there were twelve stars around her crown. Her crown was gold, and all around her was a golden haze. Emanating from her hands were different colors, but mostly white. The globe was also radiant and gold. Her mantle and dress were blowing in a breeze and waving over the whole world. Our Lady was smiling. Her light shown over the whole world.* What are you showing me, Blessed Mother? Why are you covering every area of the world?
Our Lady: I am the Mother of All Creation. I invite all my children to love one another, to live and work in harmony with one another. I am the Mother of all Creation, and I love you all, for you are my children.

October 22, 1991 *In the end there will be one Church, one people*

Jesus: I am here for you always. I have given you My Precious Body and Blood so you would be redeemed. Take My Body and be nourished. Take My Blood and do not thirst. I am your strength. I am your hope. I am your teacher. Do not look anywhere else but to Me and My Father, for here lies eternal life. This is to be your strength always.
Janie: But what about those who do not feed on the Holy Eucharist?
Jesus: Men separated because of disobedience from the very beginning. My Father made one Church, and one people. Do not worry, I am with all my brothers and sisters. In the end there will be one Church, one people.

October 22, 1991 *Open your hearts to His graces*

Our Lady: Dear children, pray to God all the time. Open your hearts to His graces, the graces with which He wishes to bless you. Children, you will never understand how important prayer is. Know, dear children, that God answers all prayers. Pray, pray, pray!

October 31, 1991 *Mother of Compassion and Love*

*Editor's note: Our Lady appears for the first time as Mother of Compassion and Love. From this day forward she continued to appear to Janie and the prayer group under this title.

Janie: *Our Lady was dressed in a beautiful robe of deep purple silk. She wore a deep purple cape with traces of gold on her cape and sleeves. Her dress was darker than her veil, and she wore a crown on her head.*
Our Lady: Dear children, I, your heavenly Mother, come to you as a Mother of Compassion and a Mother of Love. I come to you, dear children, with an urgent message: Pray, children, pray! Do not neglect my messages, for if you do I cannot help you. I will pray for you. I will pray for you. The Rosary is your weapon; pray it with faith, my children. I love you, I love you.

November 4, 1991 *You are called to love*

Our Lady: Dear children, peace and love, my dear children. Believe in my Son, for He is your strength. Listen to Him, and you will do God's Will. Dear children, I am with you. Be obedient and pray for all the world, especially the unconverted. Peace, be filled with it, and love everyone that God sends your way. Your task is a difficult one, for you are called to love and believe with your hearts. I am with each one of you in a special way all the time.

November 14, 1991 *Be converted*

Our Lady: Dear children, be converted, be converted and live my messages! I am here to help you and to guide you. Open your hearts and love one another. Thank you for listening to my message.

November 19, 1991 *These are your tools*

Janie: *Our Lady came with the Rosary and the Scapular. On the Rosary, the Cross was lit up and a real Jesus was on the Cross with drops of Blood coming from His Wounds. The angels collected the Blood dropping from Jesus and flew off. The Scapular was also in a brilliant light.*
Our Lady: My children, sin no more. These are your tools. Clothe yourselves with them.
Janie: *Her message followed shortly after this.*
Our Lady: Dear children, I have come from Heaven as your heavenly Mother. I have come to help you to be pure and holy, to prepare for the coming tribulation. Love one another. Love one another and be holy. Live a prayerful and holy life. Peace, peace and only peace.

November 25, 1991 *Many of you are discouraged*

Our Lady: Dear children, do not become discouraged. Many of you are becoming discouraged. When you feel this way pray your hardest, for the Almighty will give you His grace to go on. Dear children, take refuge in my Immaculate Heart. Ask the Holy Spirit to enlighten you in times of difficulties. I am here for you, dear children, trust in my intercession. Through prayer you will receive your answers. Trust me and love my Son, love my Son.

December 5, 1991 *The gift of love: the greatest gift*

Our Lady: Dear children, glory to God in the Highest. Praised be His Holy Name forever and ever. Amen. Prepare your hearts, little children, for My Son, for He is your salvation.

Open your hearts and keep pure during this holy time. Be like shepherds on that Holy Night. Keep watch and pray for peace. I love you, my dear children, and I am always interceding for you. Be pure and holy and ask for the gift of love, for this, little children, is the greatest gift. I am sad, because there is not enough love in this world; but you, my children, can make a difference. Be at prayer at all times and allow my Son's peace to live in your hearts. Thank you for listening to my message.

December 12, 1991 *Feast of Our Lady of Guadalupe-Love conquers evil*

Our Lady: Dear children, peace and love! I am here at your side. I have come to help you and to teach you. Rejoice and love! Love, children, love, for this is the time when love will conquer all evil. Give one another the most precious gift one can offer my Son - which is love; that is all He asks for. Strive for love, and you will learn to love. You will learn to love! Thank you for listening to my message.

December 16, 1991 *Live Heaven on earth*

Our Lady: Dear children, rejoice and be at peace. This is the time of rejoicing! Live Heaven on earth, doing God's Most Holy Will. May you spread the joy of my beloved Son to all the world around you. Dear children, open your hearts and allow the love of my Son to fill you during this Holy Season. Rejoice! Rejoice, for God is with you. Thank you for listening to my message.

Chapter Four

ABANDONING EVERYTHING TO JESUS AND MARY 1992

You are the light of the world. A city set on a hill cannot be hid. Nor do men light a lamp and put it under a bushel, but on a stand, and it gives light to all in the house. Let your light so shine before men, that they may see your good works and give glory to your Father who is in Heaven.

Matthew 5:14-16

January 6, 1992 *I hold you so tenderly*

Our Lady: Dear children, today, I come as the Queen of Peace and Queen of All Hearts. I love you all, my dear children, and I hold you all so tenderly in my Most Immaculate Heart. Pray, and be pure and holy. Love, children, love everyone. Pray for the unconverted and reach out to them with love. Pray together with your family. Thank you for listening to my message.

January 14, 1992 *Ask for a pure heart*

Our Lady: Dear children, take refuge in my Immaculate Heart, for I am here to help you and to sustain you from all the traps that the evil one is putting in your path. Love, little children, love. Ask for a pure heart in your prayers, and the Almighty will grant you this prayer. I love you, dear children. I love you all, and I am here for you. Do not turn away from Heaven, but turn toward Heaven, for in Heaven you will find your paradise. Thank you for listening to my message.

January 22, 1992 *Look toward Heaven and trust in God*

Our Lady: Dear children, come to your heavenly Mother and allow yourselves to be loved and cared for by me. Am I not your heavenly Mother? Am I not here to help you and lead you to Heaven? Do not allow yourselves to be frightened by the many problems that the evil one puts in your path.

I ask you to look toward Heaven and to put your trust in God, the Almighty and Merciful Father. I ask you, dear children, to allow yourselves to be loved by me, and I ask you to love yourselves as God loves you. In this way, when you love yourselves, you accept yourselves as God accepts you. Do not worry, little children, but trust, trust, trust! Thank you for listening to my message.

January 27, 1992 *Pray for a loving heart*

Our Lady: Dear children, today, I, your heavenly Mother, call you to pray for a loving heart. I am sad, because there is not enough love in the world. Please, dear children, help me to bring love into this unconverted world. Be obedient and spend more time in prayer. Spend time with my Son in the Most Blessed Sacrament. He will help you and refresh you. Spend more time praying and less time worrying and doubting. This world is in need of much conversion. Through your prayers and sacrifices this world will be converted. Thank you for listening to my message.

February 6, 1992 *I invite you to purity and to love*

Our Lady: Dear children, rejoice and be loving to all those souls that God puts in your path. Today, I ask you again, like never before, to live my messages and share them with others. Dear children, today, I come to invite you to purity and to love. Do not worry, but take refuge in my Most Immaculate Heart and remain under my protection. Rejoice, rejoice, rejoice, for I am with you each step of the way! Thank you for listening to my message.

February 11, 1992 *My Son died for you*

Our Lady: Dear children, today, I, your heavenly Mother, crown you, my children, with the crown of holiness. Remember, you were created in the likeness of your Creator, the Father Almighty. It is, then, your duty as a child of God to walk in holiness. My Son died for you, so that you would be redeemed to God the Almighty. Through my Son you are given new life. Love my Son, then, and listen to Him. Trust in Him Who gave up His life for you, for He will lead you to eternal life. Thank you for listening to my message.

February 17, 1992 *Do not worry*

Our Lady: Dear children, rejoice and do not become discouraged! Continue to pray and remember that God listens to your prayers.

Dear children, there are some of you who are worried about your loved ones. I am here to tell you do not worry, but pray and trust. Present all your prayers to God with faith. I love you, dear children, and I am here for you and to help you. Trust in my intercession and do not worry, but trust in your prayers. Remember, there is no room for fear and worry. Your loved ones will come to know my Son. Continue to pray for them. Thank you for listening to my message.

February 27, 1992 *I am here to take you to Heaven with me*

Our Lady: Dear children, peace and joy! Peace and joy! Be happy, little children, for I am here to take you to Heaven with me. When you pray, little children, you become like little beautiful flowers that illuminate all of Heaven. Prayer is very important. Do not forget this, my little ones. Go then, and spread your love and prayers to all without hesitation. Thank you for listening to my message.

March 3, 1992 *Seek purity and holiness of heart*

Our Lady: Dear children, today, I invite you to open your hearts to my Son and trust Him. Embrace your Savior Who gave us His love. Look upon one another with His love, and spread this love where there is no love. Look at Him Who gave up His life for your salvation. Model yourselves after my Son, and seek purity and holiness of heart. Detach yourselves and renounce everything, and accept your cross with joy. In doing this you will embrace the love of my Son and become holy and pure. Thank you for listening to my message.

March 10, 1992 *These are troubled times*

Our Lady: Dear children, I am the Queen of Peace, and I have come to bring peace to all my children throughout the world. I invite you to live this peace and share it with others. Be loving, and you will experience joy in your hearts. Dear children, I invite you to pray more. Pray particularly in these hard times when there is so much violence and darkness around you, for these are troubled times.

Pray and fast, trust God with all your heart. I am here to help you and to lead you to holiness. Pray with love in your hearts, and love one another. Thank you for listening to my message.

March 11, 1992 *Live my messages by your example*

Our Lady: My dear children, greetings to each one! I thank you for all your hard work and the suffering that you have endured. Know, my little ones, that God blesses all your efforts. My little ones, today, I continue to invite you to prayer of the heart, where you surrender all to God, Who loves you so tenderly. Rejoice, my children, and continue to live my messages by your example. Be a living testimony to others; in this way, you will help me to bring others to conversion. Prepare yourselves every day with strong prayer, and be loving to all whom God puts in your path.

Be obedient, my little ones, and listen to my motherly teachings, for I am here to teach you about the love of God. If you respond to my requests and put my messages into practice, you won't have to worry about anything, for you will be under my shadow and protection. I will take care of you and your family. I will teach you everything about love and prayer. I will lead you closer to my Son's Heart.

My little children, you must open your hearts and decide for conversion. Learn to love God with all your hearts. Then, the Holy Spirit will enlighten you in all aspects of your lives. Pray, my children, pray. I love you all. Thank you for listening to my message.

March 24, 1992 *Pray for peace*

Our Lady: Dear children, today, I invite you to pray for peace in the world. Extend your prayers to the entire world. Pray for peace for yourselves and your families. Trust in your prayers as you pray for peace. Dear children, do not despair in your difficulties, for these are the times when much more suffering will take place, especially with those you love the most. Pray, children, pray. Read Holy Scripture and live Holy Scripture, so that you may be protected from the hands of the evil one.

My little ones, I am here to help you and to teach you. You must listen and live my messages. Pray and make God the most important friend you've ever had, for He is your true friend. My children, I am the Queen of Peace and my Son is the Prince of Peace. Live this peace and share this peace with the world. Peace, peace, peace! Offer up all your prayers for peace. Thank you for listening to my messages.

March 30, 1992 *Trust in my presence with you*

Our Lady: Dear children, rejoice and pray for a joyful and loving heart. Purify your hearts through your love for my Son. During this special time, spend more time with my Son and with your family, praying together for your needs. I am here to teach you how to love and pray. Trust in my presence with you. Thank you for listening to my message.

April 4, 1992 *Live simply*

Our Lady: Dear children, peace, children, peace! Live your lives only for my Son. Abandon yourselves, abandon yourselves to God the Almighty. Live simply, and be at peace with one another. Dear children, I love you all. You are most precious to my Immaculate Heart. I look forward to being with you and praying with you. Thank you for listening to my message.

April 14, 1992 *Believe in your prayers*

Our Lady: Dear children, today, I invite you to live the Passion of my Son. Pray and fast. Pray for a pure heart and love one another. Dear children, pray to God to help you in your struggles, for some of you struggle needlessly. You struggle because you don't take time to pray. When you pray, you don't believe in your prayer.
Janie: *She meant you pray without faith.*
Our Lady: Pray and fast, dear children, for prayer opens up your heart. Pray together as a family. Pray the Rosary everyday. Thank you for listening to my message.

April 20, 1992 *Peace comes from God*

Our Lady: Dear children, peace, and rejoice in my risen Son, for He has risen to give you new life! Today, I invite you to peace and to share this peace with the rest of the world. Put all your struggles aside and pray for peace, for the world is ready for peace. Believe in this peace that I invite you to live, and share it. Put all worries and doubts aside, for these things put distance between you and God. I am the Queen of Peace, and this peace that I invite you to live comes from God. Thank you for listening to my message.

April 30, 1992 *Listen to the Holy Spirit within you*

Our Lady: Dear children, rejoice, rejoice, rejoice for I am here to help you and lead you to Heaven! All you have to do is open your hearts, and listen to the voice of the Holy Spirit within you. My little one, trust in my intercession and take refuge in my Immaculate Heart. Be at peace and pray your Rosaries, for the Rosary is your weapon. Again, I say, trust in my intercession. I love you, my children, I love you all. Thank you for listening to my message.

May 5, 1992 *Decide for conversion and accept your crosses*

Our Lady: Dear children, today, I, your heavenly Mother, invite you to a new life of prayer and purity. Open your hearts, dear children, and abandon yourselves to God. Decide for conversion and accept all your crosses with joy. My little ones, listen to your heavenly Mother, and allow your lives to be transformed into lives of prayer. Accept and follow the path that leads to eternal life. Do not be afraid to convert, but convert and God will remove all your fears. Thank you for listening to my message.

May 10, 1992 *Mother's Day - A divine jewel for your crown*

Our Lady: To all Mothers, I greet and bring the blessing from God to each of you! Special blessings are given to each one of you. I ask you to continue doing the work of my Son.

Love the gifts that you have been blessed with, which are your children. Love them and nurture their souls, and prepare them for the Kingdom of God. Know that a beautiful, heavenly crown is being prepared for you in Heaven. Each time you bring your children to God, a divine jewel is added to your crown.

Do not be afraid to be a good mother and lead your children in the right direction. I know that your job in bringing your children to God is a difficult task. It is important that you remember that God has given you all the graces necessary to be that heavenly mother that God intended for you to be. Know that I am praying for each of you all the time and helping you to bring yourselves and your family to God the Father. I ask and invite you to pray for one another; and please pray for all those poor mothers who do not know my Son and for those mothers who reject Him.

May 21, 1992 *Not tomorrow, but now!*

Our Lady: Dear children, open your hearts and allow God to help you. Pray, my children, pray, for prayer opens your hearts, and prayer brings you peace. God wants to give you His peace. Little children, there is no happiness or joy without God's peace. You pray and ask God's help, but you do not have open hearts. You ask for God's forgiveness, but you refuse to forgive others. How can God help you, my children, if you do not trust Him? Abandon yourselves, abandon yourselves and God will help you. Listen to me, listen to me, for time is running out! Come to God now, little children, not tomorrow, but now! Thank you for listening to my message.

May 26, 1992 *The midst of the great tribulation*

Our Lady: Dear children, peace, little children, peace! I come to pray for you, for some of you are fearful of the signs and wonders that surround you. Know that you are in the midst of the great tribulation. Much suffering will take place with many of your loved ones.

Do not worry, for I am here with you. Nothing will harm you if you live Holy Scripture. Rejoice, little children, and continue to pray, for prayer is your strength. I am here, I am here, do not be afraid. You, my children, are the light of the world. Allow that light to shine, shine, shine! I love you, my little precious ones. Thank you for listening to my message.

June 1, 1992 *Prepare for the coming of the Holy Spirit*

Our Lady: Dear children, I am here to help you to prepare for the coming of my Beloved Spouse, the Holy Spirit. I ask each one of you to offer all your prayers, masses, novenas, as a means of preparation. You will be blessed if you respond to my request. I love you all, my children, and I want your hearts to be open to receive all the blessings from Heaven. Rejoice and praise God, praise God! Thank you for listening to my message.

June 11, 1992 *Join the army He has been preparing throughout time*

Our Lady: Dear children, today, I, your heavenly Mother, invite you to open your hearts and prepare your hearts for my Son, Jesus. He is calling each one of you. He is gathering all people from all nations through my intercession to come and join His army that He has been preparing throughout time.

Dear children, time is short. I have mentioned this on several occasions; believe and prepare. I call you again to prayer and fasting, to conversion, to total abandonment. These are your spiritual tools that will protect you from Satan. Thank you for listening to my message.

June 16, 1992 *The harvest of salvation is here*

Our Lady: Dear children, today, I invite you to prayer of the heart. Spend time in prayer and less time talking about prayer. Be silent, and you will hear the voice of God in your hearts. Pray and fast, and be humble of heart. Love one another. Pray to God for a loving heart, in this way you will love all people that God puts in your path.

My children, the harvest of salvation is here. Believe, repent, and be converted, and you will have eternal salvation! Thank you for listening to my message.

June 22, 1992 *The importance of prayer and fasting*

Our Lady: Dear children, today, I invite you again to continue to pray and fast. I need all your sacrifices to help convert many souls. There are so many of my children who are not yet converted. My precious ones, I would not ask you for so much prayer and fasting if it wasn't of great importance. Know that as you pray and fast, your own hearts become more open to the Will of God. Prayer opens the heart and fasting brings about your own purification. Help me, my dear children, help me, and together you and I will help to bring much conversion throughout the world. Thank you for listening to my message.

June 30, 1992 *Spiritual healing in the devotion of novenas*

Our Lady: Dear children, greetings to all! Today, I want to thank you for your prayers and sacrifices. There has been much conversion throughout the world. Do not worry about anything, but pray for peace in the world. Offer up novenas as a means of penance, for there is much spiritual healing in these devotions. Offer novenas frequently in your prayers. Peace, peace, peace. I love you, dear ones. Thank you for listening to my message.

July 6, 1992 *Have courage*

Our Lady: Dear children, today, I, your heavenly Mother, invite you to return back to God. Many of you, my little children, have listened and accepted salvation in your lives. To you, I say, thank you! Continue to pray for those who refuse to accept God's love and mercy. Time is short, and the suffering continues due to lack of faith and love. To you who are struggling with your faith, have courage. Be converted, be converted! Thank you for listening to my message.

July 13, 1992 *If you do not pray, you endanger your souls*

Our Lady: Dear children, I am here to ask and invite you to continue praying for conversion, peace and love in the world. Dear children, many of you have not taken my messages of the family to heart. You continue to allow your children freedom which endangers their souls. You continue to watch endless hours of television.

Many of you have not been praying as a family. This saddens my Immaculate Heart, for I am in need of your family prayers. Please, open your hearts and decide for prayer, for if you do not pray, you endanger your souls. Today, I ask you to pray and to live as a holy family. Ask St. Joseph to intercede for you and your family. He will help you, and he will pray for you. Pray, children, pray. Thank you for listening to my message.

July 23, 1992 *God knows all your needs*

Our Lady: Dear children, pray and trust. Be at peace, for having peace in your hearts is so important. Many of you are unhappy. To you, I say, pray and trust. God knows all your needs. Be open to His love and blessings. Be at peace, and share this peace with others. Thank you for listening to my message.

August 10, 1992 *Make God's Will your own*

Our Lady: Dear children, today, I invite you to take refuge in my Immaculate Heart. Pray for a pure heart and a willing spirit. In this way you will do God's Holy Will. Make God's Will your own through your trust in Him. Remain under my mantle, and together through your prayers and sacrifices, you will help me to usher in the reign of my Son and the triumph of my Immaculate Heart. Thank you, my little children, I love you all. Thank you for listening to my message.

August 15, 1992 *I am the Glory of the New Jerusalem*

Our Lady: Dear children, rejoice, my chosen ones, and come to celebrate with me on my feast day. Come, my little ones, and bring all your prayers and sacrifices. Offer them up to God with all your love. My little ones, today, I ask that you give thanks to the Almighty Father for allowing me to be with you for such a long time. Be grateful, my children, and show your gratitude by doing all that I am asking you. Be loving, be prayerful, be obedient. Pray for purity of the heart, for when you pray with a pure heart, God answers your prayers. He loves purity.

My little flowers, you wonder how to obtain a pure heart. My little ones, you do this through the sacrament of Reconciliation. That is why I ask you to receive this Sacrament frequently. Rejoice, for today I will bless you all, my little ones, in a special way. I ask each one of you to bring me all your concerns, that I may present them to God. Rejoice, for you will feel the presence of my Beloved Son Who rejoices with me.

Be thankful on this special day for my glorious Assumption into Heaven. Love your heavenly Queen and trust in my intercession. I am the Glory of the New Jerusalem, Queen of Heaven and Earth. Rejoice, and give thanks to God, that He has blessed you with my presence on earth. I am coming to many throughout the world. I am preparing a spiritual ark, my little ones, that has been formed from your many, many prayers and offerings.

Today, I wish to thank you, my children. You have been so helpful with your prayers, and in helping me to bring many new souls to my beloved Son, Jesus. Know that each day, many souls are being converted through your prayers.

Beware! Satan is very angry, for he is growing weak. The weaker he gets, the more aggressive he becomes. His goal is to destroy your family, so pray together as a family. Love and forgive one another, for the family that prays together, grows together in faith, peace, unity and strength.

Do not be afraid of Satan, for your prayers dissolve all his evil tricks that he puts in your path. That is why, my children, I ask you again and again to attend Holy Mass together as a family.
Janie: *She means daily.*
Our Lady: Also, receive the sacrament of Reconciliation, pray your Rosary, spend time with my Son in Adoration, read and live Holy Scripture. If you do this, my children, you will have a place with me in Paradise. Rejoice, rejoice, rejoice and give glory to God forever and ever. Thank you for listening to my message.

August 17, 1992 *Respond to my call*

Our Lady: Dear children, peace and joy! My greetings to all! Today, my children, I invite you to continue to pray and fast. You, dear children, ask much of God. You must make sacrifices to receive answers to your prayers. You obtain your answers by means of prayer and fasting. God is ready to answer all your prayers according to His Holy Will.

Dear children, do not grow tired of my asking you to be converted. Conversion brings you closer to God. As you begin to convert, your hearts begin to bloom like beautiful heavenly flowers. Be obedient, my children, and respond to my call to prayer, fasting and conversion. Thank you, my little ones, thank you.

August 24, 1992 *Listen to my plea*

Our Lady: Dear children, greetings to all! Today, I invite you again in a special way to pray more and to trust God with your prayers. Spend more time with my Son; allow Him to help you to draw closer to His loving heart.

My little ones, do not be afraid to reach out to one another when you need prayers or love. You are all my children, and I want you to live together in harmony and in love. That is why I ask you to pray and to love one another.

My dear ones, I ask that you listen to my plea to pray more, to trust God with your prayer. If you do not have trust in God, you cannot pray with a trusting heart. Pray and trust, pray and trust. Thank you for listening to my message.

September 3, 1992 *My Son wants you to help me*

Our Lady: Dear children, greetings, my precious ones! You are so special to me. I thank each one for coming together to pray. Today, I wish to share with you that my Son wants to use each one of you to help me through your prayers to convert all people. My Son is calling all people to come together and form one body in Him. Be united, not only with your family but with all people. Be a neighbor to all souls that you meet. By embracing all people, you embrace my Son.

I love you, my children. God gave you all to me from the Cross to teach you and guide you to my Son. Trust in my intercession, and know that I am with each one of you. Continue to pray, trusting God with your prayers. Do not fear anything. Let there be no room for fear in your hearts, only trust. Be at peace then. Pray, pray, pray! Thank you for listening to my message.

September 8, 1992 *Our Lady's Birthday - Live the Good News*

Our Lady: Dear children, greetings to all! Thank you for responding to my call. Today, my children, the Church celebrates my feast day. You, too, are called to celebrate with the Church. I wish to share my joy with you. So many of my children are coming to God for the first time. I am so happy and joyful for your obedience, for it is through your many prayers and sacrifices that many of my children are coming to know my Son. Thank you, my children, for all your prayers. I hold you all close to my bosom. Rejoice and live the Good News. Thank you. Thank you.

*Editor's Note: Dr. Rosalie Turton, President of the 101 Foundation, along with others was organizing a pilgrimage to various places in the world. It was to be one of the most historic pilgrimages in Church history. This pilgrimage took place in October.

September 14, 1992 *Before the peace flight to Russia*

Janie: *Doctor Turton, always calm because she knew Our Lady was directing this project, nevertheless faced some seemingly overwhelming problems concerning the Peace Flight to Russia.*
Doctor Turton: Our Lord and His Mother know what is in my heart. Please ask Them if They have a word for me.
Janie: *While I was in Adoration before the Blessed Sacrament, I heard these words for Dr. Turton.* "Peace, joy and blessings from Heaven. Jesus and Mary are with you each step of the way. God is pleased."

September 14, 1992 *Feast of the Triumph of the Cross*

Our Lady: Dear children, greetings to all! I love you all for your commitment to being here today. My dear little ones, come to me, come to me, that I may console your wounded and confused hearts. Do not worry about anything, do not be afraid. I am here, I am here.

Pray to God for His strength in your difficulties. He will give you the grace to endure every trial that you are suffering. My little ones, pray for the conversion of all sinners and for those souls that do not yet know my Son. Endure your sufferings a little longer and offer them for the conversion of the world. I love you all. Thank you for listening to my message.

September 24, 1992 *God's Kingdom is within you*

Our Lady: Dear children, greetings, my little ones! I am so happy to see you. Today, I call you to peace and love. Do not concern yourselves with anything. Be at peace, open your hearts, allow God's love to enter your hearts.

God wants to share His Kingdom with you. You must remember that you do not have to search for God's Kingdom anywhere else other than your hearts, for God's Kingdom is within you. Peace and love. Thank you for listening to my message.

September 29, 1992 *Pray, pray, pray*

Our Lady: Dear children, greetings to each one of you! Welcome to my Sorrowful and Immaculate Heart. I love you all, my dearest children. Today, I ask you to pray, pray, pray!

October 6, 1992 *Do not resist your purification*

Our Lady: Dear children, greetings to all my beloved children! Thank you all for your commitment to coming today. Know that God blesses all your efforts, for He knows your needs. I invite you to receive all the gifts that God is blessing you with. Open your hearts especially to my message today. Pray your Rosaries with devotion. My time is short on earth, and I am preparing you for the tribulation. During this time, you are being purified through your suffering. Do not resist your purification, but accept it with an open and joyful heart. Love one another, and love your neighbor always. Peace, peace, peace. Thank you for listening to my message.

*Editor's Note: While Janie was in the airport in New York waiting to leave for Europe Our Lady spoke to her heart. She told Janie that from this moment on, whenever She appeared to Janie, she wanted Janie to open her eyes. Janie was obedient to Our Lady's request.

Two jumbo 747 jets flew to Europe with nine hundred and thirty nine pilgrims. They carried six tons of religious articles: Bibles, Rosaries, pictures and religious pamphlets for the people of Russia. Their pilgrimage took them to Lourdes, Lisieux, Paris, Fatima, Prague, Moscow, St. Petersburg, Warsaw and Rome. A statue of Our Lady of Fatima was crowned in Red Square!

October 11, 1992 *Lourdes, France* *You are making history*

Jesus: This is a very important event in your lives. Know that you will never understand the special event that is about to unfold. You, My dear ones, are making history that will sound around the world from nation to nation. You are proclaiming God's Kingdom on earth by joining together My Most Sacred Heart and the Most Immaculate Heart of My Mother. Through this gathering you are living witnesses that I am King of All Nations, together with the reign of My Most Holy Mother.

This event will join together your separated and long lost sister, Russia. You will be embracing one another for the first time in history. You, My children, have dissolved the Iron Curtain with your many prayers and sacrifices. Go, then, and march toward your sister and love her and share your faith with her. Go, My children. You represent all of Heaven by your heroic efforts. You are those soldiers that have been picked and blessed by the Queen of Peace herself. Go and sing loudly as you approach your sister, Russia, singing, "Onward Christian Soldiers." Go marching with the Cross of Jesus, King of All Nations, and the Queen of Heaven guiding this faith journey. Go and make peace. The heavens rejoice! The heavens rejoice!

October 12, 1992 *Lisbon, Portugal* *St. Michael is guiding you*

Our Lady: Dear children, greetings to each one of you! You, my children, have brought joy to my heart through your many prayers and sacrifices. You are all so precious to me, and you need not worry about anything. You have been chosen for this journey of faith. Yes, my children, this is a faith journey, and you must pray, for Satan is very angry, and he will try to destroy you by putting many obstacles in your path. He cannot touch you, for you have a multitude of angels protecting you. St. Michael is guiding this faith journey. Be at peace and do not worry about anything, but pray, pray, pray. I love you, my children. Remember, my little ones, the Rosary is your weapon. Thank you for listening to my message.

October 14, 1992 *Portugal* *Prayer removes all obstacles*

Our Lady: My dear children, you have the blessings of my Son, and I myself bless you to go out and have a joyful day. My dear little ones, pray more to the Holy Spirit, for God has sent you the Holy Spirit to give you His wisdom. Pray more and continue to put your complete trust in God, the Father Almighty, for He is the One Who directs all your actions.

My little ones, you will never understand the importance of prayer. Pray, my children, pray, for prayer is what will remove all the obstacles that the evil one is trying to put in your path. Prayer, my children, opens up your heart to be in complete oneness with God. So, I say to you, pray, pray, pray! Thank you for listening to my message.

October 16, 1992 *Prague* *Worry and fear distract you*

Our Lady: My dear children, greetings and love to each one of you! My children, you are reaching your destination. Prepare much with strong prayer, for the evil one continues to make your faith journey a difficult one. I am here to remind you once more: do not worry about anything.

Do not fear anything, for worry and fear will only serve to distract you from your mission. Rejoice, my little ones. Am I not here? Are you not all under my motherly mantle? Rejoice, rejoice, rejoice! Do not have the smallest worry. You should only be concerned with being in a loving and prayerful spirit. Your sister Russia, my children, needs your love and faith. My children, I, too, am embracing my children in Russia. Let us go together and embrace her with God's love. Thank you for listening to my message.

Janie: *Our Lady appeared under the title of Our Lady of Guadalupe.*

October 18, 1992 *Red Square, Moscow* *Your rewards are great*

Janie: *We were all gathered in Red Square. A small image of Our Lady of Fatima was about to be crowned by John Haffert, co-founder of the Blue Army.*

Precisely at the moment she was to be crowned, I saw Our Lady of Fatima appear over the square wearing a crown. Light streamed from her heart, flooding the square and then bouncing up and outwards in all directions.

Our Lady: Thank you for your obedience and prayers. You, my children, have overcome many obstacles by obedience and prayer. You have brought so much joy to my heart. Know that your rewards are great in Heaven, for you have pleased God. Remain small in the eyes of the world, that you may be great in the eyes of God.

October 19, 1992 *St. Petersburg (Leningrad)* *Prayer warriors*

Our Lady: My dear children, greetings to each one of you! I want to thank you for all your hard work and all the sufferings that you have endured. You have God's blessing for all your efforts. **My little ones, it is important that you remember how much I continue to need your prayers and perseverance. Many of you are getting discouraged and tired. Your frustration tolerance is low, and you have been unkind to others around you. I know you have met and put up with many difficulties, but you know the Way of the Cross is not easy.**

You must remember that you are children of the light and that light must shine for others to see. I have been with you each step of the way, just like I was with the disciples when my Son ascended into Heaven. Trust me, my children, for I will not leave you, not even for one moment. Many of you have relaxed and believe that you have accomplished your mission. My dear children, your mission has just begun to unfold.

Abandoning everything to Jesus and Mary

Remember, you are prayer warriors, and you must not grow tired of prayer. I tell you this, for many of you are not in a prayerful spirit or attitude. Beware, my little ones. Satan is trying so hard to take your peace away. He has succeeded with many of you who are questioning why you came and what you should do next. You are getting distracted with all these questions. You are here, because you have responded yes to my call, and what happens next is not for you to worry about.

My children, you have been hand picked by God for this peace journey. You came to bring God's love to Russia. She has not yet been converted. She continues to need much prayer and many sacrifices. You have seen her woundedness and how starved she is for God's love. Russia lives in darkness, and many of my children in Russia saw and felt your love, and I thank you deeply. I want to thank you again and again and ask you to please do not become discouraged.

I am with you, and all of Heaven rejoices as you continue in this peace journey, spreading your love to those souls that God has put in your path. Do not give up but pray and trust. Never forget that prayer is your strength, for prayer opens your heart to the Will of God. I love you all so dearly. Rejoice and continue serving God with a joyful heart. Thank you for listening to my message.

October 24, 1992 *Rome, Italy* *The way to the Father*

Jesus: My dear ones, peace to all! I bless each step you take. Be at peace with one another. I have sent you many small and big crosses in your journey. Some of you have accepted the crosses, but many of My children have rejected these crosses and have continued to complain. Bear your crosses a little bit longer, and you will give thanks to God for all these crosses, for the way to the Father is the Way of the Cross.

Love My Mother is what I ask of each of you, and hold Her close to your heart. Love and adore My Sacred Heart, for when each one of you learns to love and adore both Hearts, you will begin to know the love and mercy of My Father. The love of the United Hearts is what will lead you to the Heart of My Father.

My dear faithful ones, for a long time now My Mother has been preparing each one of you to take and live this peace journey. Open your hearts and do not allow your love to grow weak and tired. If you only knew the glory that you are giving My Father and the honor that My Mother receives as you continue your peace journey, if you understood the importance of your mission, you would give thanks to the Almighty Father for all the crosses and sufferings that you have endured.

Pray, My faithful ones, pray, for prayer will help you to keep the love and unity that is the focus of this journey. Do not be distracted with anything that comes your way, but pray and trust. Again, I say, pray and trust, and you will have victory over Satan. Remain pure, loving and humble, for these are the signs of God's people.

October 25, 1992 *Rome, Italy* *Vision of the Two Hearts*

Jesus: My dear ones, you have made Our Hearts radiant through your obedience, sacrifices and love, and I say to you: thank you, thank you, thank you!
Janie: *Jesus and Mary were very happy with this pilgrimage, and with all the prayers, sacrifices and sufferings that we endured, as well as those that were offered by others for the success of this pilgrimage.*

November 5, 1992 *Remain close as a family*

Our Lady: Dear children, greetings to all! Today, I, your heavenly Mother, invite you to continue to persevere in your prayers. Do not have any concerns, God knows all your needs. Trust Him. My children, seek God's Most Holy Will in everything, for His Will is different from your own will. Be content with your faith journey and remain close as a family. Pray with me everyday before the Blessed Sacrament.

Spend some time in prayer telling my Son all your needs. He will bless you, He will bless you! I love you, my children, and I am with each one of you. Remain in the spirit of prayer. God will bless you in all your efforts. Peace, peace, my little ones. Thank you for listening to my message.

November 11, 1992 *Have faith in your prayers*

Our Lady: Dear children, greetings to all! I love you all so dearly. Today, I invite you to prayer of the heart. Abandon yourselves completely to God. Have faith in all your prayers and do not doubt.

Pray to the Holy Spirit for enlightenment to do the Holy Will of God. The Holy Spirit will help you and guide you. Pray, my children, pray! Thank you for listening to my message.

Abandoning everything to Jesus and Mary

November 26, 1992 *Thanksgiving Morning - The blessings of suffering*

Jesus: Beloved child, do not be surprised at the fiery ordeal which comes upon you to purify you, but rejoice insofar as you share in My suffering. Trust Me, your Beloved Savior, and endure all your suffering for My love for you.

December 1, 1992 *How to pray from the heart*

Our Lady: Dear children, today, I invite you to empty your hearts and allow God to fill you with His love. You come to pray, because you need guidance, and you long for peace in your heart. My little ones, I am here with you in a very special way. I have come to instruct and to teach you how to pray from the heart. Prayer of the heart means being open to God's Will and trusting Him in all your prayers. Do not become discouraged when your prayer is not answered right away. Pray for faith and to be able to recognize the mercy of God, for He loves you so much and He listens to all your prayers.

I ask you to prepare in a special way when you return to your home, and to spend quiet time in prayer with God. Pray for a prayerful spirit, and be focused on nothing else except prayer. Be at peace with one another, and live in God's love. Choose the road that leads to holiness, and be converted! When you decide for holiness, you will become holy. Choose Heaven, and live as God's children, doing His holy deeds on earth. Listen to your heavenly Mother, and be attentive to all that I tell you, for the day will come when I no longer will be with you.

Little children, I want to teach you about God's love. I want to teach you about holiness and purity of heart. I want to lead you closer to my Son, Jesus. I love you, all my children.

Pray as a family, always, and never doubt in my love for you. My love and my intercession is always with you. Thank you for listening to my message.

December 4, 1992 *The family was created and blessed by God*

Janie: Praised be Jesus forever and ever. Amen. Jesus, please give me a sign that You are here. *I felt three interior joys, but I was not seeing Him.*
Jesus: My child, I am here with you. Have no doubt, but prepare to write. Are you ready to write?
Janie: Yes, My Jesus.

Jesus: Here is a teaching on the family, husband and wife. The family was created and blessed by God, therefore, the family is a holy union. God created man and woman, so that together they would be fruitful and multiply through their love for one another. In the beginning, God created all creatures to be fruitful and multiply, so it was for this reason that He created man and woman. God instructed man and woman to live in His love and to be obedient to His guidance. He provided them with everything they needed.

Both man and woman lived in peace and in true happiness, loving one another. God loved them so much that He gave them freedom, which was the free will to choose between good and evil. This was God's gift to humanity: to love all His children with unconditional love. You, My little one, teach your family about God's unconditional love. I will teach you everything you need to know, so that you may harvest the hearts of the family. This is all for now.
Janie: Thank You, My Lord. I love You, Jesus, I love You.
Jesus: And We love you.
Janie: *Our Lady was with Him.*

December 8, 1992 *Feast of the Immaculate Conception - I am the gate*

Our Lady: My daughter, you are unhappy.
Janie: Yes, My Lady, for I am depending more on myself and not enough on your guidance.
Our Lady: My daughter, I am here with you. My little one, you are suffering much for the conversion of your family and your own conversion. Do not be sad on this beautiful day. Rejoice, and prepare to write.
Janie: Oh come, Most Holy Immaculate Mary, Mother Most Holy, and fill your children with divine words from Heaven!
Our Lady: My dear children, greetings to each one of you in this Holy Season. God is calling you to prepare for the coming of my Son. Praise be to God, for all of Heaven adores Him. He Who is mighty has done great things for all of creation. Holy is His Name. My children, as you gather together on this my feast day, I, your Mother, come to teach you about prayer and how to obtain purity of heart. I am the gate that leads you to my Son, He is the Way that leads you to Heaven.

God has made me the Mother of All Humanity, Mother of Compassion and Love. In doing this, God has blessed you with His presence among you through the Two United Hearts. As the Immaculate Conception, I come to teach love and purity, for God is calling all humanity to be reconciled back to Him through my Son, Jesus. I am the gate that leads you to my Son through my Immaculate Heart.

Stop turning away from God and open your hearts to His calling, for God yearns for your goodness and purity. Come, my children, let me lead you to my Son, Who will lead you to Heaven. Come, do not hesitate, God is calling you. My dear ones, awake from the sleep of darkness and awake to the hour of great light of the love of God. Stop sinning, stop sinning and ask for my intercession for purity of heart!

To my beloved priests, assist your heavenly Mother in bringing all my children back to the love of God. For the hour will come when it will be too late! To you, my priests, I call you also, come, walk through the gate that leads all humanity to my Son through my Immaculate Heart. In the end the Two United Hearts will triumph!

My children, I am your Mother of Compassion and Love, trust in my intercession. I am here to help you to obtain purity of heart and holiness through means of prayer. I hold you all dear to my Immaculate Heart. Thank you for listening to my message.

December 12, 1992 *Feast of Our Lady of Guadalupe - Peace and joy*

Our Lady: My little daughter, why are you sad? I desire that you rejoice with me on this beautiful day. I know, my little daughter, my smallest one, that you continue to suffer, but I am here to tell you that you have found favor with God. Your husband and children are also favored by God; that is why you suffer, so that your hearts will be truly open to God, Who has called you to a mission to live the Gospel and to share it with others.

My littlest daughter, I need your help to go out and be an example (a good wife) to other families and to share with them what I am teaching you. God has graced you with a divine responsibility, and you have a mission. Therefore, do not allow yourself to doubt and grow weak. God has chosen many souls for a special calling to be examples of the Gospel and to be messengers. There are many of my children that I have come to. These are the messengers that are being visited by my Son and by me. You are one of those messengers. Trust in God, and worry about nothing, for He will never give you more than what you can handle.
My little daughter, I want you to share with others all that you are being taught by the Two United Hearts, Who are One with God. I am the Mother of All Creation. I love all my children. I came as Queen of Peace and to teach all my children to pray for peace in their hearts, for

where there is peace, there is also joy. This world is in so much need of peace and conversion and to return back to my Son.

On this day, I visited my little son, Juan Diego, and to him I asked for a church to be built in my honor. To him I came as Nuestra Senora de Guadalupe. During this time there was so much need for conversion, so much blood shed. Many of my innocent children were being sacrificed. Today, the horror continues through the sacrifice of millions of innocent infants. This horror must stop! If not, many souls will not go to Heaven.

To my little son, Juan Diego, I gave the sign of my Tilma, that to this day remains untouched by human destruction. To you, my little daughter, I have left you my image and statue that you always remember me.

To my son, Juan Diego, I asked him to remain obedient and pure, and to you, I make the same request. I love you, my little daughter, and God is very pleased that you promised to forget all your woundedness and all who have wounded you. You have a desire to begin all over, remembering no past woundedness, and to live in total abandonment, loving yourself, and your family with God's love. This humble attitude has brought much rejoicing in Heaven.

Prepare then, my little daughter, and remain small and humble, for this is the Holy Season, when God sent His only begotten Son for the salvation of the world. On that glorious night the shepherds followed the bright star that led them to Bethlehem, to a poor and humble stable, where they found the Infant Son of the Most High God, laying in a manger. The shepherds were filled with joy and peace. In this way, be like the shepherds that followed that bright star two thousand years ago. Allow that moment to come alive in your heart, for your bright star is my Son. He is the star that you must follow. Live in Him, remain in Him, be Christ-like, and you will know the peace that the world cannot give. I am the Mother of All Creation, Queen of Peace. Long live Jesus, my Son, Prince of Peace, forever and ever. To Him all glory forever and ever.

December 17, 1992 *The essence of the Holy Spirit is the Heart of God*

Our Lady: My dear children, peace and greetings to all! Thank you for your commitment to coming to be with me. You have God's blessings. My children, today, I ask each one of you to pray for peace and unity in your families, in your neighborhood, your church, and your country.

Abandoning everything to Jesus and Mary

Unity is so important, but you must have peace, then unity follows.

My children, my time with you is short. I have been teaching you and guiding you. The day will come when you will have to be with me in faith, when I will no longer be visiting you. Be strong and grow in faith and in love. I will always be with you in spirit and in prayer.

During this time I have been teaching you about the love and mercy of God. I have taught you about the importance of prayer and fasting and how you obtain answers to your prayers when you pray and fast. I taught you to be loving to one another, especially loving your family. I love you, my little ones, and I invite you to continue to be enlightened by the Holy Spirit.

Pray for the grace to do God's Will in all situations; then you will be able to embrace all your small and big crosses with the love of God. Pray every day to the Holy Spirit, Who will give you the divine wisdom and true discernment to be able to recognize things that are of God. Begin your day with the prayer to the Holy Spirit and end your day with the prayer to the Holy Spirit, for the essence of the Holy Spirit is the Heart of God. My children, do not become bored and lazy when you need to be praying. Prayer is so important, for prayer changes hearts and brings about hope. Therefore, pray, pray, pray, for God listens to all your prayers.

My children, continue to prepare your hearts for my Son during this Holy Season. Do not be concerned about the gifts you give to one another. The most important gift is the gift of love and true friendship in God. Do not waste your time in buying gifts that are expensive, but give from the heart the gift of love; it costs nothing, and it is priceless. Remain pure and humble. Rejoice, rejoice and spend time as a family, loving one another with God's love! Thank you for listening to my message.

December 22, 1992 *Talk less and pray more*

Our Lady: Dear children, greetings to all and I thank you deeply for your commitment to gather in prayer with me! I love you all so dearly. Today, I thank you for all your prayers and sacrifices. Many of you are turning more toward God and away from the world. This is pleasing to God.

My little ones, some of you are having a hard time praying. Do not become discouraged but continue to pray, and you will find peace. My children, your hearts are like beautiful flower buds that are ready to blossom. When you pray, your hearts become fully blossomed with sweet fragrance that reaches the throne of God. So pray, pray, pray!

My children, decide for conversion and for purity of heart. Listen to my messages and let them penetrate your hearts. Do not talk about my messages, but live them. Spend quiet time meditating on my messages, and ask my Son, Jesus, to help you in understanding the importance of all my messages. Talk less and pray more, and in this way the Holy Spirit will enlighten your hearts to know the Will of God.

Prepare your hearts for the coming of my Son, Jesus. In a few more days the world will celebrate the birth of my Son. It saddens my heart that many will miss the true meaning of their Savior's birth. Many do not want to acknowledge His birth. Many hate my Son and utter horrible things about Him. This pierces my heart. So, I turn to you, my children, who love my Son, and ask for your prayers. Together, our prayers will help those hearts that are full of darkness. I invite you to prepare your own hearts through being reconciled to one another and to God. This is the most precious gift that you can give my Son.

My children, Christmas is a holy day and must be honored as a holy day. Be together with your family, pray together. Do not allow Satan to distract you from the peace of my Son. Do not quarrel on this day, but pray that on this holy day you will begin a new life with my Son. Let this be a new beginning for you and your family.

I wish to thank all the parents for bringing their children. My Son has blessed all your children. To the children I say: listen and obey your parents, and God will bless you in every aspect of your lives. I pray peace, love, and holiness for all. Thank you for listening to my message.

Chapter Five

YOUR ROLE IN GOD'S PLAN 1993

Let us hold fast the confession of our hope without wavering, for He who promised is faithful; and let us consider how to stir up one another to love and good works, not neglecting to meet together, as is the habit of some, but encouraging one another, and all the more as you see the Day drawing near.

Hebrews 10:23-25

January 7, 1993 *Pray like never before*

Our Lady: Dear children, greetings! Thank you all for coming to spend time in prayer. Trust in all your prayers and have no doubt. God will bless you, God will bless you. Today, I urgently invite you to continue to pray for peace in the world. **Pray, little children, pray like never before, for Satan is very active in his efforts to separate you from God. Do not become discouraged with all your suffering and your crosses, but pray, pray, pray!**

Remember, my little ones, prayer is your strength. Trust God in all your prayers. He is always with you. He never leaves you, but when you stop praying and trusting in Him, then it is you who leaves Him. Never stop praying, for prayer helps you to remain with God forever. Thank you for listening to my message.

January 12, 1993 *Be children of the light*

Our Lady: My dear children, greetings to all! Thank you for your commitment to be here today. I thank you, again, with deep gratitude. My dear ones, today, I invite you to continue to pray for peace in the world. Pray with me, my children, so that together you and I may lead others to my Son.

Open your hearts, my little ones, and decide for conversion, for God wishes to bless each one of you. Do not allow your sufferings to distract you from doing the Will of God, for God knows all your needs. Trust Him and abandon yourselves completely to Him, that He may be able to help you. Be loving to one another and help one another. Be humble, be obedient in all that I am asking you to do. Live my messages and help your families and encourage them to trust in my intercession. I hold you all so dear to my Most Immaculate Heart.

My children, my time with you is short, so have faith in my messages. Know that my motherly task is to lead you all to Heaven. Open your hearts, allow God to inflame your hearts with the flame of His love and mercy. Be children of the light. Be prayerful, be humble, be obedient and you will shine brighter than the sun. Others will come to know that you are God's children. Pray, pray, pray! Thank you for listening to my message.

January 18, 1993 *Your role in God's Divine Plan*

Our Lady: Dear children, greetings to all! I am grateful for your coming to spend time in prayer. My dear children, today, I invite you to continue to decide for God and put Him first in your lives. In this way you will be helping me to lead you all to my Son. I love you, dear children, and you must believe that I am here helping you to decide for your own conversion. Pray to God that He may send you His peace, that you may share it with others. Pray children, pray, for only through prayer do you obtain the answers to your prayers.

My little ones, you will never understand the important role that you play in God's Divine Plan. Only through prayer will you begin to comprehend God's salvation plan for humanity. God is calling you to His peace, to His love, to His grace. Pray that your hearts will be open to God's invitation to live in His grace. God's grace is an invitation for you to repent and to be converted. So pray, pray, pray! Thank you for listening to my message.

January 28, 1993 *Each of your loved ones is a gift*

Our Lady: Dear children, greetings to all! I, your heavenly Mother, thank you for your commitment to being here. My dear ones, today, I call you like never before to take my messages of prayer and conversion seriously. I am here, my children, to teach you how to love God with your heart and soul. Do not allow Satan to distract you from living my messages.

My children, be thankful to God for His love and mercy. Be open to all His blessings and share His blessings with your loved ones. God is with each one of you, and He listens to all your prayers, so pray with faith and confidence.

My children, pray with your family and cultivate their hearts with your prayers. Your family is so special to God, and each of your loved ones is a gift from God. Love your family and pray with them. In this way Satan will not be able to touch you or separate you from God, for where there is love and prayer, Satan will not enter or dwell. So pray and love one another. I love you, my children. Thank you for listening to my message.

February 2, 1993 *Live the Gospel*

Our Lady: My dear children, greetings to each one! I, your heavenly Mother, thank you deeply for gathering here for prayer. God's blessings are with you and with you families. My dear children, today, I invite you again to decide for God. Desire only to be converted and to return back to the love of God. You should not have any other goal, but to live the Gospel and share the Gospel with others. My children, you must remember, there is no other way that you can go to Heaven if you are not reconciled back to God. So again, I say to you, be converted, and pray, pray, pray!

My children, ask God to inflame your heart and soul with His flame of love. Open your hearts, open your hearts, and allow God to possess your everything. Allow Him Who created you to be the Master of your lives, allow Him to be your everything. If you do this, my children, Satan cannot distract you from doing the Will of God. When you allow God to possess your everything, God lives in you, and you in Him. I love you all. Thank you for listening to my message.

February 8, 1993 *Decide for God*

Our Lady: My dearest children, greetings to each one! I, your heavenly Mother, thank you with deep gratitude for coming together to pray the Rosary. Know that God blesses all your efforts. My little ones, today, I call you to prayer of the heart. When you pray, open your hearts and pray with your heart. Believe in your prayer and do not doubt.

My children, God is loving and merciful, and when you pray He listens to all your prayers. Therefore, open your hearts to God's love and mercy, and He will touch the very depths of your heart and soul.

My children, know that I am with each one of you, loving you and teaching you and leading you to my Son. This, my children, is my motherly task. I ask that you help me to lead you to my Son by living all of my messages that I am giving you. I love you, my children, open your hearts and decide for God and be converted. Peace, my children, peace. Thank you for listening to my message.

February 13, 1993 *Love your husband*

Janie: *While I was praying to the Holy Spirit, Jesus and Mary came to me, and the following conversation took place.*

Our Lady: Good morning, my daughter! Your prayers are very beautiful. They bring joy to my heart.
Janie: Blessed Mother, please help me with my husband.
Our Lady: Love your husband, love him, love him. I have so many blessings for you and your family, but I cannot give you these blessings until you remain obedient and be a loving and compassionate wife. Ask my Son to inflame your heart with the flame of His love, so that you can be one love, one heart with my Son.
Janie: Blessed Mother, I will do what you ask of me. Can you give me instructions for Sr. M.? I do not have any details to what she is asking, but you know. What should I say to her?
Our Lady: Invite her to pray a nine day novena to the Holy Spirit, and at the end of her novena the Holy Spirit will instruct her on what to do.
Janie: Thank you! Could you tell me anything about whether something special will happen in our city, like other cities? Tell me only if it is God's Will that I know.
Our Lady: Yes, my daughter, your city will be a city where many of my children will flock to.
Janie: Is something special going to happen at St. John Neumann? *We held the prayer meeting there for almost a year due to conflicting schedules at St. Julia's. Our Lady gave us permission to do this.*
Our Lady: Yes! Many blessings will come upon this parish.
Janie: What about New Orleans? Do you have anything that I can share?
Our Lady: Yes, I wish to thank each one of my children for all the wonderful work that they are doing to bring others to my Son. I thank you, I thank all my children with deep gratitude. Continue doing God's work. God will bless you, God will bless you.
Jesus: My daughter, thank you for your obedience, for leaving everything and going out when My Father is calling you to give witness of the teachings you have been instructed to share with others. Know that you do not go alone on this journey, for My beloved Mother and I are always with you wherever you go. Do whatever My Mother instructs you to do. I love you, My little nothing and My little flower.
Janie: Oh Master, I love You. Thank You, thank You for coming to visit me this morning. I love You. Do You have anything for New Orleans?
Jesus: Tell My children, that I, too, thank each one of them for loving and honoring My Mother and sharing her love with others. They all have My special blessings for all the work that they are doing to share their love and faith with others. I thank you all, My little humble servants.

February 13, 1993 *An experience with Padre Pio*

Janie: *Today, I arrived in New Orleans. The people that God sent me to stay with are a wonderful family, Mr. and Mrs. S. God blessed their home. Now, I am preparing for Mass and Adoration and then my talk. Praise be to God.*

This is an account of my experience on the flight. I saw two angels, dressed in white and a burgundy red. They were huge, and each angel was on each side of the plane and supported the plane as it flew from Austin to Houston.

Later on, as I took the flight from Houston to New Orleans, I saw four angels dressed in blue and white. On their heads they each had a crown of roses. These angels were very huge and beautiful. My angel, Michael, was with me and we talked, and he shared God's love with me.

Later on after my talk, I was asking Padre Pio to intercede for me, and I asked him if I could be his spiritual child. At this, I saw a vision of a dream I had about four years ago. In this dream I was somewhere out in a field. I was preparing for Confession. During this dream I saw two confessionals, and I was going to one of the confessionals, but I heard a voice that came from the other confessional. The voice said, "I will hear your confession, for I know your sins, and your sins are not many." When I entered this confessional, there was a priest there, who later on I found out was Padre Pio. I had seen his picture in a book.

About a few months later I had another dream. In this dream I was between what appeared to be the Pope and this priest, who was Padre Pio. The Pope was in front of me and Padre Pio was behind. The crowd around me was trying to hurt me, but Padre Pio kept telling me, "Do not be afraid, no harm will come to you." This was the vision I saw. Then I heard Padre Pio's voice say to me, "You do not have to ask me if you can become my spiritual child, for when you had the first dream, you became my spiritual child."

February 14, 1993 *Mississippi Prepare for the Father's Kingdom*

Our Lady: To my beloved priests and sons, prepare, my children, for the Kingdom of the Father. Feed the flock that has been entrusted to you by the Father. Feed them spiritual food, and prepare their souls to live the Gospel. Take your calling as priests seriously, and prepare your own hearts as well, for you will be the strength that will lead your flock in the coming tribulation. So prepare with strong prayer, and know that I, your heavenly Mother, am praying with you and for you.

February 14, 1993 *Mississippi   Peace, peace, peace*

Our Lady: My dear children, I am here to bless each one of you. I am here in a very special way. I want to thank you for all your prayers and sacrifices. I love you all so dearly. Peace, peace, peace!

February 15, 1993 *Fourth Anniversary of Our Lady's Visitations*

Janie: *I woke up very early this morning and I was outside when I heard Our Lady speak these words.*
Our Lady: My daughter, my daughter, rejoice, rejoice, for my Son and I rejoice with you! How happy I am, my child. My heart is as joyful as the singing of the birds. My little one, you look to the sky as I speak these words to you, looking to see a sign in the sky. We, my Son and I, are not among the clouds. We are in your heart, your sweet and precious heart. Rejoice, my Son and I are present with you this very moment.

February 18, 1993 *Spend time alone with God*

Our Lady: Dear children, greetings to all, and thank you for being here today! My children, today, I invite you to continue to love one another and to prepare your hearts through means of prayer. Do not talk about prayer, but pray and spend time alone with God. My children, you live such busy lives, and when you leave your homes, many of you have not even stopped to give thanks to God or ask His blessing upon your daily activities. How do you expect for God to bless you, when you do not take the time to ask?

Remember, my little ones, the power of prayer: "Ask and it will be given to you, seek and you will find, knock and the door will be opened." Know that God's love and mercy is beyond your understanding. Ask God to bless you and He will. He will cover you with His love and peace. So, pray and trust God, trust God. Do not leave your homes without praying.

Oh, my little ones, listen to me! I am trying to teach you the importance of prayer, for prayer opens your heart to receive God's blessing. Pray, pray, pray, and show God your deep gratitude for all His blessings by means of prayer. Thank you for listening to my message.

February 23, 1993 *Do not wait*

Our Lady: Dear children, greetings to all! I thank each one of you for coming together to pray for one another. You have my deep gratitude for all your prayers and sacrifices.
My children, today, I call you to prepare your hearts through much prayer and fasting. Open your hearts and abandon yourselves completely to God and trust in my intercession. My children, God is calling you to return back to His love and mercy. Do not go on adding more distraction to your lives by ignoring God's calling. Decide for love and return back to God, and He will provide you with all that you need.

My little ones, I invite you, again, to prayer of the heart, where you abandon yourselves to my intercession. Pray, my children, pray. Through prayer your hearts will become pure and holy. Do not have the smallest worry. Am I not here to help you and guide you? My children, trust me, and all will go well with you if you listen to my motherly messages.

God has allowed me to remain with you for such a long time, but my time with you is short. Please, my children, waste no time and be converted, and decide for God today. Do not wait; God is calling you. I love you, my children, be converted, be converted and abandon yourselves completely to God's love and mercy. Thank you for listening to my message.

March 2, 1993 *Pray these words each morning*

Our Lady: Dear children, today, I invite you to continue to live my messages of prayer, fasting and conversion. Be loving, and accept one another with unconditional love. Open your hearts to my motherly love and share my love with your family. Do not have the smallest worry in your hearts, but trust God with all your prayers. Be witnesses of living the Gospel.

My children, many of you are experiencing much suffering in your lives. I am here to help you to turn your suffering into joy by uniting your suffering with my suffering. Offer your suffering for the triumph of my Most Immaculate Heart. I invite you to pray to the Holy Spirit, that you may be enlightened to do God's Will.

Pray each morning, these words: **My Heavenly Father, today enlighten me by the Holy Spirit, so that I may offer all that I say and do to**

Your loving care. Allow the words of the Holy Spirit to whisper softly in your ears throughout the day: **Your Will, Father, only Your Will. Amen.** Thank you for listening to my message.

March 11, 1993 *Put my messages into practice*

Our Lady: My dear children, greetings to each one! I thank you for all your hard work and the suffering that you have endured. Know, my little ones, that God blesses all your efforts. My little ones, today, I continue to invite you to prayer of the heart, where you surrender all to God, Who loves you so tenderly.

Rejoice, my children, and continue to live my messages by your example. Be a living testimony to others. In this way, you will help me to bring others to conversion. Prepare yourselves everyday with strong prayer, and be loving to all whom God puts in your path. Be obedient, my little ones, and listen to my motherly teachings, for I am here to teach you about the love of God.

If you respond to my requests and put my messages into practice, you won't have to worry about anything, for you will be under my shadow and protection. I will take care of you and your family. I will teach you everything about love and prayer. I will lead you closer to my Son's Heart. My little children, you must open your hearts and decide for conversion. Learn to love God with all your hearts. Then, the Holy Spirit will enlighten you in all aspects of your lives. Pray, my children, pray. I love you all. Thank you for listening to my message.

March 12, 1993 *Before you begin your prayers, consecrate yourself*

Our Lady: My daughter, before you begin your prayers consecrate yourself to my Sorrowful and Immaculate Heart. My child, I bring you the love of God and all His blessings. Pray for the grace of perseverance, pray with all your heart for your persecutors, and love them like God loves them.

March 13, 1993 *The Missionary Image*

Editor's Note: The Honorable Daniel Lynch is the National Guardian of the Missionary Image of Our Lady of Guadalupe. The Missionary Image is an exact photographic reproduction of the Tilma of Our Lady of Guadalupe in Mexico City.

Our Lady appeared there to Juan Diego in 1531 A.D. This image was blessed and commissioned by the Bishop of Mexico, and Our Lady said that she would bring an end to the horrible evil of abortion through this image. This image travels throughout the United States to different churches and prayer groups. Many healings and conversions along with reported closings of abortion clinics have been attributed to Our Lady in this Image. This Image has also wept tears and other miraculous incidences have been reported.

The Missionary Image came to Janie and Our Lady's prayer group and was taken to many churches and driven past many abortion clinics and planned parenthood clinics. She was also driven by the Governor's mansion and past the home of known atheist, Madeline Murray O'Hare, who has since moved out of Austin. The following message was given to Janie during the visit from the Missionary Image.

March 13, 1993 *I need all my children's prayers*

Our Lady: My child, thank you for staying up and praying with me for all my children throughout the world. My child, you cannot begin to realize the many graces and blessings that you have received through bringing my Tilma to your city. Great blessings are being given to your family and to my son, my beloved priest. As he sleeps, God is showering his heart and soul with many blessings.

My child, this morning I wish to share with you how very much God loves you. He created you, only because He loves you, and His love is eternal. You are precious to Him. Everything about you is so special to God.

Janie: Blessed Mother, why does God love me so much? He knows how sinful I am.
Our Lady: That is why He loves you, because you are a sinner. He blessed you with the gift of free will. You chose to let Him be the Master of your life.
Janie: Blessed Mother, were you speaking of your priest when you told me that your son closed the door to your Immaculate Heart?
Our Lady: Yes, my child. This has pierced my heart so. My sons, the priests, have not yet been able to fully understand that by turning away from my Immaculate Heart, they turn away from my Son. Many of my beloved and wounded sons are living impure lives. Holy Mass has become a routine. My sons are constantly in a hurry and do not spend time in prayer, especially before they celebrate Holy Mass and when

they hear my children's confessions. They rush my children that God has put under their guidance. My sons are so far away from my Son, Jesus. There is so much disobedience in the Church and many of my priests live in darkness. They indulge in drinking, smoking, using profanity, and there is no love between many of my priests.
Janie: Why are you telling me all of this?
Our Lady: My child, this is the time the Church needs much prayer because of their sinfulness. My priests are living in the time of great apostasy. There is so much division and disharmony among my priests. There is little unity in the Church. This, my child, is what hurts and pierces my Sorrowful Heart. Many of my priests are responsible for my children leaving the Catholic faith. My children are hungry for the love of God, and my priests do not have love in their hearts to love and feed my wounded children.
Janie: What about the priests that do live their vows?
Our Lady: These are my beloved priests who console my Sorrowful and Immaculate Heart. Pray for them, for they suffer much persecution from my other priests who live in disobedience.
Janie: Oh Blessed Mother, it's such a shame to see all this going on in the Church, but I promise I will pray. I promise, I too, will console your Sorrowful and Immaculate Heart.
Our Lady: Thank you, my little one, thank you.
Janie: Blessed Mother, do you want me to go to Mexico to visit your Tilma?
Our Lady: My child, I, your true Mother come from Heaven to love you, desire that you and your family make a special trip to Mexico City, while my miracle of the Tilma remains untouched or destroyed by human hands. Come, my daughter, and there I will also speak to you of many more of my motherly concerns.
Janie: What is the second part of your message? *I had received a private message earlier.*
Our Lady: My child, open your heart and listen to my request and my motherly cry. I have come to bring all my children the love of my divine Son back into their sinful hearts. I came as Mother of Compassion and Love to lead my children back to God. **My motherly task is to put an end to all the massacre of my innocent souls who cry out to God in agony when they are being murdered in their mothers' wombs. Those little innocent souls are suffering the death of my Son on the Cross in Calvary. Their Calvary is in their mothers' wombs.**

Pray, my child, please. I am begging you to pray so that this horrible evil will end. I need all my children's prayers. Together we will put an end to this horrible sin. My child, if more laws continue to be passed to kill innocent souls, many, many will go to hell. This evil has spread throughout the world like a plague. It has even begun to spread to Mexico City, where this horrible sin had stopped through my apparitions to my son, Juan Diego.

Now, many of my children have begun to commit this horrible evil again. If my children in Mexico City do not heed my request, my Tilma will vanish forever. That is why I am asking my children to turn from this deadly sin, to repent and turn back to God, Who is love. Listen to my message and let it penetrate your heart. Thank you for your time. God will bless you. God will bless you! Consecrate yourself and your family everyday to my Sorrowful and Immaculate heart.

March 16, 1993 *Believe and trust in my intercession*

Our Lady: Dear children, greetings to all! I bring special blessings to each one to thank you for your many prayers and sacrifices. Again, I say, thank you. Through your prayers many of my children are being touched throughout the world.

Continue to pray with faith and with love in your hearts. My children, I ask you to endure your trials and sufferings for the conversion of the many souls who live in darkness. Do not become discouraged when you suffer difficulties in your daily lives, but offer up everything to God, Who knows all your needs. My little ones, do not forget that I am with you in all your sufferings and in your joys. Believe and trust in my intercession and in my motherly concern for each one of you. Thank you for listening to my message.

March 22, 1993 *Again I invite you to unconditional love*

Our Lady: Dear children, greetings to all! Thank you for all your many prayers. Know that with each prayer that you say, a divine jewel is added to your crown in Heaven. Rejoice and continue praying with love in your hearts, for this world is in need of much prayer.

My children, today, I am here to tell you to love your family and accept them as God accepts you. Again, I invite you to unconditional love. Do not become discouraged when your loved ones are weak in their faith, but continue to pray for them and love them, as God loves you when you suffer from lack of faith.

Know, my little ones, that only through prayers and love in your heart will you be able to achieve your walk in faith. Today, I call you to love your family and come together for family prayer. Together, as a loving and prayerful family, you will obtain salvation. Together, you will decide for conversion. Love one another and be at peace. Thank you for listening to my message.

March 24, 1993 *Allow yourself to be loved by Me*

Jesus: My child, greetings. I, Jesus, your Master and Spiritual Spouse, bring you, My sweet Janie, My love. Do not let anything upset you, not your illness, nothing. Think only of Me, for in Me you will find and have everything.

I, Jesus, your Master, love you My little sinner, like no one else could love you. I know that your suffering has been tremendous, but it is nothing compared to My suffering for love of you. Yes, My love for you is immense. Let go of all your fears and worries and allow yourself to be loved by Me. Let My love consume you. Come into My Sacred Heart and stay with Me forever. Do not despair, My little wilted, wounded flower. In My love your sweet fragrance of purity will come to live again. Let Me penetrate every fiber of your being. Open your heart and soul to this great love of Mine.

My sweet child, I solemnly tell you that joy will overcome you, and this joy will carry you away into My arms. Allow yourself to be carried in the wings of My love for you. Learn and desire to suffer more, for it is through this suffering that I visit you daily. Yes, My love, in your suffering you meet Me, Jesus, daily. Suffer, suffer with immense pain, for I solemnly tell you that you will find your paradise in your suffering.

My child, I am here with you, and I give you a white rose which represents My love for you. My love, you have pleased Me through all your suffering. Your suffering is heavenly music to all the angels and saints, for through your suffering many souls have decided for conversion. You please Me, My child. Although you suffer with your illness, you are always giving of yourself to your family and to others. You give without complaining. At night you suffer your physical pains silently. Only I know how you suffer.

Your role as a wife brings joy to My Heart. You give your love to your husband in a special humble manner. Know, My love, that in loving your husband you love Me. I Am. Your love for your family is so pleasing to Me, that I want you to hear it again and again from Me.

Janie, My little flower, the smallest and most humble flower, you are so special to Me. I Am. I will have the angels inscribe in your heart with letters of gold that have been dipped in My Precious Blood, how special you are to Me and how very much I love you.

Prepare for more suffering and love Me as I love you. Let My love for you be your every breath. Allow My love to be felt with each beating of your heart. I love you, My love. You are Mine. No one will harm you, no one. You are Mine. I Am.

Janie: Jesus, I do feel special! Thank you! I will live and die pleasing You, My Master and My love. I love you. *I have been suffering very much with kidney stones at this time and it is very painful.*

April 1, 1993 *Build your family foundation through prayer*

Our Lady: *Dear children, greetings to all my beloved ones! I bring you God's peace and joy. Rejoice, my little ones, for God loves you. Rejoice and shout with joy, for you are blessed with God's love.*

Today, my children, I call you to take prayer seriously and to begin praying more. Some of you have given up on praying. Never stop praying, for prayer is your strength, prayer brings you peace. Today, my children, I call you to continue praying for peace beginning in your family, and then pray for world peace. Satan is growing very angry, and his goal is to destroy you and your family. Be strong, my children, and live my messages. Spend more time in prayer and less time talking about prayer. I am here to help you and to lead you closer to my Son.

I call you to more family prayer. I am sad, my little ones, you are not spending enough time with your family. You are too busy with activities and programs that do not include your family. Come together, my children, and grow together through prayer. Be a loving and prayerful family and build your family foundation by means of prayer. Pray for peace in your family, pray for God's peace in the world. Pray, my children, pray. Thank you for listening to my message.

April 6, 1993 *Keep your hearts pure through Reconciliation*

Our Lady: Dear children, today, I invite you to continue to pray for world peace and for peace in your families. God wishes to bless each one of you, my children. Be open and receive God's love and mercy.

Your role in God's plan

I invite each of you to continue to decide for conversion and to ask God to bless you with a pure heart, for when you have a pure heart you have no desire to sin. Sin, my children, is what separates you from God. Be loving, my little ones, and keep your hearts pure through the sacrament of Reconciliation.

Know, my little ones, that God's love and mercy is an invitation for you to repent and turn away from sin. Teach your children about the love of God and teach them how to pray with a faithful heart. You must not forget the importance of family prayer. As a family, my little ones, you receive an abundance of God's blessings, and your bond as a family grows in love and in unity. Pray, pray, pray! Thank you for listening to my message.

April 12, 1993 *You do not understand*

Our Lady: Dear children, rejoice, my dear ones! Rejoice, for my Son has risen! Let your hearts shout with joy for my Son's glorious Resurrection! Praised be God forever and ever. Today, my children, continue to live this joyful Resurrection and allow this joy to settle in your hearts. Share this glorious joy with others. Be happy, my little ones, for God loves you very much, and He blesses each step that you take. Again, I say, rejoice as all of Heaven rejoices.

My little ones, continue to live in my Son's peace and love, and reach out to one another. Extend this peace and love to your families and your neighbors, your community and to all the world. My children, only through my Son's peace and love will you be able to survive in this world that is in need of much peace and love.

If only you could begin to understand how important this peace and love is to the world, you would be ready to come together as God's children; but you do not understand, for many of you do not have your hearts open, so you continue to suffer. Pray, children, and ask God for His wisdom and understanding. Then and only then, will you understand my message. Only through prayer will you come closer to knowing the heart of the Father. Pray! Live in peace and love. Thank you for listening to my message.

April 22, 1993 *Do not blame God for your sufferings*

Our Lady: Dear children, today, my little ones, I invite you to continue to cultivate your hearts through your prayers. Pray for peace, pray for love, for this world lacks God's peace and love. Do not allow yourselves to become distracted by your sufferings, but offer everything to God, and He will bless you and your family. Many of you, my little ones, are enduring much strong suffering and persecution. Know that these sufferings help you in your purification, for God is calling you to purity.

My children, do not blame God when you endure any suffering, for God does not send you sufferings, but He allows such sufferings to take place in order that He may help you. Again, I ask you not to blame God for your sufferings, but cling to God in all your suffering, and He will help you to turn your suffering into joy. He will see you through everything that brings you pain, for He is a loving and merciful God.

My children, you are in the midst of the purification of the world. God is preparing all His children who are open to His love and mercy. You will see changes in this world that will frighten you, but, I tell you, fear nothing but remain children of the light and allow your light to shine, so that others around you will know that you belong to God. Remember, fear nothing, but love everyone around you with God's love. Remain close as a family and grow closer together through your prayers. Thank you for listening to my message.

April 27, 1993 *Harvest the Kingdom of God through your prayers*

Our Lady: Dear children, today, I invite you to continue to pray for peace in your families and to pray for world peace. Do not become discouraged with all the hatred and the violence in this world, but remain in the spirit of prayer, for Satan continues to declare war against all of God's children. Do not be afraid, but arm yourselves with strong prayer. Pray your Rosaries with faith and love in your hearts. Through your prayers and your love you will overcome the attacks of the power of darkness.

My children, you are living in a time where you will be rejected by your loved ones and others around you. Continue to be humble and loving, for I am with you in everything, each step of the way. I hold you all close to my bosom, and I protect you through my Sorrowful and Immaculate Heart. Therefore, fear nothing, but pray, pray, pray, and remain faithful to God. Allow nothing to distract you from praying together as a family and praying with your neighbors.

My children, again, I say, remain faithful and pray for peace and love throughout the world. God is calling you to a life of prayer, to conversion, to love one another and to live in God's peace. Continue cultivating and harvesting the Kingdom of God through your prayers. Thank you for listening to my message.

May 3, 1993 *The importance of a loving heart*

Our Lady: Dear children, today, I invite you to continue to pray for love in your hearts. Many of you suffer needlessly, for you have not yet learned to love with God's love. I am here to teach you about God's love and to tell you that a heart that loves God - this hearts knows peace, joy and divine trust. My children, love is your strength, and yet many have not understood the importance of praying for a loving heart. Pray everyday for love in your family and throughout the world.

Parents, teach your children to be loving by your examples. Reach out to each family member with love, especially those who have not yet decided to convert. I invite you to begin building family cenacles of love and prayer all around you. Begin in your homes, in your church, in your community and throughout the world. Hurry, my children, do not hesitate! Take my messages to heart and live them. My time with you is short. Live love, today and everyday; then you will begin to see hatred, pride, and jealousy vanish from your hearts.

Remember, my little ones, the teachings of Sacred Scripture concerning love.

Love is patient, kind, not conceited or jealous. Love is not selfish, it is not happy with evil or wrong doings. Love is happy with truth, love never gives up. Where there is love, there is faith, hope, and patience. Love is eternal, for love pours out from the Father's Heart upon all humanity. His love endures forever. Thank you for listening to my message.

*Editor's Note: In May of 1993, Janie was visited by St. Michael the Archangel for the first time. In 1995, the Three Archangels began to visit. All of these messages are located in the Archangel section of Vol. II of Heaven's Messages for the Family.

May 19, 1993 *Put all grudges, all hatred aside*

Our Lady: Dear children, today, I invite you to continue to pray together as a family. Learn to forgive and to love one another. My children, love settles in your hearts when you are willing to forgive those who have wounded you. Many of you suffer from wounded hearts and from lack of forgiveness.

My children, I invite you to live in God's love. Put all grudges, all hatred aside. In this way the flame of God's love will settle in your hearts. As you learn to forgive, you will begin to experience the heavenly peace and joy that God bestows on those who forgive. Your hearts will blossom like heavenly flowers. Your souls will be as pure as a newborn child.

My little ones, pray together as a family everyday. Live in the joy and peace of knowing that God has blessed you and your family. When you unite in family prayer, an abundance of graces are bestowed upon you. Pray, my children, pray. Forgive others and God will forgive you. Pray the family Rosary every day. The Rosary is your weapon. Satan flees when you pray the Rosary with love and faith. Pray, pray, pray! Thank you for listening to my message.

May 20, 1993 *A terrible darkness will absorb the world*

Jesus: My dear child, welcome to My Eucharistic Heart. Allow your Savior to embrace you in My True Presence at this moment. Rejoice on this day, the feast of My Ascension, which is a day of great joy.

My little flower, how much I love you, and how much I yearn for your complete abandonment. Give all your love to Me, hold nothing back. Be Mine, be Mine. I, your Jesus of Love and Mercy, will deliver you from all your foes. I will protect you from the calamities and pestilence that have invaded the world. The world is in such darkness, and much prayer is needed due to its sinfulness. Pray with your family and offer your prayers to console My Eucharistic Heart. Abandon your lives totally to Me, your Jesus of Love and Mercy. I Am.

My child, be open to all of My Mother's messages and live them. Be a living witness of Her messages and convey them to others around you. Pray for purity of heart and decide for holiness. I solemnly give you My word that, when the great darkness absorbs the world and its sinfulness, only those with pure hearts will live through this terrible time. There will be much fear for those that have ignored the signs of these times. Many will die in their wretchedness, for they disobeyed My Father's Commandments. My child, help you own family and teach them about My love and mercy. Bring them closer to My Heart, and My love and mercy will protect them during this terrible darkness.

Your role in God's plan

Janie: My Lord, when will this darkness happen? Is it the Father's Will that I know when?

Jesus: My child, much of what I am telling you is happening in the world, but many people are blind to the signs that surround them. You are surrounded by horrible sin. The world is reliving the time of Sodom and Gomorrah. To the world, these are My words: repent, repent! Know that you have offended My Father. His hand will come upon the world like a bolt of lightening. For you who have continued to live in sin, it will be too late! I, your Jesus of Love and Mercy, invite all to enter into My mercy before it's too late. I Am.

May 24, 1993 *Pray for your children and love them*

Our Lady: Dear children, today, I invite you to prepare your hearts to receive the gifts and guidance from the Holy Spirit. Pray with love and faith in your hearts. You will receive all the blessings from Heaven that God will pour out on you through the power of His Holy Spirit.

My children, waste no time on worldly distractions. Decide for conversion! Pray for purity and holiness of heart. Again, I invite you to pray as a family. Teach your children about the love of God. Guide them toward the road to holiness through your example as parents. Pray for your children and love them. Thank you for listening to my message.

May 30, 1993 *Teach My families*

Jesus: My child, welcome to My Eucharistic Heart. Today, a year ago, you were called to share your teachings on the family with others. God is pleased with your obedience. You, My child, have matured in wisdom and discernment. Through your prayers and sacrifices many families have decided for conversion. Many families pray together through your teachings on family prayer. I thank you deeply. You have dedicated your life to be in the service of My Father's work. Through your perseverance many souls have been renewed.

My child, you have learned to prepare well before you share with others on the teachings of the family. You pray and you fast and your teachings produce much fruit. You speak with love and peace in your heart, and those who listen to your words experience the love and mercy of God in their hearts. Your teachings move their hearts, so that they want to return back to My Father. You have done well.

Go, therefore, My child, and continue sharing with all My children, near and far, the importance of family unity, prayer, forgiveness and loving one another unconditionally. Live in harmony in My Father's love and peace. Teach my families that their only goal and desire should be to serve My Father. The only way to obtain this is through purity of heart. A heart that loves My Father has no desire to sin.

I, your Jesus of Love and Mercy, send you, My child, to share the teachings on the family to all who will hear My words. Teach husbands and wives the importance of loving one another, for many have allowed their hearts to grow cold. They must learn to love one another all over again. They must rekindle that love that they once promised to one another, those beautiful marriage vows they spoke before the altar of My Father.

Love and forgiveness must be restored in the family. Only in this way will they be able to live through the great pestilence and calamity that will cause many to perish. Share this message and continue cultivating and harvesting the hearts of the family. Have no fear; God is pleased with your obedience in this effort. He is pleased.

Editor's note: On the above date, Janie was inspired to write a family consecration to the Sacred and Immaculate Hearts and to the Holy Spirit. These prayers and others given to Janie are located in the Appendix at the back of this book.

May 31, 1993 *Pray for My Vicar and support him*

Jesus: My child, welcome to My Eucharistic Heart. I, your Jesus of Love and Mercy, thank you for your concern for My beloved brother priests. My little servant, continue to offer your prayers and fasting for My Vicar, My beloved Pope. Pray for his protection, for he will undergo a great suffering. There is much division within the Church.

Many of My brother priests have turned against one another. The schism continues to grow more and more. The schism feeds on the disobedience in the Church and the disharmony among My beloved brothers. The schism grows in strength as My brother priests rebel against My Vicar on earth. Pray for the purification of the Church. Pray for My Vicar, pray for him. Support him and love him, as I, your Jesus, love you.

June 3, 1993 *Satan's only goal is to separate you from God*

Our Lady: Dear children, today, I invite you to continue to unite in family prayer. Many blessings come upon the family that prays together. Offer your family prayers for conversion and for peace in the world. My children, do not become bored with prayer. You must pray in order to understand the importance of prayer.

Prayer is your strength and prayer brings you peace. Many of you become angry when your prayers are not answered right away. You allow yourselves to become discouraged and you stop praying. Satan takes this opportunity to fill your hearts with more lies. His only goal is to separate you from God and to discourage you from praying at all. So many of today's families have ceased praying, for they have allowed Satan to separate them from God. Remember, my children, God hears all your prayers. Pray with faith, trusting God. Do not become discouraged, but pray and be converted. There is so much need for prayer in this world that suffers from lack of faith. I love you, my children. I am with you, praying with you and for you. Thank you for listening to my message.

June 8, 1993 *Spend more time adoring my Son*

Our Lady: Dear children, today, I invite you to spend more time adoring my Son. Love one another with forgiveness in your hearts. Learn to forgive all who have caused your hearts to be sorrowful. Unite your suffering with my Immaculate Heart and take refuge. I will help you with all your trials and suffering. Through my Immaculate Heart I will lead you closer to my Son's Heart.

My children, be courageous in your suffering and trust in your prayers. Many of you are experiencing difficult times. Know that I am with you. Again, I say, have courage and faith. I will not abandon you, not even for one moment. Pray every day to the Holy Spirit to inflame your hearts with His truth and light. Pray for wisdom and guidance in all that you do. God will send His Spirit of Truth. Love one another, little children, with forgiveness in your hearts. Ask God to send you His love and peace. Be converted! Be converted! Thank you for listening to my message.

June 14, 1993 *Parents, stand by your children*

Our Lady: Dear children, today, I invite you to pray to the Holy Spirit for enlightenment, so that you may be more aware of God's love in your lives.

My children, be living witnesses of the Gospel and be a light to others. Do not become discouraged when you suffer. Pray to God to give you His grace to endure your many difficulties. My children, live as God's holy family, and be loving to one another.

Parents, love your children. Stand by them when they suffer or when they make the wrong choices. These are difficult times for all who are trying to live by God's Commandments. It is extremely difficult for all the young people. Satan is busy trying to destroy them through every temptation possible.

Parents, be patient with your children, as God is patient with you. Much prayer is needed for the family to convert. Satan will not succeed in his plan to destroy you if you pray together as a family. Satan will not enter in the homes of the family where love and prayer is their strength. God's angels protect the homes of the faithful. Be converted together as God's family. Live in harmony and in love. Pray, pray, pray, and love your children, for they are gifts from Heaven. Thank you for listening to my message.

June 17, 1993 *My beloved parents, I, your Jesus, speak to you*

Jesus: My dear children, My peace be with you, as you listen to my message that I give through My little daughter, whom I speak to, concerning the families in the world. On this day, I, your Jesus of Mercy, bless all families throughout the world. Know, My children, that time is short and soon all apparitions will cease.

Today, I, your Jesus, call each family to come and take refuge in My Sacred Heart. Let My love heal your family quarrels, your marriages. Consecrate your families to My Sacred Heart, and through My love you will be healed. My children, why are your hearts so closed to hearing My warnings, My calling you to repent and to decide for conversion? Haven't you understood My Mother's message to change your hearts and to return back to God? My Mother has called you time and time again through her messages to decide for conversion before it's too late, yet many of you have ignored her request. Now, My children, I, your Jesus, call you to amend your lives and to make reparation for all your sins.

Parents, I speak to you, My beloved: be concerned about the salvation of your children. Teach them to pray and to love themselves. Teach them to be pure. In this way Satan will not cause them to fall into his evil traps. Beloved parents, do not hesitate; protect your

children through your prayers. Know that whenever a husband and wife unite in prayer, your prayers reach the throne of My Father immediately, for a good marriage has all the blessings from Heaven. Pray, My beloved family, pray and consecrate your lives to My Sacred Heart. The family that consecrates their home to My Sacred Heart, there, I make My dwelling. That home is protected by the love of My Sacred Heart, and My graces are poured on this family.

Come to Me, all My beloved families. I speak, also, to My priests and My religious, for you, too, are called to live as a family. Live in My love, in My peace, in My joy, for I am the Way and the Light that leads to salvation.

June 18, 1993 *You must look into your souls*

Our Lady: Dear children, the peace of my Son be with you, and may His love open your hearts as you listen to my message to the families. Listen to my message, my children, and listen with your hearts. I, your heavenly Mother, have come to bring new words from Heaven. I have come to teach you about the love and mercy of my beloved Son, Jesus. Only by repenting and turning away from your sins will you come to know His love and mercy.

In order to repent, you must look into your souls. In this way you will come to understand the sinfulness that lies within your souls. You will see the things that attach you to this world. Listen, my children to the words of your heavenly Mother. Be reconciled back to God. Repent and amend your lives by making reparation for your many sins. Open your hearts, for now is the time of mercy, when my Son's mercy is being poured out on all mankind. Consecrate yourselves and your children to my Immaculate Heart, and with my motherly mantle I will protect you from my adversary and see to your safety.

My beloved children, live as God's family, loving and forgiving one another. To my beloved husbands, love your wives and bring them closer to my Immaculate Heart through your prayers. Be strong in your faith and provide the spiritual needs of your family. Do not waste precious time involved in activities which do not bring unity and love to your family. Pray to St. Joseph, to help you to be that heavenly husband, loving your family and being patient with them.

My beloved husbands, I speak to you, for God made you the head

of your family, as my Son is the head of the Church. Listen, and embrace your wives and your children with God's love. Do not be afraid or embarrassed to be humble, to be loving, to be gentle, to be forgiving, and to be patient, for these are the virtues of a heavenly husband.

To my beloved wives, listen to your husbands, be submissive and love them with God's love. Little children, obey your parents, love them, and pray for them. Take refuge in my Immaculate Heart, for I am the gate that leads you to my Son. I am your Mother, who has come from Heaven to love you and to teach you as God's family. Thank you for listening to my message.

June 18, 1993 *I am your everything*

Jesus: Welcome to My Sacred Heart. Come and take refuge in the One Who loves you the most. Let your heart be consumed with the flame of My love. Think about nothing, only be with Me, your Divine King. Embrace this moment of My Presence and allow yourself to be loved by My love. Open your heart, My little precious one, open your heart, for tonight I desire to give you graces beyond your understanding.

When you come to Me, I will soothe your aching heart with My love. I will melt away everything that worries you with My love. My love will heal you, My love will refresh you. You will realize that I am your everything; you need nothing else when you are with Me. I love you, My little one, and I desire to love you until you are completely consumed by My love. Come and take refuge in My Sacred Heart. Come and be with the One Who loves you more that anyone else. Be silent, be at peace, only feel My love.

June 24, 1993 *Do not grow tired of prayer*

Our Lady: Dear children, today, I invite you and your family to abandon yourselves completely to my Son's love and mercy. Pray, children, so that your lives may become a continuous prayer, so that through your prayers peace will reign in many hearts. Pray everyday to the Holy Spirit, that He may enlighten you in all your efforts.

Teach your children about God's love. Teach them about my motherly intercession, so that they may consecrate their lives to my Immaculate Heart. I will protect them and guide them with filial love. Do not grow tired of prayer, for prayer brings you peace. Continue praying as a family, trusting God with your prayers. Live by faith and love, praying in reparation for the sins of the world. Thank you for listening to my message.

July 5, 1993 *I beg you to spend more time with my Son*

Our Lady: Dear children, today, I invite you to pray for a loving heart. Ask my Son to inflame your heart with His love, so that you may love others with His love. My children, many of you are suffering and you wonder why God allows you to suffer. He allows you to suffer to draw you closer to Him. Much suffering is due to lack of love and forgiveness and not knowing my Son. I beg you, dear children, to spend more time with my Son. He will teach you to love, for He is love. My little ones, when you have a loving heart, forgiveness comes easy. When you forgive, you bring joy to others whom you have wounded. Please pray for all the suffering in the world.

My children, be more united as a family. Do not take one another for granted. Do not abuse one another through your lack of kindness. You live together as a family, yet you are not aware of one anothers presence. You have alienated yourselves through your busy schedules. My children, you have no time for family prayer. This pierces my Immaculate Heart. Dear children, put all programs aside. Come to know one another. Love one another and allow God's love to bless you as a family. Thank you for listening to my message.

July 15, 1993 *Pray and fast and you will discover God's love*

Our Lady: Dear children, today, I invite you to continue to pray and fast for your own conversion and for the conversion of the world. My children, I thank and praise God for the time that He has allowed me to be with you, and to draw you closer to Him.

My little ones, many of you are suffering and feeling unloved by your family. You are feeling lonely, and you have experienced much anger toward your family. I invite you to pray and fast and you will discover God's love, which will help you to accept your family with a loving heart. He will give you the grace to endure all your suffering. Know, my children, that my Son was rejected by His family. I invite you to rejoice and to open your hearts to God, Who loves you with unconditional love. Allow His love to penetrate your hearts, that you, too, may love with God's love. Thank you for listening to my message.

July 20, 1993 *The grace to pray and fast*

Our Lady: Dear children, today, I invite you to trust God with all your prayers. My dear ones, I know that there is much difficulty and suffering in your family. Know that these are difficult times, and much prayer is needed throughout the world. Satan is very active in trying to destroy all of God's children. Do not have the smallest worry or fear, for I, your heavenly Mother, am with each one of you. I protect all my children through my motherly mantle. Take refuge in my Son's Sacred Heart and in my Most Immaculate Heart, for in the Two United Hearts you will find your safety.

Every day, consecrate your lives to the Two Hearts and no harm will come to you as a family. Pray and fast for the conversion of the world and for peace. My little ones, pray to the Holy Spirit to enlighten your hearts, so that you may understand the value of prayer and fasting. Know that they are inseparable. My children, God will give you the grace to pray and fast. All you have to do is ask Him.

Learn to pray and fast, so that you may overcome all the natural disasters, calamities, and pestilence that surround you. Trust in my intercession, for I am interceding for all your needs. Thank you for listening to my message.

July 26, 1993 *Don't waste time talking about prayer, but pray*

Our Lady: Dear children, today, I invite you to continue to live my messages and decide for conversion. Open your hearts to God's blessings. Live in God's peace and put all doubts, worries and anxieties aside. **Do not waste precious time talking about prayer, but pray with faith in your hearts. Live my messages and be witnesses of living my messages. Share my messages with others.**

My children, God loves you very much. This is a time of great mercy. God is calling all His children to turn from their sins and to convert. Repent and be converted, be converted! Pray together with your family. Pray the Rosary every day! Thank you for listening to my message.

July 29, 1993 *Renew your marriage vows*

Jesus: My beloved child, I send you to My beloved families to share My love and My mercy with them. Speak to them about the importance of family prayer and family love. Invite them to return back to My Eucharistic Heart and allow My love and mercy to melt away their faults and their sinfulness. Share with them that in Me, they will find and know peace like never before, for My Heart is gentle and My peace will inflame their hearts with the fire of My love, the love that is perpetual. Share with My beloved families how they wound My Sacred Heart when they do not put their trust in Me.

Janie: Jesus, would You give the families a message?

Jesus: To the husbands and wives, I, Jesus, invite you to renew your marriage vows and to allow Me to help you live in perfect love and peace with each other by consecrating your love for one another to Me. If you respond to My invitation, your homes will be homes of joy and love where prayer will be your strength, for you will be focused on doing My Father's Will.

Your children will shine like the stars in Heaven through their obedience and purity. I will provide all that they need until they reach Heaven.

Hear My voice, My beloved families, for I, your Jesus of Love and Mercy, speak to all who hear Me. Turn away from your sins and turn back to My Father Who loves you. As My beloved Mother tells you to listen to her Son, so I, your Jesus of Love and Mercy, tell you to listen to My Mother. Live her messages; decide for conversion before it's too late.

Listen, My beloved families, hear My words: love one another, forgive so that you may be forgiven. Come to Me and bring Me all your concerns, and I will make you whole. Do not be afraid or worried about your struggles, your needs and your difficulties. Put your trust in Me, your Jesus, Who loves you and waits for you with a loving Heart.

Janie: Thank You, Jesus, thank You. My beloved Mother, do you have anything to add to your Son's message?

Our Lady: To my beloved children, listen to the calling of my Son and do as He asks of you. Trust Him and love Him. Allow Him to reign in your homes. Consecrate your marriages and your children to His Sacred Heart and my Immaculate Heart and live in God's peace, live in God's peace. Thank you for listening to my message.

August 5, 1993 *Prepare for the Triumph of My Immaculate Heart*

Our Lady: Dear children, today, I invite you to continue to pray for peace in your family and for world peace. My children, offer all your prayers and sacrifices for my beloved Pope, for his journey to visit with the youth on the feast of my glorious Assumption. God will send His blessings and graces throughout the United States through the visitation of my beloved Pope. Pray for his protection and for this holy gathering, asking St. Michael and all his angels to protect his visit to the United States.

My children, continue to consecrate your family to my Son's Sacred Heart and to my Most Immaculate Heart. Let Our Hearts be your family refuge. Love one another and live in God's peace. Pray to the Holy Spirit for enlightenment and to guide your daily walk to purity and holiness. Pray your family Rosary and accept one another as God accepts you.

My children, do not allow yourselves to be distracted from your prayer time. God nourishes your souls through your prayers. Spend time with my Son in the Blessed Sacrament. He will give you His peace that you need so much to do God's Holy Will.

My children, my time with you is short. Live my messages. Do not fear or become distracted with all the natural disasters, the calamities, and the pestilence that sweeps the world, but pray and fast. These are the signs of the times when you need to repent and amend your lives. Prepare for the triumph of my Most Immaculate Heart. Listen to my message, listen with your hearts. Live my messages. Thank you for listening to my message.

August 10, 1993 *These are the signs of the times*

Our Lady: Dear children, today, I invite you to pray and fast with a deeper commitment for the intentions of the Two United Hearts. Remain steadfast, my children, allowing nothing to distract you from praying and doing God's Will. My children, do not be sad through the difficulties that you are enduring. **Know that these are the signs of the times when you will suffer much.**

You will be rejected, ridiculed. Many will say that you are not in tune with the reality around you. Your loved ones will make it difficult for you to pray, and they will accuse you of praying too much. You will experience these sufferings and much more. Remember, you are under my shadow and motherly protection. No harm will come to you. Your heavenly Mother will protect all her children.

Remain loving, prayerful, and obedient to living my messages. Allow yourselves to endure all your crosses for the intentions of the Two United Hearts. You will not go wrong in this effort. Pray for my beloved Pope and show your gratitude to God by means of prayer for allowing His Son's Vicar to visit the United States.

I tell you, my children, God is blessing you through my beloved Pope's visit. He is truly chosen by God to be His Son's Vicar on earth. Pray for him, pray for him.

Continue to pray with your family everyday. Do not allow any distractions to keep you from prayer time. Thank you for listening to my message.

August 15, 1993 *Elgin, Texas* *Feast of the Assumption - Rejoice*

Our Lady: Dear children, today, I, your heavenly Mother, bring you heavenly blessings. Rejoice, my children, and unite your joy with all of Heaven on this glorious day. Today, I pour out my motherly blessings to all my children throughout the world. Open your hearts and embrace your heavenly Mother who loves you dearly.

Take refuge in my Most Immaculate Heart and trust in my intercession. Live my messages everyday! Do not allow any distraction to keep you from walking toward the path of purity that I traced out for you. Continue to pray and fast with a deeper commitment for peace in the world. Pray for the souls most distant from my Son, Jesus.

My children, do not become bored with prayer and fasting. Know that through prayer and fasting many souls discover God, and the fruits of your prayer and fasting is their conversion. Prayer and fasting purifies your own heart. Listen to your heavenly Mother and help me to lead you to my Son, Who loves you more than you could ever understand. Turn from your sins and be converted, be converted!

My children, I want to extend my gratitude for all the suffering and difficulties that you endured for my beloved Pope. Through your prayers and sacrifices you dissolved many of Satan's evil tricks. Your efforts protected my beloved Pope. Again, I extend my deep gratitude. God will bless you, God will bless you!

My children, continue to look toward my Immaculate Heart, consecrating everything to me. Know that I present all your needs to my Son,

Jesus. He is pouring His love and mercy to all of mankind. I invite you to enter into His love and mercy and be reconciled back to God. Love one another, and allow your love to penetrate everyone you meet. Rejoice, and let your joy move you to embrace your family and the world around you. Thank you for listening to my message.

August 24, 1993 *St. Joseph begins to visit*

Editor's Note: On this day, August 24, 1993, while praying in her prayer room, to her great surprise Janie was visited by St. Joseph, beloved foster father of Jesus. St. Joseph began to give Janie teachings to be shared with all the families. These teachings were counsel to husbands, wives and children about the heavenly roles that God had assigned them. St. Joseph came every Friday to give these teachings to the world. He visited Janie until March of 1995.

*In October of 1994, God allowed St. Joseph to visit with Janie everyday and to share with her about his life with Mary and with Jesus. In these most profound teachings, St. Joseph deals with relationships, spousal violence, importance of prayer, dysfunctional families, and the attack of Satan upon our youth, to name a few. These beautiful teachings from St. Joseph and the Archangels are in **Vol.II of Heaven's Messages for The Family**. Also included in the prayer section is a prayer inspired by the Holy Sprit to St. Joseph.*

August 26, 1993 *Allow your light to shine, shine, shine*

Our Lady: Dear children, today, I invite you to continue to trust in my intercession. Do not become discouraged with your sufferings and disappointments. I know, my children, that you are being rejected and that you are suffering much persecution. Do not worry or fear my little ones, for God is pouring out His blessings on you. He is guiding you through the narrow path that leads to Heaven. Rejoice my children, and endure all your crosses with joy. Let nothing distract you, but look to my Immaculate Heart and trust in my intercession.

My children, I invite you to spend time in prayer and to read Holy Scripture. I ask you to pray to God to send His Holy Spirit, that you may be able to imitate the teachings of the Gospel: to live without fear or worry.

Remember you are like salt that gives flavor to the world through your prayer. Do not allow your prayers to become weak through all the distractions around you. Allow your light, which is your faith, to shine, shine, shine!

My children, remember that I am with you, and that I present all your petitions to my Son, Jesus. Allow me to help you to be pure and humble. Continue to pray with your family, and teach other families to come together for prayer. Pray your family Rosary daily and abandon yourselves to God, Who knows all your needs. I love you, my little ones, and I am with each one of you. Never forget this. Thank you for listening to my message.

August 31, 1993 *Allow St. Joseph to be your model*

Our Lady: Dear children, today, I thank you for all your prayers and sacrifices. Continue to endure your trials and sufferings without complaining, for I am with you each step of the way. Continue walking toward the path of holiness and purity that I have traced out for you. Pray with your family, and be more committed to praying the Rosary together. The Rosary, my little ones, is your weapon. Through praying the Rosary, you disarm Satan and dissolve all the temptations that he puts in your path.

My children, I ask that you pray to my most chaste spouse, St. Joseph, who is an example to all through his obedience and humility. He remained faithful to God through all trials and tribulations. He looked toward God with filial trust. Nothing distracted him, for he knew that God would not abandon him. I invite you, my children, to allow Saint Joseph to be your model and to trust in his intercession. My children, live in peace and be joyful, allowing nothing to frighten you. God is pouring out his blessings on you. Allow your faith to be your strength and your love to be your foundation. I love you my children. I love you and I am with you. Thank you for listening to my message.

September 6, 1993 *The Heart of the Father is love*

Our Lady: Dear children, today, I invite you to continue to allow God's love and peace to penetrate your hearts. Allow yourselves to be guided through the Holy Spirit, and abandon yourselves completely to the love and mercy of God. My little ones, offer your prayers and sacrifices for peace in the world. Take refuge in the Sacred Heart of my son, Jesus, and in my Most Immaculate Heart, for your safety lies within the Two United Hearts.

My children, learn to live without fear or worry, imitating every word of Holy Scripture, for God is calling you to complete trust in Him. Continue to pray with your family and allow God's blessings to penetrate your heart and share God's blessings with others.

My children, I want to thank you. So many of you have matured in your love for God and for one another. You have grown in wisdom through your constant prayers and sacrifices. God will bless you and reward all your efforts. My children, embrace your crosses with joy. Live as God's pure instruments, imitating God's love and peace. I love you, my little ones, I love you. Remain joyful and loving. Pray for God's love and mercy, for the essence of the Heart of the Father is love, and mercy is His fruit. Thank you for listening to my message.

September 14, 1993 *Louisiana* *Feast of the Triumph of the Cross*

Our Lady: Dear children, I, your heavenly Mother, extend my gratitude for all your prayers and sacrifices. Through your hard work, many will receive special graces and blessings. I invite you, my children, to continue to pray together for the conversion of the world, where so many souls continue to live in darkness. Your prayers and sacrifices bring joy to my Immaculate Heart. You have consoled my heart through all your efforts. I love you, my little children, I love you. Peace, peace. Thank you for listening to my message.

September 15, 1993 *Feast of Our Lady of Sorrows - Rejection*

Our Lady: My child, I, your heavenly and Sorrowful Mother, ask that you continue making reparation for the unconverted. Many of my children continue to reject me as their Mother. They blaspheme against my virginity and spread evil rumors against my holy name. This grieves my Son for the rejection that His Mother receives. Many are the offenses committed against my virginity. Many of my children are embarrassed to claim me as their Mother. This rejection causes me much sorrow. Many are the sorrows that fill my Immaculate Heart, but your being here, visiting my Son, consoles my Sorrowful Heart.

Tonight, on the eve of Our Lady of Sorrows, pray with me to stop the horrible evil that has spread like an epidemic throughout the world: the massacre of innocent little souls. This pierces the Heart of my Son and my Immaculate Heart. Pray, my child, and make reparation for this horrible evil, asking God to forgive this terrible sin.

Your role in God's plan

September 15, 1993 *New Orleans My priests, religious, and my children*

Our Lady: My dear children, I, your heavenly Mother, wish to thank each one of you for this beautiful prayer gathering. To my beloved priests, to you I thank you with deep gratitude for feeding and nurturing the flock entrusted to your care. Continue leading all my children toward the path of holiness. My beloved priests and my children, through this gathering here tonight, you have turned my Seven Sorrows into joy. You, my dear children, have consoled my Sorrowful Heart.

To my beloved daughters (the religious sisters), thank you for coming tonight. Continue, my beloved daughters, to live in purity and in obedience looking to your Spouse, my beloved Son, Jesus. In Him you have everything. Trust Him and love Him, for His Heart overflows with love and mercy for each one of you.

To my children, thank you, thank you! God will bless all your efforts. Continue to pray. Continue to love one another. I love you all, my children, I love you all. Know that each one of you have received special blessings for you and your family. I, your heavenly Mother, bless you all. Peace, peace, peace.

September 15, 1993 *New Orleans, Louisiana Surrender all to Me*

Jesus: My child, welcome to My Eucharistic Heart. Allow My love to penetrate your soul. Come and journey with Me, and I will teach you how to love with My love. Surrender everything to Me and think about nothing else, for this time that you come to be with Me is precious. Look at My Eucharistic Heart.
Janie: *At this time I saw rays of light coming from His Heart.*
Jesus: See how much love I have to give all who come. Let Me love you totally, so that you in turn may love others. Feel the fire of My love. Come, open your heart and soul to My Eucharistic Love. I remain here for you day and night, hoping that in your busy schedule, you will find time for Me. When you come, I delight with joy and I embrace you with My love immediately. I soothe your tired and aching heart. I refresh you completely and fill you with My love, so that you can go and share My love.

I want nothing to come from your heart except My love. I want you to think love, feel love and be love. I want you to be completely Mine, heart and soul. My precious flower, don't forget what I am telling you tonight. I only desire to love you and every one of My children who come to visit Me during Adoration. Share My words, share My love. Invite everyone to come and be loved by your Jesus of Love and Mercy.

September 16, 1993 *Amend your lives before it's too late*

Our Lady: Dear children, today, I invite you to offer up all your prayers for world peace. My children, abandon yourselves completely to my Son, Jesus. Be open to His love and mercy and put your trust in Him. My little ones, open up your hearts and allow God's love to inflame your hearts. Turn to God and decide for conversion. Turn away from your sins and listen to the calling of God to repent. Do not ignore God's invitation to amend your lives before it's too late!

My children, allow your heavenly Mother to help you to be pure, to be obedient and to be humble. Pray for simplicity and live simple lives, praying and making reparation for the conversion of the world. Abandon yourselves to my Immaculate Heart and detach from the material world that distracts you from being totally united to my Son, Jesus.

My children, I desire that you be in Heaven with me; that is why I beg you to listen to your heavenly Mother. Listen to me. The world has nothing to offer you. Open your hearts, my children, and decide to live in God's eternal glory. In Heaven, my little ones, you will be happy. You will be completely filled with the love and joy of God.
Come, my little ones, allow your heavenly Mother to lead you and your family to my Son. He will lead you to the Father where you will have complete eternal happiness. I love you, my children, I love you all. Thank you for listening to my message.

September 21, 1993 *Prayer and forgiveness are the keys to Heaven*

Our Lady: Dear children, today, I invite you to live my messages like never before. So many of my children have continued to ignore my messages. **Consecrate your families to my Immaculate Heart and remain under my motherly protection. Pray, my children, pray, for Satan is busy destroying families throughout the world. Be strong as a family and pray together everyday.**

My children, do not leave your homes without praying, and do not go to bed without giving thanks to God for all of His blessings. **Begin your day with prayer and end your day with prayer. My children, prayer and forgiveness are the keys to Heaven. Allow God to take** charge over your lives, for only through complete abandonment to God will you be able to live through the great tribulation.

My children, take the message given by St. Joseph seriously and do not ignore it. You will receive special blessings in living St. Joseph's message. **Pray, asking St. Joseph to protect your family. Consecrate yourselves and your children to him everyday, for he is the protector of all families.** I love you, my little ones, I love you. Thank you for listening to my message.

September 22, 1993 *A year marked with great suffering*

Our Lady: I, your heavenly Mother, come to ask a special request of you and your family. I desire that you and your family pray for three months, beginning in the tenth month. I ask you to pray and fast in reparation and for the coming of the new year, for it will be a year with great suffering. This new year marks a time when the world will suffer with much calamity and pestilence. There will be more earthquakes and many other natural disasters that will cause the economy to suffer much.
Janie: *I saw volcanoes, tornadoes, earthquakes, floods, etc.*
Our Lady: Many will be left homeless and many will die. There will be much political struggle and world leaders will make unstable decisions that will cause the people to suffer.
Janie: Blessed Mother, this sounds serious.
Our Lady: Yes, my child, many will die from this horrible disease that continues to take millions of lives. *(She was referring to AIDS.)* This deadly disease is the result of the disobedience of many who live their lives indulging in fornication and committing adultery. This disease will claim the lives of millions of young children, because of the sins of their parents.

Young people will continue having children out of wedlock. **Much violence and evilness will grow in the hearts of the young people, for their parents have not taken the time to teach them about God. My beloved Pope will continue to suffer much for the many sins of the Church.** Many of my beloved priests will grow weak in their love for God.
Janie: *I saw that the Pope would suffer much, perhaps in a physical sense. I understood that the AIDS virus would become more serious and millions would die from this virus.*
Our Lady: My child, this coming year will be a serious year with much suffering. The family will suffer much for their lack of obedience

to teaching their children about the love and mercy of God. Pray unceasingly for these intentions for the next three months. I, your heavenly Mother, will be praying with you and your family.

September 22, 1993 *Only prayer and fasting can lessen this suffering*

Jesus: My beloved one, do not be concerned with My Mother's requests to you and your family. Abandon yourselves to her requests, for truly I, your Jesus, tell you, that this coming year is marked with much suffering and disaster, for the world has not heeded the cry of My heavenly Mother to turn from their sins and be converted. All that My Mother told you will come to pass and only serious prayer and fasting can lessen these sufferings. I, your Jesus, solemnly tell you, that unless the world hears the words of My heavenly Mother to convert, the world will only know total chaos.

Janie: Jesus, how many earthquakes will come?

Jesus: Do not be concerned with numbers, but turn quickly toward prayer and plead My Father's mercy. My child, many people are prideful and arrogant. These souls will be the ones who will suffer the most. Many will die in their sins. The world lives in darkness, for it will not commit to following the road that leads to holiness. They have ignored My Mother's requests.

My beloved one, hear with your heart My words. Pray for My brother priests and for My Vicar on earth. Pray especially for your country and plead for My mercy before it's too late! Pray to your guardian angels, for these obedient ones will help you to pray more for these intentions; they will protect you. Pray to the angel that is the protector of your country.

September 27, 1993 *Consecrate your family to my Immaculate Heart*

Our Lady: Dear children, peace my little ones, peace. Today, I invite you and your family to live in God's total peace, allowing nothing to distract you. My children, purify your lives through means of prayer. Teach your children how to pray, especially in times of difficulty, for Satan is trying to destroy your children.

My dear children, again, I ask that you consecrate your family to my Immaculate Heart. **The family that is consecrated to my Immaculate Heart is under my motherly mantle. I see to their spiritual needs and material needs. Your problems become my problems, your concerns, my concerns. I am with you everywhere you go. I am** constantly interceding for you and helping you to obtain holiness and purity. **I will dwell in your homes and at your jobs. I will be with your children and protect them while they are away from home. Trust me, my children, and consecrate your family to my Immaculate Heart. Thank you for listening to my message.**

October 7, 1993 *Through the Rosary Satan is disarmed*

Our Lady: Dear children, today, I invite you to decide for holiness and purity of heart. Open up your hearts, my little children, and live my messages. Be living witnesses of the Gospel and share your joy with others.
My children, my time with you is short. Please listen to me and live my messages. Decide for conversion and lead others to conversion. Pray your Rosary everyday and teach others how to pray the Rosary. **Remember, my children, the Rosary is your weapon. Satan hates the Rosary, for he is aware that through the Rosary he is disarmed.**

My children, there is so much sin in the world. Many of my children are not living my messages. Many have turned their backs on my Son. Please, my children, pray and decide for conversion, before it is too late! I beg you, my little ones, do not continue to offend my Son. He is already much offended. Pray the Rosary, pray the Rosary every day! Today, I bless each one present here, and I bless all your families. Be at peace and love one another. Thank you for listening to my message.

October 11, 1993 *Marian Conferences: My Mother's network*

Jesus: To My children attending the Detroit Marian Conference, I, your Jesus of Love and Mercy, have brought you here to bless you and to fill your hearts with My merciful love. Open your hearts, My little children, and accept all the blessings and graces that you will receive while you are attending this conference. Give Me your fears, all your worries and your anxieties. Give Me everything. Trust Me, your loving and merciful Savior, and abandon yourselves totally to Me.

My little children, I wait for you with My loving Heart. I will speak to you through all My children that were invited to this conference. Prepare your hearts for great graces and blessings. Many of you have come with broken and wounded hearts. I am here to heal you and to answer your prayers. Blessings will be poured out on your families back home. You have come here hurting; you will leave here rejoicing and praising My Father in Heaven.

I will flood your hearts with My love and My peace. You will return to your homes with a new heart and loving attitude. All I ask is that you trust Me. My Heart lies open for you. Come, enter into My Heart and live in My love. Listen with your hearts to all that is said here. Dismiss all doubts, for I solemnly tell you that I, your Jesus, am here with you, in everyone of you.

This conference is part of My Mother's network, her plan for conversion in the world. Pray for all Marian conferences throughout the world, so that through your prayers and sacrifices, My Mother's plan for conversion will be manifested. I, your Jesus, bless each one present here. My peace I give to you, My peace I give to you. I love you, My little children, and I am with you always until the end of time.

October 12, 1993 *Do not procrastinate in your decision*

Our Lady: Dear children, today, I invite you to open your hearts to my Son and decide for conversion. Do not delay, for every second that you waste endangers your soul. Quickly, my children, enter into my Immaculate Heart, which is the gate that will lead you to my Son. Do not procrastinate in your decision, but enter into my Son's mercy and be converted before it's too late!

My little ones, you have entered into a time when you are surrounded by violence, unbelief and much suffering. Know my little ones, that these are the signs of my times. You will see many unpleasant changes in the Church, in the families, and throughout the world. Be wise my children, and prepare your hearts and your families for the reign of my Immaculate Heart through prayer and fasting.

My children, open your hearts and live my messages. Be diligent in praying your family Rosary every day. Remember, prayer opens up your hearts and prayer brings you peace. Pray, pray, pray. Thank you for listening to my message.

October 18, 1993 *Pray for my priests*

Our Lady: Dear children, today, I, your heavenly Mother, invite you to continue to pray your family Rosary everyday. Pray for all families in the world, especially the families which are most distant from my Son, Jesus. My dear ones, open your hearts and look to my Immaculate Heart for safety and protection. Each day I am bringing you closer to God.

Dear children, I ask that you pray and fast for all my priests. Embrace my priests with the same love that you embrace my Son, Jesus. So many of my beloved priests are suffering and being persecuted for the sake of my Son. Offer up all your prayers and sacrifices for my beloved priests. Please, my children, do not resist my request but be obedient to your heavenly Mother. Pray especially for my beloved Pope, for he is my Son's Vicar on earth. Pray, my children, pray for my priests, pray for my priests. Thank you for listening to my message.

October 23, 1993 Detroit, Michigan *Message from Jesus for the youth*

Janie: My Beloved Jesus, please give me guidance on what to say to the youth. I am tired and distracted. Tell me what to say. *Jesus said that each person who reads this message should insert their name no matter what their age, for we are all His children.*
Jesus: My dear children, to you, I, your Jesus, invite you to come and be My friend, and I will be your friend. You and I will begin a friendship that will help you to understand Me and to know Me. My Name is a name that will be so impressed in your hearts.

You see, My little friend, I, Jesus, know everything about you. I knew you before you were born. I have loved you all your life. I know all about your secrets that you dare not share with others. I know about your shyness and the desire that you have in your hearts concerning your future. Let Me help you to decide about your future, for in Me you will know consolation. I will help you to trust and to love Me. Do not worry, My little friend, I won't tell anyone what you share with Me.

I will introduce you to My Mother and you will learn to trust her. She, too, will help you with your decisions concerning your future. I tell you, you don't need drugs, today's music or friends that will mislead you. You only need to know Me. Let Me be your friend, let Me help you. Come spend time with Me. Love, your friend, Jesus.

October 28, 1993 *Allow God to be the center of your lives*

Our Lady: Dear children, today, I call you to allow your lives to become lives of prayer. Allow the mercy of my Son, Jesus, to settle in your hearts.

My children, be witnesses of living my messages, so that through living my messages, you may be protected by my motherly mantle.

My little ones, allow God to be the center of your lives and faith to be your foundation. Read Sacred Scripture everyday and be examples of the Gospel! Listen to my calling to return back to my Son, Jesus, and to enter into His merciful Heart and be converted. Gather as a family everyday and pray the Rosary. Do not allow one day to go by without praying together as a family.

My children, do not become bored with prayer. Through prayer you draw closer to God and to holiness. Teach your children the importance of prayer, so that they, too, will come to know my Son in a personal way. My children, do not forget to ask St. Joseph to assist you to be models of the Holy Family. He will assist your family in every aspect of your lives. He will intercede for your family. Trust in his intercession.
My children, again, I ask that you pray for my beloved Pope and for all my priests. Come, my children, take refuge in the Sacred Heart of Jesus and in my Most Immaculate Heart. Do not fear anything around you, but live in the Two Hearts and praise God, praise God for His love and mercy. Thank you for listening to my message.

November 2, 1993 *Live my messages and do not fear*

Editor's Note: The following conversation was private dialogue between Janie and Our Lady. Janie was directed by her Spiritual Director, Fr. Henry Bordeaux, O.C.D., to share this message, because of the many questions people were asking her about the chastisements.

Our Lady: Greetings, my child, how are you this beautiful morning?
Janie: My Lady, I am not doing very well. I have concerns in my heart.
Our Lady: Tell your Mother about them. That is why I am here, to help you and to guide you. Tell me what I can do to help you.
Janie: My dear Mother, I am concerned about people worrying that they need to move and sell their homes to go to safety. I don't know what to tell them, for you haven't asked my family to move to safety and to sell our home. These people believe that they need to buy vehicles and be one hour away from the city. Please help me. This is causing me to be distracted from your teachings and the teachings of Sacred Scripture.
Our Lady: My child, I am here to guide all my children to complete holiness. My children must take refuge in my Most Immaculate Heart for their safety. I will protect all my children who take refuge in my Immaculate Heart and who trust in my intercession. My children will not fear anything if they live my messages.

I invite all my children to consecrate their family to my Immaculate Heart and live this consecration everyday. I invite my children to be examples of the Gospel and to live by faith, trusting in the teaching of the Church. I invite all my children to pray for and support my beloved Pope and to follow all his instructions concerning the teachings of the Church. I invite all my children not to become distracted by the teachings of the world but to love and follow my beloved Pope.

If my children listen to my messages and live them, they won't fear anything. Again, I say to my children, take refuge in my Most Immaculate Heart and trust in my intercession. I will protect all my children at all times, for they are under my motherly mantle.
Janie: Thank you, my dear Mother.
Our Lady: Be at peace, my child, be at peace.

November 2, 1993 *Teach your children about God*

Our Lady: Dear children, today, I invite you and your family to continue to be witnesses of living my messages. Share my messages with others who live in darkness. Pray for your own conversion and for the conversion of the world.

Dear children, abandon yourselves completely to doing the Will of God. Live the Ten Commandments, for these are the guidelines given by God to His servant Moses. If you follow and live by the Ten Commandments, you will learn to live without fear.

I invite you to spend more time in prayer and less time talking about prayer. Spend time with my Son in the Blessed Sacrament and tell Him all your concerns. Trust in the Presence of my Son in the Blessed Sacrament. The more you visit the Blessed Sacrament, the more your lives will begin to change. You will hunger for and seek holiness, instead of sin. My little ones, open your hearts and listen to my motherly teaching and follow the path that leads to holiness and purity of heart. Pray for the Poor Souls in Purgatory and offer up your masses for their intention, for they so long to be in Heaven.

My children, attend daily Mass whenever possible. Invite your children to spend time before the Blessed Sacrament and help them to know my Son. **Many parents attend daily Mass and spend time with my Son, but they do not bring their children. Teach your children about**

God, before it's too late! Pray together as a family. Thank you for listening to my message.

November 8, 1993 *Teach your children about My Son's True Presence*

Our Lady: Dear children, today, I invite you to pray for my special intentions, so that through your prayers my plan for conversion will be manifested. I invite all families to consecrate their lives to my Immaculate Heart and to pray their family Rosary for the triumph of my Immaculate Heart. I invite all my children to pray and fast for their own conversion and to put God first in their lives. Pray, my children, and ask God for a prayerful spirit and do not become bored with prayer.

Teach your children about the power of prayer and help them to pray. Teach your children about the True Presence of my Son during Holy Mass. There is so much distraction and lack of respect among the youth during Mass, and this saddens my Heart. Spend time teaching your children about the Ten Commandments and the importance of living by the Ten Commandments.

My children, listen to my motherly teaching and do all that I ask of you. God has blessed the world through my apparitions, but all is coming to an end. The day is coming when all you will have is my motherly teachings. Many of you will have to learn to live by faith and trust in God. Live my messages and allow me to help you to draw closer to God. Thank you for listening to my message.

November 18, 1993 *Provide for the spiritual needs of your children*

Our Lady: Dear children, today, I invite you to live in God's love and in His peace. Extend His love and peace to others around you. Pray together and love one another with God's love. My children, I invite you, again, to spend more time together as a family. Many of you have such busy schedules, and you don't have time to be a family or have time to pray together. My little ones, without prayer you cannot come to know God. You must pray, so that God will shower His blessings and graces upon you and your family. Prayer is the tool that will disarm Satan, who is forever busy trying to destroy you. He has only one goal and that is to separate you from God.

My children, open your hearts to my motherly teaching and guidance. You are becoming distracted from prayer, and you are not living my messages. Pray and fast, and you will obtain the answers to all of your family needs. God wants to bless you and to help you, but your hearts are so distracted. Trust in God and abandon your hearts to Him. Be apostles of His love and live Sacred Scripture. In this way others will know that you are children of the light.

Trust, also, in my Most Immaculate Heart and allow me to help you to obtain holiness and purity. Know that I protect all my children who take refuge in my Immaculate Heart. Again, I invite you to take time from your busy schedules and pray together as a family; pray especially the Holy Rosary. Do not allow your children to watch endless hours of television. Spend time together and engage in other family activities which draw you closer to God.

Parents, to you, I invite you to take your vocations as parents seriously and provide for the spiritual needs of your children. **So many parents are not aware of how much they neglect the spiritual needs of their children, and this saddens my heart. If more parents would take the time to teach their children how to pray, the violence and disrespect in the family would decrease. Pray, children, pray; time is short. Live my messages and God will bless you.** Thank you for listening to my message.

November 23, 1993 *My beloved priests are God's voice*

Our Lady: Dear children, today, I thank you for all your prayers and sacrifices. Know, my children, that already, many souls are drawing closer to My Son through your prayers. My children, I invite you to continue praying and fasting for peace in your families and for world peace.

My little ones, be thankful for all the blessings and graces that you receive from your Heavenly Father. In just a few days, the Church everywhere will be giving thanks to God for all His blessings. I invite you to take this opportunity to be charitable and share your blessings with others. Feed my hungry children, clothe them, give them shelter, see to their well-being by helping them in every way possible. Pray to the Holy Spirit to enlighten your hearts and to inflame your hearts with the gift of charity and with the gift of love.

My children, open your hearts and see with the eyes of your soul, then you will be able to see all the needs that surround you. God calls you to imitate the Good Samaritan in the Gospel and to be charitable and to love your neighbor. Be obedient and share your blessings with others.

My children, today, I invite you in a special way to love my beloved priests. Treat them with respect and love them. Do not mistreat my beloved priests; already, they are mistreated by the unbelievers. Do not say anything against them, and do not judge them, for God alone is their judge. Love my beloved priests and pray for them, for they are my Son's representatives on earth. They are God's voice and God's chosen ones. Thank you for listening to my message.

November 29, 1993 *Overcome your pride and selfishness*

Our Lady: Dear children, today, I invite you and your family to prepare your hearts for my Son, Jesus. Open your hearts and pray more as a family. Some of you pray very little. My little ones, do not become bored with prayer. Know that through praying you obtain many graces and blessings. Do not be overcome with your difficulties and sufferings, but put all your trust in God Who loves you. Trust Him, little children, trust Him. He will see you through all your sufferings.

My children, you must pray, so that through prayer you may overcome your pride and selfishness. Pride and selfishness distract you from being kind and loving. It puts distance between you and God. My children, I speak to you about pride and selfishness, for many of you are unaware that you suffer from this kind of sin. Many of you are unhappy, and you don't have God's peace, because of your pride and selfishness. Only through prayer and fasting will you overcome all the darkness in your hearts.

Today, I wish to speak to the young. To you, I, your heavenly Mother, invite you to pray more. Put your trust in my Son, Jesus. You are not alone, my little ones. God loves you very much. He wants you to be pure, and to help you and your friends to know Him in a deeper way. I love you, my young children. Pray more with your parents and love them. They need your love and support to help them to be good parents. Pray, pray, pray! Thank you for listening to my message.

December 8, 1993 *Love: it costs nothing but is priceless*

Our Lady: Dear children, today, I, your heavenly Mother, invite you to prepare your hearts for my Son, Jesus. Open your hearts and receive the joy of the nativity of the Infant Jesus. Accept the peace and joy of the birth of my Son, and allow God's blessings to help you to be pure. Today, on this my feast day of the Immaculate Conception, I invite you to choose the path that leads to purity and holiness.

My children, live in God's peace and extend this peace to others, especially your family. Continue to pray together as a family, preparing your hearts by forgiving one another. Allow this Holy Season to be a time of peace and joy in your family. Give one another the gift of love which comes from your hearts. My children, do not allow yourselves to become distracted by material things during this Holy Season. Do not worry about giving gifts that won't last or feed the soul. Give the gift of love, which costs nothing, but is priceless. Rejoice and prepare your hearts. Allow the birth of my Son to be born in each heart. Thank you for listening to my message.

December 12, 1993 *Singing: a beautiful way to prepare your hearts*

Our Lady: My children, I, your heavenly Mother, thank you for coming to be with me. Thank you so much for the beautiful songs. You, my children, have pleased your Mother through your singing. What a beautiful way to prepare your hearts to receive your Mother! My children, I know that some of you are suffering, and you are doubting that I am with you. My little ones, I am really here with you. Open your hearts, open your hearts and believe. Do not worry, my children, I will help you in your suffering. Trust in my intercession. Thank you, my children, thank you.

December 13, 1993 *Love and respect all My brother priests*

Jesus: Welcome to My Eucharistic Heart. Come and spend quiet time with Me away from all the distractions of the world. Your being here consoles My Eucharistic Heart. Today, I, your Jesus of Love and Mercy, invite you to open your heart and receive all My love and peace.

My little flower, I am pleased with all your little offerings in reparation for the world. Today, you have been fasting for My beloved brothers (the priests), and I thank you. Continue to pray and fast, especially for all the priests who are struggling with their faith. Many of My beloved brothers are struggling with the desire of wanting to leave the priesthood. This saddens My Heart, because many priests are being distracted by the world. Because of this distraction, their prayers have become weak.

Many priests do not take the time to pray before celebrating Holy Mass. The celebration of Holy Mass has become routine due to lack of preparation. Many of My brother priests lack the spirit of prayer. Their hearts and souls have become like dry trees in the winter that lose their leaves and have become barren with no sign of life in them. Many of My brother priests are dry and barren, for they have stopped loving me, the Source of their life.

Pray, My little flower, for all My brother priests. Offer your prayers and sacrifices in reparation for their hearts and souls. Through your offerings you will help My beloved brothers to draw closer to Me. Remember also, My brother priests who remain faithful and obedient to Me in all their sufferings and persecutions, for these suffer the most, for their hearts and souls are united with My Heart. Love and respect all My brother priests and never speak harshly of them, but be noble and help them through your prayers.

My little flower, you have listened patiently to My pain and suffering for My Church. Take this message and share it with others. You have consoled My Eucharistic Heart, and I bless you. Go in My peace and live in My love. I love you, My little flower. Your fragrances are your prayers and sacrifices. Go in My peace.

December 14, 1993 *Prepare your hearts for my Son*

Our Lady: Dear children, today, I, your heavenly Mother, invite you and your family to prepare your hearts for the birth of my Son. My children, open your hearts for Him. In this way your hearts will become that humble stable where my Son was born. Allow your lives to become a life of prayer, so that through your prayers many other souls will come to know my Son during this Holy Season. My children, I invite you to accept God's love and to live in His love. Do not be distracted with worldly activities, but be concerned about living my messages.

Know, my little ones, that when you live my messages, you have nothing to worry about. I, your heavenly Mother, will protect you and your family. Your needs become my needs, your sufferings - my sufferings.

I will protect you and you will take me everywhere you go, for you will be under my shadow and protection. Listen to your heavenly Mother! I want to help you and prepare your hearts for my Son. I want to take you all to Heaven with me, but you must respond to my call and live my messages.

Today, I invite all families to pray a nine day novena in reparation for all my children who do not yet know my Son and in preparation for your own hearts. Offer your novena for the Holy Souls in Purgatory, for on

Christmas day many will go to Heaven. Special graces and blessings are given to all humanity on this holy day. Pray, and prepare your hearts. Thank you for listening to my message.

December 20, 1993 *My special motherly blessing*

Our Lady: Dear children, today, I, your heavenly Mother, invite you and your family to open your hearts and receive the gift of love. Rejoice, my children, and abandon your hearts to the love of my Son, Jesus. Trust in my intercession and take refuge in my Most Immaculate Heart. I will protect you, and I will lead you to the Heart of my Son.

My little ones, today I give you my special motherly blessing that you may share this blessing with others. Do not be sad or worried about anything. Let go of everything and know that God loves you. Do not quarrel with one another, for this is a time of joy and peace. Do not allow Satan to distract you from this joy and peace, but trust God with all your prayers like never before. Convert, my children, and receive the light from Heaven and live in this light.

My children, many of you are suffering from loneliness and painful memories. Today, give them all to your heavenly Mother, and trust in my intercession. Today, receive my motherly blessing and never forget this blessing. Share it with everyone. Through my special blessing you will find it easier to convert and to love. I love you, my children, I love you. Peace and joy, peace and joy. Thank you for listening to my message.

Janie: *Our Lady asked that our prayer group embrace one another on this day and in this way the special blessing was given between us. All who have received this special blessing can pass it on to others through an embrace, extending the blessing either silently or verbally.*

December 24, 1993 *Vision of the Nativity*

Jesus: Welcome, My precious little flower, and thank you for coming to spend time with Me on this special night. You will receive a multitude of blessings while you visit, for it was I, your Eucharistic Savior, Who called you to come to Me.

Janie: Oh Jesus, I know that it couldn't be me who came on my own, especially not knowing if the church would be open. Thank You for this blessed privilege and for blessing me in this way. What is it that I can do for You, My Loving Jesus?

Jesus: My humble servant, tonight, I want you to go back into the time

when I was born in that humble stable. Journey with Me and see and experience the joy of the Nativity, the gift of love to all humanity.
Janie: *Suddenly I am alone, but I can feel God's presence all around me. I am at the stable and I see a small room with friendly animals, which appear to be kneeling. I see a very bright star shining down over this entire region where I am. It is night, and it's cold. I hear voices singing songs. The language is unknown to me. They are men's voices.*
I see shepherds a distance from me; they have many flock. A young boy is blowing on his flute and looking toward the shining star. The rest of the men are also looking at the big star, and they talk among themselves as if wondering what this big star could mean.

I feel cold, and I am wondering if I should go and warm myself by their fire. These men have a fire to keep themselves warm. I look back to the stable which is a distance away from me. I begin walking back to the stable and I see Our Beloved Mother Mary and a multitude of angels cleaning up the stable. St. Joseph is outside gathering what appears to be hay. He puts it around this small area that makes up the stable.

All of a sudden, they kneel down and begin to pray and give thanks to God for helping them find a place for the birth to take place. I listen with tears in my eyes, and I begin to pray myself. The night is clear, and there are numerous stars in the sky.

Then all of a sudden, I hear beautiful singing and a loud beautiful voice. I look to see where the voice is coming from, and I see the shepherds illuminated with great light. I look up to the sky where this beaming bright light is coming from. I see a huge angel with big golden wings. He is dressed in white. His hair comes down to his shoulders. Then I hear him say to the shepherds, "Do not fear! (The shepherds were frightened). I am here with Good News for you, which will bring great joy to all the people. This very day in the City of David, a Savior is born, Who is the Lord and Messiah. You will find a Baby wrapped in swaddling clothes and lying in a manger."

Then a great multitude of angels appeared with the angel, singing praises to God: "Glory to God in the Highest and peace on earth to those on whom His favor rests." The angels left, and the shepherds spoke to one another, saying, "Come, let us go and see this Baby which the angel spoke about."

Suddenly, once again I was at the stable. There came a great light from the stable, and I could see the Infant lying in the manger, and

Your role in God's plan

Joseph and Mary were next to Him. I felt so much love, that I began to cry with joy. Everyone was in a daze from being surrounded by this love coming from the Infant. What a gift, what a joy! How can God love me so much? Mary and Joseph look so humble kneeling down with their heads bowed down, praying and praising God. Then I am back with Jesus.

Jesus: My child, tonight you have been allowed to witness My birth and My love. Go My child and share My love with the rest of the world. Never forget what you saw here tonight.

Janie: Thank You Jesus. I am not quite sure how I will share this, for no one will believe me.

Jesus: Do not worry, but share My love with others. Peace is My gift to you. Merry Christmas, My child. I love you.

December 25, 1993 *The cup of sinfulness is overflowing*

Janie: *I was sitting at home in my living room and a great heaviness flooded my heart. I was filled with sorrow and grief. I began to cry, and Jesus was with me. He showed me the many hearts that do not know Him. I got up and went to our prayer room to pray.* Lord, help me. I pray to You for my own selfish and sinful heart. Show me how to love You, Lord.

Jesus: My child, you are sharing in My sorrow for all those souls who reject Me. Their souls are filled with sin and they have not repented. They walk in darkness; they have refused My love and My invitation for them to live in My peace. I, the Prince of Peace, came for all, young and old. I am the Prince of Peace and Truth, but many have refused to live in My truth.

There is much darkness in the world. Evil reigns in the hearts of many. The cup of sinfulness is overflowing because of the refusal to live in My truth and light. My child, this is the sadness that has filled your heart. For I, your Savior, wanted to share My sorrow with you, for I know that your heart is Mine. I love you. I love you. Pray for all that I have shown you.

December 25, 1993 *Vision of the Procession of the Holy Souls*

Jesus: Welcome, My child, and thank you for coming. Prepare to witness the great rejoicing of the Holy Souls as they are taken to Heaven. Write down everything that you see.

Janie: *I prayed to the Holy Spirit to prepare my heart. Then I was silent. I find myself in a place surrounded by great light. I see an open-*

ing in the heavens, and great light is pouring down into Purgatory. I see Purgatory as a huge cave, but to the top there is an opening which the light from Heaven is coming through. I see what appears to be a golden street or path, and to each side of the path I see thousands of angels, big and small, singing hymns and praising God.

Our Lady and Jesus, both with golden crowns on Their heads and arrayed in golden garments, escort thousands of souls to Heaven. I see priests, nuns, bishops, old and young people with Jesus and Mary leading and escorted by thousands of angels in procession, going up into this opening in Heaven.

As they enter the opening, Mary is to the left and Jesus to the right. The souls enter this light and disappear in the light. The singing becomes louder, and the rejoicing increases. The procession continues. It's like a parade of souls marching toward Heaven. All wear beautiful white garments, and as they get closer to Heaven, their garments change and become multi-colored. Then, before my eyes, the garments turn to a yellow gold, and then the souls disappear.

More and more continue in procession, and as they pass, they acknowledge my presence and smile at me and thank me. Many of my relatives are among the multitude who are in procession to Heaven. I am especially happy and thankful for all the many priests and religious that entered Heaven today. My two brothers who died years ago are going to Heaven this very day. I am surrounded by great light and rejoicing, and I am so happy to be seeing all this. To me it is like a movie with a huge picture screen with such living colors.

There are great big angels at the opening path that I think is Purgatory. These angels blow their long golden thin trumpets, and more Holy Souls come out in procession. When they get to Heaven, the angels on that end blow their trumpets as if to announce them. This procession continues and Jesus and Mary with a multitude of angels escort thousands of souls to Heaven.

The great light that surrounds me makes me feel such joy in my heart. I feel as though I myself have died and gone to Heaven. Jesus and Mary come to where I am, and these are Their words. I say Their words, because I can feel both of Their Hearts speaking to my heart; Their Hearts being One. I cannot explain, but it comes from both of Their Hearts.

Jesus and Mary: Our dear child, you have found favor with God, for

Your role in God's plan

He chose you to witness the joyful celebration of this special day, when many souls go to Heaven. You, Our dear child, pray much for the Holy Souls. Your prayers and the prayers of many others have helped to release many souls from Purgatory. Their time of suffering has ended, and now they are rejoicing with God in Heaven.

Our dear child, continue to intercede for all the Holy Souls in Purgatory, and rejoice for what you have been graced to witness. Your own heart will never be the same, for you have experienced a little of God's majesty and power. God loves you very much, for He knows that your only desire is to do His Holy Will; for this you are blessed. Go in God's peace and never forget the power of intercessory prayer. We love you, and Our love is with you everywhere you go.

Janie: *Our Lady told me that from midnight on the 24th of December, until midnight on the 25th of December thousands of souls go to Heaven.*

December 25, 1993 *When you fall I will pick you up*

Janie: *Jesus spoke to me after Confession and hearing my prayer.*
Jesus: My child, your prayer has pleased Me. My child, today, I have provided you with everything.
Janie: *Jesus meant Confession and all the other experiences that He shared with me.*
Jesus: Come and stay with Me, and you will be able to avoid temptation; for when you fall, I will quickly pick you up and rescue you from the hands of the evil one. My child, you belong to Me, and if you stay with Me, you will learn to resist temptation, for through Me you will overcome sinning. I will be your strength. Do not worry any more about your relationship with your (X). I will take care of this matter for you. You see how much I love you. Be at peace.

December 26, 1993 *Feast of the Holy Family - Consecrate your family*

Janie: *While I was going to receive Holy Communion, I saw the Holy Family where the priest was giving Communion. St. Joseph and Mary were kneeling and Jesus was giving Communion. The way that I saw Jesus giving Communion, or the way that each individual would receive Him, as they came up to receive Him, He would embrace each individual. The altar was crowded with angels who were prostrated before Jesus. Later, after Mass, I went before the Blessed Sacrament to give thanks. Dear Jesus, I saw You, Most Holy Mary, and St. Joseph. I am so happy.*

Jesus: That was a gift for you, so that you understand the importance of the Holy Family in your life. Consecrate your family to the Holy Family everyday, and you will have peace in your family. Through consecrating your family to the Holy Family, you will be protected from daily temptation. My child?
Janie: Yes, My Jesus?
Jesus: Did you notice how much holiness your heart felt as you gazed upon the Holy Family?
Janie: Yes, My Jesus, oh yes!
Jesus: When you consecrate your family to the intercession of the Holy Family, you will live in holiness.

December 30, 1993 *Help me in the battle*

Our Lady: Dear children, today, I, your heavenly Mother, invite you to continue to pray for peace in your family and peace in the world. My children, prepare through much strong prayer for the coming of the New Year, for it will be a difficult year with much suffering. I invite you to live my messages like never before and to take refuge in the Sacred Heart of my Son and in my Most Immaculate Heart.

My little ones, you are entering into a time of great tribulation where you will see much suffering and violence. You will see changes in the world and in the Church that will frighten you. The Church will undergo much suffering, and many of my beloved priests will be put to the test. Many will suffer persecution, and many will want to flee from the priesthood because of the great persecution.

I turn to you, my children, and ask you and your family to pray with me for my beloved priests. Together, through prayer these changes and sufferings will be lessened. Pray especially for my beloved Pope, for he will endure much suffering due to the persecution and suffering in the Church. Offer up all your prayers and sacrifices in reparation for the needs of all my beloved priests.

My little ones, I invite you to remain close as a family and to remain loving to one another. Protect your children through your prayers, for Satan is very active in trying to destroy the family. He is luring your children through means of drugs and unhealthy influences. It is important that you as parents demonstrate much love towards your children. Pray together everyday your Rosary. Many of you have been neglecting family prayer. You put other activities before prayer.

My children, listen to your heavenly Mother. Prayer is important, especially praying the Rosary. Prayer brings you peace. I invite you to consecrate your families to my Immaculate Heart, and I will protect you. I will lead you closer to my Son. My children, I invite you to help me in the battle to disarm Satan. Remember, these are your weapons against Satan: prayer, fasting, the Holy Rosary, Adoration, Holy Mass, and receiving frequently the sacrament of Reconciliation.

I invite you not to be afraid but to have faith, not to talk about prayer but to pray, not to talk about my messages but live them. If you respond to my request, you will help to usher in the reign of my Immaculate Heart. Through your prayers many will convert. Pray, pray, pray. Thank you for listening to my message.

December 31, 1993 *Remain in My love*

Jesus: Welcome to My Eucharistic Heart. My child, tonight, I, Jesus, bless you and your family with My love, joy and My peace. Remain in My love, so that you may be One with Me as I am One with My Father. If you remain in My love, you and your family will be able to live through these troubled times.

This new year marks a difficult year with much suffering throughout the world. Abandon yourself to My love and trust Me. Listen to My words, My child, and you will embrace all the difficulties that lie ahead with a joyful heart. My love will see you through everything. Remain in My love, and you will have joy, peace and strength. I now give you My blessing to share with your family.

Heaven's Messages for The Family

Chapter Six

PURITY AND HOLINESS OF HEART

1994

And I tell you, everyone who acknowledges Me before men, the Son of man also will acknowledge before the angels of God; but he who denies Me before men will be denied before the angels of God.

Luke 12:8-9

January 4, 1994 *Unceasing prayer and fasting to end the war*

Our Lady: Dear child, it is my desire that unceasing prayer and fasting be offered in reparation to end the war in Bosnia. If my children respond to my request, the war will dissolve through your prayers. Trust in the Two Hearts in this effort. Pray and fast unceasingly to end this horrible war that has taken so many innocent victims.

My child, you will not go wrong in this effort, but through your obedience in responding to my request, special blessings will be bestowed upon my children who join you in this effort. Trust your heavenly Mother, trust your heavenly Mother. Share this with my son.
Janie: *She meant Fr. Henry.* My beloved Mother, I will share this message with Fr. Henry. I ask that you intercede for me for enlightenment from the Holy Spirit. Blessed Mother, I will begin to invite others to join me. We will pray around the clock if it's okay with Fr. Henry. We will offer our Holy Mass, Rosary, Adoration, and fasting. We will sign up for a certain hour to pray. I will ask others to commit to one of these three: Holy Mass, praying the Rosary, or Adoration. We will pray this way until your request is met to have as many of your children praying around the clock as possible. Do you approve of this plan, My Mother?
Our Lady: Yes, my child, yes. Through this effort, my children will learn to be committed to prayer in their daily needs. My children will learn the importance of prayer and fasting. Thank you, my child, for helping your heavenly Mother.

January 4, 1994 *Hearts begin to change*

Our Lady: Dear children, today, I invite you and your family to offer all your prayers and sacrifices in reparation for the war in Bosnia. Pray for my children who are victims of this war that has lasted so long. My little ones, trust in my Immaculate Heart and turn to your heavenly Mother with all your family concerns. In this way I will protect you. Many of you suffer, and in your suffering you forget to pray. You allow your suffering to become a distraction for you.

Remember, my children, that God hears all your prayers. Through your prayers the hearts of those you are praying for begin to change. Trust in God and in my intercession with all your struggles.

My children, you have begun a new year. Let this year be a year full of prayer and peace. You know that this will be a difficult year with much suffering. Do not be afraid, my children, for I am with you each step of

Purity and holiness of heart

the way. I will never abandon you. Allow your prayers to transform your lives. In this way you will help your heavenly Mother to lead you to purity and holiness. Through my intercession I will deflect all the temptations that Satan will put in your path. Abandon yourselves to the Two Hearts, and you will overcome all fear. I love you all, my children. I am praying with you and for all of your intentions. Thank you for listening to my message.

January 10, 1994 *Convert before it's too late*

Our Lady: Dear children, today, I invite you to trust in my intercession. Take refuge in my Most Immaculate Heart, and I will lead you to holiness and purity of heart. My little ones, continue to pray as a family and live my messages. Pray for my children that live in darkness, whose hearts are closed to my Son, Jesus. My children, pray to the Holy Spirit for enlightenment in all your decisions in your daily lives. He will help you to live God's Holy Will.

My children, decide for conversion, for my time with you is short. Open your hearts and abandon your lives to the Two Hearts. Do not be afraid of the world that continues to live in sin.

Convert, convert, before it is too late! Pray for my beloved Pope, and all my beloved priests. Pray and offer your sufferings for my Church. Pray, my children, pray, so that God will help my Church to remain united to my Son during the great tribulation. Thank you for listening to my message.

January 15, 1994 *San Antonio, Texas I will help you*

Our Lady: Dear children, today, I greet each one with my motherly love. Know, my children, that I, your heavenly Mother, brought you all here to bless you. As you pray together, I will be praying with you, my children. You have brought much joy to my Immaculate Heart. My children, many of you are sad and suffering. You have come looking for answers to your prayers. Many of you have physical pains, and you are hurting. Abandon everything to my Immaculate Heart, and I will help you and bless you. Have no worry, for you, my children, are all under my shadow and protection.

January 20, 1994 *What more can I do for you*

Our Lady: Dear children, today, I invite all families to continue to pray together and to live in my Son's love. Today, I wish to thank you for all your efforts to remain strong in prayer during hard times. My children, I invite you to be living witnesses of my messages. I say this, my children, because so many of you are eager to read my messages, but you do not put them into practice.

My children, God's mercy is being demonstrated to each one of you by allowing me to remain with you for so long. Today, I ask you, my children, what more can I do for you? I have been teaching you the importance of prayer, fasting, and loving one another. I have been teaching you that through prayer and fasting, conversion will come easy for those who desire to convert. Through all my time with you I have invited you to be reconciled back to God and be converted. My children, all it takes to be my children is to say 'yes' to me and to live my messages.

Know, my children, that the most recent earthquake and its severity was lessened through all your prayers and sacrifices. Through your prayers many lives were saved, for this I extend my gratitude to all. Continue to pray and know that God hears all your prayers. Thank you for listening to my message.

January 25, 1994 *Satan is active*

Our Lady: Dear children, today, I invite you to abandon yourselves to my Son's love and mercy. Do not procrastinate, my children, but enter into my Son's love and mercy and be converted! My children, remember, prayer is your strength, so pray, pray, pray! Do not be sad and do not quarrel with one another, but love one another. Satan is active in causing so many families to quarrel. His one goal is to separate you from God and to take His peace from you. Do not give in to Satan's temptations, but pray together as a family. I say again, love one another and live in God's peace, for where there is God's love and peace, Satan has no power.

My children, listen to your heavenly Mother and take refuge in the Two Hearts; in this way no evil will harm you. Continue to pray and make reparation for the war in Bosnia. Do not abandon this effort, but be committed! Together, we can bring an end to this horrible war. Thank you for listening to my message.

January 29, 1994 *Become a slave of love*

Jesus: Welcome to My Eucharistic Heart. Come, My child, spend a

Purity and holiness of heart

few moments with your Jesus of Love and Mercy. Know that you console My Eucharistic Heart when you come to visit Me. Tell your Savior everything that is bothering you. Trust Me, and I will take away everything that distracts you from loving Me. I am a jealous Savior. I want all your love and all your trust. I want your complete attention. Allow Me to help you to become a slave of love, so that you may only have one desire: to love everyone and to have a loving and merciful heart like your Beloved Savior. Come, My child, come to your Jesus of Love and Mercy. Come, be a slave of love and remain united to My love for all eternity.

January 31, 1994 *A Mother's pleading*

Our Lady: Dear children, today, I invite you to continue to decide for conversion as a family. Pray your family Rosary everyday!

Remember, the Rosary is your weapon, and through praying the Rosary, you draw closer to God day by day. My children, again, I ask you to trust in my motherly intercession. In this way I will be able to help you and to lead you closer to my Son.

Remember, my children, that you must pray. If you do not pray, I cannot help you. Satan is busy trying to destroy you as a family. He has already separated many families, because they do not pray. I invite you, as a family, to pray for other families, so that through your prayers they may decide for conversion.

Please, my children, do everything I invite you to do, and do not delay in your decision to live my messages! My children, pray for my beloved Pope and for all my priests, that they, too, will help their heavenly Mother to lead others to my Son through their prayers and efforts.

I invite you, dear children, to open your hearts to the love and mercy of my Son, Jesus. Spend time with Him in prayer. Remember, He knows your hearts. Come to Him, little children, and be converted. Pray, children, pray, for through prayer you discover God's love. Thank you for listening to my message.

February 10, 1994 *Through prayer you discover God*

Our Lady: Dear children, today, I invite you to prepare your hearts through prayer and fasting to receive all the graces and blessings that God wishes to bestow upon you and your family. My children, I know that many of you are experiencing much suffering in your family. Many of you have allowed your suffering to become a distraction for you, and you choose not to pray. Remember, my children, that through prayer you discover God, and prayer brings you God's peace.

My little children, abandon yourselves to the Two United Hearts with filial trust. Do not allow your suffering to cause you to fear. Remember, that with God all things are possible. Trust in your prayers and remain true to serving God with joy in your hearts.

Continue praying your family Rosary and cling to God's love and mercy in your suffering. He will inflame your hearts with His Holy Spirit to help you and guide you in everything. Peace, my children, peace. Live my messages and be converted! Thank you for listening to my message.

February 10, 1994 *Rivers of living water*

Janie: *Jesus gave me this message regarding the upcoming Anniversary of Our Lady on February 15.*
Jesus: My child, be at peace, for it is I, Who am working through you. You must remain in a spirit of prayer to receive all the graces and blessings that My Father wants to give to you on that day. Ask Me for anything, for anything you ask of My Father in My Name, He will do.

There will be one angel from each choir with the child that represents that choir, and the virtue of that choir will remain in the heart of that child forever. Heaven will open up and the light of Heaven will shine this day on the community of St. Julia and on everyone who comes. All who come will carry this light. All who come are responding to My personal invitation. My Father is pleased with your work, and you will not regret anything that you are doing. It is a joy to participate in a heavenly task such as this one.

My Mother is preparing her spiritual ark in many cities and towns where she is not yet known, so that when the time comes that she will no longer be with you, her Spouse, the Holy Spirit will be with you in such a powerful way, such a powerful way!

In this way, it is necessary that when My Mother's time is up, she will usher in the Holy Spirit to every heart that has been open to her messages. As the stars illuminate the night, you will be like stars that illuminate the day - like light upon light, because God's divine light has been inflamed in your hearts by the power of the Holy Spirit.

Each person who is coming to this sacred gathering has a personal mission that they have been invested with. Many who come for the first time will discover the calling of God in a special way, and they are going to go out and fulfill their roles.

Out of this sacred gathering will result rivers of living water. In this way, long after you go to your homeland, which is Heaven, you will leave behind rivers of living water, which will be hearts illuminated with the Holy Spirit. I solemnly tell you that all that I am giving you will come to pass. I give you My word.

February 13, 1994 *Your rewards are great in Heaven*

Our Lady: My dear children, I have come to embrace each one of you and to thank you for all of your work. My little ones, you are suffering, and you are tired. If you only knew how much God loves you! If you only knew how much I need your prayers and even your sufferings.

My children, know that I am here with each one of you. Have no fear or worry. Know that you are all very special to me, and I hold you all close to my motherly bosom. Love one another and be patient with one another, for your rewards are great in Heaven. I love you, my little ones. Take refuge in my Most Immaculate Heart and be at peace, be at peace.

February 15, 1994 *Fifth Anniversary of Our Lady's Visitations*

Our Lady: Dear children, today, I, your heavenly Mother, embrace each one of you. Know that I have brought you here to bless you. My children, today is a day of great rejoicing, therefore, have no other distractions, but open your hearts to my Immaculate Heart. Little children, you are all so dear to me. You will never understand the love that I have for you. I ask that you trust in my motherly intercession and abandon yourselves to my Immaculate Heart with filial trust.

My little children, today is a very special day for you and for me. Let us together, give thanks to God for allowing me to remain with you for such a long time. For a while now, I have been teaching you how to love, how to forgive and how to pray as a family. You have pleased your heavenly Mother through your obedience in living my motherly teaching and messages. You have consoled my Immaculate Heart. You have brought joy to my Heart.

Today, my children, I want to bring God's joy to your hearts. Tell your heavenly Mother what you need. What is bothering you? How can I help you? I am here, my children. God has sent me to help you to live by His Commandments. Come, my children, enter into my Immaculate Heart, which is the gate that will lead you to the Sacred Heart of my Son, Jesus. Trust in the Two Hearts which are One with the Father, and have no fear or worry. I am here, I am here to protect you.

To my beloved priests, how can I thank you, my beloved sons? Your being here demonstrates your love for your heavenly Mother. Come, my beloved sons, come and allow your heavenly Mother to embrace you with deep gratitude. Thank you for feeding the flock entrusted to your care. Your hard work is blessed by God, and He is pleased with you.

Know, my beloved sons, that I am with you in everything. Love one another, love one another! Live my messages and be converted! Today I bless you all. Bring all your worries and anxieties to your heavenly Mother who loves you. Rejoice, rejoice, rejoice! Thank you for listening to my message.

February 16, 1994 *A path that few have chosen*

Jesus: My dear child, welcome to My Eucharistic Heart. Thank you for coming to spend time with Me, your Jesus Who loves you. My child, today is a new beginning for you. I, your Jesus, your Eucharistic Savior, invite you to journey with Me for a period of forty days. During this time, I will teach you on virtues that will help you in your own faith journey. Do you accept My invitation, My child?
Janie: Yes, My Lord, I accept Your invitation with a joyful heart. Tell me what You would have me do.
Jesus: My child, I have much to ask of you, and you have responded with a total 'yes.' Know how much you please and console My Eucharistic Heart. During the next forty days, you will journey with Me, and I shall take you through a path that few have chosen to travel. It is a hard path with much suffering, so prepare well with strong prayer and fasting.

I shall begin to teach you on virtues that will help you when you are sent out to harvest the hearts of the family. All who hear your words will know that I sent you.
Janie: Even priests, My Lord?
Jesus: Especially My beloved brother priests, for the words that come

forth from your mouth will be My words. I, your Eucharistic Jesus, will invest you with wisdom and knowledge that comes from My Father's throne of glory!
Janie: Why are You doing this? Why are You giving me this wisdom and knowledge?
Jesus: My child, you are My humble servant and you have responded with a total 'yes' to My request. You will need the virtues I invest you with, for you will be sent among rebellious and unbelieving people. Hard of face and obstinate of heart are they whom I will send you to. These whom you speak to have resisted the invitation to repent and to turn away from their sins. Know that many will contradict you and reject you, especially those who call themselves your friends. Fear neither them nor their words, nor be dismayed at their looks, for their hearts are without My light and truth.

My child, I, your Jesus, will prepare you for the responsibilities that have been entrusted to you by My Father in Heaven. Do not be concerned with what I am telling you now, but trust Me and later on you will understand. Return to your home now, My child. Go with My love and blessing.
Janie: Thank You, Jesus. I promise I won't allow myself to be concerned with anything.

February 17, 1994 *Love obedience, love obedience*

Jesus: My dear child, welcome to My Eucharistic Heart. Thank you for your obedience in coming to be with Me and allowing nothing to distract you from coming. Today, My child, I will speak to you on the virtue of obedience. This virtue will help you to carry out everything that I ask of you. This virtue will help you in all aspects of your life.

My child, obedience is a first class virtue. Obedience leads to sanctity. Through the virtue of obedience you are able to do anything that I ask of you. Obedience is something that I, your Jesus, find most acceptable. My child, you cannot offer your Beloved Savior a more perfect sacrifice than your humble and obedient heart that is ready to do everything that I ask you to do. My child, open your heart and submit to Me and always be obedient to Me.

No matter where you may be, when obedience calls, submit to it as if I, your Jesus, am bodily present at your work, at home, or wherever you are. Deny your very self and be obedient to Me by being obedient to your husband, to the needs of your family, your pastor, your Spiritual

Director, your supervisors, and friends who need your assistance. By doing this you will please your loving Savior.

My child, do not resist, but yield to My command to embrace the virtue of obedience. Love this virtue with all your heart and soul. Never neglect it as long as you live. Be obedient to others for My sake. Do it without being upset or arguing about it. Remember, you are being obedient to Me in all things, in being obedient to others. Pray for the grace to leave yourself for My sake by denying your own will. Despise your own wisdom and submit yourself to My command. Rely on Me by relying on your husband, your confessor, pastor, or Spiritual Director for assistance. Do nothing without spiritual advice from those I put in your path.

My child, live in simplicity and poverty of spirit. Renounce your very own self and all your knowledge and rely on your Beloved Savior in everything. My child, much is being asked of you as a child of My Father; that is why you must learn about the virtue of obedience. You will be able to be obedient by denying your very self. Abandon your own will and judgment, and embrace My Will - the virtue of obedience.

I love you, My child, and I am calling you to be My reflection in all things by being obedient to all My commands. Everyday, abandon yourself to My Father's Holy Will and pick up your cross and follow Me. Learn to die to yourself, that I may be born in you. Love Me and submit to being a slave to the virtue of obedience, and you will bring many souls to Me, your Jesus of Love and Mercy. As I was obedient to My Father, you, too, are called to be an obedient servant. Love obedience, love obedience.

February 18, 1994 *They do not understand My True Presence*

Jesus: My beloved child, I, your Eucharistic Savior, extend My thanks to you for being here with Me. Open your hearts to Me, Your Jesus, for I have many blessings which I wish to give to you. Tonight, I ask you to love your Eucharistic Savior with all your heart. Give Me all your love and hold nothing back. Embrace Me and tell Me what you need to help you to draw closer to My Eucharistic Heart. Tell your Savior all your worries and trust Me to help you. I shall listen to all your needs, and I shall bless all your efforts. Open your heart to Me, for this is your time to love and embrace Me with all your sufferings and difficulties.

You are sad, because others do not understand My True Presence, and they leave Me without ever noticing Me and My Presence among them. Do not be distracted with this, for I want your total attention. I shall hear your prayers for My children who do not yet recognize My True Presence. To pray for them is all I ask of you. Leave them to Me and continue giving Me all your love and attention.

My child, offer all your suffering for My sake and trust Me. I will heal all your woundedness and your broken heart. Abandon yourself to My Eucharistic Heart and surrender all to Me. Allow Me to strip you from all that you've gained and received in the world. Come to Me in the nakedness of your innocence and allow Me to clothe you with the garment of humility and purity. Allow Me to strip you of everything that the world has offered you. Come to Me and take refuge in My Eucharistic Heart. Love Me with all your heart and with every breath that you take. Trust Me and love Me. Allow nothing to take you away from My love, nothing.

Janie: My Eucharistic Savior, I surrender everything to You, everything. All I have I give You, I hold nothing back. I belong to You.

February 21, 1994 *I wish to thank all my children*

Our Lady: Dear children, today, I, your heavenly Mother, wish to thank each one of you for all your endless hours of hard work. Through your hard efforts and through your generous hearts, many of my children were received with much love.

My children, know that through your obedience to work together to honor your heavenly Mother of Compassion and Love, many of my children who came from all over received an abundance of graces and blessings. I wish to thank all my children who responded to my Son's invitation to come and embrace their heavenly Mother. God has blessed them, God has blessed them!

To my beloved priests, I, your heavenly Mother, embrace each one of you. Many of you, my beloved sons, came, even though you were tired and had busy schedules. Many of you are suffering from persecution and rejection. Do not be distracted with your crosses of suffering and persecution and rejection, but embrace your crosses with joy in your hearts.

Remember, you are all under my motherly mantle and protection. Again, I say, embrace all your crosses for the sake of my Son, Who loves you with deep love. Thank you, my sons, for embracing your Mother and for helping to lead my children closer to God. Thank you all. My children, continue being loving and compassionate and pray, pray, pray! I love you all, I love you all. Take refuge in my Immaculate Heart and I will lead you to the Heart of my Son. Thank you for listening to my message.

February 22, 1994 *Be My reflection*

Jesus: Dear child, you have pleased Me by recognizing your uncharitable attitude. Be loving always, no matter how much others hurt you. Be My reflection in all situations. Trust Me with all your difficulties. Never doubt that I am with you, especially when you feel alone and rejected, for that's when I am My strongest in you. I love you, My child.

February 23, 1994 *Television: one of the biggest distractions*

Jesus: My dear child, welcome to My Eucharistic Heart. Come, My child, and enter into My Eucharistic Heart. Allow your Beloved Savior to console your aching and sad heart.
Janie: My Beloved Lord, I need Your love so much. I wish I could always be by Your side like this in this present moment.

Jesus: What is it, My child? Although I know your heart, tell your Savior your needs. What can I do for you? This time is Ours. Speak freely My child, hold nothing back.
Janie: Oh Jesus, sometimes I wish I could be in Heaven with You and Our Lady. I guess I'm feeling sorry for myself. I just need Your love. Please Jesus, help me. I am sad, because it's so hard for me to spend time with You like I want. My schedule is so busy with my family and my job. Sometimes, I wish I could go away with You. Help me to be prudent in managing my time well. Help me to bring my family closer to Your loving and Eucharistic Heart. Help us as a family. At times, it is hard to get the family in the spirit of prayer. Tell me what to do.
Jesus: My child, share with your family how much I love them. Tell them that the only way to come to know My Eucharistic Heart is through prayer. Through prayer they come to know Me. Prayer helps them to begin a beautiful relationship with Me. As they pray more, their hearts begin to blossom like heavenly flowers. The evil one is busy at putting distractions in their path. **The television is one of the biggest distractions. Many spend endless hours watching television, and afterwards, they are too tired to pray. They retire without giving thanksgiving to My Heavenly Father Who loves them.**

Purity and holiness of heart

My child, share with your family that prayer is the spiritual food that nourishes their souls. Without prayer they are not aware of My Heavenly Father. Prayer is the key to My Father's Heart, for prayer leads to purity and holiness of heart. You have a heavy cross, My child, in bringing your family and others to My Eucharistic Heart. Do not have any concerns, but trust Me. Continue teaching your family and others about the importance of prayer. Share with them that prayer brings about an interior change that leads to conversion. Share with them, that when they pray, they speak directly to My Eucharistic Heart. Now, My little child, be at peace and continue harvesting and cultivating hearts through your prayers and reparation.

February 25, 1994 *Allow Me to refresh your suffering heart*

Jesus: My dear child, welcome to My Eucharistic Heart. I, your Jesus of Love and Mercy, thank you for your efforts to come to be with Me.

I know, My child, that you are suffering interiorly. Give everything to Me, and leave it with Me. I, your Beloved Savior, want you to have no distractions that will take your attention away from Me. This time is Ours. Speak to your Beloved Savior. Pour out your heart to Me.
Janie: Oh Beloved Jesus, I am all right. Sometimes, I get irritated when I am suffering. Please forgive Me for being such an infant. Help me to mature in my love for You and for my family. Help me to embrace my crosses without complaining. You know my heart, My Lord and my All. I only want to please You. Help me to be Your reflection in doing God's Most Holy Will.
Jesus: My little flower, how much you please your Beloved Savior. It is because of your love for Me and your desire to do My Father's Will that you suffer. Never stop loving Me and continue to do My Father's Will, for your rewards are great in Heaven. You are suffering for My sake, because you desire to live in complete holiness. This is a hard path to journey. You are doing well. Have no worry in your heart. My Father in Heaven is pleased with all your efforts. Be at peace, My child.
Janie: Thank You, my Beloved Savior. I love You.
Jesus: I love you, My child.

February 26, 1994 *I am the Prince of Peace, I am love*

Jesus: My child, welcome to My Eucharistic Heart. I, your Jesus of Love and Mercy, thank you for taking time out to come and spend time with Me. So many of My children come to Holy Mass, but they do not stop by to greet Me. Many do not understand or believe in My True

Presence. You console My Eucharistic Heart. I, your Eucharistic Savior, ask you to invite others to come and spend time with Me. Share with others how much I, Jesus, yearn to be with them.

My child, I have so many graces and blessings to bestow on those who respond to My invitation. I will refresh their hearts and souls. I will make them strong, for I will be their strength. I have so much love to give all who come. I have so much love to give all who come! I will help them to unburden all their worries and anxieties. They will leave with peace and love in their hearts, for I am the Prince of Peace, and I am love.

Janie: My Beloved Savior, I will bring others to You. I'll share what You tell me with them.
Jesus: Go in peace and let My love be your strength.

February 27, 1994 *In loving others you love Me*

Jesus: My little child, I, your Eucharistic Savior, came to be with you, for I know how you long to be with Me, so I came to you. I know My child, that you gave that time up, so that you could be with your family. This is most pleasing to My Father. My child, I am so pleased at your invitation to your husband to join you in your faith journey. It pleased Me that you offered your love and support to him and reassured him of your love for him.

You pleased Me in telling your husband that all you wanted to do was to be by My side and to love Me with every breath that you take. **It was most pleasing to Me when you told him, that in loving him, you were loving Me. How very true you spoke to your husband, for it is in loving others that you love Me. My child, your words were filled with wisdom, and the Holy Spirit was speaking through you.**

My child, you have pleased My Eucharistic Heart by sharing a special time with your husband. Share with other spouses the importance of spending time together and allowing My love to live in their hearts, so that they may love one another.

February 28, 1994 *Transform your life into My love*

Jesus: My child, today, I, your Eucharistic Savior, want to thank you for allowing My love to be your strength. My child, you have been sharing in My suffering, and you suffer without complaining. You drink from the cup of My bitter Passion, and you drink it all with a loving and open heart.

My child, I want you to remember that no one in the world loves you more than I. Know that I am always with you whether you're happy or sad, whether you are with others or alone. I know your sorrows and your joys. I know everything about you, and I love you just the way you are.

My child, your wretchedness attracts My Eucharistic Heart. Your nothingness calls Me to bless you more, for I know that you are in much need of My love and My blessings. Trust Me always, and I give you My solemn word that you will not regret it. Love Me always and allow no distractions to take you away from My love. My love will lead you to complete holiness. I give you My word that your life will be transformed into My love if you put your trust in Me, your Jesus of Love and Mercy. Trust Me, trust Me now and forever.

February 28, 1994 *Do everything St. Joseph tells you*

Our Lady: My little angel, how much you console my Immaculate Heart by following all the instructions given to you by Most Holy St. Joseph. Through his teachings you and your family have matured in wisdom and discernment. His teachings have brought your household many graces and blessings. Continue to live his instructions on the family and share his instructions with all my children.

My child, God so wanted to make your life complete in being a holy family, that He blessed you and your family with the visitations of Most Holy St. Joseph. Pray to God to give you the grace to be humble and obedient, like Most Holy St. Joseph. He is the model of humility and the obedient servant of God. Do everything that he tells you, everything!

My child, in just a short while your book with the teachings on the family will be published. This book will have a divine effect on all who read it with open hearts. Through this book many families will come to God as a family. The teachings in the messages given to you are teachings from Heaven, for God is calling all families to be reconciled to Him through being a holy family. It is important that you pray to the Holy Spirit to prepare the hearts of the many families that will read your book.

Prepare, my child, with strong prayer and fasting for the completion of the book. All my children who have dedicated their time and efforts for the completion of this book must pray and fast also, for Satan will attempt to disrupt my work in this book. That is why you must prepare every day with strong prayer and fasting for the success of my work in this book.

Trust me, my child, and do what I ask you to do. Pray to the Holy Spirit and consecrate the works of the book to Him Who will bring my work to completion. Trust me in my title of Mother of Compassion and Love, and allow me to teach you how to be the reflection of my Son, Who is compassionate and loving. I am your Mother of Compassion and Love, Mother of the True God and Mother of All Humanity. I love you, my child. I love you.

Editor's Note: This was the last message given for the first edition of the book. The first edition of this book was published in October of 1994 and included the messages of St. Joseph given to Janie up to this time. The Second edition was published in May 1998 and is called **Heaven's Messages for The Family Volume I.** *Vol II will include the messages from St. Joseph and the Archangels.*

March 1, 1994 *Pray and fast to end the war*

Our Lady: My dear child, continue to offer all your prayers and fasting in reparation for the war in Bosnia. Do not abandon the need to pray for this effort. Share with all my children that their prayers and sacrifices for this war are so important. I call on all my children to help their heavenly Mother, to pray and fast to bring an end to this war. My child, listen to me and help me by offering all your prayers. I invite all my children to offer their daily Rosary and Mass for this special intention. Thank you, my child, for your time.

March 2, 1994 *Vision of Our Lady praying to the Father*

Janie: *I was at daily Mass in Austin. I suddenly found myself in Medjugorje. I was on Mt. Krizevac, and I saw Our Lady in dazzling white light. She was kneeling below the cross, and she was praying a prayer of thanksgiving to God, Our Father, for all the time He allowed her to be in our world. At this very moment, I had a deep knowing in my heart that her time was really very short. I felt a sadness in my heart.*

In my vision it was as though Our Lady was not aware that I was there where she was praying at the foot of the cross. There was no one else around. It was late, about six in the evening or so. She was praying to God for all her children.

I sensed a sadness in her voice, and I thought that it was perhaps because there was still so much sinfulness in the world, and so many have ignored her invitation to conversion and to be reconciled back to God. I listened quietly to her as she prayed. She prayed in a different language, but for some strange reason I understood some of the words. I will write only what I understood through the guidance of the Holy Spirit. These are the words that I heard as she prayed.

Our Lady: *I have given You glory by finishing the work You gave me to do. I have made known Your Name to many who lived in darkness through those You gave me out of the world. These that You gave me to teach have embraced Your teachings with love and repentance in their hearts. They believed that all that I taught them came from You, and they have kept Your Word.*

To those You gave me I entrusted secrets pertaining to world chastisements, and to others, messages of love and repentance and a call to world conversion. They received all Your teachings entrusted to me by You. For these I pray, for they are really Yours. As long as I was with them I guarded them with Your Name. I gave them Your Word once again, and many have suffered persecution and rejection for my Son's Name's sake. I pray for Your Spirit of Truth to guide them, so that they will be protected from the evil one. I do not pray for only those You gave me, but also for those who have been touched and repented through the work of those You gave me to teach and for the many others who continue to live in darkness.

All that You entrusted to me I have done. Your Name has been glorified by many throughout the world, but many have rejected Your call to repentance. I have fulfilled Your request, and now my work on earth is completed. I entrust to You all my children, all my children, especially those who have rejected the call to live my messages.

March 3, 1994 *My children, you are called to love*

Our Lady: Dear children, today, I invite you to continue to live my messages and to convey them to others like never before. Pray, my children, so that the Holy Spirit will continue to guide you to do all that I am asking you to do.

Trust in the guidance of the Holy Spirit to help you to be children of the

light. Convey your light to others who live in darkness. Be compassionate and loving, and be the reflection of my Son, Jesus. Pray and fast in reparation for those many souls who continue to reject God's love and mercy.
My children, be strong in your sufferings and do not allow Satan to destroy all the blessings and graces that God has given you and your family. Remain loving always, in all situations, and trust in my motherly intercession. My children, you are called to love, for love will lead you to holiness. Continue teaching your children about the love and mercy of God, so that they may grow closer to God in a personal way.

I invite you all to continue to pray and fast for the war in Bosnia and to not abandon this effort. Embrace the world around you with God's love. In this way others will be helped through your love, and conversion will come easily for those who desire it. Pray and fast for my beloved Pope and all my priests who suffer so much. Pray your family Rosary and be converted, be converted! Thank you for listening to my message.

March 3, 1994 *Make the Holy Spirit your best Friend and Teacher*

Janie: Blessed Mother, will I be sad when you return to Heaven? *I meant when her time with me was up.*
Our Lady: Yes, my child, you will be sad, but just for a short while. Soon after my departure from the world, my Spouse, the Holy Spirit, will continue to guide you and all of humanity as He is now guiding you. Pray always to the Holy Spirit and make Him your best Friend and Your Teacher, as He is the Spirit of the Father and my Son, Jesus, Who are all Three in One.
Janie: Blessed Mother, will I experience your presence in my heart like now?
Our Lady: Yes, my child, in a special way, I will always be in your heart. You will not forget my time with you and your family. I shall remain in your heart with my motherly love and protection, and you and your family shall remain in my Immaculate Heart.

March 4, 1994 *Adoration: I feed your soul with My love*

Jesus: Welcome to My Eucharistic Heart, and thank you for coming to be with your Beloved Savior. My child, this time is Ours. Allow no distractions to take your attention away from Me, your loving Savior. Trust Me and have no worry or anxiety. Let Me take all worry away from your heart. I will make your heart much lighter, as I remove all burdens from your heart.

Purity and holiness of heart

My little servant, I want you to be like a child from morning 'til night, to live happily in joy and in total abandonment, not worrying about anything. You are able to do this only if you trust Me completely. My child, I shall give you heavenly food while you are here with Me. I will feed your soul with My love and you shall never hunger again, for My love will remain in you forever and ever.

You delight My Eucharistic Heart when you come to be with Me. You share in My suffering, and you console your Savior by being here with Me.

My little servant, never allow anything to separate you from My love, for in My love you have eternal life. Share all that I tell you during this time, so that others may know how much I love everyone and how I long for their company.

Pray for My beloved brother priests, that they may understand how much I want to be adored by all My brother priests. I want everybody to know My True Presence in the Blessed Sacrament. I want you to pray for this special intention. I love you, My little servant, you are a delight to My Eucharistic Heart.
Janie: My Lord and my All, I shall do all that You ask of me.

March 8, 1994 *Satan seeks to destroy you*

Our Lady: Dear children, today, I invite you to continue to pray and fast as a family and to live in God's love. Little children, I ask that you take prayer seriously and be committed to prayer. In this way you will discover God's love for you more and more everyday.

Do not allow Satan to destroy God's peace in your lives. You do this when you quarrel and stay angry at one another, refusing to forgive one another. When you do this, you alienate one another, and your prayer becomes weak. Know, my children, that Satan looks for every opportunity to destroy you and to alienate you away from God. You, my little ones, give him permission to destroy your lives when you take your eyes off of my Son, Jesus, and when you give in to his temptations.

My children, you are called as a family to be children of the light and to convey this light to other families. You are called to live by God's Ten Commandments and to live in His love. Do not allow your tribulations to draw you away from my Immaculate Heart, but trust in your heavenly Mother and abandon yourselves to my intercession. My children, live my messages and be converted! Allow your prayers to purify you, and be the reflection of my Son. I love you, my children. Come to your heavenly Mother and trust me, for I am the gate that will lead you to my Son. To my beloved priests: help your heavenly Mother bring all my children closer to God. Be gentle to all who come to you for help. Do not be cold towards them, but be loving and help my children, help my children! Remember, my beloved sons, that you are God's voice on earth, and God blesses all your efforts. Thank you for listening to my message.

March 10, 1994 *Give me your heart*

Our Lady: My dear angel, you are so special and dear to your heavenly Mother.
Janie: Oh, Blessed Mother, please hold me. I feel so sad.
Our Lady: Come to your heavenly Mother, for I know, my angel, that you are suffering and your little heart is filled with sorrow.
Janie: Yes, yes, Blessed Mother, I am very sad. *I was crying.*
Our Lady: My sweet angel, do not be sad, but be grateful to God for the time that He has allowed me to be with you.
Janie: Blessed Mother, I am trying not to be sad and not to cry, but I can't help it, I can't help it! I am most grateful to God for everything, but my heart is sad. Your time is short with me, I know this!

Our Lady: Yes, my angel, my time is short, not only with you but throughout the world, but you will never forget my time with you. It will be this way with all my children throughout the world. Your sadness will cease, for my Spouse, the Holy Spirit, will fill your heart with joy. You have a special place in my Most Immaculate Heart.
Janie: You also have a special place in my heart. Blessed Mother, I give you my heart, for it is so distracted and my prayers are weak because of my distracted heart. Take it with you and give it to God, and tell him to fix it for me, so that I may be strong in my prayers and sacrifices.
Our Lady: Give me your heart, my child.
Janie: *I saw myself giving her my heart. She gave it to a little Cherubim, who flew quickly away with my heart to present it to God. The little Cherubim came back in a flash, and Our Lady took my heart from the Cherubim and placed it back. When she put my heart back, I felt a tingling all over my being. She kissed my forehead.*
Our Lady: There, your heart has been mended by God. My child, kneel and let us pray, for our visit is about over.

March 11, 1994 *Take refuge in My Immaculate Heart*

Jesus: My child, I know that you are ill. Do not be concerned about spending time with Me in Adoration, but know that I'm always with you, always. I love you, My little humble servant. Be at peace.

Our Lady: My dear angel, I am here to tell you not to worry about anything, but do all that my Son and Most Holy St. Joseph tell you. I want to thank you for being a reflection of the Gospel and not falling into temptation. You did well, and I want to thank you for all your prayers and sacrifices. I am with you. Take refuge in my Immaculate Heart and be at peace. Goodnight, my sweet angel, I love you.

Janie: Goodnight, Blessed Mother, and thank you for your motherly care. I love you.

March 14, 1994 *Embrace all your crosses with joy*

Our Lady: Dear children, today, I invite you and your family to continue to pray and to trust in my motherly intercession.

Know, my little ones, that I am always with you, and that I never leave you, not even for one moment. Have no fear or worry, but abandon yourselves to my Most Immaculate Heart with filial trust.

My children, allow your lives to become a life of prayer, where you will discover the love of God. Pray for holiness and purity of heart. In this way you will be able to embrace God's Commandments and to live in His love and peace. Do not allow yourselves to be distracted by your suffering, but embrace all your crosses with joy in your heart. When you do this, my children, you are embracing my Son in His Passion.

Continue to pray your family Rosary and do not abandon this effort, for the Rosary is the weapon that dissolves the works of Satan. In all situations be committed to praying your Rosary and pray it with faith in your heart. Today, I bless you with God's peace. Share His peace with everyone in your path. Thank you for listening to my message.

March 19, 1994 *Love Me in the Holy Eucharist*

Jesus: My beloved one, I, your Jesus of Love and Mercy, thank you for all your hard work. Through you I have fed My families who have listened to your talk. My little flower, your heart is blossoming like a beautiful heavenly flower more and more everyday. You have become My lit-

tle flower and as of today, I, your Jesus, shall call you My little flower.
Janie: Oh Jesus, I love You.
Jesus: Today, My little flower, I ask you to lead others to the love of Holy Mass. You touched My Sacred Heart with your love for Holy Mass. Through your love to My Eucharistic Heart, others will come to love Me in the Holy Eucharist. Today you embraced Me in the Eucharist like I desire to be embraced - with your everything. You had complete abandonment. Your heart and soul were centered only on Me in the miracle of the Holy Eucharist. You came as a child with total love, knowing in your heart that in this moment while you were preparing to receive Me; this was the holiest and most important moment in your life. You received Me with your whole being.

You experienced My love today like never before, for you were open to the miracle of the Holy Eucharist. You received your Lord and Savior with an open heart. You are My little flower, for through your prayer life your heart has been transformed like a heavenly flower. Share this beauty and the miracle of Holy Mass and My True Presence in the Eucharist with all families. I bless you, My little flower.

March 24, 1994 *Allow prayer to be your daily food*

Our Lady: Dear children, today, I invite you and your family to continue to pray and to follow the path that I have traced out for you which leads to purity and holiness. My little children, it is for your sake that I have remained with you for such a long time, to help you to live my messages. I have been teaching you and your family how to pray and the importance of prayer in your everyday lives.

During this time, you have matured in family prayer through praying your daily Rosary. You have learned the importance of family love and forgiveness. Many of you have done well, because you are living my messages. Many of you continue to struggle with loving one another and praying together.

Dear children, continue to consecrate yourselves and your family to daily prayer and allow prayer to be your daily food. Let prayer be your first step in your spiritual life and persist in your prayer life. Remember, my little ones, that only through prayer will the seed of conversion be planted in the hearts of your family. Through prayer you will continue to change the laws of nature, and you will stop wars, especially the wars in your very own hearts.

Do not allow Satan to discourage you, but remain patient and constant in your prayers, and through prayer continue to fight all the evil in the world. Pray, my children, pray, so that my Son may continue to conquer many hearts. Remember, without prayer there is no peace, there is no peace. Pray, pray, pray! Thank you for listening to my message.

March 25, 1994 *Adoration: Your heart is My tabernacle*

Jesus: My little flower, welcome to My Eucharistic Heart. Thank you for coming to be with your Lord and Savior.
Janie: Jesus, I came early to pray with You and to be at Your side before the prayer group meets. I know that You will bless Our time together.
Jesus: My little flower, this time is only for you. I, your Jesus of Love and Mercy, embrace you with My eternal love. This time is yours, only yours. Allow your words to flow freely from the very depths of your heart and soul. Tell your Master everything. Hold nothing back, for I know your heart. Trust Me in My True Presence in the Blessed Sacrament.
Janie: My Lord, My Lord, how very blessed I am to be able to embrace you in this present moment. I am forever grateful, forever grateful. Today, Lord, I want You to continue to help me to detach and to teach me true abandonment, where I desire only to be with You in everything.
Jesus: My little flower, you will never understand how your words please Me, for it is only through total abandonment that you will find Me. I am pleased with your spiritual growth and your commitment to spend more time with Me in prayer and less time involved in other conversations. My little flower, your heart continues to blossom more and more each day. Your commitment to prayer has transformed your heart, where you have allowed My True Presence to live in your very own heart. You have designed a tabernacle in your heart for Me.

You carry My love enthroned in your very heart through your detachment from many things that surround your existence. I am with you in a stronger way as your love continues to grow for Me. Your hunger for My love attracts Me, for you come to your Master in your nothingness and in your littleness. You bring your woundedness to your Eucharistic Savior, and you allow your Master to mend your broken heart. Your total trust and abandonment is most acceptable to Me.

Today, My little flower, I, your Jesus of Love and Mercy, shower My love and mercy upon you and your family. I bless this prayer gathering with the flame of love in My Heart. Rejoice and remain united to the Two Hearts.

Janie: Thank You, my Master, thank You.

March 29, 1994 *Your suffering is necessary to convert the world*

Our Lady: Dear children, today, I invite you to continue to pray and fast for peace in the world and for peace in your families. Persevere in all your trials and difficulties. Embrace all your crosses with joy in your hearts. Offer all your sufferings for those who do not accept me as their heavenly Mother and for those who reject my Son.

My children, embrace this Holy Week with much prayer and fasting to prepare your hearts for the celebrating of Easter. I invite you and your family to prepare by going to Confession, so that your hearts will be pure. In this way you will present my Son the purity of your heart and soul. He will embrace each one of you in a special way.

My little children, again, I tell you to persevere in your trials and sufferings, and thank the Almighty for allowing these trials in your lives. Know that your suffering is necessary to convert the world. Continue praying your family Rosary and do not neglect this responsibility, for it is necessary for your own conversion. Pray your Rosary everyday! It is your weapon against Satan. He flees when the Rosary is prayed. Pray, pray, pray! Thank you for listening to my message.

April 4, 1994 *Within the Two United Hearts lies your salvation*

Our Lady: Dear children, today I invite you and your family to continue to seek your refuge in the Two United Hearts, for within the Two United Hearts lies your salvation.

My children, many of you are sad because my time with you has decreased, but I say to you, have courage and trust in my beloved Spouse, the Holy Spirit. He is the one who will give you His light to be prudent in all your undertakings. I will remain in each of your hearts, and when you are in prayer my motherly love will be with you in a special way. I have chosen you, my children, to be God's family, to live my messages and to share them with others. You have been chosen to help other families to come to know God through your prayers and sacrifices.

My children, you have brought joy to your Mother's Immaculate Heart. I am pleased with all your prayers and little offerings. To all my children I extend my deep gratitude. I invite you to allow my Son's love and mercy to be the equilibrium in your lives; that will help you to remain pure and holy. Each day, abandon yourselves to my Son's love and mercy with filial trust. Thank you for listening to my message.

April 5, 1994 *Mass, Rosary and Reconciliation keep you strong*

Our Lady: My child, have no fear, but write what I tell you. Continue to pray as a family without ceasing! I, your heavenly Mother, ask you and your family to commit to doing all that I am asking of you. I, your heavenly Mother, gave you and your family three forms of prayer that will help you to remain strong in your faith: daily Mass, daily recitation of the Rosary and receiving the sacrament of Reconciliation once a week. My child, this must be done as a family. It is most important for you and your family to be spiritually healthy in order to do all that I am asking of you. Share with your family my words.
Janie: Is there anything else My Lady, that we can do for you?
Our Lady: Continue to pray and fast for the war in Bosnia. Pray for the healing of the victims of this horrible war, who have suffered so much. It will be hard for these victims to forgive when they have suffered so much. Pray also for those who are responsible for this war, for they have much to account for. Pray for these intentions for three months, beginning with this fourth month.

My child, pray especially for your own country, offering every petition to God. Plead for His mercy on your country. Pray for the political decisions that continue to corrupt your country and which offend my Son so much. The cup is overflowing with violence, adultery, killing of the innocents, and lack of faith and love. Your country lies in darkness. My child, pray, for I can no longer hold back the hand of God! Plead for His mercy! Plead for His mercy!

April 19, 1994 *You have been commissioned by God*

Our Lady: My children, you have brought joy to my Most Immaculate Heart. You have opened your hearts to your heavenly Mother. You have brought joy to my Heart! My children, you have been commissioned in a special way by God to go out and harvest many hearts. You are my dear children, and you have the Sacred Heart of my Son and my Most Immaculate Heart as your sure refuge. Never forget this. I will always be with you wherever you may be. I hold you dear to my Heart. Pray, children, pray in reparation and for the intentions of the Two United Hearts. I love you. You are dear to your heavenly Mother. Have no worry or fear. I am with you and you are my children.

April 19, 1994 *Seven visions from Jesus*

Editor's Note: These visions were not included in the first edition of the book as Fr. Henry discerned that they should not yet be made known to the public. Through much prayer and discernment he has determined that now (1997) is the time for these to be released.

Janie: *In the **first vision** I saw Red China in total chaos. There were loud noises that sounded like guns all over. People were lying in puddles of blood in the streets. Houses were destroyed. I could hear screams of people, and I could see men with weapons killing people. The vision was graphic in the sense of the numerous bodies that lay in the streets and that were burning in cars. Their body parts were dismembered from the fire and the weapons. The area was filled with smoke and fire.*

*In the **second vision** I found myself in the Holy City of Jerusalem. I could hear screams of men, women and children who were being killed by men. This city was also filled with fear. The buildings were destroyed, the churches were places of refuge for the people. This was a terrible place to be at this time. No safety, no safety only fear and death.*

*In the **third vision** I saw South Africa in total chaos. People were being killed by men with hate in their hearts. These men had weapons and were running all over the city killing whoever crossed their paths. Buildings were destroyed as well as houses. Cars and trucks were all over the streets, burning, and some had people burning in them. This seems to be a war for political power.*

*In the **fourth vision** I saw Rome, Italy. I saw the Pope sitting in his chair. He was surrounded by priests who were at war with one another. The war that I saw was a war in their hearts. These priests were in complete opposition to the Pope. They meant to do him harm by refusing to follow anything that he said. God was allowing me to see the evilness in these priests hearts. Their hearts were stained with sinfulness and they wanted to destroy the Pope by turning other priests against his teachings.*

I saw the sadness and suffering in the Pope's face as if he knew of the evilness that surrounded him. I knew in my heart that these priests had separated from the love of God, and the only reason they remained in the priesthood was to destroy our beloved Pope.

The weapons of these priests were not hand guns. Their hearts were their weapons, for their hearts were filled with darkness and hate for God and His Pope. Jesus asked me to pray about this, for He said the worst kind of weapon there is, is the hatred in our hearts.
*In the **fifth vision** I saw the United States. I saw the wars in the families. I saw violence in a multitude of families. It was like the time of Noah when all the evilness was happening before God destroyed the world through the flood. These families were evil and there was no love between them.*

Children were being abused and killed by their parents and families. The youth were living in sinfulness through fornication, homosexuality, prostitution, drugs, Satan worship, etc. Spouses were committing adultery. Men were abusing their wives. Children were turning against their parents. There was profanity spoken in these families.

I knew in my heart that most of these things are already happening, but I was allowed to see all of what I mentioned happening at the same time. It was as if I was seeing a movie of a family at war with one another. Satan had declared war on the family.

*In the **sixth vision** I saw the sky and it became as if at night time only I knew it was still day time, about noon time. Yet, the day became like night. Then I saw the stars in the Heavens turn into balls of fire and they began to fall on the earth. The fire began burning the areas where it was falling. People had begun screaming in fear as the day had turned into night. People were running and trying to find safety but there was no safety. Although it was dark I was given the ability to see them.*

The earth began to tremble and it opened in many areas. The earth swallowed many people, young and old. I saw volcanoes beginning to erupt spilling their lava in different directions. I saw lightening come from the sky and destroy areas where it hit. There were tidal waves that destroyed everything near the seashores. I saw nature release its power in forms of hurricanes, tornadoes and severe weather.

There was darkness all over the world and people screamed with fear in their hearts. Many died from the fear that gripped their hearts. I saw pestilence and calamity spread like an epidemic. All of this was happening at the same time. Everything was out of control.
Jesus: My child, what you have seen are the wars that are to come. You know what will happen. Only prayer can lessen the severity of these events.

Janie: When will this happen?
Jesus: It is not important that dates or times are revealed to you. What you have seen is for you to plead for My Father's mercy through your prayers.
Janie: In the seventh vision I saw new life. I saw a garden full of life. The trees were beautiful and very green. I saw flowers of all kinds. I saw beautiful springs of water in different areas of the garden. This is the most beautiful garden I have ever seen, and I knew it was like no garden on this earth. Then I heard Jesus speak Scripture to me.
Jesus: This is the New Jerusalem. This is the new house of the people of My Father. Here there will be no more weeping, no more calling for help. Babies will no longer die in infancy and all people will live out their life span. Those who live to be a hundred will be considered young and to die before that time will be a sign that My Father had punished them.

Like trees, people will live long lives. They will build their homes and get to live in them. Their homes will not be used by someone else. The work they do will be successful and their children will not meet with disaster.

April 25, 1994 *I am always at your side*

Our Lady: Dear children, today, I invite you to continue to persevere in your prayers and love for one another. Do not allow yourselves to become discouraged or distracted by your sufferings. Pray, children, pray, for Satan continues to destroy many families because they do not pray. Allow the Holy Rosary to be your weapon and pray it with faith in your hearts.

My children, I want to help each one of you, but you do not trust in my motherly intercession. You allow your suffering to become a distraction for you. Everyday, I, your heavenly Mother, bring all your family needs before God. Everyday, I am at your side, helping you and your family to obtain holiness and purity of heart.

I love you, my children, and you are most dear to my Immaculate Heart. You have been chosen to be a loving and prayerful family. You have been chosen to be a reflection of the Holy Family and to be an example to other families. My children, do not waste precious time in quarreling with one another, but love one another. Satan delights when you give him power by falling into his temptations, and your prayers become weak. Remember, prayer is your weapon, especially the

Rosary. Pray it daily!

My children, remember, that you are called to be children of the light and to live Holy Scripture. Do not allow Satan to destroy the love and peace in your family. Be strong in your love for one another, and Satan will flee from you, for he hates love. Take refuge in the Two United Hearts, and you will be protected. Abandon yourselves to God's Holy Will, and you will have His peace. Thank you for listening to my message.

May 5, 1994 *Help your heavenly Mother*

Our Lady: Dear children, today, I invite you to continue to trust in my Most Immaculate Heart and to live my messages without hesitation.

Listen with your hearts to my words, for I cannot help you if your hearts are not open to my motherly teaching. Dear children, you must persevere in your prayers, so that you may overcome all the opposition of the evil one. He has only one goal: to separate you and your family from God and to destroy your love for one another.

My little children, take refuge in my Immaculate Heart, and I will protect you from the evil one. You are my children if you say 'yes' to my motherly teaching and if you live my messages. Arm yourselves with prayer and fear nothing around you.

Live as my little children, conveying all that I teach you to others. Allow God's love and mercy to penetrate your hearts and share it with others. My children, I need your prayers and cooperation, so that together we will help others who remain in darkness to discover God. Help your heavenly Mother, who needs your prayers to save the world before it's too late! Thank you for listening to my message.

May 8, 1994 *To My beloved brother priests*

Jesus: Dear child, write the words that I tell you, so that you may share them with My beloved brother priests. My beloved brothers, I, your Jesus, know of your great sufferings and the temptations that surround you. Many of you give in to these temptations, and many of you struggle to remain faithful to your priestly vows.

To you, my beloved brothers, I want you to discover Me, your Master and Brother in the Eucharist everyday. I invite you again and again to abandon yourselves totally to Me, and I will help you to be holy priests, for that is what you, my brothers, are called to be. Allow Me to heal you of every distraction in your hearts that keep you from being true to My Father in Heaven. Allow Me to heal you of all the poison of pride that is swelling up in your hearts. Allow Me to heal you of the fever of selfish greed that rages in your hearts. Allow Me to heal you of the itch of intemperance in your hearts.

My brothers, I, your Jesus, will heal you of everything if you abandon yourselves totally to Me in the Eucharist. In all your problems and sufferings turn to Me in the Eucharist - in that Bread, which is your Savior humbling and disfiguring Himself - and I shall teach you humility. My brothers, allow Me, your Jesus, to feed you, and you will learn generosity. My brothers, in everything that is keeping you from turning to Me completely, abandon yourselves and hasten to the Bread of Angels and allow My charity to blossom in your hearts.

My beloved brothers, I do not desire that you suffer alone, for I am with you in all your suffering. My Heart suffers when you find no consolation in Me, as you feed on Me daily. Be aware how alive I am in the Eucharist, and trust Me with all your struggles as you feed on My Flesh and Blood. Allow Me to strengthen you and to free you from everything that puts distance between you and Me.

Allow Me to be your heavenly food and feed on Me daily, and you will grow fervent. Come to Me, all you My brothers, who are troubled and suffer with the fever of impurity. Come to the Banquet of the Angels, and I will make you pure and chaste. Keep your souls pure and receive the sacrament of Reconciliation frequently. Feed on My Flesh and Blood, and you shall know Me in the breaking of the Bread. I am with you, My brothers, I am with you. Have no doubt in your hearts, but believe, and you shall know My peace.

May 16, 1994 *Recall the words of St. Francis*

Jesus: My little flower, welcome to My Eucharistic Heart. Today, My special one, I, your Beloved Savior, will bless all your suffering, as I know it's been so difficult for you. Do not despair, but listen to My words. I give you My solemn word that all your suffering will be of great help to all My beloved brother priests. Open your heart and recall the words of St. Francis to you: **"When suffering comes your way, say to the suffering, come oh suffering, come, for my soul welcomes you with the love of my Savior."**

My little servant, open the door to your heart and pave the road toward holiness for others, for your heart is like a path that through your prayers will lead others to My Mother's Most Immaculate Heart and to My Heart as well. Listen to your angel now, as he has words for you.

Janie's Angel, Michael: Behold, servant of the Most High, and remember my words. The Lord, your God, has loved you from all eternity. Pray unceasingly to Him Who is with you at this moment and for all the rest of your life. Offer your supplications with faith in your heart. Sing praises of hymns to the Eternal Who rules the heavens and the earth.

Jesus: My beloved humble servant, allow the words of your guardian angel to penetrate your heart and soul. My peace, My love to you.

May 31, 1994 *Be strong in all your suffering*

Our Lady: Dear children, peace, my little ones, peace. Today, I, your heavenly Mother, appeal to all the families throughout the world to trust in my motherly intercession. My children, so many of you are suffering with affliction of the body, with finances, with addictions which endanger your health, and your families are walking weak in their faith. Many of you are suffering rejection and persecution from those you dearly love because of your prayer life.

My children, I beg you, do not allow yourselves to be distracted by all these sufferings. I am here to protect you from everything, yes, even those deep secrets that are in your hearts. Those secrets that only God knows. I will protect you. Trust your heavenly Mother, and all fear and anxieties will leave you.

My children, continue to pray as a family, for I need your prayers to help convert my children who continue to walk in darkness. My time with you is short, so I appeal to you, my children, and I say to you: Convert! Open your hearts and accept the mercy of God, for He gives you an opportunity everyday to repent and to be converted. Listen, my children, and listen to the words of your heavenly Mother. Be converted! Be converted! Thank you for listening to my message.

June 22, 1994 *Medjugorje Prayer and penance for the Church*

Our Lady: My daughter, remove your shoes and walk in reparation and in penance for the redemption of my Church, which is so in need of conversion. Many priests are being redeemed by your humble penance. Thank you for offering your suffering for the salvation and purification of my beloved priests. So many of my beloved sons have gone astray. Their hearts are full of darkness because they have abandoned God.

Many priests have forgotten how to love, because they have chosen to separate from God and to oppose my beloved Pope and all the teachings of the true doctrine of my Church. Many of my religious' hearts are dryer than the desert, because they have abandoned their beloved Spouse, Jesus, and they are living in the world with so much sinfulness in their hearts. Oh, how this grieves my Immaculate Heart. So many of my beloved priests have been absorbed by the apostasy, and their hearts are full of darkness because of their lack of faith and love for God. Penance and prayer are so important for the salvation of my Church.

My child, through your humble efforts to being obedient to my request, many of my beloved sons hearts will change. Let your love of prayer and penance be a witness to others, so that they, too, will decide to do prayer and penance for the purification of the Church. Share with my children that many graces and blessings will be given throughout the world on my feast day. God brought you here to bless you in a special way. Accept His love and share His love with your families and others throughout the world.

June 23, 1994 *Medjugorje In the nakedness of your nothingness*

Jesus: My child, come to Me in the nakedness of your nothingness. Come to Me without attachments, so that I may bless others through you. You do not need any ornaments, for I will decorate your heart with My love. I will show you that I am all you need. I am your provider, and I will provide everything for you.

June 25, 1994 *Medjugorje Thirteenth Anniversary of the Queen of Peace*

Our Lady: My dear children, I, your heavenly Mother, greet you with God's love. I extend my deep gratitude for your hard journey and for all that you have endured to come and be with your heavenly Mother. My dear ones, how I rejoice to see the great number of all my children who have responded to my call to live my messages and to be converted. Today, my Son blesses you and all your loved ones. Today is indeed a day of great rejoicing as God blesses the whole world. Yes, my children, today is a holy day, and many will be converted in great numbers.

My children, God has heard all your prayers for your families and others who are special to you. Abandon all your prayers and concerns to God Who loves you. Consecrate this day to God Who will see to all your needs. I, your heavenly Mother, especially bless all my beloved sons, my priests, who have left all their programs to come and honor their heavenly Mother on this my feast day as Queen of Peace. I love you, my children. Today, abandon your families to God, for He loves you with immense love. Peace, my children, peace. Thank you for listening to my message.

June 25, 1994 *Adoration: Pray for my brother priests*

Jesus: My child, welcome to My Eucharistic Heart. Abandon yourself to My immense love. Stay with Me and do not abandon your Eucharistic Savior. My child, pray with Me. You have been suffering much for My beloved brother priests. You have suffered hunger and thirst. You have offered Me all your suffering for My beloved brothers.

I, your Jesus of Love and Mercy, brought you to this holy place to do much penance for My Church. You came in obedience, and your obedience has produced much fruit in the hearts of many of My brothers. My child, you have embraced all your suffering for My brothers with joy in your heart. You have not had any time for yourself. You have given all your time to your Jesus Who loves you with My merciful Heart. Oh, how the heavens rejoiced as you climbed My Mother's holy hill barefooted in the heat of the day.

Your love for Me and for My Church was put to the test, and your heart was open to everything. I sent you many of My pilgrims so that you could pray for them. I know how tired you were. You embraced all whom I sent to you. Your love for My brother priests pleases Me, and you console My Eucharistic Heart. You ask nothing except to do My Father's Will.

My child, I, your Jesus of Love and Mercy, ask you to continue to harvest the hearts of My beloved brother priests through your prayers and sacrifices. Pray and do much penance for the purification of My Church. To you, My little child, I, your Eucharistic Jesus, have revealed My own sufferings and sorrows for My brother priests. I suffer when they suffer. I take on all their pains. Pray for My brother priests, pray for them. My child, recall My Mother's first words to you. Her first words shall be the title for your book. Embrace this title.

Editor's Note: The title of the second edition of the book has been changed, with Our Lady's permission, to Heaven's Messages for the Family as they encompass messages from Jesus, Mary, Joseph and the Three Archangels. This is the first volume.

June 27, 1994 *Medjugorje Pray unceasingly*

Our Lady: Dear children, today, I invite you and your loved ones to continue to pray and to live my messages with love in your hearts. My dear ones, I invite you to convey my messages to the world around you that continues to live in darkness. Allow my messages to transform your own hearts, so that you may become a living tabernacle for my Son, Jesus. Detach from the material things that you love so much and abandon yourself completely to my Son, so that His love will transform you into heavenly flowers.

My children, I need your prayers, so that together we may bring many souls closer to my Son. The world suffers from lack of love, and the violence and wars continue to live in many hearts. Oh, how this pierces my heart. Your prayers make a difference, and through your prayers hearts are converted.

Never forget the power of prayer and pray unceasingly, so that your own hearts will not become discouraged when you suffer disappointment in your lives. Remember, that through prayer you can prevent wars, and you are able to overcome all the calamities and pestilence that spreads its evilness throughout the world. Pray, children, pray, and love one another with God's love. Thank you for listening to my message.

July 4, 1994 *Paleston, Michigan I am Flesh of her flesh*

Jesus: Today, I speak to My brother priests. Tell them, that I, your Eucharistic Savior, invite them to embrace My Mother who loves them so tenderly. It saddens My Heart that so many of My brothers, in so great a number, say that they love Me, and yet they reject My Mother. When they celebrate Holy Mass, they think only of Me, not remembering that I took My flesh from the flesh of My Mother. I am Flesh of her flesh, Blood of her blood. My Mother and I are united in the divinity of the Holy Eucharist.

My brother priests must take notice of My Holy Mother's sweet and mysterious presence when they celebrate Holy Mass. My Mother and I are inseparable. Tell My beloved brother priests to embrace My heavenly Mother every moment of their lives, and not to forget that I am the fruit of My Mother's Immaculate Womb. She is the mirror of My Father. Through her 'yes' her virginal womb became a living tabernacle for the Word made flesh. I live in her, and She lives in Me. I gave her to humanity from My Cross. Many of My brothers have embraced My Mother, but many more continue to reject her.

Today, I, your Eucharistic Jesus, tell you truly, that you cannot truly love Me if you do not love My Mother. She is the gate that leads to My Eucharistic Heart. Embrace My Mother during Holy Mass, and you will truly embrace her Son.

July 11, 1994 *Adoration: Allow Me to melt away your faults*

Jesus: My child, welcome to My Eucharistic Heart. Allow Me, your Beloved Savior, to embrace you and melt away all that hurts you. Trust Me completely and know that I am here for you. This is Our time.
Janie: My Beloved Lord and my greatest Love, today, I ask You to please listen to me. I want to talk to You, and I need Your loving attention more than anything. Please, My Lord, allow me to tell You everything, then I will be quiet so that You may speak to my heart.
Jesus: My beloved one, speak to your Eucharistic Savior and speak freely, holding nothing back.
Janie: *I told Him the concerns of my heart.*
Jesus: My child, I know what is in your heart, but by talking about it to Me, you demonstrate your trust in Me. This pleases Me: that you are concerned with how much you ask for My guidance and blessings regarding your concerns. You abandon everything to My divine assistance. That is why you are at peace in your present situation, because of your total trust in Me. Know that you have My blessings in all that you have asked of Me. My peace to you, My peace to you.

Oh, if only souls would come and spend time with Me. I would heal their woundedness, but many do not even know that I am truly present in Eucharistic Adoration. Bring souls to Me, for I long to share My love with all who come to Me.

Janie: My Beloved Eucharistic Love, I will bring You many souls. I will make You known to others. This is my promise to You.

Jesus: Thank you, My child, thank you. The healing will begin and souls will find their peace in Me.

July 16, 1994 *Feast of Our Lady of Mt. Carmel - Kiss your scapular*

Our Lady: My child, I come to you as the Lady of Mt. Carmel, and I bring my Son, Jesus with me to bless you. I extend my gratitude to you and your family for having much devotion to clothing yourselves with my garment of grace, the brown scapular.

I desire that all my children be devoted to wearing my garment of grace, for when you wear your scapular, you give witness to others around you that you are truly consecrated to my Most Immaculate Heart. All my children who wear the scapular are, for certain, under my motherly protection. My garment of grace protects those who wear it with love and devotion. They are protected from many evils. Just as it is true that those who attend Mass daily are consecrated to my Son's Eucharistic Heart, in the same way, when you wear your scapular daily, you are truly consecrated to my Immaculate Heart.

Every morning, kiss your scapular. Those who wear my scapular tell me how much they love and trust me every moment of the day, simply by wearing the scapular. It pleases me when my children wear my scapular as a mark that they are dedicated to my service. Remember my promise to St. Simon Stock: **"Whosoever dies clothed in the scapular shall not suffer eternal fire."** Each day, kiss your scapular and say this prayer: **"Our Lady of Mt. Carmel, pray for us."**

My child, remember, just as my Heart and the Heart of my Son are inseparable, this is also true of my brown scapular and the Rosary. Give great importance always to wearing your scapular and praying your Rosary.

July 25, 1994 *Pray for My Bride, pray for My Bride*

Jesus: My humble servant, welcome to My Eucharistic Heart. Today, I, your Jesus of Love and Mercy, bless you and honor all your supplications. You have been patient, accepting and embracing the crosses in your life. My Father is pleased with you.

My dear one, today I ask that you pray for the conversion of your country. Pray for those souls most distant from My Heart. I will embrace all those who turn to Me with a repentant heart. Pray for the world and its political leaders whose decisions do injustice to so many souls. My dear one, the sinfulness in the world is calling upon divine intervention. If people do not turn away from their sins, a great chastisement will come upon the world before its time.

Repentance is so needed in this world that continues to walk in darkness. My brother priests continue to live in sin, ignoring all their priestly vows. Many of My brother priests pray for peace, but they do not practice peace. Their hearts are full of hatred and vengeance toward one another. Their hearts swell with pride and stubbornness. The sins of My brothers are many, and a cloud of darkness follows them wherever they go because of the sinfulness in their hearts.

Console My Eucharistic Heart, My little servant. To you, I choose to share My suffering for My Bride. I plead with you to pray unceasingly for My brother priests, whom I love so deeply. Every time they commit a sin, they crucify their Savior all over again. Pray for My Bride, pray for My Bride. I love you, My little one. I love you. I bless your heart with joy.

July 24, 1994 *Love Me in all My brothers*

Jesus: My child, welcome to My Eucharistic Heart. I, your Jesus, extend My deep gratitude to you, for I know how tired you are from lack of sleep.
My dear humble one, today, I will guide your every effort, have no worries. Abandon everything to Me. I will pour out My love into your heart. I want you to know how much you please Me by your works of charity and mercy towards others in need. You have a generous and loving heart. You share your blessings with others, and your giving comes from your heart.

I ask your continuous prayers and fasting for My brother priests. Love Me in all My brothers that you meet. I have such love for everyone of My brothers. I find My consolation in those beloved brothers who practice holy deeds and who reflect My love and mercy. My deepest pain comes from those who have turned their backs on Me. They walk in darkness, but pretend to belong to the light. The horrible sins they commit in secret wound My Heart so much, that I cry for love of them. Pray for all My beloved brothers.
Janie: My Jesus, how You love Your priests. I wish I could do more than just pray and love them.

Jesus: My dear one, you will never comprehend how much you help My brothers by all your tireless efforts. I speak to My brothers through you, but it wounds My Heart for those who do not believe that the mes-

sages you receive truly come from Me, your Eucharistic Savior. When they ignore your messages, they ignore Me.
Janie: Oh, Jesus, let my little ways and my love, which is so imperfect, console Your wounded Heart. I don't have much, but whatever I have I give to You, My Lord and King.
Jesus: You, My dear one, have consoled My Heart through your nothingness. Thank you. Peace, peace.

July 28, 1994 *I need your prayers to help change the world*

Our Lady: Dear children, today, I invite you to pray for peace for your country, so that through your prayers your country will convert. My little ones, I need your prayers to help change the world around you. You are so dear to me, and I look to your prayers to help others to convert. Today, I ask that you spend more time in prayer and discover God more and more with each day that goes by.

Little children, I want you to be made pure through your prayers. I want to take you all to Heaven with me. I want you to have a joyful heart. Prayer, my dear ones, will help you to have a joyful heart. I love you, my children, and you are under the protection of the Two United Hearts which are one with God. Pray, pray, pray! Thank you for listening to my message.

August 2, 1994 *Live my messages and belong to me*

Our Lady: Dear children, today, I invite you to open your hearts to my motherly teachings. Allow my messages to penetrate your hearts. Decide to give more time to prayer. Pray quietly and trust God with your prayers.

Little children, I love you all, and I want you to belong to me, but you cannot if you do not live my messages. Prayer, my dear ones, will draw you closer to my Immaculate Heart. That is why I invite you to decide to give more time to prayer.

Do not be fearful or distracted by the signs of these times. Remember, I am close to each one of you. My Immaculate Heart is your sure refuge. Do not be afraid or worried. You are all under my motherly protection. Pray and trust in the guidance of the Holy Spirit, Who leads you all along the path of holiness. I bless you all. Thank you for listening to my message.

August 4, 1994 *Satan is destroying many families*

Our Lady: Dear child, today, I come to you as Mother of Sorrows for my heart is filled with sadness, for so many of my children are falling from the state of grace. Many families are in the state of turmoil, for they have stopped praying together. There is immense quarreling among the family members. The peace of God is not in their hearts, for they have stopped praying.

My child, help your heavenly Mother and pray with me. The families in the world are in need of much conversion. Parents are not aware of the damage they do when they do not teach their loved ones how to pray, how to love one another. Children are rebellious. They lack respect for their parents, for there is no love in their hearts.

Satan is destroying many families through the violence and hatred in their hearts. He wants to destroy the entire human race, but he will not succeed if families learn how to pray together. Prayer is the key to Heaven, and God's children must be willing to submit to His Holy Will. The Holy Spirit must play an important role in the family to help them draw closer to God.

My child, God allows you to join in my sorrows; that is why your own heart is sad. Your own prayers and suffering are important to help your heavenly Mother to draw others to my Son. Know, my child, that God is pouring His grace throughout the world. His grace is an invitation for all to repent and be converted. Pray and console my Sorrowful Heart, my precious angel. To you, I tell my motherly concerns for all my children throughout the world. Listen to my plea and let it penetrate your heart. Embrace your heavenly Mother and pray with me. I love you, my child, I love you. Console my Heart, console my Heart.

August 6, 1994 *Everything that concerns you, concerns Me*

Jesus: My child, I, your Jesus, call you to complete trust. Know that the devil will use anything he can to get your mind off of Me and get you confused. Stay open to Me, and allow Me to tell you whatever it is that I am calling you to. If you knew everything, you would have no need for Me. Trust Me, and allow Me to transform your heart. I will infuse My love in every fiber of your being. Give Me everything that distracts you from being totally committed to Me.

Know, My child, that everything that concerns you, concerns Me. Every suffering you suffer, I suffer. Everyone you love, I love. Be then, transfigured by My love. Allow My love to penetrate your heart. Know, that I have loved you from all eternity. Trust Me, and allow My sacrificial love to be your daily food.

August 15, 1994 *The Assumption - Distractions in prayer*

Our Lady: Dear children, today, I invite you to rejoice with your heavenly Mother on this my glorious Assumption. Today is a special day filled with heavenly blessings to all those who celebrate this special day.

My little children, you are all so dear to me, and I intercede for you each day before God. Know that I bring all your prayers to God and that you obtain special graces when you trust in my motherly intercession. Continue to pray for world peace, and pray in a special way for the conversion of your country.

My children, I am deeply concerned about your spiritual well-being. That is why I call you to much prayer of the heart. So many of you are so distracted when you are in prayer. Ask the Holy Spirit to enlighten you, so that you will be attentive to your prayer. In this way, you will pray with faith in your heart.

My children, spend this day with your heavenly Mother, praying for the needs of your family and the needs of the world. Know that I look to your prayers to help convert the world. I love you all, and I give you my motherly blessing. Rejoice and be at peace. Thank you for listening to my message.

August 29, 1994 *Don't give up!*

Our Lady: Dear children, today, I invite you to pray for the conversion of your country, so that through your prayers all the violence and hatred will cease. Plead to my Son for mercy for those souls who continue to walk in darkness and who refuse to be converted. My little children, know that I need your prayers to help me, not only to help convert your country but for the conversion of the world. Pray with your heavenly Mother and do not give up. Do not give up on my request!

So many of you are so diligent in doing all that I ask of you, and this consoles my Immaculate Heart. You bring joy to my heart when you live my messages. By doing this you demonstrate your love for your

Purity and holiness of heart

heavenly Mother. Little children, you are so dear to me, and each day I pray for you as I present your prayers to God. You are so beautiful when you are in prayer, and you demonstrate to God your love for others as you pray.

My children, I ask that you keep in mind in a special way my beloved Pope when you pray. He is so special to me as he is specially chosen for this time, when there is so much suffering in the world. Pray for his physical well-being, for he suffers so much.
Today, I bless you, my children, and I extend my gratitude for all your prayers. Continue to pray as a family, and pray your Rosary everyday! Consecrate your family to the Two United Hearts, and be converted as a family. I love you, I love you all. Pray, pray, pray! Thank you for listening to my message.

September 2, 1994 *Your little ways are pleasing to Me*

Jesus: My dear child, welcome to My Eucharistic Heart. Be at peace regarding all your needs. Allow this time to be completely Ours. Tell your Savior everything, as you abandon yourself completely to My Eucharistic Heart.

My child, you are precious to Me, and you must know that I, your Jesus of Love and Mercy, supply all your needs. I bring your petitions to My Father. You have much love in your heart, for you allow your heart to be emptied so that My love will dwell in your heart. You are wondering if you should respond to the knowing that you have been praying for these past few days. I solemnly tell you that what is in your heart has been given to you by My Father through the intercession of St. Francis.

Respond with a total 'yes' to this effort. Feed the hungry, clothe the naked, visit the sick, pray for the homeless and love them. You will not be alone in this. I, Myself, will be with you, and beloved St. Francis will help you to love all those wounded souls who are rejected by society. Do not hesitate in this effort. Know that you will be ridiculed by others. Do not allow this suffering to be a distraction to you. Keep in mind how they treated Me. Do not worry, but begin gathering food and feed the hungry.

Give to all who come and do not worry. You will be able to handle everything that will be given to you. I will send people to help you. Do not become discouraged, but trust Me. Know that as you feed the hungry, it will be Me that you are feeding. I love you, My little child. Your little ways are pleasing to Me.

September 8, 1994 *Birthday of Our Lady - Prayer dissolves all evil*

Our Lady: Dear children, today, I extend my deep gratitude for all your prayers and sacrifices for the conversion of your country. You have been so diligent in responding to my request with your prayers. You have brought joy to my Immaculate Heart. Little children, know that through your prayers, many souls are drawing closer to my Son beginning with your own family.
Little children, so many of you are experiencing hard trials in your lives with your family. Do not despair, but trust in your prayers. Satan is strong, and he wants to destroy hope in your heart. His strongest attacks are upon you and your family. Do not be afraid, but be strong in your prayers as a family. In this way, you will overcome all his attacks.

Be loving towards everyone that God puts in your path, and do not judge anyone. Be a reflection of my Son, and follow the path that he has traced out for you. Know that I pray and intercede before my Son for all your needs. Continue to pray your Rosary together as a family for all the evil that exists in your country. Know that your prayers dissolve the evil in many hearts.

Today, I invite you to pray, pray, pray, for all my intentions for my beloved Pope who suffers and whom I have chosen for this time. Know that I am united with you in prayer. I love you, my children, I love you. Pray with your heavenly Mother who needs your prayers. Thank you for listening to my message.

September 14, 1994 *New Orleans, Louisiana* Triumph of the Cross

Janie: *I was praying in the morning, and Jesus came to me. There was a Cross on the wall of the room I was praying in. Suddenly the Cross illuminated with brilliant light. Then Jesus showed me a vision. In the sky I saw a huge brilliant Cross. Rays of bright light were gushing forth to the world. A multitude of angels were around the Cross in Adoration and were singing hymns of praise.*
Jesus: My child, today I bless all hearts who lie open to Me throughout the world. The rays that you see emanating from the Cross are the graces that are being poured forth from the Triumph of My Cross. The light of My love is flooding all hearts who embrace My Cross today. I will heal all woundedness in the families who call out to Me for My mercy. Theirs is the victory of My love for them.

I am the Way, the Truth, and the Light. I lead all to My heavenly Father. I bring light where there is darkness. I bring joy where there is sadness. I bring hope where there is despair. I am Jesus, Son of the Living God. I am He Who loves the world with the love of My Father, for He is in Me and I in Him. Embrace My Cross, and I shall embrace you. I Am.

September 15, 1994 *New Orleans* *Feast of Our Lady of Sorrows*

Janie: *While I was in prayer Our Lady came. I saw her heart, and it had many thorns around it. I understood that these thorns represented the sorrow that we cause her by the offenses through which we offend her Son. She was crying tears of blood. I was so sad to see her this way.* Please tell me how can I console you?
Our Lady: Come, my child. Let me show you the reason for my sorrow.
Janie: *I saw a vision and in this vision I saw so many little infants crying out to the Lord while they were being killed in their mothers' wombs. I was allowed to hear the cry of these innocent ones that were dying such a horrible death.*

Then I saw men and women who were homosexuals. They were living lives that were most offensive to God. What I saw then was very shocking to me. I saw many priests and religious who were also living lifestyles of homosexuality.
Our Lady: Look, my child. This is how many of my beloved priests and consecrated souls offend my Son - through this horrible lifestyle. The horrible evil that is calling out to Heaven for vengeance is the massacre of innocent souls and homosexuality. These two great evils are bringing much destruction to the world.
Janie: *Then I saw families who were living in turmoil.*
Our Lady: Look at the broken families. See how many parents abandon their children and bring great pain to their little hearts. See how the violence in the family is growing stronger everyday. The violence in the family reflects a fire on a windy day that cannot be put out. There is no love or respect in the hearts of many families. My child, if my children do not repent, see what will happen.
Janie: *At this point I saw a pit of fire, and many people were consumed by the flames. I put my hands over my face and begged Our Lady not to show me any more.*
Our Lady: The sins of the world pierce my heart with sorrow. If the world does not convert and turn away from its sins, it will be condemned. My child, God will send a terrible warning to the entire world. Many will not survive this warning, for it will be too horrible for them to see the state of their souls. My child, pray for my children to repent,

repent, repent!

September 17, 1994 *Whatever you do, do it with love*

Jesus: My child, welcome to My Eucharistic Heart. Abandon yourself totally to My Eucharistic Love and be made whole. Today, My child, is truly a joyful day for you as you and your family prepare a special place in your home to live the Gospel in its fullness. Your love for St. Francis is great and you hunger to imitate him, for you know of his great love for Me. You have prayed, asking Me to fill you with the true spirit of St. Francis. You have been granted this grace from this day on.

As you walk in living the spirit of St. Francis, your life will be filled with such a joy as you embrace My Cross with love in your heart. You have a charitable spirit and love much as you embrace those who are suffering. Your heart is a compassionate and loving heart. Many will be converted through your love for Me.

I, your Jesus of Love and Mercy, bless you and your family. Go out as a family and feed the hungry, clothe the naked, visit the sick, give water to those who thirst. Embrace and love those who suffer. Be compassionate as My Father is compassionate. Be a light to others walking in darkness. Live the Gospel by being My reflection. Live simply and be humble. Whatever you do for others, do it with love in your hearts. I, your Jesus, bless you as a family and your works of charity and mercy. I love you and I bless you.

September 25, 1994 *Accept me as your Mediatrix of all graces*

Editor's Note: On this day Our Lady gave Janie several teachings beginning with the Holy Spirit.
She then taught her on the importance of consecrating oneself to her Immaculate Heart, the importance of devotion to the Angels and the importance of praying the Holy Rosary. These four messages contain a wealth of spiritual knowledge.

Our Lady: My child, invoke the Holy Spirit and His light as you wake up. Let His Name be the first prayer on your lips. Pray, **"Come, Holy Spirit, by means of the powerful intercession of the Immaculate Heart of Mary, your well beloved spouse."** I have given this same prayer to others, and now I invite you to recite this prayer throughout the day. Pray to the Father to inflame your heart with the Divine Fire of my Spouse, the Holy Spirit.

Purity and holiness of heart

Know my powerful function as Mediatrix between all my children and my Son, Jesus, is above all in obtaining for my children an abundance of graces from the Father in Heaven. I am the spouse of the Holy Spirit, and I invite all my children to be renewed by His Divine Love, and to enter into the Spirit of God's love.

My child, my Immaculate Heart is the golden gate in which my Spouse, the Holy Spirit, reaches your heart. Be filled with the fire from above and live in the fullness of the Holy Spirit. Accept the splendor of the New Pentecost in your heart. Know, my child, that when you accept me as your Mediatrix, you are then clothed with the garment of holiness. You are clothed with the Spirit of the Father, the Son, and the Holy Spirit. Associate yourself intimately with the Holy Trinity, and you will obtain holiness and purity of heart.

September 25, 1994 *The Reign of my Immaculate Heart*

Our Lady: My child, I have come to you as Mother of Compassion and Love. During my time with you, I have been teaching you the importance of praying for the grace to have a compassionate and loving heart. You have worked very hard in obtaining these two virtues, and God is pleased with all your hard efforts. You have been putting into practice all that I have been teaching you. I am deeply grateful.

My child, I want you to know the great importance of being consecrated to my Immaculate Heart. These are the things I wish to teach concerning my Immaculate Heart. Listen with your heart and allow what I teach you to penetrate your heart.

The time has come when I invite all my children to be consecrated to my Immaculate Heart. In doing this, my children will come to know that they belong to me. The time has come for my Immaculate Heart to be glorified before the Church and all humanity. I have formed you to be living witnesses of the reign of my Immaculate Heart. I have formed and prepared you to be the smallest of children, consecrated to me and completely entrusted to me, allowing yourselves to be led with docility along the path of purity, holiness and love.

My child, I am the ***Mother and Queen of the Family***. I want all families to be consecrated to my Immaculate Heart. When you consecrate yourselves as a family to my Immaculate Heart, you open your door to your heavenly Mother. I ask that families open the door of their homes, so that I may come and dwell among them. I will take part in their lives. There, where I enter, sin goes out. God's grace and divine light are always present. In the homes consecrated to me, purity and holiness dwell with me.

I will bring the husband and wife to a greater reciprocal understanding of one another. I will bring the husband and wife to an ever deeper spiritual communion and to help perfect their love, and to bring it into the Heart of my Son, Jesus. Their children will be like beautiful branches growing from their parents love and from my love. I will lead them along the path of sanctity and of joy. I will help them to always live in the grace of God.

I want to help the families to be saints, and I want to help the parents to understand that the most precious gift of a family is their children. Their children are gifts from Heaven. Parents must want their children. They must cultivate their souls like the most precious gems of a family estate.

My child, I will protect every family consecrated to my Immaculate Heart and my presence among the family will become very strong and extraordinary. I will be their consolation. I will see to all their needs.

The families consecrated to my Immaculate Heart will be hidden, small, quiet buds of my Triumph. These are my times, and families must be consecrated to my Immaculate Heart in order to have victory over my adversary. These times are times marked by my strong and great presence. My child, I thank you for being so patient and listening to all that I have said to you. I encourage all families to be consecrated to my Immaculate Heart, and I give you my motherly blessing.

September 25, 1994 *The angels are signing my children*

Our Lady: My child, pray more to your guardian angels and become familiar with them. Live always in intimacy with your guardian angels. Call upon them in times of necessity, especially invoking them in danger and in temptations. Associate them to your daily activities and tasks in your work place and recreation time. Confide to them all your difficulties, for they intervene and protect all my children in an extraordinary way.

In these times, the manifestations of demons and many evil spirits are lurking everywhere, spreading their evil in many hearts. God has given my children the protection of the guardian angels. Know that there is a great battle between the Angels and Satan. Satan is busy setting many evil traps for my children, but no harm will come for the guardian angels are signing my children with the seal of my Immaculate Heart.

The angels are clothing my children with strong armor for the battle, through means of prayer, especially the Rosary. They place themselves each day at your side, to help you, to comfort and protect you. I invite all my children to form one single entity with the angels and with the intercession of all the saints in Heaven. Everyday, pray to your guardian angels, whose only task is to lead you to Heaven.

September 25, 1994 *I mingle my voice with yours*

Our Lady: My child, do not allow a day to go by without praying your Rosary. It is your weapon against Satan, and he hates it. The Rosary is a powerful prayer and through praying it daily, conversion comes to those you offer it for.

The Rosary brings you peace. It is a simple prayer, it forms you spiritually in meekness, in simplicity, and littleness of heart. It is a humble prayer that you say together with me. As you invite me to intercede for you, I respond to your request. I mingle my voice with yours; I unite my prayer to yours.

The Rosary is a powerful weapon when prayed as a family. It is a prayer that unites your voices as a family to Heaven. What you ask of me through praying your Rosary I always obtain, because my Son, Jesus, can never say 'no' to what His Mother requests of Him.

As you pray the Rosary, you contemplate its mysteries and begin to understand the plan of my Son, Jesus, as He lived His life. You begin to understand the Incarnation to the consummation of His glorious death. You are able to penetrate more profoundly into the mystery of Redemption.

My child, as you begin to understand the mystery of love when you recite the Holy Rosary, you come to know the love of your heavenly Mother and of her Son, Jesus.

The more you recite the Rosary with faith in your heart, the more your heart will be filled with the immense divine charity of the Heart of my Son, Jesus. My child, embrace your heavenly Mother and her Son as you recite the Holy Rosary. Remember, you are united truly with the Father as you pray the prayer that Jesus taught you. You unite in adoration of the Most Holy Trinity as you recite the Glory Be. As your heavenly Mother, I ask that you make use of the Holy Rosary.

September 29, 1994 *Feast of the Archangels - Embrace the Archangels*

Our Lady: Dear children, today, I invite you to rejoice with your heavenly Mother as you celebrate the feast of the Archangels. It is a joyful day and many blessings are being poured out throughout the world. Know that you are truly blessed as you embrace the three Archangels.

Little children, I urge you to live in a union of life with the angels of the Lord. Become familiar with the angels and know that God has assigned them to protect you.

The angels take you by the hand and lead you along the path of love, of light and of holiness. They give you courage in times of difficulties. They are at your side everyday. They defend you against the continuous attacks of Satan. They help to remove the obstacles which he puts along your path. Little children, listen to my words and embrace the love that the angels have for you and trust in their protection. Pray, and know the role of the angels in your life.

Today, I invite you to embrace the three archangels: St. Michael, St. Gabriel, and St. Raphael. St. Gabriel has the duty of accepting your 'yes' to the Will of the Father. He helps you to embrace the Gospel and to live it. St. Raphael refreshes your weakness, pours balm on every painful wound, and lifts you from your weariness. St. Michael defends you from all the attacks from Satan, who is always waging war against you and your family. Today, my children, rejoice with your heavenly Mother on this glorious feast of the Archangels. Thank you for listening to my message.

October 6, 1994 *Listen to my urgent request*

Our Lady: Dear children, today, I invite you as a family to pray and fast for my special intentions for my beloved Pope. My dear children, listen to my urgent request and pray, pray, pray. Unite your prayers with me. In doing this, you will be truly responding to my urgent request. I love you, my children, and I need your prayers. I invite you as a family to pray your Holy Rosary for nine days, beginning tomorrow, my feast day. I need your prayers, I need your prayers. Pray with your heavenly Mother. Thank you for listening to my message.

October 7, 1994 *San Antonio, Texas Queen of All Families*

Our Lady: Dear child, the Rosary is the prayer of my children. Through praying the Rosary you are able to obtain from the Lord the great grace of a change of heart in those you offer it for. Through praying the Rosary and offering it for the conversion of the world, many are the souls that obtain conversion, repentance of the heart and the desire to obtain purity of heart. Through praying the Rosary you are able to snatch back from Satan whatever territory he has conquered, be it your loved ones or dear friends. Through praying your Rosary you can free an immense number of your family members that Satan has succeeded in imprisoning. Through praying the Rosary with faith in your heart you obtain peace. The Rosary possesses a potent force because it is a powerful prayer that you pray with me. In many of my apparitions I have requested this prayer and ask that it be recited.

Dear child, tonight I come as the Lady of the Rosary and Queen of All Families. Tonight I wish to teach you more about the Holy Rosary. Listen to my words. The power of the Rosary is stronger than any atomic weapon and has a powerful effect on the lives of those who recite it faithfully. The Rosary is the weapon of all my children. It is a treasure of graces and every time that my children recite it, they touch the deepest recesses of my heart. Through praying the Rosary, my children place a spiritual bouquet of roses at my feet.

The Rosary is the heavenly medicine that will heal the unconverted souls. It is a prayer that has had victory over many wars throughout time. Its power is beyond human understanding. Few are the hearts of those who have been graced to understand its power.

To my beloved sons, St. Dominic and Blessed Alan, I gave the fifteen promises of the Rosary to those who recite it. Many are the souls who embraced these fifteen promises throughout time. The Rosary is the weapon against Satan, make use of it! Know that each day in silence and in hiddeness I am waging battle against Satan together with you. Thank you for listening to my message.

October 12, 1994 *He is My Vicar, chosen for these times*

Jesus: My child, welcome to My Eucharistic Heart. Abandon yourself to My love and to My True Presence. This time is Ours. I give you My word that I am truly present here with you.
My child, I know that you are suffering from rejection. Your heart is

experiencing much sorrow. Give everything to Me. I have called you to come and join Me and My Mother in the Garden of Gethsemane. Unite your suffering with Ours for My beloved Vicar and for all My brother priests.

This is a time when the opposition against My Vicar is strong. He is My Vicar, who has been chosen for these times, and nothing will break his spirit. His heart is laced with the Two United Hearts that are One with My Father. His heart yields to the Will of My Father, and he lives in holy obedience to the Magisterium. The protection of Heaven is upon him.

My child, I extend My gratitude to you for your great love for My beloved Vicar. You submit to all that is asked of you from My Father in Heaven. You suffer in silence and at times your suffering becomes unbearable. You do not ask that your suffering be removed, but you surrender all to My Father, holding nothing back.

These next few days will be hard for you, for you will be in the Garden of Gethsemane. Your heart will feel much agony and sorrow. You will live on bread and water for these days. You will spend three hours with Me daily, adoring Me in the Blessed Sacrament. You will feel tired and weak. At times, you will want to give up, but you won't. Do not have the smallest worry, you will succeed in this effort to offer reparation and mortification for My beloved Vicar and for My Church. Allow My Eucharistic love to be your strength.

October 22, 1994 *Boyne Falls, Michigan* *I desire Perpetual Adoration*

Jesus: My child, welcome to My Eucharistic Heart. Abandon yourself totally to My love. Allow this time to be Ours, for I want to share My joy with you. Look around you, My child. I am surrounded by much love. Many of the hearts that come to spend time with Me have so much love for Me. This is so consoling to Me. Know that I am pouring My love and mercy to all who come and embrace Me, their Eucharistic Savior.

So many have come with sad and wounded hearts. I have healed so many during this holy gathering. I will continue to pour My healing love into all hearts. You see how much I love all people. I would die all over again out of My great love for all humanity. By allowing My True Presence to be here, many hearts have converted. Many hearts are now united to My love.

This holy gathering has brought much joy to My Eucharistic Heart.

Purity and holiness of heart

Many of My brother priests have responded to come and feed the flock gathered here. These beloved brothers of Mine have embraced Me through their 'yes' to coming to feed My people. To them, I, their beloved Savior, extend My deep gratitude. Their hearts are united and laced to the Two United Hearts. These are My beloved brothers on whom My Father's favor rests.

Oh, how My Mother has been honored and loved through all the people that have come. I am so happy, My child, I am so happy. I love My people and I long for their 'yes' to abandon their hearts to My Eucharistic Heart. Extraordinary graces and blessings are being poured out on all who have come. Continue to embrace Me, your Eucharistic Savior, Who loves you with immense love. Oh, how I love you.

I, your Eucharistic Jesus, desire perpetual Adoration from My brother priests. In doing this, they allow Me, their Brother, to help them draw their flock closer to Me. My child, pray for My brother priests, they are special to Me. I, your Eucharistic Savior, bless all who came, and even those who didn't come. You see how much I love everyone. Thank you, My child, for all your hard efforts.

October 23, 1994 *Boyne Falls, Michigan* Marian Conference

Janie: *During Holy Mass, as I was going to receive Holy Communion I saw a vision. As the priest put the Eucharist on my tongue I saw the Heart of Jesus and my own heart. Then, immediately before my own eyes, Jesus' Heart was transformed into an arrow and it came and pierced my heart. I found myself gasping for air and tears streamed from my eyes. I could feel the pain in my heart as if something was lodged in my heart.*

The rest of the week I could feel something like heat around my heart and much pain. Jesus confirmed my experience, that what I saw was actually what happened to my heart.

October 27, 1994 *I am truly present in the Holy Eucharist*

Jesus: My dear child, welcome to My Eucharistic Heart. I, your Eucharistic Savior, extend My gratitude for all your suffering, for My beloved Vicar. Continue to offer your sweet sacrifices for him that has been chosen by Heaven for these troubled times.
My child, invite others to come and spend time with their Eucharistic Savior. I will heal their aching and wounded hearts. I have chosen to

remain in all the tabernacles of the world as the hidden Jesus, the True Presence in the host, that small piece of bread that so many refuse to believe is My Presence. Oh, how this wounds My Eucharistic Heart.

If only many of My beloved brother priests would themselves believe in My True Presence, their hearts would begin to heal. I would not be so abandoned by many of My brother priests. If only My brother priests would believe in My True Presence, I would be honored through perpetual Eucharistic Adoration and there would be immense healing among My people. Pray, My child, so that through your prayers, others will come to believe that I am truly present in the Most Holy Eucharist.

October 27, 1994 *Do not hurry prayer*

Our Lady: Dear children, I invite you to spend more time in prayer as a family and not to allow any distractions to keep you from your prayer time. Take prayer more seriously and do not be in a hurry when you are praying. Know that when you are in prayer, God, Himself, is right by your side. He rejoices when a family unites in prayer. He listens to all your petitions with tender loving care and He gives you special graces to be able to pray more attentively. Little children, prayer helps you to draw closer to God and to one another. If only you understood the importance of prayer, your hearts would be rejoicing much more during prayer time.

Little children, my precious families, you are so dear to my Heart and your prayers are so important in helping others to convert. I wish that you, as a family, pray with me everyday for all the needs of the world. You are so beautiful when you are in prayer, and your prayers transform you into beautiful bouquets of flowers which I present to God. Pray, pray, pray! Thank you for listening to my message.

November 3, 1994 *Like fire on a windy day*

Our Lady: Dear children, today I wish to extend my deep gratitude to you for all your prayers. Many of you are persevering in your prayers, and God is giving you special graces to understand the importance of prayer. God wishes to help you in all your difficulties and suffering. He cannot help you if you do not pray. Remember, that it is only through prayer that you discover God. Pray, my children, you shall not regret it.

Little children, know that these are difficult times and that there is much suffering in the family. Satan is busy trying to destroy love and peace in the family, in the Church, and throughout the world. Pray together as a family with your heavenly Mother for peace in the world. Many continue to walk in darkness, ignoring God's love and mercy. These souls will continue to suffer much, for they have chosen the path that leads to condemnation. This pierces my Immaculate Heart.

Little children, live my messages and convey them to others. Pray to the Holy Spirit for enlightenment, for you need the Holy Spirit to help you to convey the messages to others and to live them. Little children, many of you worry so about the chastisement. Little children, I am giving you all the messages to guide you and to help you to convert. Remember, prayer and fasting help to lessen any warnings, but you must pray from the heart. Do not be anxious about the chastisement, for the chastisement is already upon you.

Look around you, little children, and see all the violence and hatred. Sin and hatred are growing like a fire on a windy day. Violence and destruction are so evident in the family and in the Church. The world has many weak leaders whose decisions are misleading many of my children.

Little children, do not allow the sinfulness around you to frighten you. Pray with me and take refuge in my Most Immaculate Heart. You have nothing to fear if you are living my messages, for my messages will help you to draw closer to my Son's Most Sacred Heart. I am the gate that leads you to my Son, and He is the pathway to Heaven.

My children, pray, trust and have no worry, for I, your heavenly Mother, am protecting all my little children who allow my messages to penetrate their hearts. I love you all dearly and I give you my motherly blessing. Thank you for listening to my message.

November 8, 1994 *Dallas Texas* *Juan Diego's intercession*

Our Lady: My daughter, I desire that my little children ask my hijito, Juan Diego, to intercede for them when they pray for the protection of the unborn from the horrible evil that pierces my Immaculate Heart. Juan Diego is dear to my heart, and he will help to bring an end to the horrible evil of the massacre of these precious souls that die such a horrible death. My daughter, tell my children that whenever they ask for my intercession under the title of Our Lady of Guadalupe, they must unite their prayers with my hijito, Juan Diego.

November 11, 1994 *Console My suffering Heart*

Jesus: My child, welcome to My Eucharistic Heart. Spend this time with Me and allow My Eucharistic love to refresh your tired soul. Abandon yourself to Me, and I, your Eucharistic Savior, will continue to pierce your heart with My Eucharistic love. Be silent and allow this time to be completely Ours, for I have much to share with you.

Console Me, My dear one, for I am much rejected by many of My beloved brother priests. They are so dear to My Eucharistic Heart. I suffer for them day and night, hoping that they will return My love by loving Me. My child, unite your suffering with My suffering for My brother priests who offend Me so.

Janie: My Jesus, truly present in the Most Blessed Sacrament, Lamb of God, Bread of the Angels, Light of the World, tell me what can I do to console Your suffering Eucharistic Heart? Tell me please, and I shall do what Thou ask of me in my wretchedness.

Jesus: Oh beloved child, pray for My beloved Bride, so that She may be purified. Offer much mortification, so that through your poor offerings and sacrifices, many of My brother priests will return back to My Eucharistic love.

My child, if you only knew all the offenses committed by many of My brother priests! How they crucify Me over and over again through their ingratitude to My Eucharistic love. Many have abandoned Me by separating themselves from My truth and denying that I am truly present in the Blessed Sacrament and in the celebration of Holy Mass.

I, your Eucharistic Savior, yearn for their return to My love and friendship. I yearn to call them friends and to offer them My friendship which can only be found in the Holy Eucharist. I yearn for their intimate union with Me in the Sacrifice of Holy Mass. Pray, My child, for My suffering Heart that is so abandoned and rejected by many of My brother priests.

Janie: *I saw Jesus in such agony, and He was crying tears of blood over all those priests and religious who have stopped believing and those who do not believe in His True Presence during the Holy Sacrifice of the Mass. This made me very sad.*

November 12, 1994 *My True Presence*

Janie: *I heard Jesus speak to me as the priest was raising up the chal-*

ice at Holy Mass.
Jesus: Come to Me! Believe in My True Presence in the Holy Eucharist and you shall have eternal life.

November 13, 1994 *Dallas, Texas* *The powerful prayers of the priests*

Janie: *Tonight while we were praying the Rosary I saw Our Lady of Guadalupe and the Child, Jesus. They were surrounded by many babies. Our Lady spoke to me.*
Our Lady: Please pray for my babies, pray for my babies.
Janie: *Earlier, I was praying with two priests. They both said a beautiful prayer for the needs of the world. Our Lady showed me a vision of how powerful the prayers of priests are. She showed me how blessings are distributed by the angels whenever priests pray. Many souls are blessed through the prayers of the Church.*

November 15, 1994 *Dallas, Texas* *Continue to pray*

Our Lady: My children, you have brought so much joy to my Heart through all your prayers. Continue to pray with your heavenly Mother and have no worry.

November 16, 1994 *Dallas, Texas* *Why do you hold back?*

Jesus: Today, My dear ones, I, Jesus, tell you: Give me your hearts like never before for I have much to give you. Trust Me, for I am truly present before you. I want to pour My healing balm into your hearts. I want to tell you just how much I love you. Why do you hold back? Why do you doubt? Don't you know that without Me you can do nothing? I am your Source of life and strength. Give Me your heart with all its sufferings, and I solemnly tell you that you will truly have a new heart - My Heart. Trust Me, for I only want to draw you into the depths of My Own Heart.

November 16, 1994 *Dallas, Texas* *The Rosary is my plan of action*

Our Lady: The Rosary is my plan of action to heal the world. Recite it everyday.

November 16, 1994 *Dallas, Texas* *I only want to be with you*

Our Lady: My dear children, today I want to thank each one of you for your continuous prayer. Know, my children, that I, your heavenly Mother, have enjoyed being united in prayer with you. Today, I want to spend time with you in a special way. I want to be here with you and to listen to your prayers. I want to pray with you, and I want you to know that I am truly praying with you.

I look to the time that you spend praying the Rosary with great joy in my Heart. I want you to know that I have accepted your invitation to come and to pray with you. Today I won't ask anything of you, I only want to be with you, my children. Let this be an intimate time with my Son and with your heavenly Mother.

November 17, 1994 *God is showing mercy to your country*

Our Lady: Dear children, what great joy you have brought to my Heart by being so generous and sharing your gifts with others! My little children, know that your prayers are helping you to love and accept others. You are learning how important it is to be charitable to others around you.

My children, my dear children, you have been so dedicated to your prayers and God is so pleased with you. You have been so committed to living my messages and conveying them to others. Know that it is because of your prayers that you are helping your loved ones to decide for conversion. It is through your prayers that God is showing mercy to your country and lessening the severity of its punishment.

Little children, your prayers have been most helpful, and this is the reason for you to rejoice in all your hard efforts. I invite you to remain committed and dedicated to your daily prayers and not to allow yourselves to become complacent in your prayers. Know that your soul is like a small seed, and your prayer is the living water that helps that small seed to blossom into a beautiful flower, giving the fragrance of purity. So, my little children, pray, pray, pray unceasingly! Rejoice, and show God your gratitude for all His blessings. Have a blessed Thanksgiving day with your loved ones and let this time be a time of great joy. Thank you for listening to my message.

November 21, 1994 *Whatever you do to the least of My little ones*

Editor's Note: On this day Janie delivered Thanksgiving groceries from the prayer group to several poor families who were not otherwise able to afford Thanksgiving dinner.

Jesus: My dear child, welcome to My Eucharistic Heart. Thank you for coming to thank Me for all your accomplishments. Know, My humble servant, that I am with you everywhere you go. Your love for others allows Me to take you into many areas that others will not travel. You saw how poor and hungry My people are. You saw their poverty, the lack of space that they live in, and the lack of privacy that gives them so little solitude for themselves.

I took you into areas in your own city that you did not know existed. You found Me in every heart you met. You saw how hungry they were to receive your love and warmth. My child, you saw many other things that frightened you deep in your heart, but you responded with a loving and trusting smile because you saw Me in every face that you met today.
Janie: *I encountered people being violent with each other and using foul language with each other.*
Jesus: My little humble servant, you have done well by visiting the poor and feeding the hungry and clothing the naked. Recall these words, **"Whatever you do to the least of My little ones you do it for Me."** I love you with immense love. Never forget this.

November 23, 1994 *Thank you, my dear children*

Our Lady: My dear children, greetings to you and your family on this day of Thanksgiving. I, your heavenly Mother, wish to extend my deep gratitude to you and your family for preparing for this moment of grace. I extend my deep gratitude to each one of you for you all have been so committed to living my message the best that you can. You have suffered as a family and have endured many crosses and tribulations. You have known hard times when the attacks of Satan have been unbearable, and yet you remained united in love and in prayer.

Many times the suffering was so strong that you thought of giving up, but you didn't. You, as a family, have grown in the virtues of faith and of love. You have, as a family, placed many bouquets of Rosaries at my feet. You have offered many Holy Masses for your own intentions as well as others.

You have offered a multitude of prayers and sacrifices in reparation for all my special intentions. You, as a family, have brought joy to my Immaculate Heart. I wish to thank each one of you for all that you have done individually.
Janie: *Here she spoke to me about all the personal things and sufferings in our family that we endured for love of her and for her Son. Our Lady said that on this day she would give an indication of the end of her*

time with us. All the prayer group prayed that God would extend our time with Our Lady. Our Lady told me that God had granted us more time with her and that she would not be leaving before St. Joseph. Praised be the Holy Trinity. We are so blessed.

December 1, 1994 *A joyful heart is a prayerful heart*

Our Lady: Dear children, today, I invite you to prepare your hearts through prayer and fasting, so that my Son's love may be born in your hearts. Little children, this is truly a time of great joy as you prepare for the birth of my Son. Abandon yourselves completely to my Immaculate Heart, so that I may help you to prepare during this Holy Season. Do not become distracted with buying gifts and decorating your homes.

Little children, allow your hearts to be pure and holy. This is the best gift that you can give my Son. Decorate your hearts with prayer and present them to my Infant Son. My little children, do not lose focus of what this Holy Season is all about. I tell you, my children, it is about the birth of my Infant Child, the most precious gift to all humanity for the salvation of the world.

Allow your heavenly Mother to help you to prepare for my Infant Child. That is why I came, to help you to prepare so that you may come to know and to desire purity of heart. I want to help you to be reconciled to one another and to learn how to love with my Son's Heart, which is rich in love and mercy.

I want to help you to be consecrated to my Immaculate Heart. In this way, your heart will be similar to my Immaculate Heart. I want to teach you how to pray so that you may discover God.

I want you to have joy in your heart, but you cannot know joy if you do not pray. Remember, a joyful heart is a prayerful heart. Let me help you, for you are so dear to my Immaculate Heart, and I want to take you all to Heaven with me. Thank you for listening to my message.

December 5, 1994 *And Jesus cried bitterly*

Jesus: My dear child, welcome to My Eucharistic Heart. Abandon yourself totally to Me, your Eucharistic Savior. Allow this time to be only Ours. Do not allow any distractions to enter into your heart, for I have so much to share with you. My child, today I want you to comfort Me in My pain that I suffer for the purification of My Bride. Come and journey with Me and write everything that I show you.

Janie: *At this time, Jesus took me to different places where I saw many different priests. First we visited priests in hospitals who were suffering from alcohol addiction.*

Jesus: Look at My poor suffering brother priests. See how they allowed alcohol to be their destruction. These beloved brothers of Mine stopped loving Me, their Source of life and strength. They became distracted with the cares of the world and forgot about My love for them.

Janie: *At this point, Jesus cried for them and for the pain that pierced His Eucharistic Heart. He cried bitterly for them. He reached out to me with His hands. I was standing to the left of Him. As He reached out to me I saw blood fall to the floor from the wounds in His hands. When I moved towards Him, His face had blood falling from the wounds of His head. Then on the floor their was a puddle of blood from the wounds in His feet.*

I embraced Him and we cried together and I felt a piercing pain in my own heart. Jesus prayed over all the priests. I also saw women who were nuns addicted to alcohol. Jesus prayed for all of them and begged His Father for mercy over their souls. I knew in my heart that perhaps many of these souls would die from cirrhosis of the liver, for many of them had yellowish looking skin which was perhaps jaundice.

Jesus: My child, each day I will show you the sufferings and the many manifestations of addictions that keep My Bride paralyzed. Pray for all these things which I have chosen to show you. Unite your suffering with Mine. Spend quiet time praying for the purification of My Bride.

December 5, 1994 *One Hail Mary prayed slowly*

Janie: *I was at home this afternoon. I took a short nap, for I was feeling a little weak. I had a lot of things to do around the house, and my spirit was slow to pray. Our Lady came to me dressed in all white.*

Our Lady: Dear child, you are suffering much. I am here to help you to pray. I want you to tell your heavenly Mother whom you desire to pray for at this moment.

Janie: *I responded that I would like to pray for my husband.*

Our Lady: My child, pray one Hail Mary with your heart and listen to the words while you are praying the Hail Mary.

Janie: *I prayed slowly and attentively, listening carefully to every word I prayed. I finished the Hail Mary and then Our Lady said to pray the Hail Mary again and to continue to listen to the words. I began to see the words coming into action as I continued to pray the Hail Mary. I finished the second Hail Mary and then Our Lady asked me to pray it* *once more. This is what I saw.*

Hail Mary - *I saw the angel Gabriel visiting Our Lady and greeting her with this sublime salutation. I understood that I was also saluting Mary with the Archangel Gabriel.*

Full of Grace - *I saw Mary's Heart filled with love, purity and holiness. There were angels placing roses around her Immaculate Heart while singing beautiful songs of thanksgiving to God for Mary.*

The Lord is with you - *I saw Our Lady being adorned with God's love. I saw oceans of graces and joys filling Mary's soul at these words.*

Blessed art thou among women - *I saw Mary in great splendor like no other woman on earth. I understood that God in His mighty power had given the world His blessed Mother with all the greatness, dignity and holiness necessary for her to be the perfect woman and Mother and to love her children throughout time and eternity.*

And blessed is the Fruit of your womb, Jesus. - *I saw the Heart of Mary and the Sacred Heart of Jesus laced together with brilliant immense light emanating from both Hearts. Then I saw one big Heart, and I understood that Mary and Jesus are inseparable.*

Holy Mary - *I saw angels placing a crown on her head, crowning her in her holiness as Queen of Heaven and Earth.*

Mother of God - *I saw God giving the world His Most Holy Mother. He gave her all the love, the tenderness, sweetness and affection necessary to be our loving and true Mother.*

Pray for us sinners - *I saw how powerful Mary's intercession is for all her children. I saw Mary praying over all who ask her for help. She comes quickly to her children's aid. I understood that when we ask for Mary's powerful intercession we lack nothing from God, for He truly has made her our most powerful intercessor. She pleads our cases for us before the throne of God and God denies her nothing.*

Now - *I saw here how Mary is with us at our side all the days of our lives and how she prepares our hearts. She helps us daily to know God's Holy Will in our hearts. She prays with all her children who invite her into their hearts.*

And at the hour of our death - *I understood how Mary prepares her children for their death through her powerful intercession. She helps us to die a happy and holy death by making sure that we die in the state of grace. At the time of our death, she makes sure that we receive all that's necessary to obtain a happy death. She is able to do this by us trusting her motherly intercession. When we die a happy death we die in the arms of Mary. What a joy it is to allow Mary to help us to die in her arms!*
Amen - *We acknowledge that we believe with our hearts that Mary is truly our advocate, our helper and our Mother.*

Our Lady: My child, you have done well and you have pleased me. Tell all my children what great joy they bring to my heart whenever they pray one Hail Mary slowly, with much love and listening to every word. When my children pray one Hail Mary, paying attention to each word, they allow me to give them a multitude of graces. I delight when my children pray the Hail Mary with reverence in their hearts. One Hail Mary prayed well gives more graces than a great many badly prayed. The graces received praying one Hail Mary with love in their hearts cannot be exhausted. The more love in their hearts, the more graces flow from my Heart to my children praying the Hail Mary.

My child, tell my children that whenever they are suffering and do not have the strength to pray, to pray one Hail Mary well said. I will be at their side to help them. The graces received by praying one Hail Mary well are indescribable.

One Hail Mary will help my children to obtain an ocean of graces, while they bring joy to my heart as I recall the holy moment of when the Archangel Gabriel greeted me at the Annunciation. Thank you, my child, for being so patient in writing everything that I have asked you to write.

December 8, 1994 *You shall begin to see results*

Jesus: My child, I, your Eucharistic Savior, extend My deep gratitude for coming with trust in your heart and honoring this hour of grace requested by My Mother. I give you My solemn word that many hearts of those represented to Me are being healed from many of their iniquities. I am truly listening to all prayers, for many are here with wounded hearts.

Know for certain that many marriages, addictions, illnesses and unbelief are being healed. I ask that you do not doubt what I, your Eucharistic Savior, tell you, but that you believe. You shall begin to see results to the requests that are being brought before My Eucharistic

Heart. I give you My word that all that I tell you will come to pass.

December 8, 1994 *Feast of the Immaculate Conception-the Gate of Hope*

Our Lady: Dear children, I invite you to rejoice with your heavenly Mother on this my feast day. I am the Immaculate Conception. I am the gate of hope for all my children who embrace me as their heavenly Mother. I am the most pure reflection of the divine light of my Son, Jesus.

Today, I invite you, my little ones, to enter into my Immaculate Heart and to be consecrated to me, for I am the gate which opens the door to Heaven and allows God's gifts and graces to be poured into your hearts. My children, know that I am the love and holiness of God. He entrusts all my children to my Immaculate Heart which will lead you to my Son.

Today, have no fear or worry and do not allow any distractions to enter your heart. Spend this day rejoicing with all of Paradise that celebrates the splendor of your heavenly Mother.

My children, many of you have concerns in your hearts about the gifts that you should give. Some of you are sad, for you don't have the material means to give to those you love. Again I tell you, my little ones, give the gift of love that comes from the heart.

My Son invites you to love and not to worry, to trust Him and not to be sad, for He is your reason to rejoice and to love. Allow me to help you so that you may enter into the heavenly garden of Paradise. Remember, I am the gate that opens to your salvation, and everyone of you must enter this gate to arrive at your own personal encounter with my Son, Jesus. My children, my presence in your midst must become more strong and extraordinary, for you need my help during these troubled times. Trust in your heavenly Mother and rejoice, rejoice, rejoice!

December 14, 1994 *Cooperate with grace*

Jesus: My child, welcome to My Eucharistic Heart. Abandon all your concerns to Me, your Eucharistic Savior. I know that you are seeking enlightenment to the desires in your heart. Tell Me everything and I shall give you My peace.
Janie: My Most Adorable Jesus, You know the thoughts and the answers that I seek, but I only want them if they are in harmony with the

Purity and holiness of heart

Holy Will of my Father.
Jesus: My little child, know that because you seek My Father's Perfect Will first in your heart, He will grant you the desires of your heart. He loves you very much and your little ways are pleasing to Him.
Janie: My Jesus and My Lord, I am so happy to be able to have You as my everything. I want to live only to please You in everything I do. Please help me to cooperate with the grace that you have given me to be truly transformed by Your love.
Jesus: My little child, I, your Jesus of Love and Mercy, give you My solemn word that as long as your heart is open to the grace given to you by My Father you will be transformed. Cooperate with this grace everyday, in everything, and you will mirror My love and mercy. Have no worry in your heart, but abandon all to Me.

December 15, 1994 *Allow your heart to be a manger*

Our Lady: Dear children, I, your heavenly Mother, invite you to continue to prepare your hearts for my Son, Jesus. The time is approaching when the world celebrates the birth of my Son. Before that time is here, it is important that you become aware of His presence in your daily lives.

He is present in all your daily suffering, when you are sick or alone, and when you feel abandoned and rejected by those you love. He is present in the loss of someone you love, when a terrible tragedy occurs, when you lose your jobs, during financial needs, in troubled times, in broken marriages, and when their is suffering in the family. He is present in your addictions and when your faith is tested. He is with you in broken relationships. He is present in all your needs. He is present in prayer and when you receive the sacrament of Reconciliation, in the Blessed Sacrament and in the reading of Holy Scripture.

Little children, I share this with you to tell you how great is my Son's love for you. He loves unconditionally and at all times. His presence in your daily lives is so immense that you cannot begin to comprehend unless you surrender and abandon yourselves to Him Who loves you. Little children, allow the awareness of my Son in your midst to penetrate your hearts.

Pray with me, so that I may help you to prepare, so that my Son's love and mercy may be born in your hearts. Prepare your hearts through prayer and allow your hearts to be a manger for my Son to be born into. Your heart and your love are the best gifts you can give my Son. He is the reason to rejoice during this Holy Season. Pray, my children, pray, and you shall have the joy of my Son in your hearts.

December 15, 1994 *Your family are my prayer warriors*

Janie: *I was praying for discernment because I had been asked to go to Mexico during Christmas with Fr. W. and Fr. H. and others.*

Our Lady: Pray and implore the intercession of Blessed Juan Diego for this special intention. All of my children must unite their prayers and fasting without ceasing. My child, when you come to Mexico, come prepared, for I have much that I will share with you.

Janie: Blessed Mother, I have never left my family during Christmas.

Our Lady: Have no worry, your family will receive extraordinary blessings for making such a sacrifice to be without you during this special time. They are giving witness to others of their love for my Son by submitting to the Holy Will of the Father. It is Our desire that you are present at my shrine during this time. Your family must intercede for you, for they are my prayer warriors. I listen to their prayers with tenderness in my heart. They give much of themselves to God by sharing your time with my children in different areas that you are called to.

December 23, 1994 *Mexico Right into my arms*

Janie: *While we were in flight to Mexico City, I was talking to D.K. and we were sharing how crazy it was to be flying to Mexico during Christmas time. I said, "Here we are flying," and at that point I looked out the window and there in the sky was Our Lady of Guadalupe. Our Lady finished my sentence saying, "Right into my arms." Her arms were extended to us. Later, I looked at the sky and there I saw a rainbow.*

December 23, 1994 *Mexico City You will receive a new heart*

Janie: *When we arrived, we wanted to go to the Basilica of Our Lady of Guadalupe and pray. We came to the gates and the Basilica was closed. I knelt at the gates looking at the Hill of Tepeyac. I went into prayer thanking Our Lady for bringing us there. At that moment Our Lady of Guadalupe came with Baby Jesus in her arms. There were tears streaming down her face.*

Our Lady: My child, my tears are tears of joy, for I am so grateful to see so many of my children who have come to be with their heavenly Mother.

Janie: Blessed Mother, we are here to do whatever you want us to do.

Purity and holiness of heart

Our Lady: I desire that all my children unite in prayer with their heavenly Mother, so that I will be able to help you to prepare your hearts for the birth of my Son.
Tomorrow, at the stroke of midnight, a miracle will happen in each one of my children. Each one of you will receive a new heart, for my Son will be born in your hearts. I ask that all my children prepare with strong prayer and offer every sacrifice, for your stay here will be difficult for some of you.
Janie: *I had a strong knowing that some of them would be disappointed in the outcome of the sonogram.*
Our Lady: Know, my children, that when you leave here you will leave here with new hearts. This is a gift from my Son, Jesus, for each one of my children for having responded to my call to come here and to be with their heavenly Mother. I ask that my children pray for the Church and for all of my beloved priests who suffer so much. Pray especially for the Vicar of my Son, for his safety and protection, for he is in much need of protection. Keep him close to your hearts through your prayers and pray with your heavenly Mother for his safety.
Janie: Blessed Mother, many have come here because of the sonogram that is supposed to be taken.
Our Lady: I do not wish that my children be distracted but to be in the spirit of prayer. Prayer is very important and I need your prayers like never before for much change is occurring in the world. There is much suffering, so much suffering. Your prayers can help change the world. Through your prayer much change will happen within the world and within your own hearts.

Again, I thank all my children for coming to their heavenly Mother. I especially wish to thank all my beloved priests who responded to their heavenly Mother and came with such faith and love in their hearts. Allow the Holy Spirit to guide you during your stay here. Offer this Mass for my special intentions.

December 24, 1994 *Mexico I came as a pregnant Mother*

Janie: *I saw Our Lady of Guadalupe. She came with Blessed Juan Diego, who was to the left of Our Lady. He was kneeling the entire time. He was so humble, and looking at him I knew that we should all model after him in his obedience and humility.*
Our Lady: My dear child, I, your heavenly Mother, am so grateful to my beloved priest, Fr. W. He came to his heavenly Mother like a little child with such faith. He has been obedient to my words and my request. He is truly blessed and has brought so much joy to my heart.

I am deeply moved by the love of all those gathered here. I wish to thank each one of them, for they all responded with faith to my request.
Janie: Please, Blessed Mother, tell me what you want us to do for you?
Our Lady: I want all the prayers of my children gathered here. I want all my children to remain faithful and to rejoice with their heavenly Mother and not to be sad or disappointed.
Janie: Blessed Mother, you said that you would tell us why you called us here.
Our Lady: My child, I want my children to pray like never before and not to give up on this effort. I want them to remain faithful to their heavenly Mother and to pray for my special intentions.
Janie: Will the sonogram take place?
Our Lady: I do not wish that my children be distracted with the results, but to prepare their hearts for my Son, Jesus, so that he may come and live in their hearts.
Janie: So the sonogram will not take place?
Our Lady: *(Smiling)* Who said it would not take place? Look, my child!
Janie: *I saw the Baby in her womb emanating an immense light.*
Our Lady: I want my children to know that when I appeared to my hijito, Juan Diego, I came as a pregnant Mother. Look, my child, look at the Divine Life within me. Know that I am the true Mother of all my children everywhere, and I came to help my children back to my Son, Jesus. Look at the Divine Life within me.
Janie: *I saw her Baby in her womb for the second time with such light coming from Him.* Blessed Mother, please help me. I am a little nervous. Am I to share this with others?
Our Lady: Look! Look, my child. Look at the Divine Life within my womb.
Janie: *I saw the Baby for the third time, only this time I saw what appeared to be a halo around His tiny head. I knew that He was little Jesus. Seeing this brought so much joy to my heart and removed any feelings of nervousness.*
Our Lady: I want all my children to return to their homes with a joyful heart. I want them to know that this mission has been accomplished. I want my children to leave here believing in their hearts that when I came under the title of Our Lady of Guadalupe, I was with Child. All my children must believe this. This is what I desire.

My child, the appointed time has come for my children to open their hearts to my Son, Jesus. He is rejected by many and this pierces my heart. Salvation cannot come to those who reject Him. Those who reject Him condemn themselves. Know that the beginning of the year comes with much suffering. Calamities and pestilence will come upon the world. This will happen in succession. Much strong prayer is needed to help convert hearts. This next year comes with much suffering that will increase in its intensity. The suffering will come in succession, so again, I beg my children to pray.

Janie: *She showed me the world, and I saw much chaos.*

Our Lady: Many of my children live in darkness and only through prayer will they come to know true repentance. I ask for special prayers for my beloved priests. **Many live in the state of darkness, for they refuse to acknowledge the True Presence of my Son in the Holy Eucharist. The schism will be strong and many of my beloved priests will perish, for they have turned their backs on my Son, Jesus. Much more will happen in the world that will put fear in many hearts. The evils of abortion and homosexuality are two great evils in the world that are destroying millions of souls involved in this evil.**

My child, I am begging my children to pray, pray, pray. If all my children respond to my request many will be saved. I wish that my children pray and trust in God's love and mercy and not be in fear. I tell my children these things, so that they will understand the horrible evil in the world and the need for strong prayer.

Janie: Blessed Mother, will I remember all this?

Our Lady: Yes, my child. I have inscribed this message in your heart.

Janie: How do I share this with all those gathered here?

Our Lady: Simply give a brief summary of my message. Rejoice also for all those souls that will enter Heaven on Christmas Day.

Janie: *Please know that I have never received a message from Our Lady saying to take a sonogram. I wish for this to be clear. I believe Our Lady said this to Fr. W., for Our Lady has chosen him in a special way. Our Lady wants us all to be humble and obedient. In doing this, we keep Satan from interfering with her plan. She wants her Son to be born in our hearts. This is why she came, to help us to draw closer to her Son.*

She also wants us to pray to the Holy Spirit and to ask the Spirit of Truth to enlighten our hearts with divine wisdom and discernment. She said there are many, many false prophets who are misleading many of my children. I have shared as much as I was supposed to. Our Lady shared some personal things with me. She blessed my Rosary for a special intention.

December 24, 1994 *Vision from Our Lady - The State of the World*

Janie: *I saw the world in chaos. There was fire everywhere. Men and women were running after each other naked. They appeared to be drunk or under the influence of drugs. There were men with men and women with women. I believe they were homosexuals and lesbians. They, too, were naked, but not all of them.*

I saw children being sexually abused as well as physically abused. Children were out on the streets and many had no one to love them. I saw abortion clinics killing babies and many of these mothers were perhaps teenagers but there were also adults. I saw marriages being destroyed by spouses abusing one another. I saw lots of family violence in the homes. Parents against their children and children against their parents. I saw violence in the streets, killings, breaking in buildings, people fighting and many of them had guns.

I saw the church in much opposition. I saw many priests telling people not to believe in the True Presence in the Eucharist. They were speaking horrible things against the Pope. These priests were involved in having sexual relationships with women and many priests were active in homosexual relationships. These were the scenes that bothered me almost as much as the ones of abortion.

Many religious women were engaging in the same activities as these priests. I understood that what I was seeing was perhaps the schism that will cause many obedient priests to suffer much. I saw many good priests and religious women praying and they had Rosaries in their hands. These souls were Our Lady's obedient priests and religious but they were suffering much, for they, too, were being scourged by other priests like Jesus was scourged. I saw priests dying for the sake of the faith and many other priests were going into hiding to keep themselves alive.

I saw volcanoes erupt, earthquakes, floods, hurricanes, tidal waves, drought, homeless people, and hunger striking many areas of the world. I saw wars in different parts of the world. I saw the world in such a state of sinfulness that it reminded me of the way that Sodom and Gomorrah is described in the Bible. All that I saw were scenes before my eyes which appeared before me just like they appear on television when the news is on and one is seeing clips of different parts of the world. Our Lady wanted me to see all this again so that I will never forget the importance of prayer for peace in our world. This message was not released in the first edition of this book. Fr. Henry discerned that now

(1997) is the time for this vision to be released.

December 24, 1994 *Mexico* Mary: *Splendor of the Father*

Jesus: My child, welcome to My Eucharistic Heart. Abandon yourself to My love, which is beyond your understanding. My child, I wish to extend My deep gratitude to My beloved brother priests for allowing My True Presence to be among those gathered here. Through the love that My brother priests have demonstrated to Me, their Eucharistic Brother, I give you My word that I will pour out My love and mercy on them and all those they are praying for.

Know that this gathering is the work of My Mother. She has brought you here to spend time in special prayer with her. She provided everything for you, so that all obstacles would dissolve before your very eyes. It was her prayers that called you here. Her love for her children is so immense.

Her Most Immaculate Heart is the gate that will lead you to My Sacred Heart. She is the golden gate, the true path to My love and mercy. My Father has confided His peace plan to her. She is the splendor of My Father, the reason why all of Heaven rejoices. My child, listen to My words and truly embrace My Mother with love and trust in your heart.

There is much that awaits the world in the coming year. The world is not ready for what they will face if they do not convert. Much prayer is needed to prepare many hearts. The prayers begin with you. Your own heart must be free from all desires of the world. Only in this way can you say that I, your Jesus of Love and Mercy, truly live in your heart. It all begins with your love for Me and your prayers.

The world is in such a state of turmoil, and the intensity of this turmoil will increase unless there is true repentance of the heart. Hate and violence must disappear from the face of the world, so that hearts may be set free. It saddens My Heart, for many will not change. They will reject My love and mercy. They will condemn themselves.

Your prayers are so needed to soften hearts. Tonight is a special time when blessings and graces will be poured out on people everywhere. I, your Jesus of Love and Mercy, will be born in many hearts. This brings joy to My Heart. Continue to prepare with strong prayer and remain steadfast. Stay close to My Mother through your prayers and you shall not regret having come here. Your own hearts will never be the same because of your 'yes' to My Mother. As she says to you, "Do whatever My Son says to you," so I, your Jesus, tell you, "Do whatever My Mother tells you to do."

Pray, asking the powerful intercession of Blessed Juan Diego for all My beloved brother priests, everywhere. I especially wish to extend My deep gratitude to My brother priests who came on this faith journey. Know that I, your Jesus of Love and Mercy, am among you in an extraordinary way through My brother priests who are with you. Pray with them and for them. They represent Me.

December 24, 1994 *Mexico City Christmas Eve*

Our Lady: My dear child, tonight is a holy night. Spend quiet time with Me in prayer. Prepare your heart well with silent prayer. Embrace this holy night and detach yourself from all other distractions. Think only of my Son and how He will bless the world. Come, be with your heavenly Mother and enter into the peace that will come upon the world through His birth.

Go back into that night, when the night was clear and the manger was being prepared by St. Joseph. Imagine yourself there in the stable with me and St. Joseph, awaiting that precious moment when the Prince of Peace would come into the world. Come, pray quietly with your heavenly Mother, so that through our prayer my Son may be born in many hearts.

The world lies in darkness and has forgotten how to know my Son's peace. Their hearts are cold because of their sinfulness. Many hate peace and choose to live in darkness. They hate prayer and persecute those who pray for peace in the world.

My child, the hour has come. Finally, that precious moment is suddenly upon you. For weeks you prepared your heart. Come now and adore Him Who is about to be born, the Savior of the World. His light will light up all darkness, and His peace will change hearts. Embrace this little Babe about to be born from my virginal womb.

December 25, 1994 *Mexico City Christmas Day*

Janie: *I entered the Chapel and I greeted Jesus by singing Happy Birthday and then Las Mananaitas.*
Jesus: My child, welcome to My Eucharistic Heart and thank you for greeting Me in such a loving and personal way. You truly acknowledge

that this is My day, when God showered the world with love. Today many celebrate this day through gifts and many other activities, yet many do not acknowledge Me as the reason for such celebration.
You, My child, make Me feel so special and loved with your salutation. Know that it is moments like this that bring such consolation to My Eucharistic Heart. Your love makes My Heart rejoice; that out of My love for humanity I chose to remain present in the Blessed Sacrament.

My child, today many new hearts have awakened to My love. Many humble souls are demonstrating their love for Me. I am especially grateful for all My beloved brother priests who embrace Me in the celebration of Holy Mass. My Vicar is one who is truly united to My Eucharistic Love. He, too, embraced Me as you did. Pray for My Vicar, for many of My brother priests oppose his teachings and this saddens My Heart.

My child, you are precious to Me and your little ways are pleasing to Me. Never forget this. Rejoice throughout this day and know that all of Heaven rejoices with you on this glorious day. My peace is being poured upon the world and many have embraced My peace. Many souls have been released from Purgatory and have entered Heaven. Rejoice with them. I love you, My child. Allow My peace and love to be the equilibrium in your life.

My peace I give to you. My peace I give to you. Not as the world gives, but as I, your Eucharistic Savior give you. Live in My peace and share it with others. I, your Jesus, give you My blessing. Go and share this blessing as well, and know that I am with you until the end of time.

Editor's Note: During this trip to Mexico, Janie also visited the Shrine of Milagro de San Miguel in Thaxcala, Mexico. The message given to her by St. Michael is listed in the section of messages given by the Archangels.

December 30, 1994 *Dallas, Texas* *Youth Retreat: There are no secrets*

Jesus: My child, welcome to My Eucharistic Heart. Thank you for coming to spend time with Me. If you only knew how you comfort Me when you come to Me. You bring such joy to My Eucharistic Heart. My child, I, your Jesus, know that you have come to ask Me to help you with your talk to the youth. Know that that's why I am here to help you. I want to do everything I can to help you to trust Me, your Jesus, more. Write down My words to the youth.

My beloved young people, I, Jesus your friend, greet you all today. What joy you have brought to My Heart by coming to spend time with Me. Yes, My beloved ones, in coming to this retreat you said 'yes' to Me, Jesus, your friend. I ask that you open your hearts to Me and do not be shy or fearful, for I know everything about you. There are no secrets between you and Me.

I know, beloved ones, that some of you did not want to come, because you don't like to pray too much, but you still came and for that you will receive many blessings. Know that you have a multitude of angels encamped around you and they will help to remove all distractions from your nervous hearts.

The Holy Family will be most present during this retreat and you will be helped in a most extraordinary way. Do not be afraid or bored with thinking that you will spend too much time here. All these thoughts come from the evil one.

Trust Me, Jesus your friend, Who has called you to come away from everything and to spend time with Me. Right now, to many of you I am just a friend, but if you trust Me while you're here with Me, by the time you leave I will be your best friend. If you choose to make Me your best friend, you shall never be alone. I will go where you go, and I will help you with everything.

Be wise My beloved ones, and abandon all your concerns to Me and you will enjoy this special time. Do not lose precious time and do not allow the evil one to put negative thoughts in your heart. He does not want you to be here with Me, and he will put every distraction before you. Trust Me, your friend, Jesus, and I give you My word as your loyal friend that you will be truly blessed.

Today My beloved ones, is a new beginning with Me in your faith journey. Do not lose the opportunity to come to know Me better. As the days progress, I, your friend, Jesus, will be among you as you enjoy all the activities that you are participating in. I love you all, My young friends and I thank you for coming.

December 31, 1994 *Dallas, Texas Youth Retreat: Jesus is the answer*

Janie: *Our Lady came to me as Our Lady of Guadalupe. I could see her Immaculate Heart, and this is the second time that I have seen her Immaculate Heart under this title. She came to me while we were pray-*

Purity and holiness of heart

ing the Rosary before the Blessed Sacrament.
Our Lady: My precious child, I am here to tell you that I am deeply grateful to you for all the prayers that you have prayed for the protection of the unborn. You have consoled my Sorrowful and Immaculate Heart, for you understand just how concerned I am about all the innocent little souls that are being killed and that die a most horrible and brutal death. Please, my child, pray for my babies. Pray for my babies!

Dear child, I wish to thank you for saying 'yes' to giving of your time to my young people. I know just how tired you are from your trip, and no one knows more than I, just how much you have suffered. Please write these words that I tell you, for I wish to speak to my young people who are so precious and special to me.

My most dear young people, I, your heavenly Mother, wish to thank each one of you for saying 'yes' to my Son, Jesus, Who loves you very much. My dear ones, I, too, love you very much, and I want to help by teaching you how to pray with trust in your hearts. Many of you have so many questions and you are looking for answers. My dear ones, my Son, Jesus, is the only answer to all your questions. Through Him you will come to understand more about yourself, your faith, your friends, and your parents with whom so many of you struggle. I love you so much and I want to help you, but I cannot help you if you do not allow me to help you.

I want to teach you about purity and holiness, but you cannot know about these virtues unless you pray with your heavenly Mother. I want to teach you all about my Son, Jesus, who longs for your friendship. I want to teach you not to be afraid or embarrassed about the things that you have done, for my Son, Jesus, will forgive you if you are truly sorry for your sins. I want to teach you how to pray the Rosary, so that everyday you and I can pray together. In this way you will come to know me and my Son, Jesus, in a special way.

My dear ones, I, your heavenly Mother, with my Son, Jesus, love you just the way that you are. I have so much that I want to share with you, and if you pray your Rosary with me I promise that you will understand how much I love you.

Listen, my dear ones, listen with your hearts to all that you are experiencing during this special retreat, for God is speaking to each one of you. He is helping you to embrace His only begotten Son, Who died for love of you. Return His love by saying 'yes' to making Him your true friend. I love you all and I give you my motherly blessing. Begin your new year with my Son as your best friend, for you will need Him to help guide you in your faith journey. Peace, my little dear ones, peace.

Chapter Seven

BECOME EUCHARISTIC 1995

And as they were eating, He took bread, and blessed, and broke it, and gave it to them, and said, "Take; this is My Body." And He took a cup, and when He had given thanks He gave it to them, and they all drank of it. And He said to them, "This is My Blood of the covenant, which is poured out for many.

Mark 14:22-24

Heaven's Messages for The Family

January 1, 1995 *Dallas, Texas* *Be living tabernacles*

Our Lady: My dear child, I wish to express My deep gratitude for all your prayers and sacrifices. You have been diligent in doing all that God has asked of you. My child, pray with your heavenly Mother and stay close to my Immaculate Heart through your prayers. Offer much prayer in reparation for the needs of the world.

This year will be in need of much prayer, for there will continue to be much suffering. The Church will continue to suffer more and more. The schism and the apostasy will be strong, and many of my beloved priests consecrated to my Immaculate Heart will suffer much. Prayer and love are so needed in the world. Much prayer.
Janie: *She looked sad as she said this.*
Our Lady: My child, help me with your prayers. I want to help my children to be living tabernacles, so that my Son may dwell in their hearts. I thank you for listening to all that I have asked of you, my little angel. I give you my motherly blessing.

January 5, 1995 *Stay close to your heavenly Mother*

Our Lady: Dear children, greetings to each one of you and thank you for being here today. Know that I am deeply grateful for all your hard efforts, and that God is pleased with all that you do to draw closer to His Son, Jesus.

My little children, I invite you as a family to allow me to help you in the beginning of this new year. Many changes will occur, and it is most important that you stay close to your heavenly Mother through your prayers. I invite all families to especially pray the Rosary and not to allow a day to pass by without you praying your family Rosary. Know that I shall be with each family as you gather to pray the Rosary.

I invite all my beloved priests and religious to pray your Rosary together and to all the faithful to recite the Rosary in the church. Know that it is through praying the Rosary along with other prayers and sacrifices that will help to draw others closer to my Son.

My little children, do not allow Satan to tell you lies about praying the Rosary. He will tell you that you don't have time, that it takes too long and that it is boring. Know that the Rosary is your weapon and through praying your Rosary, you will disarm Satan, and peace will come to those that you are praying for.

Allow this new year to be a year when you will live your consecration and abandon yourself to the Two United Hearts. I love you all, my children, and I invite you to pray with your heavenly Mother like never before. Allow my words to penetrate your heart and pray. You shall not regret it. I give you all my motherly blessing. Thank you for listening to my message.

January 21, 1995 *Big Lake, Texas* *Console My Eucharistic Heart*

Jesus: My child, welcome to My Eucharistic Heart and thank you for allowing My love and mercy to penetrate your heart. My little child, know that I am a merciful and loving Savior, and I want to inflame all hearts with My love and mercy. I love My people so much and their wretchedness attracts My Eucharistic Heart. I embrace especially those who live such sinful lives. I want to pour out My mercy in their hearts. People everywhere are miserable because of their sinfulness, but My mercy will melt away all their sinful hearts.

My child, I speak to you of My love and mercy, for this is the way that you come to know Me. You have opened your heart to My love and mercy. Your own heart mirrors My love and mercy. Others have come to Me because of your loving and merciful heart. Pray, My child, for all My beloved brother priests. I love them all with immense love. I suffer for them, for so many of them reject My love and mercy. Their love for Me has become weak. Many don't love Me or believe in Me. This wounds My Eucharistic Heart.

Embrace your merciful Savior, My child, and console My Eucharistic Heart. Tell Me how much you love Me over and over again, for I so yearn to be loved by the many in the world who reject My love and mercy. Continue to allow your own heart to be a living tabernacle where My love and mercy dwells. I love you, My little servant.

January 22, 1995 *Big Lake, Texas* *Be a slave to My love*

Jesus: My child, welcome to My Eucharistic Heart. Thank you for coming to spend one hour with your Jesus of Love and Mercy. Abandon yourself to Me. Think of nothing else except Me. Allow Me to cast out all your distractions for this is Our special time together. This is Our time when we will unite in Our love for one another.
Janie: My Jesus, My Jesus, help Me to know how to truly abandon myself to You, for I want so much to please you and to console Your Eucharistic Heart.

Jesus: My child, trust Me in everything and then you will begin to truly let go of everything for My sake. Know, My precious gem, that no one can give you eternal life except Me. I am the One Who knows the Father, for My Father is in Me and I in Him. Be a slave to My love, embrace all suffering that comes your way for My sake. Never complain, but love. Never grow weary when others reject you, but rejoice. Never doubt, but believe that I am always with you. Love, love, love everyone. Never reject anyone, never accuse or judge anyone, for My Father knows all hearts. He is the Just Judge. Leave everything to Me and I will see to all your concerns. I want you to be My reflection in everything, yes, My precious gem, only My reflection. In this way your love for Me will be a light to all those in your path. Be Mine, be completely Mine and you will have eternal joy and peace, My joy and peace. I love you, My little servant, your little ways are pleasing to Me.

January 23, 1995 *Big Lake, Texas* *Adoration: Hearts are cold*

Jesus: My child, welcome to My Eucharistic Heart. I thank you for allowing Me to be with you this morning. You had a desire and a longing to be with Me in your prayers last night. This pleased Me and it consoles My Eucharistic Heart. My precious hidden pearl, continue to put Me first everyday in your life, for I, too, long and desire to be with you. I want so much to share My love and mercy with all the world, but hearts are cold and this coldness of their hearts is a rejection to My love and mercy.

My Father is sending you among families to share My love and mercy. You are an obedient, humble servant. You go out among strangers, knowing in your heart that many will not believe that you come in My Name. My child, you are My precious hidden pearl, and many will never realize what a blessing you are to those you visit. You are quiet and have a discerning heart. Your humble ways are filled with My Father's wisdom. You see yourself as knowing nothing and you take no credit for yourself, but give all the glory to My Father. You give your total trust to Me, for you know that I will never abandon you or disappoint you.

Janie: Oh, beloved Jesus, your words are so kind, but you know that I don't see myself as You see me. I know in my heart that I am not a learned person and have no experience talking before people. You know that I prefer not to talk in any public place. I do all this for my love for You and in obedience. You reward Me in such a way, for I meet You in all the people. When people doubt that You sent me, I feel Your pain, but with God's grace I am not intimidated by this rejection of Ours and this, I know, comes from You. Thank You, beloved Jesus, thank You with all my love.

Jesus: My precious hidden pearl, continue to love Me and to console Me. Never abandon Me, but always come to Me and bring Me all those that My Father puts in your path. Tell them of My love and mercy.

January 26, 1995 *Prayer is the medicine this world needs*

Our Lady: Dear children, I, your heavenly Mother, invite you to continue to pray for love and peace in the world. Little children, the world is in a state of great turmoil and the suffering continues to increase. There is great suffering in the family, and many families are at war with one another because they refuse to forgive one another. It saddens my heart that many families are praying very little. Some are not praying at all.

My children, please understand that prayer is the medicine that this world needs. You cannot have peace in your hearts if you do not pray. Little children, please trust in my motherly intercession. Allow me to help you to draw closer to my Immaculate Heart. Allow me to teach you how to pray from your heart. You cannot say that you belong to me if you do not trust in my intercession and if you do not pray.

I know, my children, that you are living during hard times and many of you are suffering much. Know for certain that I am with you, praying for you. Trust in my intercession. I love you. Thank you for listening to my message.

January 27, 1995 *The Rosary, Adoration and obedience*

Our Lady: My dear child, I, your heavenly Mother, have come to ask you to do three special favors for me. First, I ask that you pray a Rosary everyday for my beloved Pope and all my beloved priests throughout the world. Secondly, to spend time with my Son in Adoration and console His Eucharistic Heart. He is so abandoned and He yearns to be consoled by His children. Thirdly, be obedient and do everything that God is asking of you. Know that at times things will be very difficult for you.

February 2, 1995 *Satan is becoming weaker*

Our Lady: Dear children, greetings to you, my little ones. I, your heavenly Mother, extend my deep gratitude for all your prayers and hard efforts, for I know that many of you are suffering much. Endure your sufferings and trust God with everything, you shall not regret it!

My little children, I invite you to pray especially in this second month of this new year, for I need your prayers like never before to help prepare hearts. The world continues to live in darkness, and your prayers and sacrifices are so much needed to help to avert all the calamities and pestilence that continue to spread throughout the world.

Little children, pray unceasingly so that you may remain united as a family, for Satan is trying desperately to separate you and bring division among you. He wants to take God's peace away from your hearts. He knows that he is becoming weaker through your prayers, and this makes him very angry. Pray and love my beloved Pope and all my priests, for the Church needs your love and prayers and not criticism. Remember, you are all my children and you must live in God's peace and love.

Little children, I wish to thank each one of you who is busy preparing for the Anniversary. Know that I am with you helping you to accomplish everything. This time will be a time filled with much graces and blessings. Have no worry. Continue to pray your family Rosary, and I wish to invite you to begin a nine day Novena to the Holy Spirit for this coming Anniversary.

Begin on the seventh and end it on the day of the Anniversary. This Novena to the Holy Spirit will help prepare hearts and it will also prepare hearts for this second month. Each day offer nine Our Father's, nine Hail Mary's, and nine Glory Be's. Abandon everything to my beloved Spouse, the Holy Spirit, and allow Him to renew your hearts with God's love.

Little children, do not grow tired of prayer, but pray unceasingly and know that many hearts are transformed by your prayers. Persevere in prayer with joy in your hearts. Thank you for listening to my message.

February 6, 1995 *I exchange my health for his illness*

Janie: *For more than a week my little grandson was sick with a virus, but he wasn't responding to any of the medications that he was taking. He was suffering so much with high fever. I had been taking care of him for two weeks and he had been sick. Saturday night, February 4, he spent the night with me. He was so sick that he couldn't sleep and kept crying off and on. I was praying over him and I said these words* *to Our Lord.*

Lord, please help make my little grandson well and let me take his place instead. I exchange my health for his illness. He is so little and has been through so much. Please, Lord, if it be your Holy Will, restore him back to his usual self. He hasn't been able to eat or play. I know that You are a loving and merciful God. Please hear my words. I offer myself for him whom I love so much.

My little grandson fell into a deep sleep after my prayer and did not wake up for the rest of the night. In the morning, he woke up and asked for cereal and ate two full bowls. He had not been able to eat for almost two weeks and had lost weight.

He was back to his usual self - no fever and he was full of energy. Praise God. My daughter-in-law and I were amazed by his speedy recovery, but I hadn't remembered my prayer to the Lord for I had been praying so much for him. Today, Our Lady came and said these words to me.

Our Lady: My child, know that God has granted your request that you made concerning your little grandson. You exchanged your health for your grandson's illness. The Lord heard your prayer. You offered yourself as a victim for his recovery. You are now experiencing your little grandson's illness while he is back to a joyful little soul. Embrace your suffering and offer it for my beloved Vicar and all my priests and all the consecrated souls. Peace, my child, peace.

Janie: I accept and embrace my illness with joy in my heart. Amen.

February 7, 1995 *Love even to the point of death*

Jesus: My child, I, your merciful Savior, come to you during this hour of My mercy and ask you to beg for My mercy on all those whom are in most need of My mercy in your family. I know, My child, that you, too, are suffering from seeing the lack of love in so many hearts. At times you want to give up on those that you so much love and pray for. Your own suffering becomes unbearable.

Look at your merciful Savior and see how I am crucified to the Cross over and over again by those who say that they love Me. Imagine just for one moment how much they wound My merciful and sorrowful Heart. Those who refuse to love Me by not trusting in My love and mercy, those souls wound My Heart the most. Oh, if they could only abandon their trust to Me, they would be healed.

Pray, My child, pray with Me and do not allow any distractions of frustration to infect your own heart. I know of your pain, but I beg you, do not entertain any desires to want to give up on those you love no matter how much you are rejected and ignored by your loved ones. Abandon yourself quickly to me, so that Satan will not poison your heart with his lies. You must love always, love even to the point of death. I am with you in all your suffering as you suffer for love of Me.

Pray for selfishness and control to die in hearts so that they may be able to love Me, for selfishness and control are manifestations of lack of forgiveness and trust. Hearts cannot love Me if there is selfishness or the desire to control how they should love Me. All hearts who say that they love must learn to abandon themselves to me completely without holding anything back.

My child, I come to you to comfort you in your own suffering and to ask you to console My suffering and merciful Heart. Detach yourself from all things in the world and pick up your cross and follow Me. Stay with Me and live in My Heart, so that I may live in your heart. In this way I will not allow anything to distract you from My love.

Stay with Me and don't ever leave My side. I give you My solemn word that I won't ever leave your side. I will protect you from the coldness of all those hearts that surround you. I will provide you with everything that you need. All that I ask is that you love Me and trust Me. My child, I do not want you to be distracted by anything, but I want you to stay with Me every moment of the day. My love will protect you and nothing will touch you, nothing.

Do not worry about having lost a few hours of sleep. Know that My love will sustain you and in Me you will find rest. Abandon yourself in Me and I will refresh you. Have no worry, I know your every need. Learn to love Me with all your soul so that you may learn how to suffer with Me. Never give up on loving those who wound your heart the most. Through your love for them, they will draw closer to Me. I love you, My child. I Am.

February 10, 1995 *Together We will comfort one another*

Janie: My Jesus, what do you want from me? It is late and I have not been able to fall asleep. I offered my lack of sleep for my own soul as well as poor sinners. I am here, my Jesus, please speak, for my heart is restless.

Jesus: My child, your heart is restless because it knows how much you love Me and how much you long to be by My side. Know that you are suffering so that others may draw closer to My merciful and loving Heart. While the world sleeps, I call on you to stay awake with Me so that together we will hold vigil in reparation for those who live in darkness.

I know, My child, that you are sick and tired from lack of rest. I come to you, for I know that you will not reject Me, or refuse to stay up with Me. Your obedience pleases Me and even if you didn't pray, your obedience alone is enough to convert poor souls. You see, My child, your obedience is much more pleasing to Me than all your suffering and difficulties. Love obedience always.

My child, it comforts Me to share My own suffering with you. You listen to what I tell you and you allow My words to be the food for your soul and the strength for your being. I have gone to many souls tonight, but they all rejected Me, so I came to you. You opened the door to your heart and took Me in immediately, without hesitation.

You see how much I long to be loved and consoled. Don't worry, you are not crazy. I am speaking all these words to you. Do not allow your mind to entertain doubt, for I don't want your doubts, I want your love and your warm heart. I want you to hold Me in your arms and console Me.

My child, do not fear anything, for I am here with you for I know that you, too, want to be consoled. I am here for you. Abandon this moment to Me and I will abandon Myself to you. Together we will comfort one another. Peace, My child, peace. Go now, My child, and rest. I shall be by your side protecting you while you sleep. Peace.

February 11, 1995 *My Mother and I are inseparable*

Janie: My Adorable Jesus, I come before You to be refreshed and renewed. I offer You this time to speak to my heart. Tell me, My Lord, do You have any words which you wish to speak to the people that are coming for the healing Mass and Your Mother's Anniversary? Speak Lord, for Your words are life and food for my soul.
Jesus: My child, I, your Jesus of Love and Mercy, welcome all who come to honor My Mother. It pleases Me when My Mother is loved and embraced by her children, for she is the way to My Eucharistic Heart. When My Mother is loved, I am also loved, for she is in Me as I am in My Father and My Father is in Me. Just as My Father and I are insep-

arable, My Mother and I are also inseparable. She is the Mother of All Humanity. Her Immaculate Heart is the golden gate that leads you to My Heart.

My child, know that this is a special time for all who come and many healings of souls will take place. I see the woundedness and suffering of all those who will come. It is important that they know in their heart that they will not be disappointed. All who come with paralysis of the heart and soul will be healed.

I, your Jesus of Love and Mercy, will take away all doubt, hatred, jealousy, malicious thoughts, lack of faith and all else that stands between their hearts and My Heart. All must trust Me so that they may be healed. The greater their trust in Me, the more generous I shall be, and the graces and blessings that I will pour into their hearts will be unlimited.

My child, this is the time of My great mercy. My Heart lies open to all who will come to be healed and to honor My Mother. I am especially consoled by all My brother priests who are coming to feed My lambs. By their response to come, they lay a bouquet of love before My Mother's feet and in return receive a treasure of graces from her most Immaculate Heart.

I, Jesus, will pour out My healing balm on all who come through the hands of My brother priests. I will heal My brother priests and give them new strength. The Holy Spirit will come into hearts and souls. I give you My solemn word, that those who believe will receive love in their hearts and souls. It will be to them a heavenly fire that will renew their lives.

I wish to extend my deep gratitude to My beloved brother priests for loving and embracing their heavenly Mother and who are beginning to foster devotion to My beloved St. Joseph. It is My desire that St. Joseph, too, be honored and loved, for My Father chose him as Protector of the Families and the Universal Church. Follow his guidance and teachings and I give you My word, you will become holy families. My child, to you, I your Jesus say 'afeta', for I want to heal you. Afeta and trust Me. I Am.

February 13, 1995 *The narrow path*

Jesus: My child, I, your Eucharistic Savior, thank you for your commitment to suffer with Me and to enter into My Passion with total abandonment.

Become Eucharistic

Allow Me to have My way with you for the conversion and healing of poor sinners. Stay with Me in your great suffering and do not become distracted with anything. Keep your focus on Me. I Am.

Janie: Beloved and Adorable Savior, I will give up my life for You. Take every ounce of my nothingness and help me to enter into Your Passion in my own spiritual nakedness. I resign myself to Your Holy Will. Lord, take everything from me that keeps me from abandoning myself to You. Take the poverty of my spirit and take me all unto Yourself. Help me to drink from the cup of Your bitter Passion and to drink it all. I am Yours, My Lord, do with me as You wish.

Jesus: My child, your words are pleasing to Me, for no soul knows just how much you truly suffer more than I, your Jesus of Love and Mercy. I will give you My joy so that you may continue to suffer well. I love you, My child. Oh, if you only knew the love that I have for you.

Come, My child, enter into the lonely and narrow path that leads to My Passion, for this is where you will truly meet Me, your Eucharistic Savior. Very few travel this path, for it is a difficult path. This path is filled with many crosses and thorns. Those that find it abandon it right away. This narrow path is the path to your sanctification. Embrace it, My child, for this is the path that you have chosen to follow, for you know that it leads to My Eucharistic Heart. Be a slave to My love and embrace your cross with joy in your heart. I Am.

February 15, 1995 *Sixth Anniversary of Our Lady - Love simplicity*

Our Lady: Dear children, greetings to each one of you on this glorious day that you celebrate with your heavenly Mother. Rejoice, rejoice, rejoice and give thanks to God for allowing me to be with you for so long!

Today, I, your heavenly Mother, wish to extend my deep gratitude to all my beloved priests who have abandoned all their programs and everything to come and help heal my little children. To you, my beloved sons, I say thank you, thank you, thank you. Know that I hold you all close to my bosom and that my Immaculate Heart is your sure refuge. You have pleased God through your 'yes' to your heavenly Mother. Again I thank you.

To all my little children, I want you to know how dear you are to me. Have no worry, but pray, pray, pray and live my messages. Today, my little children, I invite you to be open to all the special graces and blessings that God wishes to give you.

Be humble, my little children, and love simplicity. Be joyful with what God is giving you and do not go searching for other things. Trust God in all your prayers and you will have peace in your hearts. Do not be jealous of one another, but love one another. In this way, you will not allow Satan to take away your peace. Be holy families and be an example to others. Today, I bless you, all my dear children. Thank you for listening to my message.

February 21, 1995 *Tampa, Florida* Consecrate your families and homes

Jesus: My child, welcome to My Eucharistic Heart, and I wish to extend My deep gratitude for all your suffering. You abandon yourself to Me and you hold nothing back. Oh, how your obedience pleases My Heart. If you only knew how many poor sinners are drawing closer to Me through your obedience to suffer. You allow Me to sift you through and through, as I purify your soul. You come to Me like a little child in the poverty of your spirit and allow Me to have My way with you. Oh, how you please Me!
Janie: My Dear Lord, Your words are life to my soul. Please continue to put me through the furnace of the fire of purification, so that I may learn how to love You. I want to be totally detached from the world and united to Your Eucharistic Heart forever and ever. Amen. My Lord, do You have words for Your people in Florida? Speak only if it is the Will of the Eternal Father.
Jesus: My child, write down what I shall tell you concerning this region and this area in which I, your Eucharistic Savior, brought you to speak. Allow My words to penetrate your heart.

My beloved families, I, your Jesus of Love and Mercy, call you all to open your hearts to My love in your lives. Invite Me into your homes and I will come to make My dwelling in your homes and in your hearts. I want to be in your homes, so that you may share Me with your children and other members in your family.

I want to be a friend to you as a family, so that I may help you to overcome all your sufferings and difficulties. Please hear My words and open your hearts. Allow Me to be King and Lord in your homes. Consecrate your families and your homes to My Sacred Heart and to the Immaculate Heart of My dear Mother.

I, your Jesus of Love and Mercy, give you My solemn word, that if you heed My request you will begin to heal as a family. I will suffer with you. I will rejoice with you. When you laugh, I will laugh. When you cry, I will cry. You will never be abandoned by Me or My Mother. Know that My Mother and I are inseparable. That is why where I am there she is also. Where she is, I am there as well.

My beloved families, I know of your deep pains and woundedness. Allow Me to heal you and help you in your sufferings. I am calling everyone. I will not turn anyone away. I know your sinful hearts, you cannot hide anything from Me. Come to Me, all of you and do not fear. I will forgive your sins and heal your wounded hearts. Come to Me. Do not hesitate, for there is no time like the present time. Bring Me everything and abandon all your hurting hearts to My mercy. Come, I want to be invited into your hearts and into your homes. I invite you into My Sacred Heart. I want to nest in your hearts and for you to nest in Mine.

I invite you to foster devotion to St. Joseph, who is Protector of the Church and all families in the world. I wish that everyone understands that My words today are to be embraced by My Church and all families. My invitation is an invitation to all to hear My words and accept them. I, your Jesus of Love and Mercy, bless you all.

February 23, 1995 *Forty days of prayer and fasting*

Our Lady: Dear children, I, your heavenly Mother, wish to thank each one of you for all your hard efforts during these past few days. You worked so hard to make this sixth Anniversary successful. Know that you accomplished everything that you set out to do in order to demonstrate your love for me. Oh, what joy you all brought to my Immaculate Heart. Thank you, my precious ones, thank you all.

Little children, as you well know my time with you is short. I want you to show God your deep gratitude for allowing me to remain with you for such a long time. Know that it is for your sake that I have remained with you this long a time, to help you to draw closer to my Son.

I love you, my little children, you are all so dear to my Immaculate Heart. I invite you to remain united to the Two United hearts through your prayers and by living my messages. I invite you to allow me to help you to prepare to enter into this holy time of Lent with a pure heart. This can be obtained through the sacrament of Reconciliation. Allow these forty days to be a time of prayer and fasting.

My Son is inviting each one to journey with Him into a time of quiet prayer and reflection. Each day commit to praying the Stations of the Cross with love in your hearts. Allow my Son to share His Passion and suffering with you as you reflect on each Station of the Cross. Detach from the material things of the world and abandon yourselves to my Son. Pray and fast in reparation for your own sins and for the sins of poor sinners.

Little children, if only you could understand the importance of prayer and fasting, but you do not understand. That is why I am here to help you. Open your hearts to my motherly request, and you will pray and fast with such joy in your hearts. This world is in need of much reparation, that is why I beg you to pray, pray, pray! Everyday, pray your family Rosary and help me to draw poor sinners to my Son. I love you all. Thank you for listening to my message.

February 27, 1995 *My Bride prefers the world*

Jesus: My child, welcome to My Eucharistic Heart. Thank you for staying here with Me and keeping vigil for My Bride whom I love so much. My child, pray with Me for all My brother priests who suffer so much because they have stopped loving Me. Oh, how their sinfulness wounds My Eucharistic Heart. They trample on My love and reject My mercy.
Janie: Beloved Jesus, how can I who am nothing and know nothing console You? I am here only because I need Your strength and love.

I am sinful and selfish, only thinking of myself. You are pure love and yet You invite me, the worst sinner, to stay with You. I will stay with You because Your words are eternal life and food for my soul. I shall console You in my poor way.
Jesus: My child, your humbleness and obedience are enough to console My poor and wounded Eucharistic Heart. I love My Bride so much and I long for her purity and holiness, yet, She prefers the world with all its sinfulness. Satan has entered the heart of My Bride and has robbed her of her purity. Pray, My child, pray that she may return back to her purity and holiness before it's too late.
Janie: Dear Jesus, not all your Church is sinful, is it?
Jesus: No, My child, there is much goodness with some of My brother priests, but their numbers are few. These are My brothers that also console My Eucharistic Heart. Many of My brother priests' hearts are barren and without My love. They live in the material world and they've forgotten to trust Me and to love Me.
Janie: *Here I see a vision. I see churches that are empty. No Mass cel-*

ebrated. The Blessed Sacrament abandoned. The churches are dark. I see priests involved in activities which are not pleasing to God. Priests and religious involved in relationships that are most displeasing to God. I see priests and religious who do not believe in the sacrament of Reconciliation and speak against it. These individuals look like ordinary laity and not priests or religious. I mean I saw priests in suits and religious in clothes that appeared to be very expensive. I saw priests who no longer prepare for Holy Mass, but simply treat Holy Mass like routine work. Please Lord, do not show me this, for I cannot bear to see it. People will think that I am making this up or that perhaps I am being judgmental against priests and religious. I wouldn't do this, for it displeases You and hurts You. Please do not show me anymore. I saw other things which I will hold in my heart.

Jesus: My child, I allowed you to see how wounded My Bride is and how much prayer she needs. Do not fear of what others will say or think of you. Your responsibility is to please and to love Me. In doing this, you will do the Will of My Father.

Janie: I love You, my dear Jesus. Help me to always remember Your words.

Jesus: I, your Jesus of Love and Mercy, give you My blessing. Thank you for this hour. Go now, and attend to the needs of your family.

February 28, 1995 *Your suffering will continue*

Jesus: My dear child, I, your Jesus of Love and Mercy, know that you are suffering. I know of your desire to spend quiet time with Me, but instead you responded to being with Me through responding to a soul in need. Remember, whatsoever you do for the least of My little ones you do unto Me.

Janie: Forgive me, my Beloved and Adorable Savior. I wanted so to be with You, but I felt very weak and so I rested. Thank you for Your kind words and for coming to me tonight. I miss not going to Eucharistic Adoration to be with You, adoring You in the True Presence.

Jesus: My child, I know of your longing to be with Me, for I, too, long to be with you. Know that you will begin to suffer more and more for the purification of My Church and for families. Your suffering will continue throughout your lifetime. You will draw many as you suffer for love of my people.

Tomorrow you will spend time with My dear Mother and Myself. This will be a special time for you. My Father is pleased with all your love that you have for doing His work. It is He Who has granted you this time that you will spend daily with your heavenly Mother and your

Eucharistic Savior.

Janie: My dear Jesus, is this time private or can others join? Is there a special time for me to set aside?

Jesus: No, My child, no particular time due to your responsibility to your family. Perhaps the morning or afternoon, when you are alone at home. Your time available will be honored. Until tomorrow, My child, rest and prepare your heart for Our time together.

Janie: Thank You, my dear sweet Savior. I love You.

Editor's Note: Jesus told Janie that she would visit with Jesus and Mary on a daily basis beginning on March 1, 1995. This was a gift given to her out of God's love for his children and would continue every day until their last scheduled visit with her.

March 2, 1995 *Family prayer brings special graces*

Our Lady: Dear children, today, I invite you to continue to live my messages and to embrace them with your hearts. In this way, you are giving witness to others that you belong to me. Little children, you have begun your journey with my Son, as you embrace and enter into this time of Lent. Allow this special time to draw you closer to my Son. Let this time be a time of prayer and fasting.

Little children, walk with your heavenly Mother during this Lenten Season and allow me to help you to reflect on the changes that need to continue to occur in your hearts. Allow my Son to purify your hearts so that you may obtain the changes which you desire to happen in your life. I invite you, together with your family, to discover God through your prayers. **Live the Gospel as a family and do not become bored with family prayer time. Know that when you pray as a family you receive special graces and blessings. You grow together as a family and your love for God and for one another increases.**

Little children, I love you and I want you to truly belong to me, but you cannot if you do not pray and live my messages. I want you to help your heavenly Mother to bring light to this world that is living in darkness. I want you to have peace in your hearts as a family, so that you may be peace to others. I give you my motherly blessing. Thank you for listening to my message.

March 3, 1995 *Adoration: I am abandoned in the Blessed Sacrament*

Jesus: Good morning, My child. My Mother and I greet you with Our love.

Janie: Good morning My Lord and my dear Blessed Mother. What may I do for You today? How may I serve You?
Jesus: My child, know how much we appreciate this time that you spend with us. We know that you have much work to do for your family, everyday.

You dedicate yourself to making sure that you meet all the needs of your family. You have your visits with St. Joseph, you have all your writing to write, you attend Holy Mass and Eucharistic Adoration, and you meet the needs of those souls that My Father puts in your path. For all this we want to thank you.
Janie: Oh, Jesus, I guess I am not really aware that You know every detail of my daily responsibilities. Let me thank You and my dear Blessed Mother. I know that it is through Your love for Me that I can accomplish all these tasks. I am forever grateful.
Our Lady: My dear child, you bring so much joy to my Immaculate Heart by your willingness to do all these responsibilities with joy in your heart. You embrace your suffering without complaining. You deny yourself the things that you like to do to be at the service of others. You are growing each day in the virtue of obedience, which is most pleasing to God.
Janie: Thank you, My Lady for acknowledging the little things that I try to do for God. I offer Him so little. Please help me to do more.
Jesus: My child, My Father is pleased with your little ways. Be at peace and continue to embrace My Father in everything that you do.
Janie: My Adorable Jesus, do You have anything special that You want me to do for You?
Jesus: My child, pray for My Bride who continues to wound My Eucharistic Heart. I yearn for My beloved priests to come to spend time with Me, but many have forgotten Me. They place other worldly desires in their daily schedules, and I am left abandoned in the Blessed Sacrament. My brother priests have forgotten to teach those entrusted to them about My Presence in the Blessed Sacrament. Many go to Mass without preparing their hearts, because My brother priests are so busy that they do not take the time to teach their people about the importance of preparing to celebrate Holy Mass.

Day after day, I spend endless hours alone and no one comes to even say thank you or hello to Me. If only My brother priests would have enough love for Me, they would teach their people all about My love for them present in the Blessed Sacrament. Many of My brother priests have stopped believing in My True Presence because they do not take the time to pray. Oh, how they wound My Heart.

Janie: Beloved Jesus, I am sorry that we hurt You so much. Please forgive me for all the times that I have abandoned You.
Jesus: My child, you at least acknowledge that you have at times abandoned Me, and you are aware that this hurts Me. Many of My brother priests do not even acknowledge that their actions wound Me. You see, their hearts are closed to My love.
Janie: But My Lord, how do they remain priests?
Jesus: My child, many of My brother priests are bored and tired of being priests. They have forgotten their priestly vows at the time of their Ordination. Please pray with My Mother and Me for the purification of My Bride whom I love so much. Love and pray for My beloved Vicar whom I love and who loves Me.
Janie: My dear Blessed Mother, do you have a request?
Our Lady: My dear child, my request is the request of my Son. Pray for all my beloved sons and daughters. Love all priests and religious always. Never criticize the Church, but abandon all your concerns quietly to my Son.
Jesus: My child, Our visit has come to an end for today. Until tomorrow, remain united with us through your prayers and sacrifices. You have Our gratitude. I, Jesus, give you My blessing.
Our Lady: And I give you my motherly blessing. Go in God's peace.
Janie: I will be with You in prayer.

March 5, 1995 *Wimberly, Texas* *The presence of the Holy Family*

Jesus: Greetings, My child, on this beautiful day. Know that My Mother and I know that you were praying that you could have your visit while you and your husband were visiting your land. We responded to the desire in your heart.
Janie: Dear Jesus and My Lady, yes, I had prayed that it would be nice if I would be visited by both of You while I was here. I just thought that it was too much to ask.
Our Lady: My dear child, know that the desires of your heart are important to us, so do not hesitate to ask. We love you and we want you to be happy. Know that this land is a gift to you and your family. God is pleased with your future plans for this beautiful, peaceful place. Many souls will experience peace in their hearts as they visit here.
Janie: My Lady, this land is consecrated and dedicated to your Son.
Our Lady: Yes, My child, I, your heavenly Mother, know this. Much family conversion will take place here because of your love for my Son. The love and mercy of my Son will dwell in this land. Have no worry concerning your goals for this land. God will provide everything that you need. Trust Him with your plans.

Jesus: My child, I am honored to have this land consecrated and dedicated to Me. For this great love you have shown for Me, I give you My word that the presence of the Holy Family will dwell here. Now, My child, your husband has finished his work. Our visit with you was a joyful one. Peace, My child.
Janie: Thank You. I am grateful.

March 6, 1995 *We are united to you in your life's journey*

Janie: Good afternoon My Lord and My Lady.
Jesus: Good afternoon, My child. How are you doing this afternoon? Know that We are here to help you.
Janie: Thank You, my Adorable Jesus. I am truly blessed to have the honor to visit with both of You at the same time. Praised be God.
Our Lady: My child, We know that you are suffering interiorly, for the visitations of St. Joseph will soon cease. You are suffering quietly, but know that We are with you in your suffering. What may We do to help you during this time?
Janie: My Adorable Jesus and my beloved Blessed Mother, just by Your being here with me is all the help I need. You help to console my heart and bring me God's peace. I never imagined that it would be so hard for me to have my visits come to an end. Sometimes I wish silently in my heart that I would have not been chosen to have such a privilege to be blessed in such a loving way. I acknowledge that I am unworthy and how much God loves all His children.
Our Lady: My dear child, God chose you to have these visitations. It was His Holy Will that you would have these experiences and to help draw others closer to Him. Know that long after these visits are over your heart will remain united to Our Hearts.
Jesus: My little humble servant, you work so hard for your own conversion and for the conversion of your family. You suffer rejection, coldness of hearts, ridicule, persecution and loneliness all for the love of Us. This so pleases My Eucharistic Heart and the Immaculate Heart of My Mother. You have a loving and generous heart.
Janie: Thank You both. I wish I could do more for You, but I recognize my human limitations. I abandon myself to Your service of loving and helping others, for I know that God provides everything I need to do His work.
Jesus: My little child, remain united to Us in prayer, for We are united to you in your life's journey.
Janie: Please intercede for me before God, so that I may have the energy to take care of my family and to help them. Please pray for my oldest son and his family, please. Also help my Spiritual Director and

enlighten him. He needs Your guidance.
Jesus: Have no worry. We will see to everything you requested. Now, My child, I, your Jesus of Love and Mercy, give you My blessing.
Our Lady: My precious angel, I, your heavenly Mother, bless you also. Peace, my child, peace.
Janie: Praised be the Name of God forever and ever. Amen.

March 7, 1995 *Trust Me*

Janie: Good morning, My Lord and my dear Blessed Mother.
Jesus: Greetings and peace to you, My child. How are you doing this morning?
Janie: I am doing quite well thank You. I went to Holy Mass and then I went to Confession.
Our Lady: My precious angel, God is so pleased with all your hard efforts. Know that we know just how much you are giving of yourself to help your son and his family's situation. You have abandoned yourself to God, trusting Him in your suffering.
Janie: Oh, Blessed Mother, I am aware that all I truly have is God and all of the powerful intercession of Heaven. Sometimes I wonder if I am truly doing God's Will. I pray that I am.
Jesus: My little humble servant, know that when you abandon yourself to the Will of My Father, you are indeed trusting in His Will. Have no doubt. Now, My little suffering soul, what can We do to help you?
Janie: I beg You, my Adorable Jesus and my dear Blessed Mother, to pray for our situation concerning (X.) Please guide my Spiritual Director and enlighten him with the wisdom and discernment from God so that his decision will be what God wants.
Jesus: My dear child, know I am with My suffering brother and I will help him to do My Father's Holy Will, for I know that My beloved brother wants to please My Father. I know that there is much suffering because of this situation, but all that I, your Jesus of Love and Mercy ask, is that you trust Me and I will lead you and My beloved brother to the truth of this matter and help you to make a decision.
Janie: I will abandon this situation into Your hands.
Our Lady: My precious angel, know for certain that We are standing by you in your suffering. This situation saddens Our Hearts, but do all that my Son is telling you to do and your Spiritual Director will have peace.
Janie: Thank You both so much. I feel the peace from your guidance. I love You. Thank You for all your help. Oh, my Adorable Jesus, please heal my little granddaughter and please do not allow her brothers and sisters to get her illness. Please also heal all their family problems and

woundedness.
Jesus: Be at peace, My little humble servant. I will bring My peace into their hearts. My little servant, Our time with you is up. Let us pray together as I give you Our blessing.
Our Lady: I love you, my angel. Peace to you.
Janie: I love You both. Pray for us.

March 8, 1995 *Dismiss all anxiety*

Janie: Good morning, my Adorable Savior and my dear Blessed Mother. Thank You so much for blessing me and my family by your visit.
Jesus: My little suffering servant, allow Me, your Jesus of Love and Mercy, to embrace you. Abandon yourself to My love and mercy with filial trust. Dismiss all anxiety from your heart, for My dear Mother and I will help you during this difficult time.
Janie: Oh, Jesus, the anguish that I feel in my heart is so painful. I feel so all alone although I know that You and my Blessed Mother are with me. My Adorable Savior, am I in the desert?
Jesus: My little humble servant, you are experiencing My sorrowful Passion. Your suffering will be manifested in different ways. You will continue to experience the loneliness, the anguish and agony in your soul. You will suffer physically as well as emotionally, but know that you have been given the grace to endure your suffering as you journey with your Savior during this time of My sorrowful Passion.
Our Lady: My precious angel, you have been chosen to be a suffering soul for the conversion and the purification of the Church. You will suffer for the conversion of families throughout the world. My angel, you will suffer much during your life, but you will rejoice in Heaven. Know for certain my angel, that my Son and I will always be by your side. Take refuge in my Immaculate Heart, for my Immaculate Heart is the path that will lead you to Heaven, to the Heart of my Son. I love you so much. Never forget this.
Jesus: My little humble servant, allow Our words to penetrate your heart and know that We are with you until the end of time. Now, let Us pray together as I give you My blessing.
Our Lady: Kneel down, my angel, as I, too, give you my motherly blessing.
Janie: Glory to God forever and ever. Amen.

March 9, 1995 *When doubt comes, invoke St. Thomas*

Janie: Good morning, my Adorable Savior and my dear Blessed

Mother. Praised be God forever and ever. Amen.
Jesus: Good morning, My little humble servant.
Our Lady: Good morning, my angel.
Jesus: How are you doing this morning? My Mother and I are here to give you strength through Our love. Abandon yourself into Our love and allow Us to impregnate your heart and soul with My Father's peace. Speak freely to Us and hold nothing back.
Janie: My Adorable Savior, I am having problems with being distracted during prayer or whenever I am at Holy Mass. My mind wanders and this bothers me. I know that this is part of being human, but I don't remember being this distracted before. Tell me, is something wrong? Help me to handle this.
Jesus: My little humble servant, do not allow your being distracted to make you believe that you are not in prayer. When this happens ask the powerful intercession of your guardian angel. He will help you overcome your distractions. Do not dwell on this, but do what I, your Jesus tell you to do.
Janie: I will do as You say, my sweet Adorable Jesus, for I know that Your words are life to my whole being. Thank You for helping me. I have peace in my heart now.
Our Lady: My angel, you bring joy to Our United Hearts through your obedience to submit to what you are instructed to do by Our teaching. You yield to the Holy Spirit and surrender yourself through your abandonment. Know that this is why Satan cannot touch you, because of your total surrender to the Holy Will of God. My angel, know that everything that you are doing to bring peace and unity to your family is pleasing to God. Never abandon your efforts to work for the Kingdom of God through your prayers and sacrifices. Many are drawing closer to my Son through your hard efforts.
Janie: My Blessed Mother and my Adorable Savior, sometimes I think that I am crazy and that I am making up all that is happening to me. I don't see how I could, because I am so busy most of the time with my family, but I wonder about it.
Jesus: My little humble servant, you are not crazy. You have been chosen by My Father throughout all eternity to have these mystical experiences. You were chosen before you were conceived in your mother's womb. This is My Father's plan for you. Part of your doubt is your cross. Know that all the saints in Heaven suffered as you do.
Recall My own apostles. Remember how they all doubted in many of the things that I said to them. They were with Me, they knew Me, they lived with Me, ate with Me, they spent hours, days and many months with Me, yet they abandoned Me at the time of My great persecution and death. They were able to recover from their doubt and through them

the Gospels were written.

Do not be hard on yourself. When doubt comes your way, invoke the power of the Holy Spirit and call upon the intercession of the apostles, especially St. Thomas, for he doubted as you do. Remember, a tree is known by its fruit. Through your love and obedience, much fruit is being produced. This should be your proof of your mystical experiences. My humble servant has this helped you?
Janie: Yes, thank You so much.
Jesus: Until tomorrow, let Us pray together and I will give you My blessing.
Our Lady: I will bless you as well, my angel.
Janie: Praised be God forever and ever. Amen.

March 10, 1995 *During your childhood, St. Joseph was at your side*

Janie: Thank You so much for waiting for me, my Adorable Savior and my Blessed Mother.
Jesus: My little humble servant, We know today you are suffering, that is why We wanted you to get rest, so that you will be able to accomplish your family responsibilities.
Janie: My Adorable Savior, I am most grateful for Your love and mercy. I am feeling very weak. It hurts for me to walk or just to do anything. I am having a hard time breathing. Please forgive me, my Precious Jesus, I am not complaining.
Jesus: My little humble servant, I, your Jesus of Love and Mercy, know that you are suffering. I know exactly how you feel the pain throughout your body. You are united in My sorrowful Passion.
Janie: It is an honor for me to suffer for love of You. Will my suffering cease after You cease to visit me?
Jesus: My little humble servant, you will continue to suffer My sorrowful Passion throughout your life. You have been chosen to suffer for My Bride and for poor sinners. Your suffering will be much more intense during My sorrowful Passion.
Janie: Will I know when I suffer for your special intention? Right now, I know when You ask me to suffer for a special intention, because You ask me and inform me when and why I will suffer.
Jesus: Your guardian angel will inform you.
Our Lady: My angel, listen with your heart to all that my Son is telling you. Embrace every word and allow His words to lodge in your heart. Allow your heart to be a tabernacle for my Son. My little child, We know that things are hard for you. We know of all the pain in your heart. Allow Our love to soothe your aching heart. As the last visit of St.

Joseph grows near, your heart becomes more sorrowful. Know that it's all right for you to feel this way. Know that St. Joseph's heart is also sad for he loves you very much.

My angel, I, your heavenly Mother, wish to tell you something special about your childhood. Remember how you suffered as a young child? Recall how joyful you were? How you loved to sing and you made people happy through your singing?
Janie: *I saw a vision of my childhood. I was about four or five years of age.* Yes, I remember all this, but why are you sharing this with me?
Our Lady: My angel, during your childhood, St. Joseph was at your side. Remember how you used to feel that someone was with you and at times you thought you saw someone. You knew it was a friendly man. This was St. Joseph. He was with you all during your childhood. He guided you in your adolescent years.

My angel, I share this with you for it is time that you understand more clearly that St. Joseph was allowed to come to you as a child. This was the joy that you felt in your heart and why you were loved by your neighbors. Remember how you used to love to help older people? This was St. Joseph guiding you to love and help those who couldn't help themselves.

I share this with you now to assure you that just as St. Joseph was with you as a child, he will continue to be at your side until you go to Heaven. Know that you will see St. Joseph as you recall your time with him.
Jesus: My little humble servant, embrace these words which My Mother has shared with you and rejoice in the love that My Father has for you. Until tomorrow, pray with Us as I, your Jesus, give you My blessing.
Our Lady: I give you my motherly blessing.
Janie: Praised be God forever and ever. Amen.

*Editor's Note: When Janie was small there was a glass factory not far from her home. At times she would go to the glass factory and slide down the pile of glass on cardboard for fun. She used to play in that area and she would sometimes see a man smiling at her in a protective way. Then he would be gone. Our Lady explained to her that this was St. Joseph and that he had been with her throughout her childhood.

March 11, 1995 *I will take care of everything for you*

Jesus: My suffering servant, know that I know your pain and anguish.

I am with you in all your suffering. Trust Me, your Jesus of Love and Mercy.
Janie: My Adorable Savior, I do trust You. Please help my (X). This soul is so wounded, please hear my cry.
Jesus: You have My solemn word that I will respond to your cry for this situation. Abandon all this to Me. I will take care of everything for you. Now, listen to My Mother's words.
Our Lady: My angel, I, too, am with you and I am praying with you. Abandon yourself to my Son's Heart and to my Most Immaculate Heart. Together We will unite Our prayers with yours. Trust totally in my Son and do not lose courage.
Jesus: My little humble servant, you have a busy day ahead of you. We will make Our visit short. Rejoice and embrace My Father in His love and mercy. Rejoice! Peace.

March 12, 1995 *If only souls would cooperate with grace*

Janie: Thank You, my Beloved Lord and my dear Blessed Mother for being with me.
Jesus: Good morning, My little humble servant.
Our Lady: Good morning, my precious angel. Did you have a good night's rest?
Janie: Yes, I believe so, although I woke up a few times, I feel rested. Thank You so much for asking. My Adorable Savior, please thank Your Father for all four of my sons. I am so happy that my other son who is in the service came to visit. Seeing him makes me realize how much I really miss him. Yesterday during the Baptism of our grandson, I was so happy to see the interaction between all four sons. They filled my heart with joy. Praised be God for giving my sons to me. Please, Jesus, watch over them and guard and purify them by Your Precious Blood.
Jesus: My little humble servant, I, your Jesus of Love and Mercy, give you My solemn word, I will pour out My love and mercy into their hearts for the love that you have for Me and My Mother and St. Joseph. Know that your family is under Our love and protection.
Our Lady: My precious angel, it brings joy to Our Hearts to see how hard you work for the conversion and to keep the peace in your family. You are aware of your family's emotions and you help them to talk and to solve their problems. We want to thank you for your tireless sacrifices and efforts.
Janie: Thank You both for recognizing the little things that I do for my family. I am grateful to God for saving me from the fires of hell. I am forever grateful.
Our Lady: My angel, yes, God is merciful but you cooperated with His

love and mercy and repented, that is why you have the Father's joy in your heart. Oh, if only souls would cooperate with the graces that God gives them, conversion would come to those who desire it. It saddens my heart that many souls continue to reject God's mercy and continue to desire darkness in their lives. If only souls would pray, they would come to realize that God's Will for them is their sanctification. His grace is an invitation for them to repent. Pray, my angel, pray with Us for poor sinners.
Janie: I will, I promise!
Jesus: Now, Our little humble servant, pray with Us so that We may both give you Our blessing.
Janie: Thank You both, I love You. Pray for us and for our world.

March 13, 1995 *Love is your reason for living*

Janie: Good morning, my Adorable Jesus and my dear Blessed Mother. I love You both so much.
Jesus: Good morning, My little humble servant. How are you doing this morning?
Janie: I am doing all right. Thank You for asking.
Our Lady: My precious angel, We know that things are hard for you. It was hard for you to see your son leave yesterday.
Janie: Yes, it was very hard, but I am grateful that I saw him and that we spent some time together.
Janie: Blessed Mother, why did you give me the date of when you and Our Lord would be leaving on my wedding Anniversary? My friends wonder why did you choose this particular day? I also wonder myself.
Our Lady: My precious angel, this day was already designated by God. He knew that you would be able to accept this day. He knew it would be a great suffering for you, but know that your suffering is bringing about much conversion for your family and others. My angel, We know that your suffering is increasing, know for certain that We are with you.
Jesus: My little humble servant, abandon yourself to Our love and know that We are with you each step of the way. **Remember, when someone mistreats you, return their maltreatment with loving words. You can do this if you do it for love of Me. Be like an innocent lamb being taken to be slaughtered and remain loving until the end. Remember, love is your whole affair in life and your reason for living.**
Janie: I will do as You say, My Lord, no matter how hard it is. Please help me.
Jesus: Have no worry. We will help you. We will be with you tomorrow. You have our blessing.

Become Eucharistic

Janie: Thank You both. I love You.

March 15, 1995 *Trust in Our love for you*

Jesus: My little suffering servant, I am here to console your wounded and suffering heart. I know that your suffering has been severe, but believe that My Mother and I are with you.

Janie: Oh, Jesus, my only Love, I have behaved so foolishly at times. My heart was filled with doubt and lack of trust. Please forgive me, for I only want to be a fool for love of You.

Our Lady: My precious angel, We understand your suffering. Do not be too hard on yourself, for We love you so very much. We are with you and all things will work out. Your (X) will recover, but continue to offer your prayers with love in your heart for this special intention.

Janie: Please, I beg both of You, help me not to fall into Satan's evil traps. I don't want to sin. Please help me.

Jesus: We are with you. Trust in Our love for you. Bring all your concerns to Us and do not allow anyone or anything to distract you. Be at peace. We will be with you as you visit with St. Joseph who is here at this moment.

Janie: At this time St. Joseph is present.

March 17, 1995 *Satan is waging war on you*

Jesus: Good morning, My sweet humble servant.

Our Lady: Good morning, my angel.

Janie: Good morning to both of You. Thank You for being so patient with me.

Our Lady: My angel, your cross is heavy, but you are embracing your suffering with joy in your heart.

Janie: Oh, dear Lady, how can I be embracing my suffering with joy in my heart when I have been angry and weak?

Our Lady: My angel, for everyone who has hurt you during these past few days you have remained charitable, and have initiated peace with them no matter how you are hurting inside. You do this for the love of my Son. Oh, how you please God.

Janie: *My Lady, I have never had so many people verbally attacking me in succession like this before. Tell me, what I am doing so that I can change it.*

Our Lady: My angel, know that it is Satan, who is waging war on you because of all the poor souls that are drawing closer to God through your suffering.

Janie: But I have been angry and at times unkind.

Our Lady: My angel, you are reacting to the insults and the hard attacks against you; this is normal. You are aware of your actions and you correct them. This is what God wants from all His children, to make amends for their actions and to repent. This is what you are doing. This is a very hard time in your life and you are suffering much.
Janie: Blessed Mother, will I always suffer the Passion of your Son?
Our Lady: Yes, my angel, yes. You will continue to drink from the cup of the bitter Passion. Your suffering will increase during Lent, but you will suffer other times as well.
Jesus: My child, after you recover from your sadness from St. Joseph, I, your Jesus of Love and Mercy will begin teaching you on the Holy Eucharist. Through the Holy Eucharist, those who believe in It will have eternal life.
Janie: Oh, Jesus, I am so sorry that I've missed daily Mass, but I couldn't help it. Sometimes my family responsibilities tie me down. Sometimes when I am suffering, I cannot drive. This hurts me very much.
Jesus: My humble one, I know that you do your best, but if you cannot go to Holy Mass in the morning, go during the day. Do not ever miss Mass for the sake of just missing it. Make every attempt.
Janie: I will, my Adorable Savior, I will. Is this why You woke me up early?
Jesus: We wanted to spend more time with you to comfort you. Lately Our visits have been short because of your family responsibilities. We know that you long for more time with Us as well.
Janie: Jesus, I have missed visits with You, Our Lady and St. Joseph, because of my family. This upsets me and yet I know that I am doing the right thing. Am I?
Jesus: Yes, my little humble servant, yes. Now Our time is about over. Prepare for Holy Mass.
Janie: Jesus and my dear Blessed Mother, I recommend to You my grandchildren: Jessica, Maria, Monica, and little Jesse in a very special way. Please protect them from the suffering which their parents are inflicting on these innocent little souls.

Please promise me You will protect them. Help and heal this marriage so that these precious children won't suffer so much.
Jesus: I give you My word, your grandchildren are under Our constant protection. Know that if you didn't offer your constant assistance these children would suffer greatly. Thank you, My child, for loving so much when it's hard to love. Thank you.
Janie: Jesus, this was a good visit. Thank You both. I love You. Pray for us.
Jesus: We love you, We love you.

Become Eucharistic

March 18, 1995 *We are with you*

Janie: Beloved and Adorable Savior, please forgive me, but my hands are hurting. I cannot write much.
Jesus: My little humble servant, do not worry, for My Mother and I are here to tell you that We love you and that We are with you. We know your pain as you await the visit with St. Joseph. Have no fear, We are with you.

March 19, 1995 *Be strong*

Jesus: My little humble servant, My Mother and I are here with you. Be strong for you have been given the grace to endure all that you are suffering. We love you and We bless you.

March 20, 1995 *No words were spoken*

Janie: *Our Lord and Our Lady came to bless me when I had my last private visit with St. Joseph. No words were spoken.*

March 21, 1995 *Have no fear*

Jesus: My little humble servant, We are here with you in your suffering, have no fear.

March 22, 1995 *Draw your strength from Our love*

Jesus: My little humble servant, We are here. We have come to tell you that We love you. You are suffering much. Draw your strength from Our love. We know that your heart is sad for you miss St. Joseph. Recall his words that he is with you in prayer.

March 23, 1995 *Take My hand and enter into the narrow path*

Janie: Please, Dear Jesus and my Blessed Mother, help me. My suffering is so heavy and I feel weak. I am concerned because I can't even do my house work. I am feeling like I do not want to be around anyone when I am suffering, for I do not want to be a distraction to anyone. Please tell me what to do.
Jesus: My humble suffering servant, you are suffering for all the sins and the purification of My Bride. She has allowed herself to be soiled with sin and She is in need of much prayer in reparation to be reconciled back to My Eucharistic Heart.

Janie: Please, My Lord, tell me, how is my suffering helping Your Bride?

Jesus: You have been chosen to suffer for My Bride and as you suffer, many of My beloved brother priests and consecrated souls are being helped to repent for their lack of obedience to live their vows as priests and religious. You will never understand how much your suffering is helping My Bride. Do not be afraid of your suffering, for it is a gift to you from My Father. He will not test you beyond your limits. Abandon yourself to Me, your Eucharistic Savior and fear nothing

Janie: I will do as You say, My Jesus. I would like to request a time away from everyone and to be relieved of some of my responsibilities to the prayer group when I am suffering, for I do not want people to see me like this.

Jesus: My humble servant, it pleases Me that you do not want to be a distraction to anyone. I, your Jesus of Love and Mercy, together with My Mother, will honor your request. In doing this, you demonstrate your humility and your love for Me. Share this with My beloved brother who is your Spiritual Director.

Know that you will spend more and more time alone, except for the times that you are called out to go and evangelize the hearts of the families. Your suffering will continue, but your strength lies within the Holy Eucharist and Eucharistic Adoration. This will become more and more your only source of strength, for no one will truly understand your suffering. You will be renewed as you abandon yourself to Me in the Holy Eucharist and in Eucharistic Adoration.

You will become more aware of My powerful True Presence in the Holy Eucharist and in Eucharistic Adoration as your suffering increases. You will long for Me more and more as I become more known to you during Holy Mass and Eucharistic Adoration. This is where you will spend much time, for I, your Eucharistic Savior, long to be with you as well.

Rejoice, and enter into the narrow path which many reject and avoid. This path is traveled by few, for not many can endure the thorns and crosses in this path. This narrow path leads to salvation, but it requires much perseverance, much trust, love and prayer. It requires total abandonment and true detachment from the world. Come, do not fear. Take My hand and allow Me, your Eucharistic Savior, to walk with you. Trust Me.

Janie: Jesus, My Lord and my All, I am Yours to do with as You wish. I will die being a slave to Your love. I will embrace You in my suffering, for in my suffering I shall come to know perfect joy. I trust in You,

I trust in You.
Our Lady: My precious angel, your true abandonment is most pleasing to God. We are with you, nothing will happen to you. We love you and give you Our blessing.
Janie: Thank You, thank You, pray for me.

March 23, 1995 *Joy and strength in suffering*

Janie: *Our Lord came to me again in my suffering. I have been suffering so much that I could hardly pray, but I forced myself to remain in prayer no matter how weak I felt. I prayed from three to ten after four in the morning. Our Lord woke me up at two in the morning to have my visit with Him and Our Lady.*

After the visit I remained in prayer. I decided to make a cup of coffee and I realized that although I was still suffering, my spirit was stronger and more joyful.
Jesus: Prayer drives all evil away.
Janie: Praised be God for His love and mercy.

March 24, 1995 *Holy Mass: the holiest time of your life*

Janie: Praised be God forever and ever. Thank You, my Lord Jesus and my Beloved Holy Mary for being here with me.
Our Lady: My angel, my Son and I are here with you to help you, to strengthen you in your suffering. Cling to Our love and abandon yourself to God Who loves you with immense love.
Janie: My dear Blessed Mother, please, I beg you and your Son to truly help me to abandon myself to God. My only desire in life is to be united with His Holy Will.
Jesus: My humble suffering servant, you please My Father in desiring to be totally united to His Holy Will. Know that you obtained this through unceasing prayer, especially through being sustained through Holy Mass, for this is the ultimate prayer.

My humble servant, know that when you attend Holy Mass, you obtain graces and blessings that last throughout your life time. When you are in Holy Mass, feeding on the Holy Eucharist, this is the holiest time in your life. It is the most important time in your life. Nothing in your lifetime can compare to the time that you are feeding on the Bread of Life which is My Holy Eucharist. Nothing in the entire world can compare to the holiness and importance of this time you spend with Me in Holy Mass.

When you attend Holy Mass with a pure heart, you allow Me to heal you and draw you closer to My Eucharistic Heart. Holy Mass and Eucharistic Adoration is a continuation of My love. There, I, your Jesus of Love and Mercy remain for you day and night. My love is immense.

My humble servant, I know that you are weak from your suffering. Rest before attending Holy Mass, and then keep Me company for one hour, for I have much to tell you.

March 24, 1995 *Adoration: He wept and wept*

Janie: *I had attended the funeral of a young person that had been killed and this young person was with child. As I was praying, Jesus was before me, crying.* Oh, Jesus, I know that You are sad for this family and what happened here.
Jesus: Oh, how it saddens My Heart that this world does not know true Divine Love. The love that they know is the love that they find in self satisfaction - the love that puts distance between their hearts and Mine.
Janie: *He wept and wept.* Oh, my Beloved Savior, please forgive us, please forgive us for wounding You so much. Help us, please help us.
Jesus: Oh, dear child, how can I help when the world does not want My help. They turn to Me only in times of great suffering, but when they overcome their suffering they quickly forget about ever asking for My help. Yet, I am grateful for this moment that they spent with Me.
Janie: My Beloved Savior, I know that we need so much purification, please do not abandon our world.
Jesus: Dear child, it is not I who abandon the world, rather it is the world who abandons Me. I remain in the Holy Eucharist daily, so that I will draw those who come to My Eucharistic Heart. I remain present, hidden in the host, and I call out day and night to all who come in faith.

Dear child, I am most present in Eucharistic Adoration night and day. I yearn for all My beloved brother priests to become Eucharistic in their hearts and to have Eucharistic Adoration. Oh, if only that Eucharistic Adoration would exist in My beloved brothers' churches, the people entrusted to them would begin to heal. The graces and blessings received are beyond their comprehension. Pray with Me for Eucharistic Adoration and console your Eucharistic Savior.
Janie: I will pray for this special intention, I promise.

March 25, 1995 *Have no fear*

Janie: Good morning, My Lord and my Blessed Mother. Praised be

Janie at the Marian Conference in Merida, Mexico, with the Bishop and attending priests.

Marcelino and Janie Garza atop Mt. Krizevac in Medjugorje.

Bishop Garmendia blessing Janie.

Some of the members of Our Lady's prayer group in Austin, Texas.

Janie took this picture in June of 1997 of the statue of Our Lady which is in front of St. James Church in Medjugorje. A perfect Pillar of Cloud appears next to Our Lady signifying the Divine Presence of Yahweh.

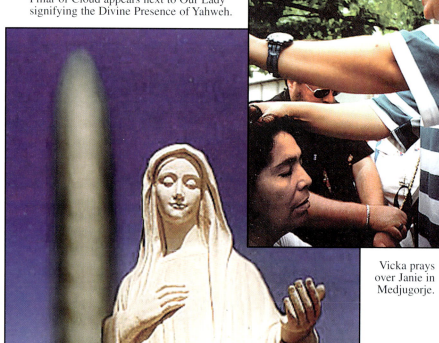

Vicka prays over Janie in Medjugorje.

Janie and Vicka in Vicka's prayer room in Biakovici. Vicka wrote words for Janie's book, see page 444.

Fr. Gerald Haby and Janie during the Lenten mission at St. Michael's Church, Mt. Pleasant, Texas. Janie was there for five days giving talks and ministering to the people there.

Fr. Henry (Janie's spiritual director), Janie and Fr. Walter Winrich having coffee at San Giovanni Rotondo, Italy.

Marielle (front left), Lucille (front right), Lil, Ann, Janie, Judy, Bernie, Kathie and Tina on Apparition Hill (Podbrdo) in Medjugorje.

At this moment Janie raised her hand to release a white dove which had flown to her from Our Lady. Notice the white circle in the upper center of the picture.

Janie's last scheduled visitation with Our Lady, Oct. 7, 1995. Feast of Our Lady of the Rosary on the Garza's land in Wimberley, Texas.

Five of Janie's grandchildren, Jessica, Jesse Jr., Maria, Alex and Monica. Not pictured Robert, Marissa and Veronica.

Janie in her living room. Two Pillars of Cloud appear. Photo taken by Rita Andrich, Archangel Press.

Pillar of Cloud signifying the presence of Yahweh appears again on the painting of Our Mother of Compassion and Love accompanied by a column of smoke (top right) signifying the presence of Our Lady.
Photo taken by Cindy Forman of Omaha, Nebraska.

Pillar of Cloud appears in the tight hand side of this picture. Photo taken by Rita Andrich, Archangel Press.

Professor Courtenay Bartholomew, M.D., with Janie on the Garza's land in Wimberley, Texas.

Marcelino and his sons building their home. The Garza family are building their own home in Wimberley, Texas.

Janie and her four sons, Mitchell (front), Marcelino, Janie, Armando and Jesse.

Fr. Richard Beyer, Mitch, Fr. Henry, Janie, Marcelino and Msgr. Povonka on the Garza's land, Aug. 15, 1997. Their new home was enthroned to the Two Hearts on this day.

Janie and Fr. Henry, in Ancona, Italy, waiting for the ferry to Split, Croatia.

Janie and Marcelino, Lisa, Fr. Christopher Scadron (Tucson, AZ.), Glenn and Kathie, and Sherry and Bob in Austin, Texas.

Pillar of Cloud appears by the Child, Jesus, and the Column of Smoke leans on the arm of her Son (top right), in Janie's prayer room at home. Photo taken by Cindy Forman of Omaha, Nebraska.

Janie being blesses with the glove of Padre Pio by Fr. Alessio Parente, OFM, at San Giovanni, Italy.

God forever and ever. Amen.
Jesus: Good morning, Our dear humble servant. We wish to extend Our gratitude for waking up early so that you may have your visit with Us before you leave on your trip. Know that through your obedience to go wherever We send you, many families will be blessed. Conversion will come to those who desire to convert. Have no fear or worry as to how your talks will be. The Holy Spirit Himself will speak through you. Your guardian angel will be right at your side. We are with you wherever you may be. Go with Our blessing.
Janie: Thank You both.

March 25, 1995 *Mt. Pleasant, Texas* *Hungry for love*

Jesus: My child, I, your Jesus of Love and Mercy, come to you to tell you thank you for coming to this town to give of yourself to My people. Know how this pleases Me, that you respond in obedience to My call to go wherever I send you. My child, My people are so in need of My love and mercy. You see how wounded they are. Many are hungry for love, but they do not know where to find love. They do not know about true Divine Love which they find only in Me.

I send you to give witness of your faith journey with Me and to share of your own personal family struggles with My people. I know that you experience some nervousness while preparing for your talks, but this is normal. What pleases Me is your true abandonment to trust Me through everything that I ask of you. I, your Jesus of Love and Mercy, ask you to continue cultivating and harvesting the hearts of My people through your witness of your love for Me and of My Mother and St. Joseph. Thank you, My child, thank you.

March 26, 1995 *Mt. Pleasant, Texas* *The impossible is possible*

Jesus: My humble servant, know We love you very much and all of your hard efforts are blessed. Abandon yourself to Our love and rest in Our love. Know that although at times things you have to do may seem impossible to accomplish, all things are possible with My Father. He makes the impossible possible.
Janie: Beloved Savior, thanks for bringing these concerns to my attention. I will remember this at times when I am struggling.
Our Lady: My precious angel, you are so precious in the eyes of the Lord. He is always with you wherever you go. Open your heart and fear nothing, but be ready to go whenever God calls you. Remember when He guides, He provides all that you need. Trust Him always.

Jesus: Now, My humble servant, We give you Our blessings for you have much work to do today. Remember, We are with you.

March 27, 1995 Mt. Pleasant, Texas *Stubborn and cold hearts*

Jesus: My humble servant, know that you are suffering for all those souls that are drawing closer to My Eucharistic Heart. Continue to abandon yourself to My love, for I am your strength. Embrace your suffering with joy in your heart.
Our Lady: My precious angel, listen to every word that my Son speaks to you, for His words are eternal life.
Janie: I will do as you say, my dear Blessed Mother. Intercede for me so that I may endure my cross with joy.
Jesus: My humble servant, I brought you here so that through your words, your prayers, and your hands, I could heal many who desire to be healed. There are many who live in darkness because of their refusal to repent. I, your Jesus of Love and Mercy, will touch their stubborn and cold hearts because of your obedience to come here. Have no worry, My humble servant, leave everything at My disposal. We give you Our blessings. Rest for now and remain with Me in the Blessed Sacrament. I will bless you, I will bless you.

March 28, 1995 Mt. Pleasant, Texas *Harden not your hearts*

Jesus: Tell My people these words: "If today you hear My voice harden not your hearts." My humble servant, talk to My people about My Mother.
Janie: *At these words, I saw the image of Our Lady of Guadalupe.*

March 29, 1995 Mt. Pleasant, Texas *Extraordinary graces*

Jesus: My humble servant, you have just experienced My pain and how I felt when My own people rejected Me. Do not dwell on this situation, but pray and love all my people everywhere. In loving them, you are loving Me.
Janie: Lord Jesus, I am so tired, please strengthen me.
Jesus: I know, My child, that you are tired but rest in Me through your prayers. I am with you. Do not become discouraged, but trust Me. My Mother and I brought you here to Our hurting people. We will not abandon you.
Our Lady: My precious angel, many are the miracles of conversion that are taking place through your obedience to come to this area. Rejoice, my angel, rejoice and pray, pray, pray. Continue to teach oth-

ers about the importance of prayer. I shall come to bless my children tonight and my Son will also come with me. Tonight, extraordinary graces will be poured into all my children gathered here. Now, my angel, allow this time for prayer. We will be praying with you.

March 29, 1995 Mt. Pleasant, Texas *Convert as a family*

Janie: *Tonight Our Lady came under the title of Our Lady of Guadalupe.*
Our Lady: My little children, I, your heavenly Mother, give you my blessing. I am here to help you to pray together as a family. You must pray everyday. In this way God will help you to convert as a family. Little children, I rejoice to be here with you, but my heart is sad, for many of you do not pray together as a family.

Understand, my little ones that a family that does not know God suffers much from many difficulties. I am sad because you do not trust in my motherly intercession and many of you reject the love and mercy of my Son. Allow me to help you, my children, to become holy families by praying together as a family. Be converted, be converted! Thank you for listening to my message. I love you all dearly.

March 30, 1995 *Satan hates family prayer*

Our Lady: Dear children, today, I invite you to continue to pray with me for the peace that is needed in your family. Know that I, your heavenly Mother, am aware of all the suffering in your family. Pray with me and together we will dissolve the attacks of Satan.

Little children, remember, you cannot say that you belong to me if you do not take the time to pray. Many of you are so busy and you do not have time to pray. How can I help you if you do not pray? Know, my children, that the reason for the darkness in the world is because many do not take the time to pray.

Little children, do not allow Satan to lie to you and tell you that you are too tired to pray. He confuses you with his lies, for he knows that prayer drives all evil away. He hates prayer, and he works very hard to put many distractions in your path to keep you from prayer. He especially hates family prayer, so pray, pray, pray and you will have God's peace in your hearts.

Little children, I love you all and I am constantly praying for you as a family. Learn, too, about my spouse, the Holy Spirit. Many of you do not ask the Holy Spirit to help you to give you the gift of prayer of the heart. Ask for the gifts of the Holy Spirit and He will lead you to God's truth. He will enlighten your heart and help you to pray with love and faith in your heart. Listen to what I am telling you, my children, and trust in my words. Thank you for listening to my message.

March 31, 1995 *Pray*

Our Lady: Pray, pray, pray.

April 1, 1995 *Live and die for Divine Love*

Janie: Good morning, My dear Lord and my dear Blessed Mother.
Our Lady: Good morning, Our dear child, good morning. Sit down and visit with Us.
Janie: Oh dear Lady, there is so much suffering everywhere and I see that it's all due because of the coldness of peoples' hearts. Why don't many people realize it when they hurt other people? Am I making sense, my dear Mother?
Our Lady: Yes, my angel, We understand what you mean. The reason that many have coldness of heart is because they do not pray well. When they pray, they pray for their own benefit and their prayers are not in line with the perfect Will of God. Others never pray. This saddens Our hearts.
Janie: Oh, Blessed Mother, please help me. Sometimes I feel like I am going crazy because I am aware of so much pain in people's hearts. I don't even have to touch people to know their pain. Many times I experience this in stores or wherever I may be. I don't like knowing or experiencing all this. Am I going crazy? What is happening to me? Sometimes I just want to run away and hide.
Our Lady: My precious angel, God has given you this gift to be able to know the pain in many hearts. He wants you to pray for all His children. This gift is not given to everyone. Embrace this gift and pray, pray, pray for all those wounded souls which God puts in your path. You are not going crazy, but you are foolish in love with my Spouse, the Holy Spirit who enlightens your heart.
Janie: Oh, I do love your Spouse, the Holy Spirit, for I know that He is the breath of the Father and the Son and you are One with Him.
Our Lady: My angel, do not ever fear anything, but continue to pray for the gift of Divine Love, which is above all other gifts, for God is love and when you pray for the gift of Divine Love you are uniting your heart with God's Heart which is love.

Janie: I will pray for this gift everyday. My dear and Adorable Savior, do you have anything that I can do for You?
Jesus: Remember, My humble servant, the words of St. Francis to you: **"Divine love is the rule to live and die for."** I, your Jesus of Love and Mercy, know that you are suffering for the plight of the world. I want you to abandon yourself into Our love and pray with Us. We are always with you, always!
Janie: Oh, my Most Adorable Savior, I abandon myself to You. Strip me of everything that keeps me attached to this world, for I want nothing. All I want is to be united to Your Eucharistic Heart.
Jesus: Then it shall be as you ask. Rejoice and continue being a slave to love and allow Our Divine Love and prayer to be the food of your soul. Peace, Our dear child, peace.
Janie: Thank You both, thank You. Pray for my special intention.

April 2, 1995 *Embrace your suffering with joy*

Jesus: My dear humble servant, I am with you. Embrace your great suffering with joy and abandon yourself to Me, your Jesus of Love and Mercy.

April 3, 1995 *Keep your focus on My Eucharistic love*

Janie: My Lord and Savior and my dear Blessed Mother, please pray for me and protect me from all the evil that surrounds me and my family. We have been so much under the attack of Satan.
Jesus: My humble servant, be aware of all the evil around you, but do not allow yourself to become distracted with it. **Keep your focus on My Eucharistic love and arm yourself with strong prayer. This is the weapon that will destroy all his evil tricks.**
Our Lady: My angel, do not be afraid and listen to my Son's words. Do all that He instructs you to do, you shall not regret it. Know that many of my children are under attack, for Satan is angry, for he is aware that he is becoming weaker through the prayers of the faithful. My angel, attend to your grandson. My Son and I will continue Our visit with you. Your little grandson needs your attention. Go to him.

April 4, 1995 *God will reward your hard efforts*

Janie: Dear Lord, and my dear Blessed Mother, please forgive me for waiting so long to visit with You. I have been quite busy with my sick grandchildren. Please help me to prepare for my pilgrimage to Garabandal. I haven't had a chance to even begin to pack. I need spe-

cial graces for this.
Jesus: My humble servant, do not be concerned about your faith journey to these holy special places that you are going to. You will be ready.

You have a generous and giving heart, as you busy yourself with caring for your grandchildren. God, Who knows all hearts, will bless and reward all your hard efforts.
Our Lady: My angel, as you journey to these holy regions, my Son and I will speak to you and give you special messages to help others on this journey. Do not be afraid, but go in peace.
Janie: My Blessed Mother, pray for me, my family and all people.

April 5, 1995 *Reach out with compassion*

Janie: Thank You, My Lord and my All and thank you my Blessed Mother, for coming to comfort me.
Jesus: My humble servant, We know that you bear a heavy cross and for this you suffer much, but know for certain that We are with you each step of the way.
Janie: Oh my Adorable Savior, sometimes I am torn up on what to do concerning my family needs. My grandchildren suffer so much, for they are torn between their family situation. My grandchildren need that nurturing love to help them to develop spiritually healthy. My Lord, I try to be here for them and to pray, but in doing so I miss attending Holy Mass, and this is a great suffering for me. Tell me what to do.
Jesus: My humble servant, recall My words that you would suffer much during this Holy Season of Lent. The times when you are in your great suffering and when you feel like you are taking your last breath, know that I, too, felt this way when I was carrying the Cross to Calvary. I was extremely exhausted, My flesh torn open and I bled excessively to the point of death. You, My dear one, are experiencing My Passion in a most extreme manner. It is My Father's Will that you suffer this way.

As for you missing Holy Mass because you are in charge of caring for your grandchildren who are ill, do not worry. We are with you right where you are. I, too, love your grandchildren, and it please Me that you are charitable. You abandon yourself to My love when you reach out to others with compassion and love.
Our Lady: My precious angel, know that We love you and that We bless all your hard efforts. Your family will receive many special graces and blessings as you go on your pilgrimage. You, too, will be blessed for your obedience to go against your own will. My angel, remember, holy obedience is a first class virtue and when you abandon yourself to

holy obedience, the graces and blessings given to you and your family are without limit.
Jesus: My humble servant, embrace your suffering with joy and know that Our hearts are your sure refuge and the path that will lead you to Heaven. Peace, peace.
Janie: My Lord and my All and my dear Lady, it will be as You say. I abandon myself to the Most Holy Will of God. I love You both.
Jesus: We love you.

April 6, 1995 *Unite your prayers with my children in Medjugorje*

Our Lady: Dear children, today, I invite you as a family to continue to persevere in your prayers. God wants to bless you and to help you to understand the importance of loving and forgiving one another, but He cannot do this if you do not pray together.

Little children, do not be fearful and weak when crises come your way, but stand steadfast in your prayers. Satan is trying very hard to destroy your faith and to take God's peace away from your hearts. Know that I am truly with each one of you in everything, and that I protect you through my motherly mantle.

Pray with your heavenly Mother for all those who are so far away from God's love. Again I tell you to be strong in your sufferings and crises and always to have the Holy Rosary as your weapon. Everyday, pray one Creed, seven Our Father's, seven Hail Mary's and seven Glory Be's. Offer these prayers along with your Rosary, for peace, for physical and spiritual suffering. Know that my children in Medjugorje pray these prayers daily for peace. Unite your prayers with them and embrace one another through your prayers.

Little children, I invite you to prepare for Holy Week through your prayers. In this way, you, too, will experience my Son's Resurrection. I give you my motherly blessing. Thank you for listening to my message.

April 8, 1995 *The Upper Room*

Janie: *This morning I woke up at 5:45 a.m. I got ready and my husband took me to the airport. I checked in about 7:00 a.m., then I went to get coffee and a muffin. I began my morning prayers and prayed for one hour and forty five minutes. I got to my gate and called a special friend. We talked and said our good-byes. I am aboard the plane headed for Houston, Tx. I am very tired, but the plane is not too full. I will* *rest in the hearts of My Lord Jesus, and my Holy Mother and St. Joseph, my three dear friends.*

After I had landed in Houston, I sat down and began to pray. I was praying to the Holy Spirit, and as I was praying I found myself in the upper room with Jesus and all His apostles. Jesus was speaking to His apostles.

Jesus: Peace I leave you, My peace I give to you, not as the world gives do I give to you. Let not your hearts be troubled, neither let them be afraid.

Janie: Oh Lord, help me to be like Your apostles, obedient to Your truth. *I looked around the room where they all were sitting, then I found myself back at the cafe at the airport. I saw my guardian angel who was standing right by me.*

April 9, 1995 *Lisbon, Portugal St. Anthony's Birthplace*

Janie: *As I prayed before his crypt, St. Anthony spoke these words to me.*

St. Anthony: Little child, I, St. Anthony, am deeply grateful for your deep love and devotion that you have for me. For this great devotion, God has granted you a special favor to come here to my birthplace. Your novena will be fulfilled.

Janie: *Then little Jesus spoke.*

Jesus: My little servant, I, Jesus, will continue to visit with you until December 25, 1995. This is a gift to you for all your suffering for love of My Bride the Church, and My people.

April 9, 1995 *Santarem Site of a Eucharistic Miracle*

Jesus: Have no worry, for I, your Eucharistic Savior, know of your weariness. Abandon yourself to Me and I will give you rest and will refresh you.

Janie: *I was blessed with the Holy Eucharist and I immediately recovered from everything that I was feeling. Praised be the Name of the Most High God.*

April 10, 1995 *Fatima Site of Apparition of St. Michael*

St. Michael: Behold, this ground that you stand on is holy ground. Take this water and drink it, for this is water that will help to purify your soul.

Many who drink of this water will be converted, many will be physically healed. Behold, believe what I am telling you and let it penetrate your heart.

April 10, 1995 *Fatima Site of Apparition of Our Lady*

Our Lady: Come, my children, come to your heavenly Mother. Let me lead you to my Son, Jesus.
Janie: *She was smiling at the pilgrims.*

April 10, 1995 *Fatima Site where St. Michael gave Lucia the Eucharist*

St. Michael: Behold your Savior in the Holy Eucharist. Love Him Who died for love of you. Embrace Him in the Holy Eucharist. He wants to give you Himself with all His love and mercy.
Janie: *I saw the host in the Angel's hand come alive, a real Host.*
St. Michael: Behold your Savior and love Him.

April 10, 1995 *Fatima Words from St. Michael*

St. Michael: Behold, I, St. Michael, come to you here in Fatima to tell you that all this area is holy ground, for Lucia, Jacinta and Francisco have walked these grounds. This is a place of prayer and reverence.

Embrace and show God your gratitude for giving you the grace to be here. All who come receive a multitude of graces. Behold, I, St. Michael, have spoken. Share this with others. It is important that God wants to heal all His people, but He cannot if people do not have faith and they do not pray.

April 10, 1995 *Fatima Words from Jacinta and Francisco*

Janie: *While I was praying at the site where Jacinta is buried, I went to Jacinta first, then to Francisco. As I prayed, I saw both children standing in front of me and Francisco said these words to me.*
Francisco: Our little sister, we have heard your prayers and we will intercede for you. Everyday, consecrate yourself and your family to the Immaculate Heart of Mary and she will lead you to Jesus. Live Holy Mass everyday and pray your Rosary, and you will truly belong to Our Lady and to her Son.
Janie: *They both smiled and then Jacinta spoke.*
Jacinta: Pray for families everywhere.

April 10, 1995 *Fatima* Chapel of the Sacred Family

Janie: *I went to the Chapel of the Sacred Family for Mass. The Holy Family was present to me.*
Jesus: Pray, My little humble servant, and bring all families to Us. We will help all families that desire holiness in their lives. You have Our promise.

April 10, 1995 *Fatima* Apparition Chapel

Our Lady: My precious angel, live Holy Mass everyday and be transformed by the Holy Eucharist. Receive my Son everyday, and your life will become Eucharistic. My angel, you have come to know through your prayers that my Son is the Way, the Truth and the Light. He gives His light to a world walking in darkness and His mercy is unlimited.

Imitate the lives of the children, Lucia, Jacinta and Francisco, and you will continue to desire purity and holiness in your heart. Holy Mass is the ultimate prayer and the Holy Rosary helps to dissolve the works of Satan. Live my words and allow them to be inscribed in your heart and soul.

April 10, 1995 *Fatima* Praying the Way of the Cross

First Station: *Jesus is condemned to death.*
Jesus: Look at Me, My humble servant. See how I was condemned for love of you. I was innocent and yet the world found Me guilty, guilty, guilty.
Second Station: *Jesus carries His Cross.*
Jesus: I took the sins of the world upon My shoulders. As I was carrying the Cross, I was seeing those souls who would be redeemed and those souls that would refuse to be redeemed through My act of love and mercy. I saw every soul that truly would love Me and those who would hate Me, but I carried My Cross for love of all.
Third Station: *Jesus falls the first time.*
Jesus: As I fell the first time, while I was on the ground I felt the woundedness of many hearts and how through their woundedness many would choose to separate from Me. As I got up, I saw those souls that would be healed through embracing My Cross and suffering.
Fourth Station: *Jesus meets His Mother.*
Jesus: As Our eyes met, I could see the pain and sorrow in My Mother's Heart, but with her sorrowful Heart she told Me, "It's all worth it my Son," and she gave Me strength. Trust in her intercession.

Fifth Station: *Simon helps Jesus carry the Cross.*
Jesus: My Heart was sorrowful as I carried My Cross. I was weak with sorrow to see how many would refuse to be charitable to others and allow them to suffer alone. Simon, though unwillingly, picked up My Cross. In doing this, He was converted and his conversion represents those who will be converted as they embrace My Cross.

Sixth Station: *Veronica wipes the face of Jesus.*
Jesus: Look at Veronica. See the sorrow in her face as she saw Me suffering. Embrace your suffering Savior Who loves you.

Seventh Station: *Jesus falls the second time.*
Jesus: I fall for the second time, for My love for you grows deeper and deeper. Come, help Me to get up again through your love. As you embrace Me when I am down, so too, will I embrace you in your suffering.

Eighth Station: *Jesus consoles the women of Jerusalem.*
Jesus: Look, look at the loving hearts of these women of Jerusalem, how they weep for Me. As I consoled their sorrowful hearts, know that this is how I console you when you are in your most desperate moments.

Ninth Station: *Jesus falls the third time.*
Jesus: Again I fell, for the third time. My whole body was weak as I bled excessively. My flesh was so disfigured from the scourging. I could barely walk for I was to the point of death, but I had to accomplish the Will of My Father through My obedience to carry My Cross to Calvary. You, too, must persevere in doing My Father's Will, no matter how severe your suffering is. Always do the Will of My Father.

Tenth Station: *Jesus is stripped of His garments.*
Jesus: Behold your Savior as you see Him being stripped and treated like a criminal. Know that My being stripped of My garments represents My total abandonment to My Father. Abandon yourself and imitate your Savior, and be stripped of all that stands between you and My Father.

Eleventh Station: *Jesus is nailed to the Cross.*
Jesus: Behold your suffering and dying Savior. Abandon yourself to Me and embrace Me as I am nailed to the Cross. Feel the piercing pain that I am feeling in every fiber of My being. Embrace your Cross with joy in your heart, for only through suffering will you know perfect joy.

Twelfth Station: *Jesus dies on the Cross.*
Jesus: Behold your Savior Who has died for love of you. Pray that you may also learn to die to yourself for love of Me, so that I may truly live in you and you in Me. Be one with Me as I am One with the Father and the Father is One in Me. You will only experience My Resurrection when you die to yourself completely. Then I will come and dwell and nest in your heart.

Thirteenth Station: *Jesus is taken down from the Cross.*
Jesus: Behold My Mother as she holds her lifeless Son in her sorrowful arms. Embrace My Mother and love her. Comfort her in her sorrow and you will comfort Me.
Fourteenth Station: *Jesus is placed in the tomb.*
Jesus: Behold your Master as I am placed in the tomb. Come and rest with Me. Do not be sad for all this had to happen in order for Me to bring redemption to all of humanity. Remember, do not fear, for I am with you until the end of time.

April 10, 1995 *Fatima Adoration: Healing of the soul*

Jesus: My humble servant, welcome to My Eucharistic Heart. Come and abandon yourself to My Eucharistic Heart. This is Our time together. Allow nothing to distract you from being totally united to Me.

My child, today has been a day filled with special graces and blessings for you. You have been blessed with the visits of little Jacinta and Francisco. St. Michael came to you as well. Recall that I said to you that it was My desire that you come on this journey of faith, for I had much to give you. Now you are beginning to understand more why I, your Jesus of Love and Mercy, called you on this journey.

My child, many come to Fatima hoping that a miracle will happen. Many come with their loved ones who are sick, hoping and praying that they will be cured of their illness. It saddens My Heart that many do not ask for spiritual healing, for healing of the soul is the most important healing of all. When the soul is healed, people are truly converted; yet many do not know this.

My humble servant, share with others My words. I, your Jesus of Love and Mercy, want to heal all people, but it cannot happen unless they desire to leave their evil ways. My child, I know that you are tired from your busy and prayerful day. I, your Jesus of Love and Mercy, extend My deep gratitude to you for coming to spend time with your Eucharistic Savior. I give you My peace and My blessing.

April 10, 1995 *Fatima Chapel of Apparitions*

Janie: *I went to say goodnight to Our Lady before leaving Fatima, for we were leaving early in the morning.*
Our Lady: My child, my child, oh how I love you. I hold you close to my motherly bosom. I am always with you, never forget this. My

angel, thank you for saying 'yes' to my Son, Jesus, Who loves you very much. Goodnight, and I give you my motherly blessing.

April 11, 1995 *Fatima Share these blessings*

Our Lady: My angel, do not be sad that you are leaving Fatima, for my Son and I are with you wherever you go. You have received an abundance of graces and blessings during your stay here. Share these blessings with others.

April 11, 1995 *Coimbra, Portugal The Angel's greeting*

Janie: As we arrived at Coimbra, a huge angel greeted us. He was above the city of Coimbra. Here we had Mass and I gave my granddaughter's letter to one of the sisters to give to Sister Lucia. She said that she would give it to her right away.
The Angel: Greetings! I am a messenger of God. I am here to welcome you to this holy place.

April 12, 1995 *Salamanca, Spain We are here at your side*

Jesus: My humble servant, My Mother and I are here to comfort you in your suffering. Abandon yourself to Our love and allow Our love to be your strength. Good night, Our dear one. We are here at your side.
Our Lady: Rest, my angel, rest.

April 12, 1995 *Leaving Salamanca Angels everywhere*

St. Michael: Behold, see all the multitude of angels that encamp around you as you travel.
Janie: *I see angels all over the fields as we travel.*

April 12, 1995 *Burgos, Spain Repent, repent, repent*

Janie: *I saw the sky open, then I saw a huge throne. I saw a big man sitting on the throne, but I could not see His face. He was dressed in a white robe that came all the way to His feet. Then, I saw Jesus carrying a huge Cross across the sky. Blood was dripping from His head, His hands, and His side, and where He walked He left puddles of blood. Then* I heard these words: "Repent! Repent! Repent!"

April 12, 1995 *Cathedral of Burgos* *Prayer to the Father*

Jesus: My humble servant, abandon yourself to your Eucharistic Savior. Spend quiet time with Me just for a few moments, for I know that you have little time before attending Holy Mass. I want to teach you a prayer. Listen quietly to My words.

Every morning before getting out of your bed, pray this prayer: **My Father, Who are in Heaven, I, a miserable sinner, abandon myself to your mercy. I come in the Name of Your beloved Son, Who is One with You as You are One with Him. My Eternal Father, listen to the cry of this miserable sinner and send me Your Holy Spirit, so that this very day, I may walk in Your light. Pour Your love into my miserable heart so that I may be transformed into Your likeness.**

My Eternal Father, only You know the many crosses that await me. Only You know all the temptations that will come my way. My Father, no harm may come to me if only Your love enfolds me. I recognize that without You I can do nothing, but with You I will accomplish all things.

Take this poor miserable sinner into Your loving arms and let Your love dissolve all my misery. Breathe Your breath into my sinful heart, that I may be strong in You. Let me walk with You, not behind You or in front of You so that I may not separate from Your love.

Take my hand, Eternal Father, today and everyday of my life, so that I may know Your Will, be Your Will and live Your Will. I ask this, my Eternal Father, in the Name of Your Son, who is King and reigns forever and ever. Amen.

April 13, 1995 *Salamanca, Spain* *Remain in the spirit of prayer*

Jesus: My humble servant, We are here to comfort you in your suffering.
Janie: My Lord, do I have a virus?
Jesus: No, My child, you are suffering for My Bride and for the conversion of poor sinners. Know that your suffering will increase, but you have been given the grace to endure your suffering.
Janie: Lord, do you have any words for the people on this pilgrimage? What do You want me to share with them?
Jesus: Share these words. Beloved ones, I, your Jesus of Love and

Mercy, know of your sufferings. Many of you are suffering with physical pain, for you are in poor health. Many of you are physically tired, and some of you are suffering from sleepless nights. Some of you have experienced anger and have been uncharitable to one another.

Trust Me, My beloved ones, for I know all your needs and your concerns. I have called you to this faith journey to bless you and to help you. Know that your family is benefiting from all your prayers and sacrifices. Remain in the spirit of prayer, and love one another. In doing this, you will love Me and My Mother. A multitude of angels encamp around you as you continue on your faith journey.
Our Lady: Tell my children to offer all their prayers and sacrifices for love and peace in their families and throughout the world.

April 13, 1995 *Garabandal, Spain* Site of Apparition of St. Michael

St. Michael: Behold, daughter of the Most High God. Pray and make reparation for poor sinners. The world is in need of much repentance and time is short. Those souls that pray and repent, they will be safe. Those who refuse will condemn themselves. The justice of God will come like a thief in the night. Repent before it's too late!

April 13, 1995 *Garabandal, Spain* Site of First Apparition of Our Lady

Our Lady: I, Mother of the True God, welcome all my children who come with faith in their hearts. I invite all my children to unite their prayers with their heavenly Mother for the conversion of all my children everywhere, and for peace in the world.

April 13, 1995 *Garabandal, Spain* Holy Thursday

Janie: *I was with some friends on the mountain of Garabandal and we had been there praying all day. We were to meet some people, a group from another bus, to go back to our hotel because we did not want to leave early. We were on the way to meet with our friends, but we decided to stop first at the pine trees where Our Lady had appeared to the children of Garabandal. This is what took place.*

I was praying there at the pine tree, looking at the picture of Our Lady. I was praying and asking her to help the people on the mountain who had come from so far away. I was also praying for some special intentions for my family. Then, suddenly, Our Lady was there. I don't recall what happened around me, but Our Lady greeted me. She was very happy and we said a prayer together, and then she began to share the following words with me.

Our Lady: My dear child, I am so happy to see all my children coming to visit here on this mountain where I appeared many years ago. It brings so much joy to my Sorrowful and Immaculate Heart to hear all the prayers of my children gathered here. My children have journeyed to this mountain from all four corners of the world. Oh, what faith they have in their hearts. I wish to express my deep gratitude to everyone here today and to tell them how much I love each one.

My dear child, share with all my children that God has truly blessed them for the great act of faith that they demonstrated in coming here. God will not disappoint them. He will give to them what they need for their sanctification. He will bless all their personal intentions as well as the intentions of their loved ones.

My children must know that this is a holy place and that by coming here, they receive extraordinary graces and blessings. Share with them to dismiss all their fears and anxieties. Share with them that I am with them wherever they may be, and to know for certain I hold them all dear to my Immaculate Heart. Oh, what joy I have in my heart to see all my children praying together with such fervor! I give my motherly blessing to all.

April 13, 1995 *Garabandal, Spain* *The greatest miracle*

Jesus: Beloved ones, rejoice on this glorious and holy day. Today is the birth of the priesthood, when I, Jesus, instituted the Holy Eucharist when I was with My apostles. I offered Myself as ransom for the redemption of all humanity. I died so that you may have life and have it more abundantly.

Beloved ones, know that the greatest miracle is the miracle of the Holy Eucharist. This is the greatest act of love and mercy for the world. I, your Jesus of Love and Mercy, chose to remain with you, present in the Holy Eucharist so that you may be reconciled back to My Father. Pray to God with all your might so that you may be transformed by My Body and My Blood and become Eucharistic. In doing this, you will be truly united to My Eucharistic Heart, and you will demonstrate your love for Me, your Jesus of Love and Mercy.

Beloved ones, be people of love and faith and do not doubt in My love and mercy. Many of you came to see a great miracle. Know that the miracle is the faith that you demonstrated in journeying to this holy place where My Holy Mother appeared. Many of you have overcome many sufferings and sacrifices just to be here. You came to receive a special healing. You came representing your loved ones. Abandon yourselves to My love and mercy and to the Sorrowful and Immaculate Heart of My Mother. Know that it is for your own sake that she has remained with you, to help you to decide for conversion!

Beloved ones, the world is in need of repentance. This is the reason for the apparitions throughout the world. Many miracles are occurring in many parts of the world. I tell you truly, the greatest miracle is the Holy Eucharist. Never forget this, beloved. Embrace your Sorrowful Mother and know that she is praying with each one of you. Through her prayers, many of you will receive spiritual healings and physical healings, for you are walking on holy ground. The miracle will be in your heart and soul. Abandon yourself and trust in My love and mercy, for I know all your needs.

April 14, 1995 *Loyola Monastery St. Ignatius' presence*

Janie: *Today as we visited the monastery where St. Ignatius lived, I could feel his presence. I was so thankful to God for doing this for me. I could feel all his prayers and his love that he had while he was alive.*

April 15, 1995 *Lourdes, France Rejoice in My glorious Resurrection*

Jesus: My dear child, welcome to My Eucharistic Heart. I, your Jesus, rejoice in seeing you here visiting the One Who loves you more than anyone else. You come to keep Me company. You come with a pure and joyful heart for you have been forgiven for all your sins. Always be purified through the sacrament of Reconciliation. In this way, you will truly be united to Me and to My Mother.

My humble servant, you have received many graces and blessings as you continue in your faith journey. You have visited many holy places where My beloved Mother has appeared. Today, you are here in Lourdes, a most holy place. You have been granted your request by My Mother. Always remember this moment as long as you live. Love My Mother who loves you, and do whatever she asks of you and you will truly be doing My Father's Will. I, your Eucharistic Savior, love you. Live in My love and share My love with others.

Janie: Dear Lord, do you have words for the people on this pilgrimage?
Jesus: These are My words. Beloved ones, I, your Risen Savior, invite you to rejoice in My glorious Resurrection when I am crowned as King. During these last forty days you have prayed and offered many sacrifices. You have journeyed in My Sorrowful Passion. Now, beloved ones, rejoice in My Resurrection and allow My Resurrection to penetrate your hearts.

Take My love and share it with everyone you meet. Love and embrace your risen King Who has died and risen for love of you. Be loving, be compassionate, forgive so that you may be forgiven. Be charitable and represent your risen Christ and King through your love. Beloved ones, remember, I am the Way. Only through Me will you obtain salvation. Come to your risen Savior and embrace Him, Who loves you with immense love.

April 16, 1995 *Lourdes, France* *Easter Sunday-The crown of obedience*

Jesus: My dear humble servant, welcome to My Eucharistic Heart. Come and embrace your risen Savior. Rejoice with all the angels and saints as I am crowned with the crown of obedience for having fulfilled My Father's plan, to die and resurrect for the salvation of the world. Always live My glorious Resurrection and allow nothing to separate you from My love.

My child, I wish to extend My deep gratitude for the obedience that you have demonstrated by coming on this faith journey. You have embraced the virtue of obedience with your heart. In doing this, you have allowed Me to pour My love and mercy into your heart. Never separate from My love and you will know that I always keep my promises.

I, your risen Savior, promised you much during this faith journey and you have received much. Live always in my love and allow My love to transform you into My reflection. You wonder if this can be done. I, your risen Savior, give you My solemn word that if you live in My love you will be My reflection. Trust Me and listen with your heart to every word that I speak to you. I, your risen Savior, have much more to give you, so much more.

April 16, 1995 *Lourdes, France* *Prayer gives light to the heart*

Janie: *On Easter morning, Our Lady asked me to go to the grotto to have my visit with her. I arrived there with some friends just before the*

Become Eucharistic

candle light procession. I lit my candle and then I waited there for Our Lady and then she came. St. Bernadette was also present.
Our Lady: My dear child, I your heavenly Mother, called you to come here to this holy place where I appeared to St. Bernadette. I wish to extend my deep gratitude for your 'yes' to my Son to coming on this faith journey. Pray, my child, pray much in reparation for sinners. There is so much darkness in many hearts because they do not pray.

My child, look at the light of the candle that you are holding in your hands. Just as this light gives light to darkness, prayer gives light to the heart. Prayer is the key to the light that illuminates the heart. Pray always, my child, so that your heart may shine brighter than the sun. Prayer helps to change sinful hearts. Pray, do much penance for those souls walking in darkness.
St. Bernadette: Do all that our Mother is asking of you. I will intercede for you always.

April 17, 1995 *Montserratt, Spain* Be a vessel of prayer

Our Lady: My dear child, greetings to you. My child, you are tired from your faith journey. You have suffered from having the food that was unsatisfying to you. Know, my child, this was a great sacrifice. Pray and do means of mortification for the conversion of poor sinners. Pray always, for there is so much need for prayer.
Jesus: My humble servant, be a vessel of prayer and offer your prayers and penance in reparation for the world. We give you Our blessing. Sleep now. We bless your journey back home. We will be with you.

April 18, 1995 *Leaving Montserratt, Spain* Obedience is the key

Our Lady: My dear child, know that We are here to bless you. We will be with you as you travel to your destination. Again We ask you to pray, do penance and mortification in reparation for sinners, so that through your obedience to embrace others through your prayers and sacrifices they will be converted.
Jesus: My humble servant, We give you Our blessings and remember, We are with you each step of the way. Be a vessel of love and prayer.

April 18, 1995 *Aboard the plane to the U.S.*

Janie: *I have been suffering today right after leaving the monastery. I have been in prayer all this time. When we boarded to go to the U.S., I felt like I was going to faint. I knew that I was suffering for the Lord. I* *couldn't eat a thing and I asked the Lord to help me to sleep and He did.*

I was aware of the noise on the plane so I was semi-awake. I kept praying the Lord's prayer over and over, but I heard an interior voice say to me, "You have been praying much, now be silent and rest." I fell asleep, but was still aware of all the noise. As I was waking up I heard Our Lady's voice.

Our Lady: You are suffering for the desecration of my Son in the Holy Eucharist. You are suffering for the ingratitude given to Him through the lack of reverence when souls receive Him in the Holy Eucharist.

Janie: *Then I heard Our Lord's voice.*

Jesus: Look at the way they receive Me with their souls so impure filled with sinfulness. It hurts Me to see how My brother priests do not take the time to teach the flock that has been entrusted to them about the sacredness of the Holy Eucharist.

Janie: Lord, I submit myself to You. Send any suffering my way in any manifestation in which You choose, so that I may console You in a small way. *Saying this, I woke up and I was not suffering anymore. Praise be to My Lord for all His goodness and mercy. Amen.*

April 27, 1995 *We are God's family*

Our Lady: Dear children, today, I invite you to continue to live my messages which I am giving you as a family. I want you to understand in your heart how important your family is to God. He created you so that you could be His family, and to love one another as He loves you. He wants you to be witnesses of the Gospel and to live good lives, trusting Him in everything you do as a family.

Little children, God has granted me to come to you as a family, and to help you to become holy families. He has given you holy instructions through St. Joseph to bring you closer as a family. I have come to you as a compassionate and loving Mother to help you to obtain holiness. Open your hearts to God's love and mercy.

Little children, you must help me through your prayers to draw families that are living in darkness to the Sacred Heart of my Son. Pray and help your heavenly Mother to dissolve the violence in the family.

Help me to dissolve all the divorces that Satan uses to destroy the family. Help me to put an end to the horrible evil of abortion, adultery, drug abuse, homosexuality and the wars that exist in many parts of the world.

Become Eucharistic

My children, there is so much sinfulness in the families all over the world. Many husbands and wives are leading their children to condemnation because of their sinful lives. Families must turn from their sins and be reconciled back to my Son before it's too late!

Pray for all my priests who have turned against my Son and have abandoned Him. God will bring His justice to all these priests who are leading many to perdition. Little children, do not be frightened by all that I am sharing with you. I only wish to present the condition of the world in all its sinfulness. Pray with me, do penance in reparation for your family, my beloved priests and all the world. Remember, the Rosary is your weapon. Let it always be in your hands so that you will disarm Satan. I give you my motherly blessing. Thank you for listening to my message.

April 28, 1995 *Dallas, Texas* Hearts infected with sin

Jesus: My child, I, your Jesus of Love and Mercy, come to you and to the world as your loving Savior. I want to heal all of those souls that have a desire to be healed. Know that in order for Me to heal My people, they must be sorry for all their sins. You see, My child, many souls desire to be healed but they do not repent. How can I heal them if their hearts are infected with sin? Look at all those souls who are condemning themselves because they refuse to repent.
Janie: *I saw hell and many souls were falling into these great flames of fire.*
Jesus: My child, tell My people to repent from their sins truly from their hearts and I will heal them.
Our Lady: Listen to the words of my Son and convey this message.

April 29, 1995 *Dallas, Texas* Healing the broken-hearted

Jesus: My sweet child, oh, how you console My Eucharistic Heart when you embrace My love. You console Me when I hear you tell Me, "My Jesus, I trust You with all my heart." When I hear these words, I immediately consume you with My love and mercy. Little child of Mine, never stop telling Me how much you put your trust in Me. You see, it is those souls that wound my Heart the most who do not trust. Oh, how they wound their Eucharistic Savior.

Know, My child, that My love and mercy is without limit. I want to heal all who come to Me. I will not turn anyone away. I will pour My love and mercy into every heart that comes to Me with a repentant and sorrowful heart. I, your Eucharistic Savior, give you My solemn word I will turn no one away. I want to heal every broken heart. I yearn to be loved

by all My people.
Our Lady: My little angel, convey this message to all my children. Tell them to embrace my Son Who loves them with immense love.

May 2, 1995 *You are a child of the Eternal One*

Jesus: My wretched servant, suffer for love of Me. Embrace all the rejection imposed on you by those whom you love. Embrace all the loneliness that surrounds you, all the coldness of hearts. Abandon yourself to My love and allow My love to be your strength. Do not be overcome by all the temptations that Satan crowds your mind with. Do not entertain such wicked thoughts, for these are evil temptations from the world of darkness.

You belong to the light, for you are a child of the Eternal One. No darkness will overcome you unless you permit it to happen. Being a child of the Eternal One gives you such an inheritance of special graces and blessings to conquer anything that is trying to destroy your love for others. I love you, hear My words, I love you. I am with you and My grace is enough for you. Trust Me, your Eucharistic Savior.

May 3, 1995 *Adoration: I am the Way to the Kingdom of My Father*

Jesus: My child, welcome to My Eucharistic Heart. Thank you for coming to visit with Me. During this time you will have the honor of visiting with My Mother as well, for she has much to share with you. Abandon yourself to Our Hearts which are One with the Father.
Janie: Please, my Adorable and Eucharistic Savior, teach me to lead a holy life. Help me to only be focused on You. I desire to be Your reflection with each breath that I take.
Jesus: To lead a holy life you must live a good life. You must never point a finger of accusation at anyone. You must not condemn, you must forgive, you must love unconditionally, you must be charitable to everyone. You must feed the hungry, clothe the naked, visit the sick, the imprisoned and give shelter to the homeless.

You must live the Gospel, but to live the Gospel you must read Holy Scripture. Many have abandoned Holy Scripture, and many who read Holy Scripture do not live it. **My child, in order to do all the things which I mention to you, you must pray unceasingly. Your life must be transformed by prayer. You must do much penance and fasting for your own heart to be transformed. You must embrace My Cross with joy in your heart.**

Janie: Help me to understand more clearly.
Jesus: My child, come to Me everyday and eat of My Body and drink of My Blood. Allow yourself to be transformed through eating My Body and drinking of My Blood and become Eucharistic, for only through Me and the prayers of My Mother will you obtain holiness in your life. I am the Way to the Kingdom of My Father. I am the Light that came from Heaven to give light to a world walking in darkness. Do everything which I have shared with you, and you will be united to the Two Hearts which are One with the Father. Now, My Mother will speak with you.
Our Lady: My precious angel, how you bring joy to your heavenly Mother when you ask only for graces and blessings that will help you to grow in holiness and purity of heart. This is what I desire for all my children all over the world. I want to take all my children to Heaven, though it saddens my heart for many do not want to be good and live good lives.

Many of my children believe that they can live a life of sin and still go to Heaven. Oh, how they will suffer when they are judged before the Divine Judge. Pray, my angel, with your heavenly Mother for all my children walking in darkness. Pray with me for their conversion before it's too late! Satan is taking many to hell because they have refused the love and mercy of my Son.

Janie: Oh, my Dear Holy Mother, help me to truly belong to you and to bring my family closer to you and your Son by my love and example. Help me to pray from the heart and to truly fast, please!
Our Lady: My precious angel, I will help you for the desires in your heart are pleasing to God. Now, my Son and I will give you Our blessing. We bless you in the Name of the Father, the Son and the Holy Spirit. Amen. Go in my Son's peace and in Our love.

May 4, 1995 *Never grow tired of prayer*

Our Lady: Dear children, today, I invite you as a family to pray with your heavenly Mother for my special intentions for world peace. I need your family prayers so that together we will help those souls that continue to walk in darkness. Little children, never grow tired of prayer, for it is only through praying that you will discover God. Each day, spend quiet time with God away from all other distractions. Come to know God more and more by allowing Him to speak to your heart.

Little children, many of you have been so good in living my messages and praying your family Rosary, but some of you have

stopped praying as a family; this saddens my heart. Know that family prayer is powerful and that it helps to protect you as a family and drive all evil out. Many temptations and dangers are dissolved by your family prayer.

Know, my precious ones, that the Holy Family is present with many angels when you gather for your family prayer. Pray together everyday and God will bless all your family efforts, and He will help you through all your suffering and difficulties. I give you my motherly blessing. Thank you for listening to my message.

May 5, 1995 *Adoration: this time is Ours alone*

Jesus: My humble servant, welcome to My Eucharistic Heart. Thank you for coming to spend time with Me, for I know how tired you are from all your responsibilities to your family. Abandon yourself to My love for this time is Ours alone. Do not permit any distraction to enter your mind. I want your complete attention.
Janie: My Lord, whatever you ask of me I will do. By the way, thank St. Theresa for the beautiful rose. I really appreciated her quick response.
Jesus: My little nothing, it pleases Me when you trust in the intercession of the saints. Through their intercession you will obtain many favors and answers to prayers.
Janie: My Jesus, please watch over little Alex, my grandson, and help my son, Marcelino, so that he may take good care of his little son. My son is so young and inexperienced about caring for babies. Watch over both of them and heal my little grandson.
Jesus: My child, do not concern yourself with this matter. I will take care of everything for you. Now, I wish to invite you to sit quietly with Me.

May 8, 1995 *You have all the intercession of Heaven to help you*

Our Lady: Our dear child, you have pleased God through your obedience to respond to what was expected of you as a wife. Praised be God forever and ever.
Our Lord: My child and humble servant, you have pleased your Eucharistic Savior in listening to My beloved brother who loves Me so much. He guided you well and he pointed out your error without hesitation. He humbled himself through his sorrowful tears because you had not listened to the Holy Spirit. My beloved brother was courageous as your Spiritual Director. He knows that Satan was trying to mislead

you and your family. My beloved brother helped you with such gentleness.

My child, you recognized My voice through your Spiritual Director and you immediately repented. This was most pleasing to My Eucharistic Heart. Always rely on My voice through your Spiritual Director and you will have the blessings from My Father for your obedience to your Spiritual Director.

These are My words to your husband and your family. Beloved ones, never give up in times of great adversities, but remain in the spirit of prayer. Never allow Satan to defeat you through his evil attacks. Beloved ones, Heaven has chosen you as a family, both young and old. Your task is to embrace Me and My Mother in one another. Never fear, but always love and forgive one another no matter how great your suffering may be.

My Father has found favor in you as a family to help other troubled families. Many souls will be saved through your family prayers and sufferings. Marriages will be restored and healed, and forgiveness will take place in troubled families. Beloved ones, Satan will not destroy you unless you lose courage and allow him to defeat you. This is why family love and prayer is your weapon against Satan. Together as a family you will defeat him. Remember that My Mother and I are always with each one of you.

Abandon yourself as a family to Our Two United Hearts and draw all your strength from Our love and Our prayers. Yes, beloved ones, My Mother and I pray for you as a family. You have all the intercession of Heaven to help you. Trust, beloved, trust in Us and never doubt Our love for you. Remain a loving family and know that you will be tempted by Satan as a family. Reject all his lies and he will flee from you. Remember your love for Us and for one another. Your prayer is your strength. We give a family blessing.

May 8, 1995 *A special favor*

Janie: *Our Lady had words for me concerning a pilgrimage to Medjugorje, Assisi and Rome.*
Our Lady: My angel, since February you have asked me for a special favor, to return back to Medjugorje before my visits with you would decrease. I have granted you this request. I know that you do not like traveling. Have no worry, We will be with you. God has many blessings

for you and your family. This will be a special time for you. I give you my motherly blessing.

May 9, 1995 *Your writings will live on*

Jesus: Good morning, Our dear child.
Janie: Good morning, my dear Lord and my dear Blessed Mother. *We prayed together and then they talked with me.*
Jesus: My humble servant, it is good to see you joyful once more.
Janie: Thanks be to God for giving me my Spiritual Director to help me through the enlightenment of the Holy Spirit.
Jesus: You have a good Spiritual Director. He is dear to Our Two United Hearts.
Janie: My Adorable Savior, You asked me to write down every conversation that I have with You and Our Blessed Mother because my writings would help others. Do You mean after I leave this world?
Jesus: My humble servant, your writings are already helping others, however, your writings will continue helping families and priests long after you leave this world.
Janie: Oh Jesus, I always wanted to be a writer and even as a child I knew that I would write a book about my life. Do You remember this about me?
Jesus: Yes, My humble servant, I remember. Your heart was given the knowing that you would one day write these conversations that you have with us, but you couldn't understand it in your mind.
Janie: Blessed Mother, I have always felt that simplicity meant that one is dumb and that to be humble meant to be ignorant.
Our Lady: My angel, simplicity and humility are characteristics noticed in the lives of all the saints while they existed in the world. These are two great virtues and you have these virtues.
Janie: I guess I should be happy, but I really don't understand fully what you are saying in my heart. I don't believe that I am simple or humble, but if you say it then it must be true.
Our Lady: Be at peace, my angel, and embrace what my Son and I speak to you.
Jesus: My humble servant, I ask that you pray and embrace all my brother priests who suffer for love of Me. Please remember them in all your prayers. Pray for all the religious communities that are obedient to My Vicar on earth, for they, too, suffer for love of Me.
Janie: I will pray and offer my sacrifices for Your special intentions for the Church. Do you have any special intentions Blessed Mother?
Our Lady: Pray for my Son's special intentions and for all my children throughout the world.

Become Eucharistic

Jesus: We bless you and your family to help you to live God's Most Holy Will.

May 9, 1995 *Adoration: let Me speak words of Divine Love*

Jesus: My child, welcome to My Eucharistic Heart. I delight in your coming to console Me by visiting Me. I welcome you with all the yearning of My Sacred Heart. Come and let Me speak words of Divine Love into every fiber of your being. This time is Ours.

My child, I am so grateful that you believe in My Eucharistic Presence and that you come and embrace Me, just by being here. Your being here is a proof of your love for Me. While you are here adoring Me, I shall clothe you with a robe of glory. I shall pour into your soul graces and mercy. I shall bathe your soul with My Eucharistic love.

My child, let Me demonstrate all my appreciation to you for taking time for Me, by increasing Our union together with a deeper relationship in My Eucharistic love. I love you, My child, I love you. Thank you for having spent time with your Eucharistic Savior.

May 9, 1995 *The Importance of Eucharistic Adoration*

Janie: *This vision was shown to me by Jesus for me to understand the importance of having Eucharistic Adoration. I saw this vision during Eucharistic Adoration.*

I saw angels blowing their trumpets announcing my arrival. As I entered Eucharistic Adoration, two angels quickly came and clothed me with a garment of Jesus' glory. Although it was a spiritual garment, I could see it in a physical sense.

I saw myself as the angels put a golden cape over my shoulders that went all the way down to my feet. I understood that this garment of Jesus' glory represented the joy in the Sacred and Eucharistic Heart of Jesus for my coming to visit Him.

I saw angels prostrated all around where Jesus was being honored as Eucharistic King. Then, two angels put a golden ring on my left finger and escorted me to where Jesus was being adored and honored by a multitude of angels.

I prostrated myself and then the angels helped me up. They then brought a beautiful chair all covered with golden cloth, and I sat on this chair. In front of me was Jesus, smiling at me and thanking me for coming to spend time with Him.

Two angels stood by Jesus and two angels by me, fanning Us with four big fans with beautiful colors. I could feel the breeze from these fans penetrate my very soul. The angels did this while Jesus and I visited together. The other angels remained prostrated before the feet of Jesus.

This vision reminded me of the story of the prodigal son in the Bible, and how we are all prodigal children who wander away from Our Lord. Yet, God in all His love and mercy remains waiting for us, as did the father of the prodigal son until his return home. In this vision I was embraced by Jesus just as the prodigal son was embraced by his father. Oh, if only everyone could see this vision that I was given the grace to see, every person would run to be with their Eucharistic Savior in Perpetual Adoration.

Jesus: This is how I, your Eucharistic Savior, embrace all who come to be with Me. No matter how many times you come in one day, you are received by Me and the angels in the same way. My humble servant, you were allowed to see this vision so that you would understand the importance of Perpetual Adoration. I, your Jesus, desire Perpetual Adoration in every Church. If only My beloved brother priests would understand its importance and would have Perpetual Adoration, all those entrusted to them would begin to heal as a community.

Janie: *This vision was given so that we could truly understand the True Presence of our Eucharistic Jesus in Perpetual Adoration. May all who read this vision embrace it with their heart and soul. Amen.*

May 12, 1995 *Yearn to be holy through prayer, fasting and sacrifices*

Jesus: My child, welcome to My Eucharistic Heart. Thank you for coming to spend time with Me and to console My Sacred and Eucharistic Heart. This time we spend together is special. Abandon everything to Me. I will listen to all your concerns. Tell Me everything.

Janie: My Lord and my All, You know my sinful heart. Help me to truly become transformed by Your love, so that I may be everything that God wants me to be. This is all I want and yearn for. With Your grace I can handle all other concerns. I know that You are always with me and that is enough for me to know.

Jesus: My humble servant, your response pleases Me so. You are growing in wisdom and your love for sanctity is maturing. The more you pray, the more you grow in My Father's love.

Our Lady: My angel, continue to always yearn to be holy. Nurture this longing through your prayer, fasting and sacrifices. God has so much that He wants to give you.
Janie: Blessed Mother, I am going to the House of Loreto, what a gift. Thank you for this pilgrimage.
Our Lady: My angel, this will be a special time for you. Embrace this pilgrimage with love in your heart.
Janie: I will, I promise I will.
Our Lady: My angel, we know that you have errands to finish before your family returns home. Go with Our blessings. Be gentle and loving with your younger son. He is in much need of prayer, for Satan is trying hard to destroy him. He must be careful in his choices and in his decisions. Tell him to pray, pray, pray and tell him that we want to help him.
Janie: I love You, my Jesus and my Mother.
Our Lady: We love you!

May 13, 1995 *Teach children the importance of Mass and Confession*

Jesus: My humble servant, welcome to My Eucharistic Heart. Thank you so much for helping your son to prepare to make a good Confession. If you only knew how much you console My Eucharistic Heart by helping your son. If only parents would take the time to bring their children to Holy Mass and teach them the importance of a good Confession, their children wouldn't suffer so much.

It saddens My Eucharistic Heart, for so many parents are only seeking their own interests and pleasures. They have forgotten the importance of family prayer. Many parents suffer because they do not come to Holy Mass. In their suffering they turn to worldly pleasures and seek answers in alcohol, drug abuse, adultery, divorce, and many other interests that lead to condemnation. Parents have forgotten the sacrament of Reconciliation, where they are reconciled to My Father and to one another. Pray for families everywhere. Again, thank you for helping your son make a good Confession. My Father is pleased with you and him. I give you both My blessing.

May 14, 1995 *Mother's Day - God answers a Mother's prayer quickly*

Our Lady: Good evening, my angel. Greetings to you and happy Mother's Day! My angel, I know that you have been busy and had much company. You haven't had time alone, but my Son and I waited

until you had a little time alone for Our visit.
Janie: Blessed Mother, I haven't had a very good Mother's Day, but I accomplished much around our home. You said that you would give a Mother's Day message?
Our Lady: Yes, My angel, I have a message for all mothers. Write what I tell you. To all Mothers, I, your heavenly Mother, wish to give you a blessing from God on this day when your loved ones honor you in many special ways. I wish to tell you all how much I love you and how dear you are in God's eyes. You are a delight to God, because you care and give of yourself constantly to your family.

You have very little time to yourself, but you do not mind because you love your family. At times you wish God had made two of you so that you may accomplish all your responsibilities. Know, beloved mothers, that God hears all your prayers, yes, even those unspoken prayers in your heart.

Today, God has showered you with an abundance of graces and blessings to continue being the loving and caring mothers that you are. Know, that I, as your heavenly Mother understand your struggles and family sufferings. I am always interceding for you because I love you very much. My beloved and dear mothers, do not lose courage when things are not going well in your family, but love your family and pray for them.

Know that a mother's love and prayer is so special to God, and He answers your prayer quickly, for He knows that you only want the best for your family. That is what God wants as well. His Heart is united with yours always. Pray always for your family and love them with God's love. Remember mothers, God loves you very much. Happy Mother's Day to all mothers. You are in my prayers. I give you my motherly blessing.
Janie: Thank you, my Most Blessed and Holy Mother, for this holy message of love to mothers everywhere. Happy Mother's Day to you, for this is the month when the Church honors you. I love you. Thank you.
Jesus: My humble servant, I give you and all mothers My blessing as well.
Our Lady: Goodnight, my angel, and Our little workers of the Church and of the family. Thank you, also, for praying for the Holy Souls.

May 16, 1995 *A loving wife and mother*

Our Lady: Our dear angel, We know how tired you are from taking care of your little grandson and from cleaning your house. Do not worry about not being able to spend too much time with Us, for in everything that you do out of love for your family, We are with you in a very special way.

Know Our angel, that God is truly pleased with all your hard efforts. He loves you very much, for you are a good and loving wife and mother. You have much love and patience for your family, and by having love and patience you keep God's holy peace in your family.

Good night Our dear angel. Sleep now little child of the Most High God.
Janie: *Jesus was also present.*

May 17, 1995 *St. Anthony's intercession*

Jesus: Good morning, Our humble servant. We are here to bless your day as we know you are honoring St. Anthony (his death). We will bless your family as well, and pray love and peace in your day. My humble servant, do not be concerned about not being able to go to Holy Mass because of your little grandson. Take him to Mass with you, for the angels will help you with him. You should not miss Holy Mass.
Janie: Thank You, my Adorable Savior. This brings joy to my heart for today is Tuesday, and this is when St. Anthony died. I want to offer my Holy Mass and Confession in his honor. I love him so much.
Jesus: St. Anthony loves you My child, and he will help you through his intercession.
Our Lady: My angel, I want to tell you that the joy that you feel in your heart is Our love for you for all your prayers and sacrifices. You give so much of yourself for the love of my Son. Bless you, my angel, God bless you.
Jesus: Now, We give you Our blessing.

May 18, 1995 *Pure and holy prayers*

Our Lady: Dear children, I, your heavenly Mother, bless each one of you with my love. I am here to help you as a family to live good and holy lives. I am here to teach you how to offer God your gratitude for all His blessings. I am here to teach you how to pray well, so that your prayers may be pure and holy.

Today, little children, I invite you to pray with your heavenly Mother for my Son's Vicar on earth. Love him and embrace him through your prayers. Be obedient to all his teachings. Pray for all my Marian Movement of Priests and for all my beloved priests whose hearts have grown cold towards my Son, Jesus. These beloved priests are leading many towards the road to perdition.

Pray for all parents who reject their children and abandon them for worldly pleasures. These parents are leading their children to perdition. These parents are leading most sinful lives. Pray, please pray for the unconverted world that continues to walk in darkness. My little children, pray everyday with your heavenly Mother who loves you. I intercede for all your intentions. I give you my motherly blessing.

May 23, 1995 *Jesus' prayer to the Father for Janie*

Janie: *Our Lord and Our Lady came to me. I was suffering and I asked Our Lord to pray to the Father for me. I was suffering about a family matter. When I asked Our Lord to pray for me, He began praying right then because my suffering was so great and I was doubting God's love for me.*
Jesus: God My Father, My Mother and I thank you for granting us the favor of coming to your daughter Janie, to teach her of the immense love that you have for her family and families everywhere. Thank You My Father, for allowing My Mother and Me to come to your daughter and give her teachings on the family. Thank You that you chose her and her family to become your vessels, to help the family to become holy families through their love and prayers.

My heavenly Father, Your daughter has suffered much, and she has met with many difficulties, rejections and persecutions in helping to cultivate the hearts of the family. She is strong in her love for You and her perseverance is without limits. She battles with Satan through her prayers and sacrifices. She is drawing many families closer to You, My Father.

Give Your daughter all the protection and graces that she needs in the times when she is weak. She is your beautiful rose that has blossomed in your heavenly garden. Thank You, My Father for listening to Our prayer. Amen.
Janie: *Our Lady was also present.*

May 24, 1995 *Prayer: the key to My Father's Heart*

Janie: Good morning, My Lord and My Lady.
Jesus: Good morning, dear child, how are you this morning? Sit down and write what We tell you.
Janie: *I was kneeling when Jesus was talking with me.* My Precious Lord and Savior, I am so happy this morning, although I haven't had much sleep. I feel very rested and joyful.
Jesus: My humble servant, you woke up praising My Father in Heaven. You united yourself with Heaven through your prayers. My Father quickly responds to a prayerful heart, for He is prayer. As you opened your eyes, you abandoned yourself completely to the intercession of all the saints and angels in Heaven as you gave praise to My Father. This is the reason for your being happy and having much joy in your heart. Remember, a soul that is prayerful always finds peace and joy. This is why My beloved Mother begs her children to pray always, so that they may discover My Father.
Janie: Thank You so much my Adorable Savior, for teaching me the importance of prayer. Does Satan keep us from prayer? How does he do this?
Jesus: **My humble servant, Satan hates prayer, for he knows that through prayer comes peace, forgiveness, love, hope and compassion and many other beautiful virtues. Prayer is the key to My Father's Heart. One who prays unites their soul with My Father, and one's soul begins to transform as one perseveres in prayer.**

Satan knows that prayer helps souls to convert and to draw closer to My Father. He becomes very angry when this happens. He becomes disruptive by telling lies about prayer. He fills the minds by telling those souls that are praying that prayer takes too long, that it's useless to pray, that My Father does not hear their prayers. He plays tricks on their minds by telling them that they are tired, feel sick or that they have other more important things to do. He disrupts through disagreements between the family and numerous other disruptions. He is evil, and he hates My Father and anyone who prays.
Janie: Lord, please help us to pray more. I want to grow in prayer, but sometimes I am not sure that my prayers are strong. What makes prayers strong My Lord?
Jesus: My humble servant, your faith and perseverance strengthens your prayer. Prayer helps you to grow in love as you draw closer to My Heart. Prayer brings you peace, and your faith helps you to trust in your prayers. Perseverance helps to bring about hope in your faith. Do not be concerned, My little humble flower, My Father hears all prayers.

Trust in all your prayers.
Janie: Thank You, My Lord and my All.
Jesus: I give you My blessing.

May 25, 1995 *Begin and end your day with the Holy Spirit*

Jesus: Good morning, Our humble servant. Today is the day when the Church celebrates My Ascension into Heaven. Today is a day of great rejoicing for the people of faith. Today, you begin your faith journey to holy places where My Mother and I will be taking you. Today is the day that I, your Jesus of Love and Mercy, call all people to accept My love and mercy before it's too late!

Today, I, your Eucharistic Savior, repeat the same words that I said to My apostles: Go out, My child, to places near and far and in My Name share My messages about repentance and forgiveness of sins. Tell all families you speak to that they must repent and forgive one another.

I ascended to My Father so that the power of the Holy Spirit would come into all of humanity and inflame their hearts with My Father's love. Today the Holy Spirit lives in many hearts and is enlightening those souls who call upon Him to know and live the truth. My child, always call upon the Holy Spirit to guide you, as a family, closer to Our United Hearts. Begin your day with the Holy Spirit and end your day with the Holy Spirit, and the attacks of Satan will dissolve before your eyes.

As you begin your journey, know that you will be visited by St. Michael, St. Francis, St. Clare and Padre Pio. You will see many visions, and the saints will share important things with you.

You will see St. Joseph. My Mother and I extend Our gratitude for your obedience in saying 'yes' to these places in which you will journey with Us. We give you and your family Our blessings. Know that this faith journey is under Our protection.
Janie: *I saw Jesus clothed in a dazzling white robe. Our Lady did not speak. She stood by her Son, listening to everything that He was sharing with me. They were both so beautiful. Praised be God forever and ever.*

May 26, 1995 *Medjugorje: A faith journey*

Jesus: Greetings, Our humble servant. Today you begin your faith journey. We are here to bless you and to tell you that this faith journey

is under Our protection. You will experience many difficulties and many crosses, but do not be concerned. Dismiss all anxieties, fears and frustrations, for We will be with you throughout this journey. A multitude of angels will encamp around you the entire journey. St. Michael will lead and protect you. We ask that you abandon yourself completely to Our Two United Hearts. You will receive extraordinary graces and blessings to help you to continue to follow the path that We have traced out for you.
Our Lady: My dear angel, know that this message does not only pertain to you, but to all my children who have embarked on this faith journey. We bless everyone on this journey and all their families. Embrace this journey with faith and trust in your heart. We give you Our blessing.

May 26, 1995 *In flight to New York*

Janie: *We are on our way to New York. I am very tired, but I am very grateful that God is with us.* Dear Father, I praise your Most Holy Name. Thank You for loving me so much. Help me to return this love by being obedient in doing Your Holy Will. Lord, I am ignorant, my words are limited, therefore, I need You to teach me, because I belong to You. Amen.

May 27, 1995 *Rome, Italy Adoration: Be humble and forgive*

Jesus: My child, welcome to My Eucharistic Heart. I extend My deep gratitude to you for coming to this holy place where My beloved Vicar lives. I have shared with you how dear he is to My Eucharistic Heart. Embrace him and love him through your prayers. Much suffering awaits him.

My child, pray hard with faith in your heart for all my people on this faith journey. There will be much suffering before this journey is over. The only way to dissolve the attacks of Satan is to remain strong in the spirit of prayer. Many are weary, frustrated from the crosses that you have already endured.

Beware, Satan will attack you when you are weak. He will cause division and anger towards one another that will cause uncharitable attitudes. When these sufferings occur, be humble and forgive one another. In this way, Satan will flee from you. Know, My child, that this faith journey is under Our protection. Pray together, love and forgive one another. Your prayers will dissolve the attacks of Satan.

May 27, 1995 *Medjugorje* An oasis of peace

Janie: *I am going to be visiting Medjugorje for the third time. I am feeling physically sick and discouraged. I feel in my heart joy to be here once again, for I know this will be a powerful time for me. I will spend time alone praying with Our Lord and Our Lady.*
Our Lady: My child, have no worry for I know what's in your heart. Pray with me and my Son while you are here. Be open, for there is much that We want to give you. Welcome back, my child, to this oasis of peace.

May 28, 1995 *Medjugorje* Jesus on the way to Calvary

Janie: *As I took my shoes off to climb Mt. Podbrdo, Our Lord came to me. I looked up and I saw angels standing along the path that I was to climb. This brought tears of joy to my heart. As I began to climb Mt. Podbrdo Our Lord began speaking to me.*
Our Lord: My child, rejoice as you feel the pain of the sharp and pointed rocks under your feet. Offer the pain that you will suffer for My Bride that is in much need of prayer. The apostasy is destroying many of My brother priests. My Bride is in a state of great turmoil. Offer this pain in reparation for families that have no room for Me and My Mother in their lives and who criticize My Mother.

While you climb with your bare feet in the heat, know that this penance you are offering will help My Bride and families everywhere. Many youth are being destroyed by Satan, and this great suffering of yours will help them as well. The Holy Souls will also benefit from your obedience to suffer with joy in your heart.

My child, the higher you climb the more your pain increases. I, too, suffered when I was carrying My Cross to Calvary. I was so weak from loss of blood from the scourging that I begged My Father to help Me to make it to Calvary. While I carried My Cross I felt like fainting. I felt like I was going to die before reaching Calvary. As I approached Calvary, it seemed to me that I wouldn't make it.

You, too, are experiencing these thoughts in your heart this very minute. Rejoice as you reach your destination, for your suffering is helping the world. You are almost there, be strong for love of Me and My Mother.

Now, you are here in this holy area where My Mother appears. Give thanks to My Father that you endured your pain for your love of My

Bride and families. You are very tired from your climb; in an instant the Holy Spirit will refresh you.
Janie: *I was instantly refreshed and I wasn't tired. My feet were not hurt in any way.*
Our Lady: Welcome, my angel, to this holy place. I wish to say thank you for responding to my Son's special intentions. Kneel and pray with your heavenly Mother.
Janie: *We prayed together and then she blessed me. Our Lord also blessed me. I remained on Mt. Podbrdo and prayed in thanksgiving to God for His love and mercy for me and the world.*

May 28, 1995 *Medjugorje* Awaken to my presence

Our Lady: My angel, convey to my children to awaken to my presence in the world, for the Triumph of my Immaculate Heart is about to take place.
Janie: *At these words I felt the earth tremble.*

May 29, 1995 *Medjugorje* The earth trembled

Our Lady: My angel, convey to my children to awaken to my presence in the world, for the Triumph of my Immaculate Heart is about to take place.
Janie: *Again at her words I felt the earth tremble.*

May 29, 1995 *Mt. Krizevac* Give thanks to My Father

Jesus: Our humble servant, We are here to bless each one as you climb this mountain. It brings joy to Our Two United Hearts that you are united in prayer and in love. Know that your prayers are helping your loved ones back home. Continue to pray together, for this world is in much need of prayer. Give thanks to My Father for all the blessings and graces that He is showering you with. We give you Our blessing.

May 30, 1995 *Medjugorje* St. James Church during the Rosary

Our Lady: My child, you have made your Mother very happy in your hard efforts to truly purify your heart and soul.
Janie: *I had gone to Confession and Our Lady was very happy. We make her very happy when we try to keep our souls clean through Confession.*

May 30, 1995 *Medjugorje Our Lady answered my prayers*

Our Lady: Good evening, Our dear angel.
Janie: Good evening My Lord and My Lady.
Jesus: My child, you are sad this evening.
Janie: Yes, My Lord I am kind of sad.
Jesus: Do not worry. My Mother and I are here to comfort you. Open you heart to Our love for you.
Janie: Lord, what is wrong with my hip? Is this a penance?
Jesus: Yes, my child. You will suffer much from this pain. I, your Jesus of Love and Mercy, ask you to offer it for the purification of My Bride, for suffering in the family, for the destruction of the youth, for the souls in Purgatory who suffer and for the massacre of the precious innocent little souls that die a horrible death.
Janie: Jesus, My Lord and my All, I will suffer and do my penance in this way for Your intentions.
Our Lady: My precious angel, tomorrow you will meet with my daughter Vicka. Know that this is my desire. I will be with you and her as you meet in my Son's Name.
Jesus: My humble servant, We are asking much of you, but you have been prepared for this new suffering. There will be much physical pain. At times you will not be able to walk or move around much. This will be hard on your family, to see you suffering, but their love and prayers will help you to suffer with joy in your heart.
Janie: Thank You, my Adorable Savior, for giving me an opportunity to do something small for You. I'll do anything You ask of me.
Our Lady: My precious angel, do not worry. Your guardian angel will help you to get all your writing done. Now, my Son and I give you Our blessing. Goodnight, Our precious angel. We love you.
Janie: Goodnight, my Beloved Savior and heavenly Mother. I love You with all my heart.
Janie: *Tonight I was in my room praying and we heard some bombing. It was late and people came out of their rooms to see what it was. The shots got louder and louder. People were getting scared. I prayed so that Our Lady would intercede for us. I said to her, "Blessed Mother, make them stop. They are really scaring the people."*

I saw in the sky a yellow orange light which appeared like a long comet with a bright tail. It came down from Mt. Krizevac and it disappeared before my eyes. Then the shooting stopped. Our Lady answered my prayers.

May 31, 1995 *Renew living my messages*

Jesus: Our humble servant, We are here to bless you and all those who join you in this faith journey. Know that We cover you with Our protection. Embrace My love and mercy and the intercession of My Mother.

Our humble servant, do not be concerned about your health. Offer it up in reparation for Our special intentions. We will be with you throughout the day. Pray to the Holy Spirit, for His presence is strong with you as you continue this faith journey. Have no worries or anxieties; abandon yourself completely to the power of the Holy Spirit. He shall enlighten you in everything you must do. Embrace the protection of St. Michael and all the army of his angels. Peace, Our dear one, peace. We give you Our blessing.

Our Lady: My child, pray with your heavenly Mother, for I need your prayers for my special intentions. Pray for my beloved Pope and all the Church. Pray for all my children who live here.

Janie: Blessed Mother will the war hurt Medjugorje?

Our Lady: This place is under my protection, and I am here with all my children in a special way. My children here suffer in reparation for the war that exists around them. Unite your prayer with my children here. I have brought you back to this place so that you realize truly in your heart the importance of prayer. Convey the message that I am giving my children here to your country. Tell all my children that they must renew living my messages so that they may realize the importance of God's presence in their lives. This is my message today.

May 31, 1995 *Medjugorje   Prepare well for the feast of Pentecost*

Our Lady: Dear children, today I call you to renew living my messages. Many of you read my messages, but quickly dismiss them from your heart. Many of you grow tired of hearing my message on the importance of praying unceasingly. Little children, how can you understand what I am telling you about conversion if you do not pray? Prayer helps you to discover God. Then, you begin to see the sinful lives that you live. Know that God's plan cannot be realized in you as a family if you do not pray.

I have remained with you as a family for your own sake, to help you to convert and to bring you closer to God. My children, I visited my cousin Elizabeth when she was in need, for she was with child. I stayed with her a few months, then I returned home. In the same way, I have come to visit you as a family, for you are in much need of prayer. I have come to help you to discover God through your prayers, so that you may have His peace in your hearts.

I have remained with you for such a long time, helping you to rediscover the path that my Son has traced out for you, but soon I must leave you to return to Heaven. My children, pray with me to my Spouse, the Holy Spirit, to enlighten your hearts as a family. He will help you also. Everyday, invoke His assistance in your lives. Thank you for listening to my message.

Janie: Blessed Mother, what did you mean when you said that the triumph of your Immaculate Heart was about to take place? Russia has not yet been converted.

Our Lady: My daughter Russia will be converted soon and the Triumph of my Immaculate Heart will reign in many hearts. Time is short my child, time is short. Listen to my words and let them penetrate your heart. Prepare well for the feast of Pentecost through your prayers for on this special day, my Spouse will set many hearts on fire from Heaven. I give you my motherly blessing.

May 31, 1995 *Embrace all that you have received*

Jesus: Our dear child, you have but a few hours left here in this holy place. Embrace all that you have received here and take it back to your family, your church, your community and to wherever We lead you. Take this message of peace, prayer, penance, conversion, fasting, Holy Mass, Holy Scripture and praying the Rosary together as a family. Much has been entrusted to you to help to harvest the hearts of the family. Continue to pray and do much penance in reparation for the Church, especially the beloved Pope. Pray for him always. We give you Our blessing.

Our Lady: My precious angel, thank you for returning to this holy hill where I appeared to my children. Pray for my children here, for they have much work to do, as you have.

You see, my angel, how my Son and I arranged for your meeting with my daughter Vicka. Know that all the messages that you have received which are in the book have Our blessing through the hands of Our daughter Vicka. Embrace the message which We gave you through her. She is dear to Our Two United Hearts. Pray for her and her tireless work. Those souls that read the messages concerning the family and embrace them will be enriched in their lives. We give you Our blessing.

June 1, 1995 *Medjugorje* *Trust in Our perpetual protection*

Jesus: Good morning, Our humble servant. We are here to bless your faith journey as you continue to draw closer to Our Two United Hearts. Do not be sad that you are leaving this holy place, for this holy place lives in your heart. Rejoice and be grateful to My Father for all the special graces and blessings.

Know that as you continue your faith journey, the special graces and blessings that you will receive are without limit. Open your heart and trust in Our perpetual protection. Continue your faith journey without fear or worry. Know for certain that We are with you each step of the way. Be at peace with yourselves.

Our humble servant, it is important that you know that the special graces and blessings that you are receiving are being bestowed on your family and all the special intentions of your dear friends. Remain in the spirit of prayer and you will continue to overcome all the obstacles that Satan will put in your path.
Our Lady: My precious angel, convey this message to all my children. We give you Our blessing.

June 2, 1995 *Rome, Italy* *Pray one Hail Mary and Satan flees*

Jesus: Good morning, Our humble servant. We are here to bless your day and to help you as your faith journey continues.
Our Lady: My precious angel, today continue to offer all your prayers and sufferings for Our special intentions. Convey to my children to continue to be prayerful. In this way Satan will not take their peace away. My children must know that Satan is very angry with them for coming on this faith journey. He will continue to put negative thoughts in their minds. He will distract them with many, many obstacles. My Son and I desire that Our children become habitual prayer warriors. In this way Satan's attacks will be dissolved.

My precious angel, many of my children are concerned with their spiritual journey and how it is affecting their lives. They are concerned with the decisions that they have to make. They are concerned with how they are going to continue to serve God. Share with my children, that God knows all their concerns. All God wants is for my children to trust Him. He will never test them beyond their limits. Tell them to have no worry, for God will help them. He will never abandon them.

Share with my children to pray to the Holy Spirit who is guiding this faith journey in a strong way. Share with them that when Satan puts negative thoughts in their minds, to pray one Hail Mary from their hearts and Satan will flee from their sight.

June 2, 1995 *San Giovanni, Italy I saw my sins*

Janie: *Today we arrived at San Giovanni. We all prepared to go to the church where Padre Pio's tomb is. We got there and began our tour. First we went to the gift shop where we were with the priest who took care of Padre Pio when he was alive. He gave us all a blessing with Padre Pio's glove before he took us down to the tomb.*

I was trying to pay for some items I had purchased and I got left behind. The last I saw of the group was at the tomb. I was in such awe on seeing the tomb, because Jesus had brought me here before in a vision and I had seen this tomb before coming to San Giovanni. I never could get back with my group. I became very angry and frustrated, because I hadn't come all this way just to be left alone. I kept finding myself back at the tomb of Padre Pio and also found myself kneeling and praying in front of his confessional. I was attacked so badly, but I couldn't see it as attack. I continued being angry and Padre Pio spoke to me.

Padre Pio: Why are you allowing Satan to take away your peace? Pray and he will flee from you.

Janie: *I tried to pray but I couldn't concentrate. I was so overcome with anger that I wanted to be as far away from the tomb of Padre Pio as possible. I left the church in tears, because I knew that the group was seeing the area where Padre Pio lived. This made me angrier. As I was walking home, Satan kept telling me to throw away my Rosary and everything that I bought that was about Padre Pio.*

I got to my room and I cried some more. Then I asked God to forgive me and to help me. At this point, Padre Pio was in my room kneeling behind me. Jesus was in front of me. My soul was illuminated, and I saw sins in my soul that caused me to weep bitterly. Jesus and Padre Pio gave me strength and once more I had God's peace. Fr. Andre, who was my spiritual director for this pilgrimage explained to me why this had happened to me.

June 3, 1995 *Rome, Italy We are here to bless your day*

Jesus: Our dear humble servant, We are here to bless your day. Remain

in the spirit of prayer, for We have much to give you.
Janie: *They blessed me and this was the end of my visit.*

June 3, 1995 *Lanciano, Italy* Sanctuary of the Eucharistic Miracle

Jesus: My humble servant, welcome to this Eucharistic Sanctuary where you can see the miracle of My Body and Blood. I, your Eucharistic Savior, have brought you here to witness My love and mercy that I have for all of humanity. This great miracle of My True Presence in Holy Mass has been investigated throughout time. Many of My brother priests continue to doubt in My True Presence in the Holy Eucharist. Oh, how this wounds My Eucharistic Heart.

My humble servant, pray with My Mother and Me, so that the world may come to believe that Holy Mass is a continuation of My Calvary. Offer much penance for this intention that we are begging you to suffer for, so that through your little sacrifices hearts will be open to My True Presence in the Most Holy Eucharist. **Oh, if only hearts would love Me, they would be healed through the sacrifice of Holy Mass. I, your Eucharistic Jesus, have given My Bride many Eucharistic miracles in numerous ways, yet many of My brother priests doubt. They must know that only through eating of My Body and drinking of My Blood will the world be healed.**

The sacrifice of Holy Mass is My True Presence, which only My beloved brother priests have the power to do. Oh, love My brother priests and pray for them, for they need your prayers to overcome the attacks of Satan. My humble servant, I, your Eucharistic Jesus, have entrusted much to you. Please tell My people that the Holy Eucharist is My Real Body and the wine My Real Blood.
Janie: Oh, My Jesus, with all due respect to You, how can anyone believe me if many do not believe in Your Eucharistic miracles?
Jesus: My humble servant, you have experienced My True Presence. Tell them what you have seen during the sacrifice of Holy Mass. Please tell them.
Janie: My Eucharistic Savior, I will do as You say.
Jesus: My humble servant, your little ways are pleasing to Me.

June 3, 1995 *Italy* St. Michael's Cave

St. Michael: Daughter of the Most High God, I, St. Michael the Archangel, greet you and welcome you to this holy place. I, St. Michael, brought you here to strengthen you in your time of suffering and to tell you that you are under my perpetual protection. Behold, little vessel of the Most High God and listen to my words. The world must convert and turn away from their sins. Time is short and for those who do not repent and turn away from their sins, see what will happen to their souls.

Janie: *I saw hell and the many souls that would be condemned.*
St. Michael: I, St. Michael, Chief and Commander of God, command you, little vessel, to do much penance in reparation for the sinfulness in the world. Embrace my words and let them penetrate your heart.
I, St. Michael, consecrated this cave to help all souls who will come and enter this cave with a penitent heart. Many are the saints that have come to visit this holy cave where my presence dwells.

All my army of angels are under my command and they go where I, St. Michael, command them to go. Devotion to the Guardian Angels in the world is most important. These heavenly spirits have but one task, to help souls to obtain holiness and purity of heart. Trust in their intercession. Behold the world in its sinfulness.
Janie: *I saw many sins in the world.*
St. Michael: Little vessel of the Most High God, the world must repent before it's too late! This is a time of great mercy. Embrace this mercy and be converted. I, St. Michael, have spoken all that you need to know for today. I give you my gratitude, little vessel of God, for coming here. He is pleased with your hard efforts

June 4, 1995 Lanciano, Italy *Be open to the Holy Fire of love*

Jesus: Greetings, Our humble servant. We are here to bless you on this special feast day of Pentecost. Open your heart and be filled with the power of the Holy Spirit. Today you will receive many blessings and gifts from the Holy Spirit. Today you will experience the power of the Holy Spirit in an extraordinary way. Prepare with strong prayer and unite your prayer with all the angels and saints. Consecrate yourself to the Holy Spirit and be open to the Holy Fire of Love from above. Know that as you journey to the Holy House of Loreto, there, My Mother will delight your heart with heavenly favors. Pray, and prepare your heart.
Janie: *Our Lady and Jesus gave me Their blessing. Our Lady did not speak. She stood by her Son.*

June 4, 1995 *The blessing of the Holy Family shared through a hug*

Janie: *I prayed with the angels all day as we journeyed to the House of Loreto. As we were going there, I saw many angels in the sky. They*

Become Eucharistic

were all in prayer so I prayed with them.
I have no idea what awaits me. I know I will see the Holy Family. We arrived at the House of Loreto. It was breathtaking, just being in this holy place. I felt so unworthy and yet so grateful. Then I saw the Holy Family before me. They welcomed me. I cried just to see St. Joseph once again.

Our Lady: Our dear angel, we welcome you with Our love to this, Our home. My child, you have such love for the Eucharist that God wishes me to tell you that He is pleased with your love for His Eucharistic Son. He has favored you with two heavenly gifts. He asks that each day you set one hour aside to spend with His Son in Eucharistic Adoration.

During this hour you spend in prayer with my Son, you will unite in prayer, praying to God for the purification of the Church and for the families. You will not see my Son interiorly or in the way that God allows you to see Him. You will only hear Him in your heart. This will take place after His last visit with you. In times when you cannot spend time with Him in Eucharistic Adoration, He will come to you. God has done this for you because of your love for His Son.

St. Joseph: My little one, you see how much God loves you. All your hard efforts are rewarded.
Janie: *I cried to hear him speaking to me once more.*
Our Lady: My angel, the second gift that God has given you is this. Today you will receive a blessing from us as the Holy Family. This blessing will come to you through Our embrace (a hug). You are to share this embrace with all families that God puts in your path. As you share this heavenly embrace with families, We, the Holy Family, will bless those families through you.
Janie: My Lady is this not calling attention to myself?
Our Lady: My angel, you have been chosen by Heaven to be a humble vessel and suffering soul for the family and the Church. God has entrusted you with this responsibility. My child, do not question what God wants to accomplish through you but respond obediently with a loving heart.
Janie: At this point I was embraced by the Holy Family and received a heavenly blessing to share with all families by simply embracing them. I cried with joy to be in the presence of the Holy Family in the House of Loreto. What a gift. I shared this with Fr. Andre.

June 4, 1995 *Assisi, Italy St. Francis' presence*

Janie: *We arrived at Assisi after leaving the House of Loreto. We pre-*

pared for Holy Mass. I saw St. Francis right beside the altar as Fr. Andre was celebrating Holy Mass. I could see all the angels around the altar. I saw the angels taking the petitions up to Heaven. I saw the Crucified Savior, and from His five wounds came rays of light that penetrated the host and wine. Immediately, there was Jesus before us. What a gift! The Holy Spirit was so alive in every heart. Holy Mass was powerful and the presence of the Holy Spirit was very powerful. Everybody was crying and rejoicing. Praised be Jesus. When Fr. Andre was blessing us, St. Francis was kneeling by the altar.

June 5, 1995 *Many doubted my Son*

Janie: *Both Our Lord and Our Lady greeted me.*
Jesus: Our humble servant, We are here to bless your day. We will be with you as you endure your suffering. Spend time in quiet prayer away from all other distractions. Prayer will bring you peace. Stay close to Our Hearts through your prayers.
Our Lady: My angel, your suffering will help many others whose hearts are cold to the love and mercy of my Son. My angel, you will suffer much persecution, for many will not believe that my Son and I are visiting you. Do not allow this to be a distraction. Remember, many doubted my Son and His teachings. Listen to my Son's words and stay close to Our Hearts through your prayers. We give your Our blessing. St. Francis and St. Clare will be united with you as your pray in this holy place.

June 5, 1995 *Assisi, Italy Come, oh sister suffering*

Janie: *I spent all my free time in prayer before the tomb of St. Francis. Here I prayed fifteen Rosaries for the special intentions of Our Lord and Our Lady. There were obstacles in the group that required much prayer. St. Francis spoke to my heart through these five hours that I spent before the Blessed Sacrament.*
St. Francis: My spiritual daughter, it is only through suffering that you will embrace the Cross. Prayer and fasting will help you to welcome your suffering with joy in your heart.
Janie: *St. Francis spoke to me a second time.*
St. Francis: My spiritual daughter, you have been in unceasing prayer for a few hours now. Embrace all suffering that comes your way from Heaven. Your heart and soul blossom like a beautiful heavenly flower as you abandon yourself to your suffering. Say to sister suffering, "Come, oh sister suffering, come, for my heart and soul welcomes you with the love of my Savior."

Janie: *I visited the birthplace of St. Francis and prayed there. I could feel St. Francis' love for His Savior. I was with St. Clare and saw her incorrupt body. This was such a holy time in my life. We celebrated Mass at the crypt (tomb) of St. Francis and I could see him in my heart the entire time. I was so grateful to God for allowing me so holy an opportunity to come and pray in this holy place. Blessed be Our Lord forever and ever. Amen.*

June 6, 1995 *Assisi, Italy* Quiet time in prayer

Jesus: Our humble servant, We are here to bless your day. Again We ask that you spend quiet time in prayer.
Our Lady: My angel, We will be with you. Pray, pray, pray for my special intentions.

June 6, 1995 *Assisi, Italy* St. Mary of the Angels Church

Janie: *I visited the church that St. Francis rebuilt. We had Mass there. I was so thankful to God for everything that He was giving me. I saw the rose bushes which St. Francis threw himself on when he was experiencing a temptation through a distraction of the flesh. These are the only rose bushes in the world without thorns. I also visited a statue of St. Francis that was in the rose garden. This statue has two live doves that are nesting in the hands of St. Francis. This truly is a miracle. Here, St. Francis spoke to me.*
St. Francis: My spiritual daughter, it is the wish of St. Clare and myself that when you return home you build an altar in our honor. We will help you to truly obtain prayer of the heart. At this altar, you will be united with us in your prayers.
Janie: *I thought, my house is so small, where will I have this altar? But, I knew the Holy Spirit would guide me. I did say to both St. Francis and St. Clare,* "I will do this for you, but please help me to find holy pictures of yourselves so that they will hang over this altar." *I went to the gift shop and I found two pictures. I got them and had them blessed. I went to the rose garden where the statue of St. Francis with the two doves was. I touched the pictures to the wall. Then I said these words to St. Francis:* Thank you! My spiritual father, would you bless these pictures? I will climb up to where you are with the doves so that these pictures may touch your hand, but you have to keep everyone from coming in. Otherwise, I won't be able to climb up to where you are. *For about five minutes no one came in. I climbed and touched the pictures to the hands of St. Francis. Praised be God forever and ever. Amen.*

June 7, 1995 *Rome, Italy Empty your heart and soul*

Jesus: Our humble servant, you are on your way back to your country. Allow all the graces and blessings you received in this faith journey to penetrate your heart and soul. We will be with you as your journey to your final destination.
Our Lady: My angel, you have done well during this faith journey. Empty your heart and soul. Allow no other distractions to take you away from Our Hearts. You are dear to Our Hearts. Never forget this, my angel. Fear nothing. We give you Our blessing.

June 7, 1995 *Rome, Italy Through the eyes of Our Lord and Our Lady*

Janie: *We are aboard the plane heading for New York. I am so happy. I discovered areas in my soul that need much prayer and fasting. I saw people through the eyes of Our Lord and Our Lady.*

June 7, 1995 *The journey home*

Janie: *I just left Chicago and I am about to finish my twelfth Rosary. This pilgrimage has required much prayer as just about everyone was attacked by Satan. I am very tired from flying and my mind is numb. I keep praying to Our Lady to intercede for me as I journey home. There has been much turbulence as we head to Houston, Texas. I can't wait to get to Austin. Tomorrow is the prayer meeting and I hope that I won't be experiencing jet lag too badly. I am in God's hands.*

June 8, 1995 *Tools to obtain holiness and purity as a family*

Our Lady: Dear children, today I invite you to pray with your heavenly Mother for my special intentions for all my children in Bosnia. Offer your family Rosaries and prayers so that together we may overcome all the attacks of Satan. Little children, do not grow weary of prayer. Know that through prayer, you remain close to God. Prayer covers you with God's love and protection.

My children, open your hearts and allow my messages to come alive in your hearts. What the world offers you is only temporary, but what God offers you is eternal life. **Live as holy families, praying together everyday. Read Holy Scripture, receive the sacrament of Reconciliation once a month, attend Holy Mass together, pray your family Rosary everyday. Love one another and forgive one another.**

These are your spiritual tools to obtain holiness and purity as a family. These are the tools that will help you to follow the path that my Son has traced out for you. Little children, I want to take you all to Heaven with me, but I cannot if you do not live my messages. I give you my motherly blessing. Thank you for listening to my message.

June 9, 1995 *Continue to offer your suffering*

Jesus: Our humble servant, you are suffering from the results of your faith journey. Continue to offer your suffering in reparation for My Bride and families throughout the world. We give you Our blessings.
anie: Thank You, My Lord and my Blessed Mother, thank You.

June 10, 1997 *My deepest gratitude*

Jesus: Greetings to you, Our humble servant. We are here to bless you and your family.
Janie: Good morning, My Lord and My Lady. Thank You for being here with me. My Lord, I did what You asked of me concerning my (X).
Jesus: My humble servant, I, your merciful Savior, extend My deepest gratitude to you. Know that I was right at your side as you carried out My request. This meeting was under Our protection.
Janie: My Adorable Savior, please forgive me. I have not been able to make it to Mass for two days. My family has missed me and I them. Please forgive me.
Jesus: My humble servant, I know that your family was happy to have you back home. Do not be concerned. We are pleased with all your little sacrifices.
Our Lady: My precious angel, I wish to tell you that my Son and I are most pleased with all that you do to draw others to Our Two United Hearts. Know that We are always at your side, We never leave you. You are dear to Our Hearts. My angel, We will end our visit with you for you have much to do. We give you Our blessing and We bless your family as well. God's peace to you Our dear one.

June 11, 1995 *Offerings for their special intentions*

Our Lord: Our humble servant, continue to offer your suffering for Our special intentions. You have received many graces and blessings during your faith journey. Embrace this time. We give you Our blessing.
Janie: Thank You, My Lord and my dear Blessed Mother.

June 12, 1995 *Little ways are pleasing to God*

Our Lord: Our humble servant, We are here to bless you and to comfort you as you pray your morning prayers. Rejoice Our little one, your little ways are pleasing to God.

Continue to pray for poor sinners for their conversion. We give you Our blessings.
Janie: Thank You so very much, My Lord and My Lady.

June 13, 1995 *Pray the complete Rosary together as family*

Jesus: Good morning, Our humble servant. We are here to bless you and your family. Our dear one, We know that you are not doing well today. We know you are suffering. Know that We will give you the grace to carry out your family responsibilities.
Our Lady: My precious angel, know how grateful We are that your family has committed to praying the complete Rosary in gratitude to their heavenly Mother. What joy this brings to Our Two United Hearts. My sweet angel, know that this is a result of all your prayers and sacrifices for your family's conversion. The tireless hours that you have spent going to Holy Mass, all your numerous Rosaries and everything that you have done has helped draw your family closer to God. You are witnessing the fruits of your labor for your family. We deeply thank you.
Janie: My Lord and My Lady, I am also so happy that we are praying the complete Rosary as a family. I can feel the presence of all of Heaven while we are praying our Rosary. My family has such a good attitude about it. Oh, how blessed we are.
Jesus: Our humble servant, perseverance in prayer brings about an interior change of heart. Continue to pray unceasingly and you will continue to reap much fruit of conversion. Now, We give you Our blessing so that you may rest. Know that We are always at your side.
Our Lady: Peace, my precious angel.

June 14, 1995 *My children will announce it to the world*

Jesus: Good morning, Our humble servant. We are here to bless you and your family.
Janie: Good morning, my Adorable Lord and my most loving Mother. Thank You for blessing our family. Blessed Mother, will any harm come to the village of Medjugorje? I love that place, it is so peaceful. I can really feel your presence there in my heart and soul. No matter

where one goes in the village your presence is everywhere.
Our Lady: My precious angel, have no worry, no harm will come there for I have chosen that place to make my presence known in a special way.
Janie: Blessed Mother, is your time there going to end soon?
Our Lady: My angel, you will know, for my children there will announce it to the world. Pray for them as they continue to carry out all that I am asking them to do for me.
Janie: Will I visit there again?
Our Lady: Do you wish to return back to Medjugorje?
Janie: Yes, but with my family!
Our Lady: Then pray very hard for this intention and I shall pray with you.
Janie: My Beloved Savior, please bless my (X) so that she might listen with her heart to your guidance!
Jesus: My humble servant, continue to pray for her for she is much confused. Love her and let her know that you will always be there for her, no matter how much what she is doing hurts you. She is in need of much love. My Mother and I are praying for her in a special way.
Janie: Please help me today, so that I can maintain my fasting. I have much work to do and You know of my physical suffering.
Jesus: My humble servant, offer all your pain and sufferings of this day for the war in Bosnia and other troubled areas in the world. My Bride is in need of much prayer as many of My beloved brother priests are leading many souls to perdition through their disobedience to follow the teachings of My beloved Vicar. Pray and suffer especially for this intention.
Janie: My Beloved Savior, I will do what You ask of me. Give me the grace to pray lots of Rosaries from the heart. Oh, yes, and please tell St. Francis and St. Clare to pray for me so that I may understand all their writings.
Jesus: My humble servant, I will take your message to the two saints.
Janie: Also give St. Joseph a big hug for me.
Jesus: I will give St. Joseph a big hug for you, My humble servant. We give you Our blessing. Peace to you and your family.
Janie: I love You both very much! Thank You for everything.
Jesus: You are welcome. We love you Our dear one.

June 15, 1995 *My Son, too, was a humble servant*

Jesus: Good morning, Our humble servant. We are here to bless you and your family and all your hard labor for today.
Janie: Good morning, My Lord and My Lady. Thank You for coming

and blessing us. We did have much to do today. Please help us to keep our peace as we work together.
Our Lady: Our dear one, be at peace for you will have many angels encamped around you as you work together.
Janie: Blessed Mother, should we pray our Rosary first, because I feel that we will be too tired to pray the complete Rosary later on.
Our Lady: Praying the Rosary will most certainly give you special graces and blessings. Yes, my angel, it would be wise to pray your Rosary first.
Janie: Blessed Mother, please pray for me for I have had a hard time going to Mass. Please help me to arrange my time wisely. I feel like I am always busy around the house and that I hardly have time for myself. Of course I am always praying no matter what I am doing.
Our Lady: My precious angel, you are called to be a servant to others, especially your family. Know that everything that you do out of love for others pleases God. Sweet little angel, never become discouraged of being a humble servant, my Son was a humble servant. He worked very hard ministering to all people, all His work was out of love to God and for all those He met. Like Him, my angel, you should imitate Him and always pray unceasingly. God has entrusted much to you for He knows that you will be able to manage all that He gives you. All your hard efforts are pleasing to Him.
Janie: My Most Loving Holy Mother, I will do everything that God wants me to do. Thank you for helping me. Beloved Savior, You are quiet.
Jesus: Yes, I am suffering for all my brother priests. Pray for them.
Janie: *I could see tears in His eyes. I prayed for His special intentions. I cried also.*

June 16, 1995 *Fasting on Wednesdays and Fridays*

Jesus: Good evening, Our humble servant. We are here to bless you and your family.

Janie: Good evening, my dear Savior and my dear Mother. Please pray for us (my family), so that we may be able to overcome Satan's attacks. Today was awful. Satan was so active trying to take away our peace.
Jesus: Our humble servant, you are suffering for all the good that you are doing for your family. **Satan is very angry at you for helping your family to pray more. You are fasting on bread and water on Wednesdays and Fridays, the days that my Mother has requested. You are trying very hard to detach from those little things that bring you pleasure.**

Our dear one, you are maturing in wisdom and knowledge. Your focus is on being of service to others beginning with your family through works of charity. Satan hates all that you are doing. This is why he is attacking you and your family. We are with you, have no worry.

Janie: Oh, Jesus, thank You so much for loving me and my family. I wish that I was with You in Heaven so that I wouldn't sin anymore. I hate sin.

Our Lady: Our precious angel, your heart is full of love and you want to live a good life. This is why you suffer when your family is under attack. Your heart wants to love and to share God's joy with others, but sometimes the family forgets to go on being loving especially during suffering. Continue to pray, for prayer dissolves all the attacks of the enemy. Now, Our dear one, my Son and I will give you Our blessing so that you may have enough time to prepare your beloved husband his dinner. We love you Our sweet angel.

Janie: And I love You forever.

June 17, 1995 *Continue praying when Satan distracts you*

Janie: Good morning, My Lord and My Lady.

Jesus: Good morning, Our humble servant. We are here to bless you and your family.

Janie: Oh Jesus, please teach me to pray well. My soul yearns always to be in prayer, but sometimes I become distracted.

Jesus: Our humble servant, Satan will always try to interrupt your prayer through distractions. Do not allow him to distract you when this happens, but continue praying. He will leave you if you persist and do not become discouraged.

Janie: Thank You, My Lord. You're so kind and loving. Help me to live a good life and to be an example to others.

Jesus: Continue to follow the path that I have traced out for you and live My Mother's holy messages. Do this and you shall live a good and holy life.

Our Lady: Our sweet angel, we know of your deep pain in your heart for your (X). You are hurting because of your love for this soul. Do you wish to talk to Us about it?

Janie: Oh My Lord and My Lady, sometimes I am not sure that the things that I do to help others is the best thing for them. Sometimes I just wish that I could be all by myself and this way I wouldn't see people suffering. Right now there is much sorrow in my heart for these people. I just want to pray for myself and for them, for I know that prayer is the only medicine that helps to heal the soul. Thank You both

for asking. I didn't want to bother You with this. You give me so much and I have little or nothing to give You.
Our Lady: Our sweet angel, you do much for Us through all your suffering. Never forget that We are always at your side. Speak to Us freely as you speak to Us when We are visiting you. Our precious angel, you have said 'yes' to be a suffering soul for the conversion of your family and of the world. Your suffering will end when you leave this world. Be at peace and offer all your prayers and sacrifices for Divine Love and peace in the world.
Jesus: Our humble servant, you are most dear to Our hearts. Know that We are with you in all your prayers and sacrifices. We give you Our blessing, Our love and Our peace.
Janie: Oh My Lord and My Lady, I love You so much. Help me to suffer well for God. I love You so, so much. Thank You both. I'll see You tomorrow.
Jesus: We are with you in everything.

June 19, 1995 *Never rely on emotion*

Jesus: Good evening, Our humble servant. We are here to bless you and your family and to bring you Our peace.
Janie: Good evening, My Lord and My Lady. Thank You so much for helping me today through my prayers.
Our Lady: Our precious angel, continue to persevere in your prayers and in your suffering. You are going through a very difficult and painful time. We are with you in a special way.
Janie: Blessed Mother, I want to do the Will of God but my emotions get in my way. This causes me to make poor judgments. Please help me.
Jesus: Our humble servant, never rely on what you are feeling. Rely on divine faith and reason. Recall what we said to you a few days ago concerning trusting in divine faith and reason. Feelings can mislead you in your decisions. Pray to the Holy Spirit for discernment, and you will not go wrong. He will guide you.
Janie: My Dear Lord and my Blessed Mother, I just need Your love and prayers. I will do what You guide me to do. I ask that nothing be taken away as far as my suffering. Let me embrace this suffering both in my heart and soul.
Jesus: Our humble servant, know that your nothingness pleases Us. We give you Our blessing, for We know that you have things to do. Peace, Our dear one, peace.
Janie: Pray for my special intention.
Our Lady: Have no worry, Our dear angel, We will pray for you.

Become Eucharistic

June 20, 1995 *'Our humble servant'*

Janie: Good morning, my Beloved Savior and my beloved Holy Mother. Thank You for being here with me.
Jesus: Good morning, Our humble servant. We are here to bless you and your family and to bring you Our peace.
Janie: Beloved Savior, why do You call me Your humble servant? I don't have an ounce of humility in my entire soul.
Jesus: Our humble servant, you do not recognize humility as We (My Mother and I) know it. You understand it as the world understands it. You are humble and simple and you have a loving and forgiving heart. You recognize yourself as nothing. You believe in your heart that you are the worst sinner in the world. Not many people are able to say this about themselves. You come before Us knowing in your heart your nothingness.

You understand in your heart and soul that without My Father's grace you can do nothing. You want nothing for yourself, your only desire is to please My Father by doing His Holy Will. These are the makings of a humble servant. Now do you understand?
Janie: Yes, but I don't like people telling me that I am humble.
Jesus: This continues to demonstrate your humility.
Our Lady: Our dear angel, I wish to extend my deep gratitude for being committed to praying your Rosary as a family. Last night you gathered your family to finish praying the last part of the Rosary even though you had been working hard on your yard. You, as a family, brought joy to my Immaculate Heart.
Janie: Thank you for saying this. I wanted us to keep our promise to you as a family to pray the complete Rosary on a daily basis.
Our Lady: Our precious angel, you will never comprehend the blessings and graces that you reap by praying the complete Rosary as a family. In doing this, you will obtain holiness and purity of heart as a family. Oh, my Sorrowful and Immaculate Heart yearns with desire for all my children to pray the entire Rosary as a family. Wars would end, family violence would be no more, many evils in hearts would cease only through praying the Rosary as a family.
Janie: Oh, my Adorable Savior and my Most Holy Mother, I desire that this happens as well. I don't understand this in my heart in the way that You know it, but I see the peace and the calmness in my children's hearts.
Jesus: Our humble servant, continue to teach your family the importance of family prayer. Share what We teach on family prayer with all families whose hearts are open to hear this important message; that will

help change their lives.
Janie: Beloved Savior and my Most Holy Mother, today my husband and I meet with the lawyer. We need Your prayers.
Jesus: We will be with you during this meeting. Now, We give you Our blessing to begin your daily duties to your family. Peace to you Our dear one.
Janie: Thank You both. I wish I could stay here with You all day. *They both smiled as they left.*

June 21, 1995 *Special guidance from St. Michael*

Janie: Good afternoon, my dear Lord and my beautiful Holy Mother. Thank You for coming, thank You for loving me so much, thank You, thank You, thank You!
Jesus: Good afternoon, Our humble servant. We are here to bless you and your family and to bring you Our peace. Sit down and prepare to write what We tell you.
Janie: *I was kneeling on the floor when Our Lord said this to me.* Oh dear Jesus, thank You for helping me earlier this morning. I seem to have a dark cloud over me.
Jesus: Our humble servant, you are enduring much suffering for your family's conversion. These are the things which you are experiencing that you don't understand. Today you are fasting for Our special intentions and Satan will try to put many distractions in your path. Remain in a prayerful spirit and he will flee from you.
Our Lady: Our sweet angel, you had requested special guidance from St. Michael while you were in prayer. St. Michael will come to you between the third and fourth hour in this afternoon. Prepare to receive his visit.
Janie: Oh, Blessed Mother, thank you so much for interceding for me for this request. I will prepare.
Jesus: Our humble servant, I, your loving and merciful Savior, ask that you rest after Our visit, that your mind will be clear when St. Michael comes to you.
Janie: Do You mean for me to sleep?
Jesus: Yes, that's what We want you to do. You have been working very hard for several days. You have also endured much suffering. Rest will help you.
Janie: Very well, I will do as You say. I love You both.
Jesus: We love you Our dear one. Peace, Our suffering servant, peace.
Janie: *St. Michael came later this day to give me personal guidance.*

June 22, 1995 *Proclaim the teachings on the family*

Janie: Good morning, My Lord and my beloved Holy Mother.
Jesus: Good morning, Our humble servant.

We are here to bless you and your family and to bless your trip as you go out to give witness on the teaching on the family. Know that the Holy Spirit will be most present with you during this time to enlighten your heart.
Our Lady: Our sweet angel, do not worry about having not slept. We are grateful for all your prayers that you offered during the night.
Jesus: We give you Our blessing to go out and proclaim the teachings on the family to all who will embrace these heavenly messages. Go with Our peace.
Janie: Thank You, My Lord and My Lady.

June 23, 1995 *Half Moon Bay, California* *Take refuge in Our love*

Jesus: Our humble servant, We are here to bless you. Know that We will be with you to help you to prepare for your talks. Have no worry as to what you will share about St. Michael; everything has been inscribed in your heart.
Our Lady: Our precious angel, know that you will touch many souls as you give witness of your love and devotion to St. Michael and the angels. Through your witness, many of my children will foster devotion to St. Michael and all the angels. Abandon yourself to Our Two United Hearts and have no worry.
Our Lord: Our humble servant, take refuge in Our love. We give you Our blessing.
Janie: Thank You My Lord and my Holy Mother.

June 24, 1995 *Half Moon Bay, California* *Your simplicity brings joy*

Jesus: Our humble servant, We are here to bless you and to embrace you with Our love. Today, be open to all that the Holy Spirit gives you. He will infuse your heart with Divine Love as you witness to Our people about your faith journey. You will touch many hearts as you share some of your most painful experiences regarding your family.
Janie: My Lord, I trust in Your and my Holy Mother. I will abandon myself to the Holy Spirit for divine guidance. Come, oh Holy Spirit of God, infuse my heart and soul with divine wisdom and discernment.
Our Lady: My precious angel, you are most dear to Our Hearts. We will unite Our prayers with your prayers. We will remain with you

throughout your time here to give you strength.
Janie: Thank You both. I love You with all my heart.
Jesus: We love you, Our dear little one. Your simplicity brings joy to Our hearts. We give you Our blessing.

June 25, 1995 *Half Moon Bay, California* Total surrender

Jesus: Good morning, Our humble servant, We are here to bless your day and to give your Our strength.
Janie: Thank You, My Lord and my Holy Mother. I am tired. I will abandon myself to Your love.
Our Lady: Our precious angel, you have witnessed to many of our children, you have touched many hearts. My Son and I are pleased with your total surrender as you give your time to all who wish to talk to you and to meet you.
Janie: It's a joy for me to be able to share my love for you and your Son with all these precious souls, who are so hungry for God's love and mercy. It's truly a great honor for me.
Jesus: Our humble servant, you are a delight to Our hearts. We love you and we give you Our blessing.

June 26, 1995 *Strengthen me in my suffering*

Jesus: Good morning, Our humble servant. We are here to bless you and your family and to help you in your suffering.
Janie: Good morning, Our Lord and Our Lady. I thank You for being with us (my family and me). I ask that You strengthen me in my suffering so that I may be strong.
Our Lady: Our sweet angel, today will be difficult for you and you will suffer much, but have no worry, we will help you. Spend quiet time in prayer.
Jesus: Listen to the words of My Mother and do as she asks of you. We give you Our blessing.
Janie: Thank You, My Lord and my Blessed Mother.

June 27, 1995 *Spend quiet time in prayer*

Jesus: Good morning, Our humble servant. We are here to bless you and your family.
Janie: Good morning, My Savior and My Lady. Thank You for coming to help me and my family. Please help me with my special intentions.
Our Lady: Know, Our dear angel, that we will intercede for your special intentions. Spend quiet time in prayer. This will help you to endure

your suffering.
Janie: Thank You, My Lord and My Lady. I will do as You ask of me.
Jesus: We give you Our blessing.

June 28, 1995 *Lukewarmness in the Church*

Our Lady: Our sweet angel, We are here to bless your day. You are suffering for all the woundedness in the Church and this suffering is hard on you. Offer your suffering for all the lukewarmness in the Church. The spirit of apostasy is strong. We give you Our blessing.
Janie: *Our Lord and Our Lady appeared very sad today because of all the sinfulness that is within the Church. I had a vision of many priests and religious who no longer believe in the Holy Sacrifice of Holy Mass.*

June 28, 1995 *Do not let suffering distract you*

Janie: Good evening, My Lord and My Lady.
Jesus: Good evening, Our humble servant. We are here to bless you and your family.
Janie: My Dear Lord, please pray for me. I need your strength.
Jesus: Our humble servant, do not allow the persecution that you are enduring to distract you from My love and mercy. The evil one is busy trying to bring every distraction your way. He will succeed only if you allow him.
Janie: My Lord, I won't allow him to distract me from Your love. I am tired and when I am tired, I become distracted. Thank You for helping me.
Our Lady: Our precious angel, We know that you are tired, but have no fear for We are at your side protecting you.
Janie: Oh, Blessed Mother, thank you for your reassuring words. My husband and I are going away for a few days. Please bless our time together.
Our Lady: Our sweet angel, you and your husband will have a blessed time together. My Son and I will be at your side to help you to enjoy your time together.
Janie: Thank You, Blessed Mother and my Beloved Savior.
Jesus: Our humble servant, We give you Our blessing, for you need to be with your family.
Janie: *My son and my husband had arrived at home.* Thank You both, I love You.
Jesus: We love you.

June 29, 1995 *Console Our Hearts through your suffering*

Janie: *Today Our Lord and Our Lady asked me to continue to suffer for the sinfulness and the division in the Church.*
Jesus: Our humble servant, console Our sorrowful Hearts through your suffering for My Bride.

June 29, 1995 *Satan prowls throughout the world*

Our Lady: Dear children, today I invite you to continue to pray with me, so that I may be able to help you in your daily walk with God. Know, my little ones, that this is why I am here, to help you to be reconciled back to God. Little children, Satan is so very busy trying to destroy you as a family and to keep you in sin. He prowls throughout the world seeking the opportunity to destroy many souls. Those souls that do not believe in God are his primary victims. He devours them with his lies and temptations.

Little children, do not allow this to happen to you as a family. Pray, everyday, and consecrate yourselves to my Most Immaculate Heart. In doing this, you remain in my motherly protection and Satan's attacks on you as a family will melt like the snow on the mountain tops on a sunny day. He will not harm you.

Pray, my children, pray everyday with your heavenly Mother. Never forget that the Rosary is your weapon. Pray it everyday! I give you my motherly blessings. Thank you for listening to my message.

June 30, 1995 *A sharing of hearts*

Jesus: Our humble servant, tonight stay up with Us and pray for Our special intentions.
Janie: *I stayed awake with Our Lord and Our Lady to pray. They shared many things with me which I hold dear to my heart concerning the importance of being a holy family.*

July 1, 1995 *Family prayer builds family faith*

Jesus: Our humble servant, We are here to bless you and your family.
Our Lady: Our sweet angel, spend time with your family and pray for Our special intentions for families throughout the world.
Janie: *Our Lord and Our Lady shared with me how important family*

prayer is. Family prayer is what helps families become the reflection of the Holy Family. Family prayer is what helps to build family faith.

July 2, 1995 *Please help our family to pray*

Jesus: Good morning, Our humble servant. We are here to bless you and your family.
Janie: Good morning my dear Lord and my Blessed Mother. Thank You for coming to bless us. Please help us to continue to pray our complete Rosary.
Our Lady: Our sweet angel, it pleases God that you have committed to praying your family Rosary. Know that you receive special blessings and graces.
Janie: Thank You for sharing this with me.
Jesus: We are pleased with your efforts as a family. Continue to pray as a family. We give you Our blessing.

July 3, 1995 *Prayer is heavenly medicine*

Jesus: Good morning, Our humble servant. We are here to bless you and your family as you begin your day. Rejoice and enjoy your time together.
Janie: My Lord and my dear Lady, help us as a family, especially help my oldest son and his family.
Our Lady: Our sweet angel, have no worry concerning your oldest son and his family. Continue to offer your prayers and sacrifices for them. Prayer is the heavenly medicine that helps convert their wounded hearts.
Janie: Thank You, My Lord and my Blessed Mother.
Jesus: We give you Our blessing.

July 4, 1995 *Independence Day*

Jesus: Good morning, Our humble servant. We are here to bless your day as you prepare to have a family celebration.
Janie: Good morning, My Lord and my Blessed Mother. Today is the fourth of July. A day of independence for our country. I will prepare a brisket, ribs, chicken, potato salad, beans and many other family favorites.
Our Lady: Our sweet angel, you and your family will have a most blessed day. We give you Our blessing.
Janie: Thank You both.

July 5, 1995 *Persevere in family prayer*

Jesus: Good morning, Our humble servant. We are here to bless you and your family.
Janie: My Dear Lord and My Lady, I praise God for Your coming. Please pray for me and my family, so that we may be able to resist the attacks of Satan. Help especially my family to remain in a prayerful attitude during his attacks.
Our Lady: Our sweet angel, we will help you and your family through these difficult times. Persevere in your family prayer. Know that We are with you each step of the way. We give you Our blessing.

July 6, 1995 *Peace for the world*

Jesus: Our humble servant, We are here to bless you and your family. Today We ask that you offer all your prayers and sacrifices for peace in the world. Pray, so that souls may repent and be truly sorry for the sinful lives that they live.
Janie: I will pray for these intentions.
Jesus: We give you Our blessing.

July 6, 1995 *Through prayer you learn to love and forgive*

Our Lady: Dear children, today, I invite you and your family to continue to love one another with God's love. Persevere in prayer together during your family trials and tribulations. In this way, you will overcome all your suffering.

Little children, be grateful to God, for He has allowed me to come to you and your family to help you. Be open to all that I tell you and do not become tired or discouraged with living my messages. Know that everything that I invite you to do is for the good of your soul. I want you, little children, to know God, but you can only do this through prayer. In prayer, you meet God in a personal way and you become good friends. Through prayer you learn to love, to forgive others and you come to know God's peace.

Little children, you, as a family, are so dear to my Immaculate Heart. Please, I beg you, allow me to help you to be holy families by doing all that I invite you to do. Thank you for listening to my message.

July 7, 1995 *Pray for this intention*

Jesus: Good morning, Our humble servant. We are here to bless you and your family.
Janie: Thank You both for blessing us.
Our Lady: Our sweet angel, did you have a restful night?
Janie: Yes, My Lady, I rested well. How are you and your Son this morning?
Our Lady: We are doing quite well and We are joyful to share this time with you.
Janie: Thank you so much. You are so kind and loving to me. I am forever grateful. Tell me, do you have any special intentions which you wish me to pray for?
Our Lady: Pray for all souls to desire to lead good lives. Pray for God's peace to be known in the world in a special way, so that souls may desire to convert. Many in the world have forgotten about God's love and mercy. Pray for this intention. We give you Our blessing.
Janie: I will do as You ask of me My Lord and My Lady. *Our Lord and Our Lady smiled at me as the visit ended.*

July 8, 1995 *Father, forgive them*

Jesus: Good morning, Our humble servant. We are here to bless you and your family. Open your heart and allow Our words to penetrate your heart.

Our dear child, you are suffering much for your son and his family. Your heart is breaking as you embrace the suffering of your grandchildren. We are here to tell you that We are pleased with all the love and your time that you are giving to these precious little ones. Continue to embrace your painful suffering with joy in your heart. Offer it in reparation for those souls that are most distant from My Sacred Heart and the Immaculate Heart of My Mother.
Our Lady: Our precious angel, We know that you are having a difficult time in having a loving attitude towards (X). You must not allow Satan to put all his lies in your heart. Recall the words of my Son as He was dying on the Cross, as He prayed to God the Father, "Father forgive them for they know not what they do." Our sweet angel, know that we are with you and with your family in your suffering. Continue to pray the Rosary together as a family. Do not allow Satan to distract you from your prayers.
Jesus: Our humble servant, know that many families are suffering, that is why your prayers are so important. Unite your prayers with Our

prayers. You are a delight to Our Two United Hearts.
Janie: My Beloved and Most Adorable Savior and my beloved and Holy Mother, thank You for Your love, for it gives me strength. I will continue to do as You ask of me. I love You both.
Our Lady: We love you, Our precious angel. God's peace to you and your family.

July 9, 1995 *Pray for all My beloved brother priests*

Jesus: Good morning, Our humble servant. We are here to bless your day.
Janie: Thank You so much, My Lord and My Lady. Do You have any special intentions for me today?
Jesus: Our humble servant, pray for all My beloved brother priests who are suffering from persecution because of their love for Me.
Janie: My Lord, I will pray for all the Church today.
Jesus: Thank you, Our humble servant. We are grateful. Until tomorrow, We give you Our blessing.

July 10, 1995 *Do not become discouraged*

Jesus: Good afternoon, Our humble servant. We are here to bless you and your family. Our dear one, We know of your great suffering. Know that We, too, are suffering with you. Do not become discouraged, for you are not alone; We are with you in your suffering.
Janie: My Lord and my Blessed Mother, I feel so alone, like nobody understands my pain. I so much desire to be a saint, but here lately I feel like I'll never become a saint. There is so much suffering all around me, it seems like people do not believe in prayer.
Our Lady: Our precious angel, you are under the attack of Satan. He is busy polluting your mind with lies. Pray, pray, pray! Have no worry.

July 11, 1995 *The grace of this present moment*

Jesus: Good morning, Our humble servant. We are here to bless you and your family.
Janie: Oh, my Beloved Savior and my beloved Holy Mother, I thank God for the grace of this present moment. I so need Your love and comfort, for my suffering continues to surround me and my family. Your presence with me is so important. Please help me to embrace my suffering with joy in my heart.
Jesus: Our humble servant, We are with you. Unite your suffering with Ours. Until tomorrow, We give you Our blessing.

Janie: Until tomorrow.

July 12, 1995 *How unworthy I am*

Jesus: Good morning, Our humble servant. We are here to bless you and your family. We are here to comfort you in your suffering and to help in your discernment.

Janie: *I was praying to the Holy Spirit for enlightenment on personal family issues.* Oh, my Beloved Savior and my Holy Mother, I am so thankful to God for His immense love and mercy. I know how unworthy I truly am and therefore, I do not deserve His goodness. Lately my prayers are few and I have not been dedicated to praying my Rosary like I usually do. I feel awful and what hurts me is that I have not really trusted in Your help. Please forgive me. I am so sorry from my heart.

Our Lady: Our precious angel, you have been under such attacks from Satan. Your whole family has been suffering much, but you, Our dear one, have endured much, much suffering. Recall the words of my Son to you when you were suffering and could not pray: **"My child, your suffering is a prayer."** You attend Holy Mass daily, therefore, your soul is in the state of grace, for you take such good care of your soul in going to receive the sacrament of Reconciliation once a week.

Our precious angel, you have allowed your soul to embrace prayer in such a way that your soul hungers to be united in prayer with each breath that you take. This is why you think that you are not praying during the time of your suffering. We are here to tell you that you have nothing to worry about in the area of prayer. Our precious angel, prepare to go to receive the sacrament of Reconciliation and to attend Holy Mass. We will continue Our visit later as you visit my Son in the Blessed Sacrament.

Janie: *The visit with Our Lord and Our Lady at the Blessed Sacrament was private.*

July 13, 1995 *Trust the intercession of the Holy Souls and the Saints*

Jesus: Good morning, Our humble servant. We are here to bless you and your family. Embrace the grace of this moment and be filled with Our love and peace, then go out to share this love and peace.

Janie: Good morning, my Beloved Lord and my Holy Mother. Thanks be to God for everything.

Our Lady: Our precious angel, you are doing much better today. It brings joy to Our hearts to see how you remain steadfast even in your greatest suffering. Your prayers, suffering and love for your family is what is helping your family to overcome their many attacks. Our precious angel, you will continue to suffer until God calls you to your heavenly home. Recall God's invitation to you to be a victim soul to suffer for the conversion and purification of your family, the Bride of my Son and sinners throughout the world.

You have endured almost seven years of great suffering and God is pleased with you. Pray for the intercession of the Holy Souls in Purgatory to help you in your suffering, for they truly know suffering. Trust in the intercession of all the saints, for they too, suffered greatly during their lifetime on earth.

Janie: My Beloved and Holy Mother, I don't mind suffering, but I become concerned when I cannot pray while I am suffering. I understand that my suffering is a prayer. Sometimes, I wish I had a cave where I could be praying and offer my sacrifices for my own purification. Sometimes I only want to be left alone so that I may hear more clearly what God is telling me through the power of the Holy Spirit.

Jesus: Our humble servant, take refuge in Our Two United Hearts, allow Our Hearts to be your cave. We are always with you in a special way.

Janie: My Lord and Savior, what do You mean when You say that You are with me in a special way?

Jesus: Our humble servant, because My Father in Heaven has chosen you to be a vessel and victim to suffer for the world, He has blessed you with special graces to endure your sufferings. Through these special graces given to you to suffer, My Mother and I are always with you, for We, too, suffer. We help you when your suffering is intense. Our love gives you the strength to suffer with joy in your heart.

Janie: I understand, thank You so much for taking the time to explain this to me. My Lord, will You give me a message for the people in Odessa, Texas? Do You have any guidance for my son?

Jesus: Our humble servant, I will give you a message for the people that you will be visiting during My Mercy Hour. Tell your son that the Holy Spirit will be his guide. Now, Our humble servant, We give you Our blessing.

Janie: Thank You both, I love You.

Jesus: We love you, Our little vessel.

July 13, 1995 *Odessa, Texas* *Many suffer because they do not pray*

Jesus: My humble servant, I, your Jesus of Love and Mercy, will give you guidance on what to share with My people in Odessa. Talk to them about the importance of love, prayer and forgiveness. The Holy Spirit will enlighten your heart each day. Here are My words to My people.

Become Eucharistic

Beloved, I, your Jesus of Love and Mercy, invite you to embrace Me as your Lord and Savior. I am here with each one of you, because of My immense love for you. I yearn to be called your friend and for you to invite Me into your heart. In doing this, I will make My dwelling in your heart and in your home.

Beloved, many of you are enduring much suffering. Many of you are suffering from physical illness, there are loved ones who suffer with addictions, there is divorce in your family. Many of you do not pray, therefore you have no faith. There is violence in your family, many of you do not attend Holy Mass, many of you have separated from My Father. You have so many crosses in your life, and because of this you have become discouraged.

Those of you who remain united to My Sacred Heart through your prayers, you have helped your loved ones. Beloved, come to Me, all of you, with your wounded hearts, with all your crosses, and I will refresh you. Trust Me completely and abandon your troubles to Me. I give you My solemn word that you shall not regret it.

The graces and blessings that you will receive are without limit, for I am generous to you, My beloved. Bring Me all your loved ones and I will heal your hearts. I will pour My love and mercy into your hearts and you shall be healed.

Hear My words beloved, and embrace My love and mercy. Love and forgive one another, and you will be set free. The Holy Spirit will come and infuse your hearts with the Fire of My love. Come to Me, your Jesus of Love and Mercy, and I will heal you as a family. All I ask is that you trust Me.

July 14, 1995 *Odessa, Texas* *Your request is the Will of My Father*

Jesus: My child, welcome to My Eucharistic Heart and thank you for coming to spend time with your Savior. Abandon yourself to My Eucharistic love and embrace the grace of this moment. My humble servant, I, your Jesus of Love and Mercy, invite you to continue to pray for all My brother priests.

My Bride is in need of much prayer, for many of My brother priests and consecrated souls are suffering from lukewarmness of heart. Their faith is weak for they pray very little. It wounds My Sacred Heart to know how little My brother priests trust Me. They do not come to Me during their times of suffering. If only they would comprehend that it is only by putting their trust in Me that they will have My strength. Pray with Me for them. In doing this, you will console My heart.

Janie: My Adorable Jesus, I will offer my masses, prayers and sacrifices for Your special intentions for Your Bride. Please pray for me so that I can continue my fasting. Help me to remain obedient to my promise to my Holy Mother to pray my Rosary everyday. I want to do everything that You and she request of me.

Jesus: My child, you will receive the request that you seek, for your request is in harmony with the Will of My Father. I give you My blessing.

Janie: Thank You, My Lord and my All.

July 15, 1995 *Odessa, Texas St. Michael and the St. Benedict Cross*

Jesus: Our humble servant, We are here to bless you as you prepare to give your talk to Our people. Abandon yourself to Our love and trust in the Holy Spirit for enlightenment. He will speak through you. Know that those souls that will come to listen to your testimony will be blessed with graces to help them to embrace the teachings of the Holy Family.

Janie: *Later this same night Our Lord and Our Lady came.*

Jesus: Our humble servant, We are here to tell you that We are pleased at the way that you abandoned yourself to the Holy Spirit.

Janie: *Tonight Satan came into my room to distract me while I was reading. I could hear his voice. At first I felt scared but I quickly called upon St. Michael, and I took my St. Benedict Cross and embraced it. I heard Satan's voice three times and then he stopped.*

July 16, 1996 *Odessa, Texas Feast of Our Lady of Mt. Carmel*

Jesus: Our humble servant, We are here to bless you. Do not allow Satan to distract you. He is most angry with you, for you are drawing souls to Us. Know that We are with you.

Janie: My Dear Lord and my Dear Mother, I will do as You say. Although Satan does frighten me, I will trust in You. Please bless all the people that are coming this afternoon. Bless in a special way Fr. B. He is so kind and loving. Bless him abundantly.

Our Lady: Our precious angel, We will intercede for your special intentions. We give you Our blessing.

Janie: *Later on Our Lady came as Our Lady of Mt. Carmel. She had her Infant Son. Both held a brown scapular. These were her words concerning the brown scapular.*

Our Lady: My dear angel, today I came to you under this title to remind you of the importance of wearing the brown scapular. This is my garment of grace. To wear it means to be in my service, and you are constantly reminded that you belong to your heavenly Mother. I want all my children to wear my brown scapular. I say 'my scapular,' for it is my garment of grace. Those who wear the scapular always will die in the grace of God, because they have demonstrated their confidence in being under the protection of their heavenly Mother by wearing the scapular.

Recall my promise to St. Simon Stock: **"Whosoever shall die wearing this badge of my Confraternity, shall not suffer everlasting fire."** I know, my child, that wearing the scapular is inconvenient and at times embarrassing, especially when souls that do not understand consider you strange, and they laugh at you.

Know that by wearing the scapular you will never be without prayer, for I plead to God for all my children wearing the scapular as the perfect Mother, and to the perfect Mother God refuses nothing. Wear your scapular always and never be without it. Thank you, my angel, for listening so patiently. I give you my motherly blessing.

July 17, 1995 *Reparation for the sins of the world*

Janie: *I prepared myself for my visit with Our Lord and Our Lady by prostrating myself on the floor. This way of preparing myself was inspired by my guardian angel. From the very first time that Our Lord and Our Lady invited me to be a victim soul, I have suffered in different ways. All my suffering is for the purification of Our Lord's Bride (the Church), families everywhere, for all the innocent souls (infants) that are murdered in their mothers' wombs and for the Holy Souls. My suffering helps to purify me as well, for I am a great sinner.*

Today as I was praying and visiting with Our Lord and Our Lady, I asked them to help me to offer my life to do great penance in expiation for the sins of the world, beginning with my own sinfulness.

Jesus: Our humble servant, We are here to bless you and your family and to help you with your request to live the rest of your life doing penance in reparation for the sins of the world. My child, on Mondays you offer your fasting for My Bride's purification. Beginning today, I ask that you pray fifteen decades of the Rosary while prostrated on the floor. Do this three times a day.

The first time, pray five decades of the Rosary, the second time pray five

more decades of the Rosary and the third time pray five more until you have prayed all fifteen decades of the Rosary. Pray it in honor of the Holy Trinity, God the Father, God the Son and God the Holy Spirit. Offer this Rosary for my Vicar on earth who suffers for all His flock that continues to separate from the true teaching of the Church through the spirit of apostasy.
Offer it all for My brother Cardinals, Archbishops, Bishops, priests and religious who need your prayers. Do not forget the holy souls. On Wednesdays, offer your fasting for the intentions that We give you and to make St. Joseph more known, for We know that you desire this. We, too, want him to be more known. On Wednesdays and Fridays We ask that you prostrate yourself on the floor while praying your Rosary. Pray your Rosary each time with five decades of your Rosary until you complete the fifteen decades of your Rosary.

On Fridays, offer your suffering and fasting for My Sacred Heart and the Sorrowful and Immaculate Heart of My Mother, for all the innocent infants that are killed in their mothers' wombs, for your family and families throughout the world. You will pray your Rosary this way while prostrated on the floor three times a week. Each time offer it in honor of the Holy Trinity.

My Mother and I will be with you to help you in your suffering as you pray and offer your Rosary. We will come three times on those days that you suffer by doing penance. In October, My Mother's visits will cease, but I will continue to come to you three times on those days until December 25th. The three Archangels with St. Francis and beloved Padre Pio will be with you on those days that you suffer in reparation for these intentions that I have mentioned.

Janie: Dear Lord, Our Lady said that after Your last visit on December 25, I am to spend one hour each day in Eucharistic Adoration with You for the rest of my life. She said that when I cannot go to be with You, that You would come to me. She said that during this time I will have thoughts in my mind and that I am to write these thoughts because these will be You speaking to me. What does this mean? She said I won't see interior visions of You during these holy hours. Please explain this to me.

Jesus: My child, these thoughts will be what the world refers to as inner locutions. It is another way that I will continue to communicate with you on a daily basis.

Janie: For how long My Lord?

Jesus: Do not be distracted with this concern. I will let you know when the time comes. Now, We give you Our blessing.

Janie: Thank You, My Lord and my All and my beautiful Holy Mother. Amen.

July 18, 1995 *Holy Mass: the strongest form of prayer*

Jesus: My child, welcome to My Eucharistic Heart. Abandon yourself to the grace of this moment for I have much to share with you. Arm yourself with strong prayer, for the evil one will try to put many temptations in your path. My child, you must pray unceasingly and not allow any distractions to keep you from spending quiet time in prayer.

Holy Mass is your strongest form of prayer. Make every effort to attend Holy Mass on a daily basis. Be prudent with your daily responsibilities and use your time well, so that you may please your husband and keep your commitment to the things that My Mother and I are requesting of you. Know that your guardian angel will help you in carrying out your daily tasks and your spiritual commitments. My child, the world is in need of much prayer. The evil one is trying to destroy many souls. This is why We invite you to pray with Us. I love you, My child.

July 18, 1995 *Do not allow television to be a distraction*

Our Lady: Our precious angel, We thank you for coming to spend time in Perpetual Adoration. We need your prayers in a special way. Do not allow the television to be a distraction to you for Satan wants to distract you from your prayer. Spend time with Us praying, for Our time with you is short. See the condition of the world around you.

Janie: *I saw the many sins in the world.*

Our Lady: Pray with Us for the Bride of my Son, for so many bishops and priests are leading many to perdition. Pray for holy and obedient bishops and priests so that through their prayers my Son's Bride will be purified, and all those souls entrusted to them will convert.

Our dear one, the spirit of apostasy is destroying the love and faith of many priests and religious. Pray for love and faith in a Church that is under Satan's attack. We love you and We beg you to spend time in prayer for these intentions. We give you Our blessing.

July 19, 1995 *Continue to pray and fast for others*

Jesus: Good morning, Our humble servant. We are here to bless you and your family.

Janie: Good morning, My Lord and My Lady, thank You for being here with me. We are so blessed.
Our Lady: Our precious angel, We want you to know that We are truly grateful for all your tireless efforts and your prayers for the conversion of my Son's Bride and for the family. Know that God blesses all your work.
Janie: Blessed Mother, thank you for sharing this with me. Sometimes I feel like I do so little to help draw other souls closer to your Son's Heart.
Our Lady: Our precious angel, if you only could understand how you are helping to draw many souls to my Son's Heart, you would rejoice.
Janie: I am sorry, Blessed Mother, I don't understand how much I am helping other souls. Maybe I am not praying enough, however I will rejoice at what you tell me on how I am helping many souls draw closer to your Son.
Jesus: Our humble servant, you have much suffering to endure as you draw souls to me. Do not fear, you have been given special graces to endure your suffering. Continue to pray and fast for the conversion of others. Until tomorrow, We give you Our blessing.

July 20, 1995 *Inflame my heart and soul*

Jesus: Good morning, Our humble servant. We are here to bless you and your family.
Janie: Good morning, My Lord and My Lady. Thank You for coming. I am so excited as I wait to visit with St. Joseph on my birthday.
Our Lady: Our precious angel, your heart will be filled with great joy as you visit with St. Joseph. God will bless you with special virtues on this day.
Janie: Oh Blessed Mother, I cannot wait. I am so excited, but I am a little nervous.
Our Lady: Our precious angel, why are you nervous? We will be with you to help you.
Janie: I know this, my dear Holy Mother, but people being around me when I have my visits makes me a little tense. These visits are so special to me and I feel like I call attention to myself. I do not wish to be a distraction to anyone.
Our Lady: Be at peace, Our dear one, you are not a distraction to anyone. Your obedience to respond to Our request is pleasing to God. It is He Who wishes to bless His people through Our visits with you.
Janie: Thank you for helping me. I do so want to do the Will of God, so I will do anything that He asks of me. ***Oh, Holy Spirit, inflame my heart and soul with your Divine Love so that I may love my God with***

every beat of my heart and with every breath that I take. Amen.
Our Lady: Our precious angel, your prayer is most pleasing to God. Until tomorrow, We give you Our blessing.
Janie: Until tomorrow, I love You both.
Jesus: We love you.

July 21, 1995 *Follow the path that leads to holiness*

Jesus: Good morning, Our humble servant. We are here to bless your day.
Janie: Oh, thank You so much for blessing us. Today is my son's birthday. Please shower a bouquet of special graces and blessings upon him. He has gone through so much, he really needs your help.
Our Lady: Our precious angel, We will bless your son in a special way. Tell him to continue to follow the path that leads towards holiness and to abandon everything else. We are with him in a special way. Rejoice with your son on his birthday. Until tomorrow, We give you Our blessing.
Janie: Thank You both.

July 22, 1995 *Thank You for bringing God's blessings*

Jesus: Good morning, Our humble servant. We are here to bless you and your family.
Janie: Praised be God forever and ever. Thank You both for bringing God's blessings to our family. I am so grateful to God for His great love and mercy. I can see my family growing closer to God through our prayers. We remain strong for one another especially in times of crisis.
Our Lady: Our sweet angel, God has blessed you and your family by choosing you as His vessels to help other families. Pray for families throughout the world.
Janie: Blessed Mother, we will be forever grateful that God chose us as His vessels to help families and to pray for them. We will pray everyday in thanksgiving for the love and mercy which God has poured into our hearts.
Our Lady: Our sweet angel, your family prayers are pleasing to God. Until tomorrow, We give you Our blessing.

July 23, 1995 *A beautiful tribute to St. Joseph*

Jesus: Good morning, Our humble servant. We are here to bless you and your family.
Janie: Good morning, my Beloved Savior and my Holy Mother. I am

so excited because in three more days I'll visit with St. Joseph.
Our Lady: Our sweet angel, your birthday will be a most joyful day with many graces and blessings. Embrace this day with gratitude in your heart, for God has truly blessed you and your family with the visits of St. Joseph.
Know that not many souls have been so privileged to have visits from St. Joseph. This is truly a great honor to have St. Joseph teach you as a family holy instructions on how to pray, so that through your family prayer, you will reflect the Holy Family.
Janie: Blessed Mother, many are saying that St. Joseph will play an important role during these times. Is this true?
Our Lady: Our precious angel, St. Joseph has always played an important role in the world. He was chosen by God to be the foster father of God's only begotten Son and to care for me before the birth of my Son, Jesus.

St. Joseph has always been the Protector of the Church and all families throughout the world. Many souls throughout time have had devotion to St. Joseph, especially many of the saints.
Janie: Blessed Mother, not much has been written about St. Joseph.
Our Lady: This is true, my angel.
Janie: But why?
Our Lady: This was God's plan for St. Joseph. God demonstrated the importance and greatness of St. Joseph simply by choosing him to be the foster father of His Son. St. Joseph was a prayerful and humble man who lived his life doing the Holy Will of God. He was quiet and dedicated to his work as a carpenter. He was admired and loved by all the people that knew him. He never refused help to anyone.

He was most talented in his work, and many people sought him out to do work for them. He worked very hard to please God. He dedicated his entire work for the glory of God, for he knew that God had gifted him with his talent. He arose very early to begin his day by spending much time in prayer and thanksgiving to God. Everyday he offered all his daily work and activities to God with joy in his heart. He loved God very much and lived a pure and holy, prayerful life. This is why he was chosen to be the protector of the Holy Family.

St. Joseph has played an important role in the history of the Church and many souls have honored him throughout time. He will always play an important role as Protector of the Holy Family to all who invoke his powerful intercession. His greatness is demonstrated in his humility to be referred to by many as the silent St. Joseph, Protector of the Holy

Family, most chaste spouse of Mary and foster father of the Child, Jesus.

Know, my angel, that God is the one who chooses souls such as you and your family to make St. Joseph more known as a humble and loving spouse who is the perfect model of what a husband and father should be. The holy instructions given to you will help many souls.

Janie: Oh, Blessed Mother, thank you so much for telling me so much about St. Joseph. May I continue to ask you more at other times?

Our Lady: Certainly, my sweet angel. We will help you to know more about St. Joseph. Until tomorrow, We give you Our blessing.

Janie: Thank You, oh, thank You.

July 27, 1995 *St. Joseph must be asked*

Jesus: Our humble servant, We are here to bless you and your family.
Janie: Good morning, My Lord and my Blessed Mother. I am so grateful that You are here to bless us, for we truly need Your blessings.
Jesus: Our humble servant, you have a joyful heart from your visit with St. Joseph.
Janie: Yes, My Lord, I am most joyful for having spent time with my beloved friend, St. Joseph. He is so special to me. I have much love for him. His picture is so beautiful.
Jesus: Know that you are special to St. Joseph, for it was he who asked My Father's permission to come and give you holy instructions on the family. He has much love for you. He has been with you throughout your life, even though you were not aware of his presence in your life. He was with you when you were a little child because of your great suffering. He protected you in a special way.
Janie: My Savior, isn't St. Joseph with everybody?
Jesus: Yes, he is, My dear one. He protects all families in the world, but he has to be invited into people's hearts through prayer. Although you don't remember much about your childhood, your godmother asked St. Joseph to protect you and to be at your side. St. Joseph always responds to those who ask for his intercession.
Janie: Thank You, my Beloved Savior and my Blessed Mother.

July 27, 1995 *Try very hard to lead good lives*

Our Lady: Dear children, I invite you to continue to pray as a family. Satan is strong and he wants to destroy you. Prayer is your weapon against his evil attacks. Little children, I want to help you to draw closer to God through your prayers. It is important that you trust in my motherly intercession and allow me to help you.

Little children, you are so special to me and I want to take you all to Heaven with me. Love one another and try very hard to lead good lives. Do not become discouraged in your suffering, but pray with faith in your hearts. God listens to all your prayers. Trust Him in everything. I love you, little children. I give you my motherly blessing. Thank you for listening to my message.

July 28, 1995 *Not even breathing is as important*

Jesus: Good morning, Our humble servant. We are here to bless you and your family.

Janie: Good morning, my Beloved Friends and Helpers. You are everything to me and I look to these visitations to regain my strength as I continue to suffer for the sake of love. Beloved Savior, please enlighten me with knowledge on the Eucharist. I look forward to morning Mass because this is when I am truly united with You, my Savior. When I cannot attend Holy Mass, my soul suffers. Tell me why do I feel this way?

Jesus: Our humble servant, the Holy Eucharist is life to you. In the Holy Eucharist you find Me, your Eucharistic Savior, hidden in the host which becomes My Body and the wine that becomes My Blood. To receive Me daily means to be united with Me through My Body and Blood. My immense love and mercy flows through every vein and every fiber of your being. Not even breathing is more important than being united with Me by simply eating of My Body and drinking of My Blood daily.

Those souls who nourish themselves with My Body and Blood daily, suffer from lack of heavenly food when they cannot receive Me. This is why you feel the way that you do when you cannot attend Holy Mass. Until tomorrow, We give you Our blessing.

Janie: Oh, Beloved Savior, thank You so much for this lesson on the Holy Eucharist. Will You continue to enlighten me with more heavenly knowledge on the Eucharist?

Jesus: I will help you with whatever you need, for this is what draws you closer to My Eucharistic Heart.

July 29, 1995 *Do not be distracted with this concern*

Jesus: Good morning, Our humble servant. We are here to bless you and your family.

Janie: Good morning, my Adorable Lord and my Holy Mother. How are You doing this beautiful morning?
Our Lady: Our precious angel, Our Hearts are joyful to be here with you. Our dear one, you are most happy this morning.
Janie: Yes, I am because my joy continues to linger from my visit with St. Joseph. I love him so much, and I am most grateful to God for allowing St. Joseph to come to us. What an honor and blessing!
Jesus: Our humble servant, St. Joseph is indeed a blessing to you as a family, and to all those who are embracing his holy instructions on the teachings of the family. Through these holy instructions many will foster devotion to him, and he will be embraced by many families. Those souls that have devotion to him will rejoice to know that this most humble saint is being embraced by many. St. Joseph will live in many hearts and the youth will embrace him as well.
Janie: Beloved Savior, this is a great blessing to our world. Will he come to other souls like he did me? If I am not supposed to know this, please forgive me for asking. Many are saying that St. Joseph is supposed to start appearing in certain places, this is why I ask. I know that there are many false messages and I love St. Joseph very much. I pray that he will continue to help us if he is to appear to others.
Jesus: Our humble servant, do not allow yourself to be distracted with this concern, but continue to live the holy instructions given to you by St. Joseph. We understand your love for him. Abandon all to Our Two United Hearts. Until tomorrow, We give you Our blessing.
Janie: Thank You both.

July 30, 1995 *Continue in prayer for Our special intentions*

Jesus: Good morning, Our humble servant. We are here to bless you and your family.
Janie: Good morning, my Beloved Lord and my Holy Mother. Thank You so much for coming to bless us.

Our Lady: Our precious angel, today We ask you to continue to unite with Us in prayer for Our special intentions. We give you Our blessing.

July 31, 1995 *Clothe your family with love and prayers*

Jesus: Good morning, Our humble servant. We are here to bless you and your family.
Janie: I praise God for this moment of grace. Please pray for us so that we may make Holy Scripture our rule for everyday living. I embrace this way of life, but I'm not sure that my family clearly understands this.

Our Lady: We will intercede for your special intentions. Continue to clothe your family with your love and your prayers; this will help them. Until tomorrow, We give you Our blessing.

August 3, 1995 *If you only understood the graces of family prayer*

Our Lady: Dear children, I invite you to continue to pray as a family everyday, especially the family Rosary. If you only understood the graces that you receive when you pray together as a family. Little children, you are so special to my Immaculate Heart. I am always present with you as you pray together as a family. I ask that you trust in all your family prayers, especially when there is great suffering in your family.

Know, my little ones, that prayer brings you God's peace. When you unite as a family in prayer, your love grows stronger for one another. So my dear children, pray, pray, pray! Live Holy Scripture and be a living witness of the Gospel to those around you. Do not allow Satan to distract you from prayer time. Live everyday, loving one another and praying for one another. I love you, my dear children, I love you. Thank you for listening to my message.

August 11, 1995 *God is showering your country with great blessings*

Jesus: Good morning, Our humble servant. We are here to bless you and your family.
Janie: Good morning, My Lord and My Lady. Thank You for coming. Please help me and my family to do God's Holy Will.
Jesus: Our humble servant, We will help you and your family. For now, rest, for We know how tired you are from your suffering. We will return this evening to visit with you. We give you Our blessing.
Janie: Thank You. I am very tired. I will rest. *Our Lord and Our Lady came later this evening as they said.*
Jesus: Good evening, Our humble servant. You have had a very busy day.
Janie: Yes, My Lord and My Lady. I have been cleaning and doing much laundry. You see, my sons have a habit of leaving their soiled laundry in their room. Today they discovered just how much their soiled laundry had accumulated. I was thankful to God that I remained peaceful with them through this whole ordeal. My sons and I cleaned the house together and we enjoyed being together. This was the last day of their jobs as school will soon begin. We prayed our family Rosary and had a great day, but I am not tired.
Our Lady: Our precious angel, you are a good and loving mother.

Your children love you very much, for they know what a treasure they have. Know that your prayerful life is what helps you to remain peaceful during difficult situations with your family. Pray always, unceasingly, and you will overcome great difficulties.

My sweet angel, continue to pray for your country, for God is showering your country with great blessings. Many of my children in your country are converting through the prayers and sacrifices of my faithful children that spend much time praying for peace and conversion. This brings joy to my Immaculate Heart.
Janie: Blessed Mother, I am so happy to hear this about our country. I'll share this with others.
Our Lady: I, your heavenly Mother, desire that my children continue to persevere in their prayers for peace in the world. Know that praying for world peace helps your country as well.
Janie: My heavenly Mother, it's been so hot and many have suffered from this, some have died. Is this what you meant in December of 1995 while I was visiting the Basilica in Mexico, when you told me about the pestilence and calamities that will occur in succession in our country and throughout the world?

Our Lady: Yes, my precious angel, this is why I ask for much prayer for those who will suffer from such disasters. Continue to pray for these special intentions. Now, We give you Our blessing.
Janie: Blessed Mother, give St. Clare a hug and kiss for me and tell her happy feast day.
Our Lady: I will, my angel.

August 12, 1995 *Janie's prayer to the Eternal Father*

Jesus: Good morning, Our humble servant. We are here to bless you and your family.
Janie: Good morning to the both of You and thank You, My Lord and My Lady for being so kind to us.
Jesus: Our humble servant, We had your guardian angel wake you up before your family's day begins, so that We could spend time with you. We have special things which We wish to share with you.
Janie: Oh, My Lord and My Lady, please tell me whatever You wish to share with me, for my heart and soul are open to the things which You will tell me. Please allow me to pray to the Eternal Father first, before You share with me.
Jesus: Pray, Our humble servant, pray to My Father Who loves you with the greatest love.

Janie: Oh, my Heavenly and Eternal Father, I wish to thank You for creating me with great love. Help me to return this great love by loving others around me, especially My family. My Eternal Father, no one could love me more than You. Help me to abandon myself to Your love and mercy. Help me to abandon the spirit of the world and to embrace the spirit of Your Son and His Most Pure Mother and St. Joseph, for they are Your reflection. Help me to be love, to know love and to love with Your love. Amen.

Jesus: Our humble servant, My Father is pleased with your prayer. Today, I, your Jesus of Love and Mercy, ask that you unite your prayers with Me and My Mother for My Vicar and all My brother priests. There is so much division among My brothers and those souls consecrated to Me. There is little harmony and unity in their relationships with one another. This truly wounds My Eucharistic Heart. Oh, if only My brothers and consecrated ones would turn to Me in their great need.

I would refresh their aching and wounded hearts. I would console them like never before, but I cannot do this for them, for many do not trust Me. Many do not believe in My True Presence. How can I help them? Pray for this special intention and embrace My Vicar who suffers out of great love for Me.

Janie: Oh, my Beloved Savior, I guess I can relate to You in a very small way. I, too, feel this pain about my family, knowing that many of my distant relatives are not consistent with the teachings of the Church and many do not go to Church. I feel great pain for this, but I, too, am a great sinner, so please have pity on my sinful soul. I will offer my sacrifices and prayers for Your intentions. I promise.

Jesus: Our humble servant, this consoles My Eucharistic Heart. Thank you for listening to My pain for My Bride.

Janie: You are very welcome with all my heart. Thank You for sharing with me.

Our Lady: Our sweet angel, I, your heavenly Mother, ask that you intercede for families throughout the world, so that more families will consecrate their family to the Two United Hearts. Pray and offer your prayers for my beloved Pope.

Janie: My heavenly Mother, please help me to accomplish all the things that I need to do concerning the book of St. Joseph. I am always so busy with family responsibilities. Help me to manage my time well and to put things in proper perspective.

Jesus: We will help you, Our sweet angel. Now, We give you Our blessing. We love you.

Janie: Thank You both and I love You both.

August 13, 1995 *The Mercy Hour*

Jesus: Good morning, Our humble servant. We are here to bless you and your family. Our humble servant, today you will suffer much. Know that We will be with you, for your suffering will be intense. Your suffering will be in reparation for a soul who has lived in darkness most of his life.
Janie: Good morning to my Two Dear Ones, Whom I love so much. Thank You both for helping me to understand the reason for my suffering. I know that You will give me the grace to suffer with joy in my heart. Do I know this soul?
Our Lady: No, Our sweet angel, you do not know him.
Jesus: Our humble servant, prepare well with much prayer and trust in Our love for you. I tell you this, for today you will become discouraged during your suffering.
Janie: My Adorable Savior, I will do my best to remain peaceful when I become discouraged in my suffering. Today we are going out to visit our land. Please help my husband with all his plans for our home which he plans to build soon.
Jesus: Our humble servant, I give you My solemn word that all will go well with this effort. Tell your husband to trust in his prayers and St. Joseph's intercession.
Janie: Oh, I will tell him My Lord. This brings so much joy to know that St. Joseph is interceding for us.
Our Lady: Our sweet angel, know that St. Joseph loves you and your family very much. He will be at your side in a special way, helping your husband in all his needs.
Janie: Blessed Mother, my husband and I asked the intercession of St. Anthony and St. Francis also.
Our Lady: Our sweet angel, know that St. Anthony and St. Francis will help you and your husband in this effort.
Janie: Thank you, Blessed Mother, for reassuring me.
Our Lady: You are most welcome. We give you Our blessing. My Son will be with you in a special way today.
Janie: *Later on this same day I was praying the Chaplet of Divine Mercy with my husband and a special friend. After we finished praying the chaplet, I told them We must continue to pray, for we are still in the mercy hour.*

We began to pray the Rosary, and Our Lord came to me in the second mystery.
Jesus: My humble servant, know that my mercy is great during this hour. All who ask for My mercy receive it.

August 14, 1995 *If they would only turn to Me*

Jesus: Good afternoon, Our humble servant. We are here to bless you and your family. We are here to comfort you in your suffering.
Janie: Good afternoon, My Lord and My Lady. Thank You so much for helping me to be strong and to endure my suffering for all Your beloved priests and religious.
Jesus: Our humble servant, know that as you suffer for My Bride, you are helping many of My brother priests in their own great suffering. Offer your suffering with joy, so that My Bride will overcome many of Satan's attacks. Many of My brother priests and souls consecrated to Me are having a difficult time trusting Me. They turn away from Me and blame Me for all that is happening to them.

Oh, if only they would turn to Me in their pain, I would strengthen them. I would pour out My healing love into their souls. The spirit of apostasy is strong among My brother priests and religious. Please, My humble servant, make much reparation for My Bride. In doing this you will console My Eucharistic Heart and the Immaculate and Sorrowful Heart of My Mother.
Janie: My Wounded and Beautiful Savior and my Precious and Loving Mother, I will pray much for this intention. I will do my best not to cause You any pain or sorrow. I will love and pray for my family so that they, too, will love You more and more each day. I'll pray unceasingly for all souls all over the world, so that many souls will love the two of You very, very much.
Jesus: Our humble servant, you have a generous and loving heart. We are honored by all your heroic efforts.
Our Lady: Thank you, our sweet angel, for your words of comfort. You are most dear to Our hearts. We give you Our blessing.
Janie: Thank You both from the bottom of my heart.

August 15, 1995 *Feast of the Assumption   Mary: The Glory of Paradise*

Janie: *Our Lord and Our Lady came. Jesus was in brilliant light and Our Lady was arrayed in her beautiful golden garments, and she wore a golden crown surrounded by twelve stars. She was beautiful and very joyful. Jesus gazed upon His beautiful and Holy Mother with such love in His Heart. They both greeted me.*
Jesus: Our humble and suffering servant, We are here to bless you and your family on this glorious day. Rejoice beloved daughter, for God has chosen you to bring divine peace and love to your family and families

everywhere. Know that Satan is most angry with all the blessings that My Father is bestowing upon families who embrace your testimony of your own conversion through the visits of My heavenly Mother. Rejoice, rejoice, rejoice!

Janie: My Beloved Savior, Our Lady looks so heavenly beautiful. Thank You for this great joy. I promise that I will continue to suffer with joy in my heart. I promise to live Holy Scripture with each breath that I take, for I know in my heart that this is the Holy Will of God.

Our Lady: My precious angel, you are so dear to Our Two United Hearts. We know, Our beloved one, that you suffer much for the sake of your family and families everywhere. Know dear one, that this is your task, to pray, to fast unceasingly in reparation for unconverted families and for the Church. This is a difficult task and at times this suffering brings such sorrow to your poor little heart, but your suffering is bringing about great victory over those souls that convert. Unite your suffering with Our Two United Hearts and allow Our love to be your strength.

Janie: Thank you, my dear Mother, for never leaving my side, for being united to Your Two Hearts is life giving to my entire being. Oh, praised be the Eternal Father for having created me in His own likeness. May He be praised forever and ever. Amen.

Jesus: Know that your praises come straight from your heart. This was a beautiful response. My Father is pleased.

August 15, 1995 *Live in the Paradise of Her Immaculate Heart.*

Jesus: My humble servant, today I, your Eucharistic Savior, invite you to rejoice with all the angels and saints as the Heavens embrace their heavenly Mother and Queen on her glorious feast day. Today I, Jesus Christ, the only begotten of the Father, invite all of humanity to embrace their heavenly Queen who assumed into the glory of Paradise even with her body. She is the one chosen by My Father throughout eternity to be the Mother of Him Who would bring salvation to a world walking in darkness.

She was the one who was chosen to be the Spouse of the Holy Spirit and from the fruit of her virginal womb the Light would come into the world. That Light was the Son that she gave birth to, the Salvation of the world. It was her 'yes' that made it all possible for the Son of God to be born. In all her humility she abandoned herself completely to the Holy Will of My Father. She is the perfect example of humility, yet, in her humility her great love for My Father is demonstrated through her response to St. Gabriel: "I am the handmaiden of the Lord, let what you say be done according to His Will."

She is the perfect model of love who loves with immense love. She is indeed the 'woman clothed with the sun, with the moon at her feet,' who is crowned as Queen of Heaven and Earth. She is the one that I, Jesus her Son, gave to the world from the Cross before My death. She was the one who remained with the apostles to help them to follow all that I taught them and instructed them to do. She, in all her littleness and humility, helped to form My apostles through her great love.

I, your Jesus of Love and Mercy, invite all to embrace your heavenly Mother who is appearing in many places throughout the world to help lead you to My Eucharistic Heart. Her appearance in the world is to help guide all her beloved priests, religious, and all her children during these bloody and difficult times. Her glorious body is shining on you as you struggle with all the suffering in your life. She is pointing out to all humanity the path that all must follow. She is calling you to prayer, to love, to purity, to suffering and to holiness. She is the glory of Paradise, she is your heavenly Mother who loves you dearly.

I, Jesus, invite the world to embrace your heavenly Mother and to live all her messages. Take refuge in the Paradise of her Immaculate Heart and allow her love to illuminate your life. She is the gate that leads you to My Eucharistic love. Beloved, be like little children and take My Mother into your hearts. Trust in her intercession for you are her offspring, whom she nourishes through her motherly love. Allow yourselves to be loved and to be cared for by her. Live in the Paradise of her Immaculate Heart. Embrace My heavenly Mother on this her feast day, and you will embrace Me, your Jesus of Love and Mercy.

August 15, 1995 *My motherly mantle protects you day and night*

Our Lady: Dear children, today I invite all my children to embrace their heavenly Mother who loves you. Rejoice on this day and love one another. Live in God's peace and fear nothing. I am with you in all your suffering. You are never alone, for my motherly mantle protects you day and night.

Little children, allow the light of my motherly love to guide you gently towards the path of holiness. Look towards your Mother with heavenly trust. Do not become discouraged when you are in the midst of great suffering, but pray, pray, pray. Today and everyday rejoice with your heavenly Mother. Unite your love with my love. Allow me to lead you as a family, closer to the Heart of my Son. Allow my heavenly light to come down from Heaven and illuminate your way.

Little children, make Heaven your goal and live heart and soul in the paradise that my Son, Jesus has prepared for you. Be at peace and allow nothing to disturb you as a family. My adversary is most angry, and he is waging war on all my children. Do not be afraid, for I, your heavenly Mother will protect you. Satan cannot harm you if you allow yourselves to be led by your heavenly Mother.

Little children, I know that for many of you these are painful and difficult times. You are afraid of the times that surround you. Take refuge in the garden of my Immaculate Heart, and you will be strengthened through my intercession. My little children, on this glorious feast day, I, your heavenly Mother, will cause a heavenly shower of blessings and graces upon each one of you. Embrace your heavenly Mother who loves you with great love.

August 17, 1995 *Darkness comes from lack of prayer and love*

Jesus: Good morning, Our humble servant. We are here to bless you and your family.

Janie: Thank You, Beloved Savior and my Most Holy Mother. I am grateful to receive all these divine blessings. What can I do for You today?

Do You have any special intentions for me to pray for?

Jesus: Our humble servant, it is most kind of you to be concerned about Our needs for the world. There is so much darkness in the world. Only prayer can bring light into many hearts. The darkness comes from lack of prayer and love, which many do not understand.

Janie: Dear Jesus, are there many people who really do not believe in You?

Jesus: Yes, there are many, especially among My brother priests.

Janie: But how can they be priests if they don't believe in You? I don't understand, please explain to me.

Jesus: My humble servant, there are many of My brother priests who no longer believe in Me, but they are still priests. Once a priest takes his priestly vows, he will always be a priest. My humble servant, a priest remains a priest until his death.

Janie: I guess I understand My Lord, I just thought that one who is a priest is one who believes in You.

Jesus: My humble servant, the reason that many of my priests do not believe in Me is because they no longer believe in My Presence in the Eucharist. These are the priests which I ask you to pray for. These are the ones who sadden My Heart.

August 18, 1995 *Pray for your country*

Jesus: Our humble servant, We are here to bless you and your family.
Janie: Good morning, my dear Savior and my Blessed Mother. Thank You so much for blessing us. We so need Your blessing.
Our Lady: Our sweet angel, We look forward to Our visits with joy in Our hearts. You are most dear to Our hearts. Today, We ask you to pray for your country, so that through your prayers and the prayers of others, there will be much conversion in many hearts.

Janie: Blessed Mother, I will pray for my country so that many will convert.
Our Lady: Our precious angel, pray with your family and be grateful to God for giving me permission to come to you as a family. He allowed me to come and to help you as a family, how to discover God through prayer, how to love one another and how to forgive. You have drawn much closer to God and to one another. This brings joy to my Immaculate Heart.
Janie: Blessed Mother, we thank God for your having come to help us. We are most grateful to God and to you.
Our Lady: Our sweet angel, continue praying as a family, and you will overcome all your many difficulties which Satan puts in your path. We give you Our blessing.
Janie: We will do as You say. I love You.
Our Lady: We love you.

August 19, 1995 *Satan attacks parents first, then children*

Jesus: Good morning, Our humble servant.
Janie: Good morning, My Lord and My Lady. Thank You for coming.
Jesus: Our humble servant, We are here to bless you and your family. We are here to console you in your suffering in reparation for the difficult times in your family.
Janie: My Dear Lord, please help me, for I need Your love and Your patience more than ever to be able to embrace my family in their struggles. It's so hard to remain loving when my loved ones refuse to be helped.
Jesus: Our humble servant, remember, the evil one is trying desperately to break up your family. He knows that you and your husband are strong together, and that he cannot bring division between you. He then attempts to destroy your children. Remember, your weapon against him

is perseverance in prayer. He knows that your love and your prayer for your family is strong. He hates this. Do not allow his attacks to make you weak. He cannot harm you.
Janie: Jesus, my Adorable Lord, I think I know this, but would you clarify this for me. Do my prayers protect my family and those I pray for?
Jesus: Our humble servant, your prayers are your weapon. In the world, people use other means to protect themselves.
Janie: *He meant guns, etc.*
Jesus: People of faith use prayer as their weapon. Your prayers protect your loved ones and others that you pray for. Your faith is the shield that keeps the attacks from Satan away from you and your family.
Janie: Oh, Jesus, thank You. Please pray for me. I find my prayers to be very weak. I am in the desert. Please help me.
Our Lady: Our sweet angel, you are suffering for the purification of those that you love so much. Endure your suffering and call upon the intercession of St. Francis, for he loves you very much. Through his intercession, you will suffer with joy in your heart.
Janie: Oh, Blessed Mother, I will ask St. Francis to intercede for me. Nobody knows my suffering more that you and your Son. Please do not leave my side and help me to remain prayerful, please.
Our Lady: We will remain with you. Do not fear but pray, pray, pray. We give you Our blessing.
Janie: Thank You so much.

August 20, 1995 *In anticipation of St. Joseph*

Jesus: Good morning, Our humble servant. We are here to bless you and your family.
Janie: Good morning, My Lord and My Lady and thank You so much for helping us to draw closer to Your Hearts. Beloved Savior and my Holy Mother, I am so happy to know that in a few days I'll have a visit from St. Joseph.
Our Lady: Our precious angel, that day will be a joyful day for you, and all who come will be blessed through the intercession of St. Joseph. God has many graces that He will bestow on those who come and embrace St. Joseph on your Anniversary. Healings will come to those who are wounded. Conversions will take place as well.
Janie: Oh, Blessed Mother, please help me to prepare well for this day.
Our Lady: Our sweet angel, prepare through means of prayer. We give you Our blessing. Until tomorrow.
Janie: Thank You both. I love You.

August 21, 1995 *Never hold anything back from Us*

Jesus: Good evening, Our humble servant. We are here to bless you and your family.
Janie: Good evening, My Lord and My Lady. Please forgive me for not being able to meet with You sooner, but I had my little grandson and he keeps me busy.
Our Lady: Our precious angel, do not be concerned, for We know how dedicated you are to taking good care of your little grandson. God is pleased that you gave him all your attention. Your grandson has been ill and he needed your complete attention. Know that my Son, St. Joseph and I are always with you in a special way.
Janie: Blessed Mother, I wish to thank You, the Holy Family, for always being with me. I guess I know this in a way, but it's good to hear it from You. I know that I'll miss our visits together, for you have helped me and my family so much. I guess my heart is beginning to experience separation anxiety. Please help me.
Jesus: Our humble servant, We will never abandon you. When Our visits cease, you will experience Our presence with you in a special way. Rejoice for you are special to the Holy Family; you are Our humble servant.
Janie: Oh Jesus, my sweet Savior, I love You. Please forgive me for acting like a child.
Jesus: Our humble servant, We see you as Our child. Do not apologize for your behavior, for you are only expressing what is in your heart. Know that We desire to hear all your concerns, so never hold anything back from Us. Our visits with you are to help you and to strengthen your faith.
Janie: Thank You both, You are so kind to me.
Our Lady: Our precious angel, you are most dear to Our Two United Hearts, never forget this. Now, Our sweet angel, We give you Our blessing. Rest well tonight.
Janie: I love You, goodnight. *They smiled and said 'goodnight.'*

August 22, 1995 Queenship of Mary - This is the decisive moment

Our Lady: Dear children, today, I invite you to give God thanks for allowing me to remain with you for such a long time. Know that God is demonstrating His great love and mercy to you through my visits with you.
Rejoice with your heavenly Mother who loves you dearly. I invite you to pray with me every day, so that through our prayers, this world will come to know God's peace. Little children, your prayers are so impor-

tant for the conversion of the world. I pray for all my children, and my motherly prayers protect you. Know that I will always be with each one of you and that I am helping you to draw closer to my Son. Embrace the path towards holiness and desire to be the reflection of my Son, Jesus.

Little children, I am your heavenly Mother and leader. Allow yourself to be led by me for I am here to lead you all to Heaven, to be with me and my Son, Jesus. This is the very reason that God made me the Mother of All Humanity, so that I may lead you all to your heavenly home to be with your heavenly Father and my Son, Jesus. Accept the way to conversion which I invite you to, my dear children, and do not waste precious time. This is the decisive moment to repent and be converted. Thank you for listening to my message.

August 22, 1995 *I could talk to you all night*

Jesus: Good evening, Our humble servant. We are here to bless you and your family. You have been very busy preparing yourself and your family for your Anniversary with St. Joseph. That day will be most special for you and all who join you in celebrating your Anniversary with St. Joseph.
Janie: My beloved Savior, I am excited and joyful about my Anniversary with St. Joseph. I love him so much with a special love. I cannot wait for Thursday to be here.
Our Lady: Our sweet angel, St. Joseph will give his special blessing to all who come. He will help them in their faith journey. St. Joseph will intercede for all those who embrace him and foster devotion to him.
Janie: *This morning when Our Lady came I forgot to wish her happy feast day.* Oh, Beloved Holy Mother, I forgot to greet you on your special feast day. You are so heavenly beautiful. Thank you for saying 'yes' to God. I really mean this from the bottom of my heart. My heart and soul are filled with joy to know that at last I love you as my heavenly Mother. I am so blessed to have you, your beloved Son and St. Joseph helping me in my daily walk with God.
Our Lady: Our sweet angel, you are special to Us, the Holy Family. We shall always be with you in a special way.
Janie: Oh thank You so much. Help me to be a good wife and mother and to lead a good life. My only desire is to do the Holy Will of God everyday of my life. I want to love everybody in the world. I want to love with God's love. Please pray for me, so that God will flood my heart and soul with His love.
Our Lady: Our sweet angel, know that God will grant you the desire

to love with His love. Now, Our sweet angel, We give you Our blessing. Good night, Our dear one.
Janie: Goodnight, my Beloved Savior and my Most Holy Mother. I wish Our visit wouldn't have to end. I could talk to You all night.
Our Lady: Our sweet angel, you have much to do tomorrow. You need your rest.
Janie: *They both smiled when I said that I could talk to Them all night.*

August 23, 1995 *Thank you for my Spiritual Director*

Jesus: Good morning, Our humble servant. We are here to bless you and your family.
Janie: Good morning, Dear Lord and Blessed Mother. Please help me, because I am tired and I have so much to do.
Jesus: Our humble servant, do not worry. You will accomplish everything. We will help you, and your guardian angel will also help you. Be at peace.
Janie: Beloved Savior, tomorrow is my Anniversary when St. Joseph will come. I am a little nervous. My Spiritual Director will also arrive later on today. Thank You so much for him. He is a treasure to me. I would never have known that I would be so blessed to have a Spiritual Director like him. I recommend him, his family and his special needs to You both.
Our Lady: Our precious angel, your Spiritual Director was chosen by God to help you and your family. He is dear to Our Two United Hearts. We will pray for him. We know you have much to do. We give you Our blessing.
Jesus: Good morning, Our humble servant. We are here to bless you and your family.
Janie: Thank you so much for blessing us.
Our Lady: Our precious angel, you are sad, and your heart is filled with sorrow. We know how much you are suffering.
Janie: Oh Beloved Mother and my Adorable Savior, how can I be so sad after being so joyful yesterday. Today has been a most difficult time for me. My little grandson is suffering so much, and this brings great sorrow to my heart. Please tell me what to do.
Jesus: Our humble servant, abandon yourself to Our love and know that We are with you. Recall that We shared with you that a great suffering would cause much sorrow in your heart?
Janie: Yes, I remember My Lord. Please help me to suffer well. I love my family, and I will do anything for them. I just wish that little children did not have to suffer.
Jesus: Our humble servant, children are victims of their parents' sin-

fulness and choices that they make. Parents forget just how precious their children are. They forget that they are gifts from Heaven. Our hearts are sorrowful for all the children who suffer so much because their parents do not have love in their hearts.

Children are at the mercy of their parents. These little treasures are totally dependent on their parents to love them, to protect them and to provide for them. Many children are being neglected by their parents; they are abused by those they trust the most. Parents do not know the evil that they do against their children when they abandon their responsibility as parents. The day will come when they stand before My Father and have to give an account for what they do to their children. It will not go well with them on judgment day.

Our humble servant, pray for all parents throughout the world who do evil to their children. Always love all children and help them in any way that you can. Children are precious gems. Love them and pray for them.

Know that you will endure much suffering for all the children who suffer from the neglect of their parents. Rejoice, for as you suffer for them; their own pain will become lighter and your prayers will console their little wounded hearts. Unite your suffering with Ours. Until tomorrow, We give you Our blessing.

Janie: Beloved Savior and my Blessed Mother, I will embrace all children throughout the world through my love and prayers. *Our Lord and Our Lady showed me in a vision, how many children were suffering throughout the world. I saw children alone, being abused. I saw children in the streets, hungry and cold and scared. I saw children with illnesses such as AIDS and other illnesses brought on by parental neglect. This was so painful for me to see.*

August 26, 1995 *Today has been very hard for me*

Jesus: Our humble servant, We are here to bless you and your family. We are here to comfort you in your suffering.
Janie: Thank You Beloved Savior and my Holy Mother. Today has been very hard for me. I have been very busy with my little grandson. I am trying to keep my house extra clean so that it's safe for him when he crawls on the floor. He really enjoys crawling. He is also taking steps. He brings so much joy to my heart.
Our Lady: Our sweet angel, you are doing well with taking care of

your little grandson. We understand that you are busy and that you are also suffering for him. We are with you helping you to accomplish all that you need to.
Janie: Beloved Savior and Blessed Mother, please intercede for me so that I may do God's Holy Will. Please pray for my special intentions.
Jesus: Our humble servant, your request will be granted. We know you are busy with your little grandson. We give you Our blessing.

August 27, 1995 *Holy Spirit, pour your strength into our hearts*

Jesus: Our humble servant, We are here to bless you and your family.
Janie: Thank You so much. Please intercede for me, so that I may take good care of my family and my little grandson.

Our Lady: Our precious angel, you are doing well with all your responsibilities, have no worry. Continue to pray and ask the Holy Spirit to pour out His strength into your heart. Know that We are with you. We give you Our blessing.

August 28, 1995 *All the graces and blessings being given*

Jesus: Good morning, Our humble servant. We are here to bless you and your family. Special graces are being given to you to help you with your little grandson.
Janie: Good morning, and thank You so much for helping me. I appreciate all the graces and blessings. My little grandson is a handful. He is so precious! He loves to play. I have a good time with him. I am getting attached to him. Help me in this area please.
Our Lady: Our sweet angel, your love is helping your little grandson. Your love makes him happy and joyful. He knows in his little heart that you love him very much. Do not worry about anything. Enjoy your time with him. We give you Our blessing.

August 29, 1995 *Suffer for the sake of love*

Jesus: Good morning, Our humble servant. We are here to bless you and your family.
Janie: Thank You so much for blessing us. We are in great need of blessing.
Jesus: Our humble servant, continue to endure your suffering for the sake of love for all the children that suffer throughout the world.
Our Lady: Our precious angel, your prayers are so important to help these innocent little angels that suffer so much. Today as you take care

of your little grandson, offer all your pain and suffering for all children and infants throughout the world. We give you Our blessing.
Janie: I will do all that You ask of me. I will suffer for the sake of love.

August 30, 1995 *Today my heart is so joyful*

Jesus: Our humble servant, We are here to bless you and your family.
Janie: Thank You both and good morning. Today my heart is so joyful. I am going to Confession and Holy Mass with my son and my little grandson.
Jesus: Our humble servant, today you will continue to feel joy in your heart. We give you Our blessing now so that you have time to get to Church in time. We will be with you.

August 31, 1995 *Visit from the Holy Souls*

Jesus: Good morning, Our humble servant. We are here to bless you and your family.
Janie: Good morning, My Lord and My Lady. Thank You so much for blessing us.
Jesus: Our humble servant, Our visit will be short, for We know that you have a busy schedule. We give you Our blessing.
Janie: *This morning I was with my husband and a friend who had stopped by when I heard a knock on the door. When I went to answer it I could only see great light like an outline (silhouettes) of persons. Then I heard these words: "We came to thank you for your prayers. We are on our way to Heaven. There are ten of us." This happened again later on this evening, ten more souls going to Heaven. They promised that they would pray for me. The first knock was heard by my husband and my friend.*

August 31, 1995 *Pray as a family like never before*

Our Lady: Dear children, today, I invite you to embrace prayer as a family like never before. Satan is on the prowl seeking to destroy you as a family. Let prayer be life for you, and do not allow one day to go by when you do not pray together as a family.

Little children, my time with you is short so it is important that you do all that I am inviting you to do. Allow me to help you as a family, for you are so special to me. Take refuge in the Paradise of my Immaculate Heart and embrace me as your heavenly Mother through your prayers. Know that the Holy Family is most present when you gather as a family for prayer time. Family prayer is so important because it helps you to draw closer to God, and prayer strengthens you as a family.

Little children, when you are at prayer, you are transformed into beautiful heavenly flowers, and this brings joy to my Heart. Begin your day as a family with prayer, and end your day with gratitude to God for all His blessings and graces.

Little children, I am your Mother come from Heaven to love you, to teach you how to pray as a family. I am your Mother of Compassion and Love. I have come to help you to convert, to teach you about family compassion and love which the world has forgotten. I have come to bring peace into your hearts as a family. Pray, pray, pray. Thank you for listening to my message.

September 1, 1995 *Offer your pain for all the suffering children*

Jesus: Good morning, Our humble servant. We are here to bless you and your family.
Janie: Good morning, My Lord and My Lady. Thank You so much for blessing us.
Jesus: Our humble servant, We know just how much you are suffering because you miss your little grandson. Your pain is deep in the very depth of your soul. Offer your pain for all the children that suffer throughout the world.
Janie: Oh Jesus, I am so sad. I miss my little grandson. Please take care of him and protect him. He is so special to us. We love him so much. My heart is lonely for him.
Our Lady: Our sweet angel, We are with you in a special way. Unite your suffering with us. We give you Our blessing for We know how much you are hurting. We know that you would like some quiet time alone. We respect that. We are at your side.

September 2, 1995 *Janie's guardian angel speaks*

Jesus: Our humble servant, We are here to bless you and to comfort you in your suffering. Have no worry, We are with you and we know the pain in your heart.
Janie: Beloved Savior and Blessed Mother, please give me a blessing, for it is so hard for me to write.
Jesus: We will bless you, and you will be able to write some tomorrow. Know that your suffering will increase and at times you will not be able to do anything without your family's help. Offer your suffering for My

beloved Vicar on earth. Until tomorrow.
Janie: Oh my guardian angel, please help me to suffer well for My Lord and Blessed Mother.
Janie's guardian angel, Michael: Do not worry my dear friend. I am here to help you in your suffering. I never leave your side. I pray for you when you suffer and when you are unable to pray. Know that we guardian angels never stop helping those souls that we are assigned to. My dear friend, tomorrow I will help you to write more. I am at your side.

September 3, 1995 *Do not be sad, my angel*

Jesus: Good evening, Our humble servant.
Janie: Good evening, My Lord and My Lady. Thank You for being so patient with me. Lately I've been having a difficult time. It seems that everything is going wrong. I feel like I am in the desert, my soul feels parched and dry. Please help me, because I am really feeling sad about October 7th when I have my last daily visit with you, Blessed Mother. I know that you will come on special feast days, my birthday and in times of suffering, but I'll miss you.
Our Lady: Our sweet angel, you will suffer from sadness in your heart. This is normal for you to experience these emotions. I, too, have sadness in my Heart, for I look forward to our visits. I have been visiting with you for over six years. We have shared much and I will miss our visits, but I shall be with you in special times. Do not be sad, my angel, but pray with your heavenly Mother who is always praying for you.
Janie: I will pray, Blessed Mother, and I'll try not to allow myself to be sad.
Our Lady: Our sweet angel, We shall always be with you. We give you Our blessing.
Janie: Thank You both.

September 4, 1996 *Husbands and wives, spend time together*

Jesus: Good evening, Our humble servant. We are here to bless you and your family.
Janie: Good evening, My Lord and My Savior. Please forgive me for meeting with You so late, but I have been busy spending time with my husband. He had some time off, and we went to many places and had a good time.
Jesus: Our humble servant, you must always know that spending time with your husband is most important. My Father blesses you as husband and wife when you spend time together. Many marriages grow

weak because spouses do not spend time together. Did you enjoy yourself Our little one?

Janie: Yes, I did very much, but at times Satan attempted to come between us and make us disagree on certain things, but we knew that it was him. We had a wonderful time, and I think that we found someone to help us get our home on our land started. We are happy about that.

Our Lady: Our sweet angel, it sounds like you and your husband had a joyful time together. You have accomplished much these past few days. You and your husband must pray much to the Holy Spirit, so that He will help you with the building of your new home.

Janie: Oh, Blessed Mother, I think that we are also going to be working on the Cross and pouring the foundation for the Chapel. I am a little nervous.

Our Lady: Do not have any worry. All will go well. Continue to trust God with this project and abandon all concern to Him. Remain in the spirit of prayer as a family. It is late now Our angel. We give you Our blessing. Until tomorrow.

Janie: Oh thank You so much for helping me. Until tomorrow.

September 6, 1995 *Your love is constantly being tested*

Jesus: Good evening, Our humble servant. We are here to help you and to comfort you in your time of suffering.

Janie: Thank You so much My Adorable Savior and My Holy Mother. I feel so alone and detached from everyone and everything. I have so many doubts in my mind, but I know that it is the evil one.

Our Lady: Our sweet angel, your love is constantly being tested for your family. You will endure all your suffering for your family. Know that Satan is strong trying to destroy your faith by placing many temptations in your family's path. Continue to persevere in your prayers and your love for them, for God is listening to your prayers.

Janie: Please pray for me so that I may stay focused on God's Holy Will for us as a family. I am truly struggling, please help me.

Jesus: Our humble servant, your suffering is helping your family. Do not despair, for We are with you. It is important that you know that Satan is angry for all the work that you are doing, helping many to convert. Satan wants to distract you and your husband from the project that you are working on. All will go well and everything will proceed as scheduled, have no worry.

Remain in the spirit of prayer and do not allow Satan to distract you from the path which I have traced out for you and your family. Remember your family Rosary is your weapon, and your love for one

another will drive all of Satan's attacks far away from you. Remain in the spirit of prayer. We give you Our blessing.
Janie: Thank You both.

September 7, 1995 *Decide for conversion before it's too late*

Our Lady: Dear children, today I invite you as a family to continue to pray together everyday. I am pleading to you my children so that together our prayers will help to bring peace to those many souls that continue to walk in darkness.

Little children, there is so much evil in the world because many do not believe in prayer. They have forgotten about my Son, Who died on the Cross for their redemption. Many have abandoned my Son completely and say that there is no God. I beg you to please pray for all these poor sinners who have this mentality, for they are truly on their way to perdition.

Little children, your conversion is so important to me, that is why I invite you to decide for conversion before it's too late! Satan is so active, destroying many families because they do not believe in prayer. Many of the youth are on their way to perdition for the lifestyles they have chosen, because their parents did not teach them about God and about prayer.

These young souls do not know or recognize that the lifestyles that they have chosen are evil, because their parents did not take the time to teach them about God's goodness and His great love that He has for all of humanity.

Little children, I share these concerns which cause much sorrow to my Immaculate Heart, so that you will pray for all troubled youth in the world. Pray, children, pray for all the evil in the world, for prayer is what will heal many souls. Thank you for listening to my message.

September 8, 1995 *Birthday of Our Lady - This evil cannot be ignored*

Our Lady: Greetings, my precious angel.
Janie: Happy Birthday again my Most Holy Mother. You look so heavenly beautiful. *She was dressed in all gold and had a crown. She was surrounded by angels.*
Our Lady: My precious angel, you have been suffering all day and

your heart is sad. Tell your Mother everything.

Janie: I am sad for the ruin of many of the youth, for the children that suffer so much and all the slaughtering of the unborn babies. These babies are so precious. Why are they not wanted by their parents?

Our Lady: My angel, it is because God's love does not exist in their hearts. Their hearts and souls are infected with darkness. There is no light in these souls who participate in the killing of their unborn babies, these precious treasures from Heaven. My precious angel, pray for this horrible evil to end, for many, many who participate in the abuse of their children and the killing of their unborn children are truly on their way to perdition.

Janie: Oh, my Blessed Mother, I do not wish to talk about this evil in the world on your birthday. I do not wish to see you sad.

Our Lady: My sweet angel, this evil cannot be ignored and go unnoticed. This evil is most offensive to God and He will pass judgment on these souls. Their punishment is eternal damnation. Those many souls that continue to neglect their responsibilities as parents and abuse and kill their children, they are on their way to perdition.

Janie: Blessed Mother, can prayer really stop this evil?

Our Lady: Yes, my angel, prayer is the only answer. Prayer softens and melts away the darkness that exists in many souls. Pray much for poor, poor sinners. Please pray for this intention. I give you my motherly blessing.

Janie: Thank you, My Lady, thank you. I love you.

Our Lady: I love you.

September 9, 1995 *The Illumination*

Jesus: Good morning, Our humble servant. We are here to bless you and your family. We are here to comfort you in your suffering.

Janie: Good morning, My Lord and My Lady. Thank You so much for blessing us and for bringing comfort to my heart.

Our Lady: Our sweet angel, you are suffering, for you've seen all the evil in the world through the visions which God allows you to see. You have seen many of the things that are to come. You have seen the suffering in the families and the suffering in the Bride of my Son. These visions which you embrace with your heart and make reparation for, this is the reason for your great suffering.

Janie: Blessed Mother, I don't mind my suffering, but I am affected by knowing of all the suffering youth, the children and the killing of the unborn babies. Please pray so that I will pray unceasingly for the poor sinners in the world. Could you tell me about the illumination which St. Joseph talked to me about. Will people suffer much?

Jesus: Our humble servant, the illumination that will take place will be for a short period. During this time My Father will allow all of humanity to see the state of their souls as My Father see their souls. This will be a time of great grace when many souls will repent and return to My Father. Those souls that die will die from great shock to see the state of the darkness which exists in their souls.
Janie: *Beloved Savior, will the illumination scare people?*
Jesus: The fear that will inflame their hearts is the holy fear of the immense power of My Father, especially for those many souls that have continued to deny the existence of My Father. These will be the souls that will experience tremendous fear.
Janie: *Will all people convert?*
Jesus: Many will convert, but many will not.
Janie: *Oh, Jesus, will this happen very soon?*
Jesus: Our humble servant, this will happen within a short period. Do not be distracted with dates, but prepare everyday with strong prayer. Many who worry about these times will not live to see these things take place. This is why Holy Scripture warns everybody not to be concerned about tomorrow, for tomorrow is promised to no one. The present day has enough trials and crosses.

Know that when We speak about such things to come; this is for the people to convert and abandon their evil ways. Everyday is an opportunity for souls to convert. People should not wait for such things to come to convert, but they should convert now, before it's too late! The very fact that such judgments will come is because people refuse to convert and continue to live in darkness.
Janie: Oh Beloved Savior, please continue to pour Your love and mercy into our souls so that we accept You as our Savior truly in our lives. I love You both.
Jesus: We love you, and all your prayers, your sacrifices and your little ways are pleasing to Us. We give you Our blessings. Until tomorrow, remain in the spirit of prayer as a family.
Janie: We will, we truly will.

September 12, 1995 *The Archangels will come*

Jesus: Good afternoon, Our humble servant. We are here to bless you and your family.
Janie: Thank You so much for blessing us. I need your help more than ever to help me to embrace my cross truly with love in my heart.
Jesus: Our humble servant, never be distracted with the crosses that will help others to convert, especially your own family. We know that

your suffering is a heavy burden; that is why We come to you everyday, to help you to embrace your daily crosses.

Janie: Oh, Jesus and Mary, what will happen to me when You are no longer coming everyday? Will I still be able to embrace my daily suffering?

Our Lady: Our precious angel, the Holy Spirit will continue to give you His strength and the Three Archangels will themselves come to you on a daily basis to help you.

Janie: Oh, I didn't know this. Gosh, I am so grateful. I understood that after your last visit (Blessed Mother), the Archangels would come in your place.

Our Lady: Our dear one, this will happen as well, however, the mission and responsibility given to you for the family is so important that the Archangels and other angels will help you in your mission to help families throughout the world.

Janie: How will this happen?

Our Lady: Every day when you pray your chaplet to St. Michael the Archangels will flock to you and you will be aware of their presence. The Holy Spirit and the Archangels will always be with you whenever God asks you to go to speak to the family. Know that the Holy Spirit will be very strong in your life. Everyday, the Holy Spirit will help you to grow in His truth and His wisdom. You must abandon yourself to the Holy Spirit so that you may truly die to yourself and live completely in His truth. Our sweet angel, Our own presence will be strong in your life, but the Holy Spirit will enlighten you with visions of things to come. The Archangels will also tell you of things to come.

Janie: Blessed Mother, when will the visits of the Archangels and the angels stop?

Our Lady: You will know this at the appointed time. We ask you to prepare yourself with strong prayer and fasting. Do all that we ask you to do so that my adversary's attacks on you will melt as soon as he comes with his evil attacks. After Our visits cease, you will continue to be as if We were coming to you daily. Have no worry, remember, We will come to you on your birthday, anniversary days, special feast days and in times of great suffering. Meanwhile, remain in the spirit of strong prayer. Until tomorrow, We give you Our blessing.

Janie: Thank You.

September 13, 1995 *The wedding banquet*

Jesus: Good morning, Our most humble servant. We are here to bless you and your family.

Janie: *They embraced me as They greeted me. I had finished my morn-*

ing prayer of total abandonment to Our Lord.
Jesus: Your morning prayer is truly pleasing to My Father. Our dear one, you will suffer much throughout your lifetime, but you will find great joy in your suffering, for it will be in your great suffering that you be united with Me in the garden of Gethsemane.
Janie: *I felt heat all over my entire body after my prayer.* Good morning, my Precious Heavenly Friends and Teachers. Oh, how I love You, God only knows how much. My heart aches with joy to be so blessed to have You come. Praised be the Most Holy Eternal One, for loving us so much unworthy as we are.
Jesus: Our humble servant, you and your family are truly most blessed to receive visits from the Holy Family, to help you to grow in holiness as a family. Embrace this heavenly blessing and show My Father your gratitude by praying together and loving one another.
Janie: My dear Savior and my Most Holy Mother, do You have some special intentions which You wish for me to pray for?
Jesus: Our humble servant, this morning We wish to share with you the importance of praying everyday, so that you and your family will be prepared. Pray for all those who do not believe in prayer, for it will not go well with them in the days to come. Daily, My Father continues to prepare a banquet for all to come and to share in His great love, but many continue to ignore His invitation.
Janie: *The Lord allowed me to see the vision of the Wedding Banquet which is written in Holy Scripture. Matthew 22:1-14.*
Jesus: Everyday My Father dispatches His servants, the angels, to summon the invited guests, humanity, but the guests refuse to come. They continue to put other affairs before My Father's invitation. Oh, how these poor sinners will suffer, for they have refused to eat from the banquet prepared by My Father. Pray, Our dear one, for these poor sinners.
Our Lady: Our humble servant, pray with Us so that through Our prayers poor sinners may convert!

September 14, 1995 *In the very early hours of the morning*

Jesus: My child, know that you have pleased Me in your response to take care of your little grandson when you know that you have busy days ahead. You abandon yourself to My trust and you respond with a 'yes' to help out, because you know that this pleases Me. Your heart is full of love and holy charity and you extend your help to all.

You were concerned for the young mother of your grandson who called you in her most desperate need, and you responded with love. You offered to take care of your grandson in his illness so that his young

mother would not lose a day of school. My humble child, you have brought joy to My Eucharistic Heart in your little humble ways.
Janie: *I was so thankful that God notices all that we do in our lives, even the smallest of things. God is love Himself and He invites us all to be transformed into His love through our works of charity. God sees everything, let us live to please Him.*

September 14, 1995 *Triumph of the Cross*

Jesus: Our humble servant, We are here to bless you and your family. Today We invite you to rejoice in the Triumph of My Resurrection.
Janie: Thank You so much for helping me to be inflamed with such joy. I shall be united in the joy of Your glorious Resurrection. I love You, My Lord and my All.
Jesus: We give you Our blessing.

September 14, 1995 *Jesus' visit to the prayer group*

Janie: *I saw Jesus with great rays of light over the Cross on our land. There was a multitude of angels all around the Cross and all over our land. Jesus was most beautiful, and His garments were dazzling white. Rays of different colors were emanating from His Heart and hands. The colors were gold, red, blue and many other different colors.*

He filled my heart with such joy and love. He talked with me about the great victory that we have in His Cross, and how He died and resurrected for love of us. I saw rays come from His Heart to all the people that were there, and the rays were plunged deep into their hearts and souls. Jesus shared with me how all our prayers are heard, even the smallest prayers. In all our suffering and sorrow, He is with us and we are never alone.

His holy Cross is our triumph and our victory. He died so that we may have life and have it more abundantly; and by His stripes we are healed. Nothing is lacking in us if we believe with faith in the Triumph of Our Lord's Cross. We should be a people of great joy, for Jesus Christ, the Son of the Most High and Living God, has paid the price for us and through Him we are victorious.

September 14, 1995 *Embrace My Cross with joy in your hearts*

Jesus: Beloved of My Father, behold the Triumph of My Cross. Know that today is a day of great rejoicing for the faithful people of My Father, for today My Bride celebrates the Triumph of My Cross. Today is a day of great victory for all those who believe in My death and Resurrection, for My Father so loved the world, that He gave His only Begotten so that everyone who believes in Him may not die but have eternal life.

Rejoice, beloved, rejoice with your Beloved Savior Who paid the price with His life for you. I took the sins of the world upon Me, for I came that you may have life and have it more abundantly. It was through My death and Resurrection that salvation came into the world. Beloved of My Father, embrace My Cross with joy in your heart, for it is only through embracing My Cross that you will truly embrace your Beloved Savior.
I, your risen Savior, say to you, fear nothing, but only believe in the Triumph of My Cross. Beloved, I, your risen Savior, have prepared everything for you, everything! If you believe in what I am telling you then you understand the great victory in the Triumph of My Cross. I, your risen Savior, have paved the way for you with My life.

My suffering was great, more than what you could ever understand, but I did it out of love. I came to give light to a world walking in darkness and to redeem mankind back to My Father. Beloved, yours were the sins I carried but by My stripes you are healed. Beloved, embrace the healing in faith and rejoice with Me on this glorious day. When you gaze upon My Cross, recall the great victory behind the Triumph of the Cross and rejoice, rejoice, rejoice!

September 15, 1995 *Know for certain that We are with you*

Jesus: Our humble servant, We are here to bless you and your family and to help you in your suffering, when your heart is experiencing doubt.
Janie: Thank You so much for helping me. I admit that I believe that I must be out of my mind in believing that I am being visited by You, My Lord, and you, my Holy Mother. Please pray for me for I need much help.
Jesus: Our humble servant, know that you are constantly in Our prayers. You are suffering because you recognize your unworthiness, and yet you have been chosen to carry out a heavenly task. Abandon all worry and believe that you are not out of your mind. Know, for certain, that we are with you. We give you Our blessing, for We know that you are tired.
Janie: Thank You both. Please forgive me for my doubts.

September 15, 1995 *Feast of Our Lady of Sorrow - Her bloody tears*

Our Lady: Dear children, today, I invite you to embrace your Sorrowful Mother who weeps bloody tears for all my children that live in darkness. Little children, I need your continuous prayers and sacrifices to help those many souls who continue to ignore the call to conversion. You are living in times of great suffering, when my adversary is waging war and bringing the destruction of many, many souls.

Today, I come to you as Mother of Sorrows and beg you to repent before it's too late. Today, I continue to cry bloody tears for the slaughter of all the little unborn babies that suffer a most horrible death. Their little souls cry out to Heaven for Divine Intervention. This evil must stop, for if it continues, nations will self-destruct, for God's justice will be done.

Today, I cry bloody tears for the destruction of the troubled youth who live sinful lives, and for all the abuse of children everywhere. Today, I cry bloody tears for the violence in the family, the wars among nations and for the sinfulness in the Church. Today, I cry bloody tears for my Son's Vicar on earth, and for his own suffering that he endures for all those priests and religious that oppose him and disobey him. This causes such sorrow in my heart.

Little children, those of you who embrace me as your heavenly Mother console my Sorrowful Heart. Your love and prayers help to remove that sharp sword from my Sorrowful Heart. I love you, my children, I love you. Embrace your Sorrowful Mother and console me with your love.

September 16, 1995 *Enflame my heart with the fire of your Son's love*

Jesus: Good morning, Our humble servant. We are here to bless you and your family.
Janie: Good morning, my Adorable Savior and my Holy Mother. Thank You so much for helping me with my prayers. Today I'd like to ask for extra graces to accomplish certain virtues in my daily walk with You.
Jesus: Our humble servant, what would you like My Father to grant you today? Ask for whatever in My Name, and it shall be done unto You.
Janie: I do ask the Father in Your precious and Most Holy Name. **Eternal Father, today I come to you in the Name of Your Son, My Lord and Redeemer, and I ask that You inflame my heart with the fire of Your Son's love that He demonstrated in taking our sins upon**

Himself, and in dying for us a most horrible and brutal death.

Give me the grace to have that very same love that He had at Calvary and that He continues to have. Though His death was enough for us, He, out of great love for us, chose to remain hidden in the Most Holy Eucharist, the Holy Bread of the Angels. Eternal Father, this is the love which I wish to have in my heart and soul, so that I may love as He did, forgive as He did, and to model after Him all the days of my life.

Eternal Father, I do not wish to cause anybody sadness. I do not wish to anger anyone. I do not want jealousy or envy to dwell in my heart. I want to love everyone with unconditional love. I want the love of Your Son to dwell in me. I want to live and die for His love. I want Him to live perfectly in me so that all I do will be according to Your Most Holy Will. Please, my Eternal Father, hear my prayer. Inflame my heart and soul with Your Spirit of Truth, so that I may perfectly live by Your Truth, loving as Your Son loves. Amen.

Jesus: Our most humble servant, know for certain that this grace is yours from this moment on, for your prayer is most pleasing to My Father. We give you Our blessing.

September 19, 1995 *Abandon yourself to Our Two United Hearts*

Jesus: Good evening, Our humble servant. We are here to bless you and your family.

Janie: Thank You so much and please continue to bless my son as he goes on celebrating his birthday. Please also pray for my special intentions.

Our Lady: Our precious angel, We know that you have been suffering much. Know that We are with you. Abandon yourself to Our Two United Hearts and allow Our love to give you strength. We will intercede for all your special intentions.

Janie: My Dear Lord and My Lady, please ask God to grant me special graces to endure my suffering. Please help me.

Our Lady: We will help you, do not worry. We give you Our blessing. Until tomorrow.

September 20, 1995 *My soul feels empty and dry*

Jesus: Good evening, Our humble servant. We are here to bless you and your family.

Janie: Good evening, my Beloved Savior and my dear Mother. Thank

You for coming.

Our Lady: Our precious angel, you are sad tonight. Tell us what can We do to help you?

Janie: I really don't know, I feel so unlike myself. I am tired of everything. I cannot explain. I know that I am not making much sense. I need Your prayers, my soul feels empty and dry.

Our Lady: Our dear angel, your soul is not empty or dry. You are experiencing a little of what my Son did before He was put to death. God is allowing you to experience this agony to help draw you closer to Him.

Janie: But I have so much doubt in my heart about truly receiving divine visitations. I feel like I am misleading people who believe that I am having visitations from Heaven. The last thing I want is to mislead anyone. It's not that I am ungrateful, but sometimes I wish that I hadn't been chosen in this way because of my doubts. Please forgive me for saying this. I just don't want to blaspheme against God.

Our Lady: Our sweet angel, you do not need to apologize. God understands your deep pain. You have been chosen and with this gift comes a great responsibility. Have no worry, you haven't done anything wrong, you are only speaking what is in your heart and what God already knows. He loves truth. In this way He can help you in your suffering. Know that those few chosen souls that truly receive heavenly visitations also doubt. Be at peace and abandon yourself to Our Two United Hearts. You are also not feeling physically well, but you will be all right. Trust in Our help. We give you Our blessing.

Janie: Please help my Spiritual Director with his special intention and my friend's grandson.

September 21, 1995 *The flowing of the Holy Spirit within my soul*

Jesus: Good evening, Our humble servant. We are here to bless you and your family.

Janie: Thank You both. I am so happy that I am doing better. Thank You both for your prayers and strength.

Jesus: Our humble servant, these next few days will be filled with many graces and blessings for all the people with whom you will be sharing your life. Many families will be enlightened by what you share with them. Abandon yourself to Us during this time, and the Holy Spirit will enlighten you in all that you will share concerning the family. Trust in Us completely and through your trust in Us, many families will be helped.

Janie: My Beloved Savior and my Dear Mother, I promise that I will abandon myself to Your intercession. I will be completely open to the

flowing of the Holy Spirit within my soul. I will trust Him totally.
Our Lady: Our sweet angel. We give you Our blessing.

September 22, 1995 *Corpus Christi, Texas* *Prayer and forgiveness*

Jesus: Our humble servant, We have brought you to this city to give witness to the teaching of the Holy Family. Know that those souls who listen with their hearts and embrace these heavenly teachings will receive blessings as a family.
Our Lady: Our sweet angel, share with my children the importance of family prayer and forgiveness. I want to help all my children, but I cannot if they do not pray. The Holy Spirit will speak to their hearts through you.

September 22, 1995 *Corpus Christi, Texas* *Not the smallest worry*

Janie: *Our Lady and her Son came tonight while I was at Holy Family Church giving my talk.*
Our Lady: My dear child, tell my children not to have the smallest worry for my Son knows their needs. We came to bless each one of them as well as their loved ones whom they invited, but did not come. Convey to them that We love them very much and that We are with them, protecting them through Our prayers.

September 23, 1995 *Corpus Christi, Texas* *Abandon yourself*

Jesus: Our humble servant, today We bless you as you continue to suffer in reparation for all those souls who will come to hear your sharing on the teaching of the Holy Family. Know that We are with you in a strong way and that the Holy Spirit will speak through you. Continue to prepare yourself with strong prayer.
Our Lady: Our sweet angel, know how much you are pleasing God through all your hard efforts. Abandon yourself to His love and mercy and you will remain united to us.

September 23, 1995 *Corpus Christi, Texas* *At the Hospital*

Janie: *Our Lady of Guadalupe came when I was at the hospital visiting a very dear friend whose husband was very ill.*
Our Lady: Convey to my daughter and her children these words: My dear children, I come to you in your great suffering to comfort you and to console you. I am here to bring you my love and to tell you, do not be worried or anxious about anything. Am I not here, who am your

Mother? My little ones, nothing will harm you, nothing will bring you distress if you but listen to my words and allow them to penetrate your heart.

September 23, 1995 *Corpus Christi, Texas* *Your love consoles Me*

Janie: *Later that day I went to two dear friends to spend a few silent moments at the beach. We prayed the Chaplet of Divine Mercy. In the sky*

I saw the Sacred Heart of Jesus and His Heart was dripping blood. I saw little angels collecting the blood, and then they would pour it over the entire city of Corpus Christi and all over the world. Then I heard Jesus say these words.

Jesus: See how great is My love for all of humanity? Oh, if souls only would realize how much I suffer for love of them. Console Me, My daughter through your love. Console your Beloved Master, console Me.

September 24, 1995 *This priest is most dear to our hearts*

Jesus: Our dear humble servant, We are here to comfort you in your suffering. Today you will continue to give witness of your love for Us. Know that you are protected by Us and all the angels that encamp around you.

Janie: Sweet Jesus and my Dear Mother, please give an abundance of blessings to Monsignor for inviting me. He is so special to You, and he loves You two so much. I am grateful to be here with him. He is so prayerful. I love that in a priest.

Jesus: Our humble servant, My beloved brother is truly prayerful. He works hard to teach the flock entrusted to him. We indeed are at his side day and night. He is most dear to Our Two United Hearts.

Janie: Thank You so much for Your kind words, my Dear Savior and Master.

September 24, 1995 *Corpus Christi* *Blessings to a homebound soul*

Janie: *Later that day Our Lady of Guadalupe came again when we went to visit a sweet special soul who is homebound.*

Our Lady: My sweet daughter, I am here to thank you for all your many prayers and your great suffering. Know that you are helping many souls through your prayers and sacrifices. I give you my motherly blessing. I love you dearly.

September 25, 1995 *Allow Our love to refresh you*

Jesus: Our humble servant, We are here to bless you. We know how very tired you are. Rest and allow Our love to refresh you as you sleep. We are most grateful for all your hard efforts.
Our Lady: Our sweet angel, you have worked so hard to help draw souls closer to Our Hearts. Know that God will reward all your hard efforts. You are so dear to Our Hearts. Many families are deciding for conversion because of your hard work. God is most pleased with your total surrender and obedience to go out and be a witness to His Kingdom and to His love and mercy.
Janie: My Lord and my Blessed Mother, I am most happy to help souls know all about God. I am so very grateful for all His graces and blessings, especially my family.

September 26, 1995 *Your faith will be your strength*

Jesus: Good evening, Our humble servant. We are here to bless you and your family.
Janie: Thank You both so very much. I so need Your blessing.
Jesus: Our humble servant, We know that you are suffering and that you are having a difficult time knowing that in just a matter of days, you will be having your last scheduled visit with My dear Mother.
Janie: Yes, my Beloved Savior and My Lady. I am having a very difficult time accepting this. I know that you, my Holy Mother, will visit me on certain days, but between these times I will miss you. I have gotten so used to being with you on a daily basis. Deep down in my heart, I want to beg you to stay, but I will be obedient to God's plan for me.
Our Lady: Our precious angel, I know this is most hard for you, but recall what my children in Medjugorje said to you, that your faith will be your strength.
Janie: *This was told to me by one of the visionaries in Medjugorje, that when Our Lady stopped visiting me, my faith would be my strength.* My Blessed Mother, I know this, but I cannot help myself; I am having a difficult time. I don't want to be around anybody, I don't want to do any house work. I have to force myself to keep up with my daily duties as a mother and a wife. However, I am doing the best that I can.
Our Lady: Our precious angel, We know that you are going through all these most difficult days, but know that We are with you helping you to endure this suffering. I, too, am sad, but We must both submit to God's Most Holy Will, so that We may please Him. You will help your heavenly Mother won't you, my angel?
Janie: Oh, yes, with all my heart and I promise to be strong. Whatever

pain I may have, I will offer it up for my own purification. Please forgive me, I didn't mean to complain.
Our Lady: Our precious angel, you are not complaining, you are sharing what's in your heart. Pray very hard in these next few days. I shall share something that will make you very happy in a few days. Until then remain patient, my sweet angel.
Janie: I promise that I will be patient.
Jesus: Our humble servant, know that you are dear to Our Two United Hearts, and that We will see you through these difficult times. Trust Us and abandon yourself to Us.
Janie: My Beloved Savior, I will do as You say. Could You tell me if I will continue to suffer physically? Lately, I have been suffering physically on a daily basis. Could You explain to me if this suffering will increase?
Jesus: Our humble servant, your physical suffering will increase and your suffering will become more difficult. Offer your suffering for the sins of My Bride, for She will undergo a great suffering. Your suffering and prayers will help My Bride. Now, We give you Our blessing.
Janie: Thank You, I love You.

September 27, 1995 *Unite your prayers with Ours*

Jesus: Good morning, Our humble servant. We are here to bless you and your family.
Janie: Good morning, my Beloved Savior and Mother. Thank You so much for Your blessing.
Jesus: Our humble servant, you are doing much better this morning.
Janie: Oh, yes, I am indeed doing great. Your visit last night strengthened me so much. I don't have words to express my deep gratitude.
Jesus: Our humble servant, We will always be right by your side to help you in your faith journey. Know that you will continue to suffer My most bitter Passion throughout your life. At times your suffering will be most difficult; you will have to remain at home. You will suffer on Monday's, Wednesdays and Fridays. This is the time when your suffering will increase. Other times you will suffer as well.
Janie: My Beloved Savior, what will I offer my suffering for during these times?
Jesus: My humble servant, your guardian angel will tell you. Know that the three Archangels will help you in many ways. They will come to you twice a month. They will take the place of My Mother. They will tell you many things to pray for and they will show you visions of things to come. You must write everything they tell you.

Janie: I will be obedient to everything You and my beloved Mother ask of me. One thing I ask is a favor if You will. Ask God to give me the grace to pray the Creed, the Our Father, the Hail Mary and the Gloria in Latin. I would like this very much.

Our Lady: Our sweet angel, you will know these prayers, have no worry. We ask that you continue to unite your prayers with Our prayers, so that God's plan will be realized in the world.

Many souls continue to ignore my messages, and they remain in their sinful lives. Please pray for these prideful souls who ignore the call to conversion, for it will not go well with them if they choose to remain in their sin.

Janie: Blessed Mother, I will pray for all these intentions. I love You, my sweet Savior and my dear Blessed Mother. I shall do everything for Your special intentions out of my love for You and poor sinners. I shall never grow weary of doing God's Most Holy Will.

Jesus: Our humble servant, know that throughout your life you will be visited by the angels, by saints and the Holy Souls. You will not be left without the consolation of Heaven. Know that you have been prepared to help many souls during the time when souls suffer. Your suffering will help many and your gift to know certain struggles in souls will increase. You will be given more wisdom in this area in your life. Your gifts will be numerous for you will need these gifts to help souls.

Janie: Will I know these gifts?

Jesus: Yes, for the Holy Spirit of Truth will reveal all this to you. Your faith journey will be a difficult journey, but you have been enclothed with the grace to endure everything.

September 28, 1995 *Prayer, fasting, Rosary, Eucharist, Holy Scripture*

Our Lady: Dear children, today I invite you as a family, to embrace your heavenly Mother who loves you with immense motherly love. Open your hearts and allow my messages to penetrate your hearts. Time is short, my little ones, and I desire that you be obedient to living all my heavenly messages as a family.

Little children, allow yourselves to be led by me, for I cannot help you if you ignore all that I am teaching you as a family. I love you so much and my heart suffers so when you mistreat one another, when you quarrel. Be a loving family and allow your love to be a witness to others around you.

Do not be sad or fearful because soon I won't be with you as I have

been during this time. **I will never leave you, my little ones. I will be with you in your prayers.** You will feel my love as you embrace my messages and continue to apply them to your everyday lives. I will be with you when you pray your Rosary as a family.
I will protect you with my motherly prayers. I will not leave your side, not even for one moment! **My children, remember the spiritual weapons that I have given you: prayer, fasting, the Rosary, the Eucharist and Holy Scripture. These are your weapons to help you to lead good lives and to follow the path which my Son traced out for you. My Spouse, the Holy Spirit, will help lead you towards holiness.** I love you. I love you all. I give you my motherly blessing. Thank you for listening to my message.

October 1, 1995 *Suffer for those souls who hate my Son*

Jesus: Our humble servant, We are here to bless you in your time of great suffering. Abandon yourself to Our love, for We are here to help you to suffer with joy in your heart.
Janie: My Beloved Savior and Most Holy Mother, I thank You for blessing me, but I am really doing well. I know that I am suffering, but I want to welcome this suffering with all my heart. I want to offer God all my suffering for my own sinfulness and for the sins in every soul.
Our Lady: Our sweet angel, your response is most pleasing to God.
Janie: Dear Lord and Blessed Mother, please help me and pray for me, so that I may always desire to please God. Also pray for me, because it's so difficult for me to write because of my physical suffering. It's truly so hard for me to write. I write so messy.
Our Lady: Our sweet angel, We know that writing is very hard and painful for you. Offer all your suffering for all those poor souls who hate my Son and who speak against His Most Holy Name. These poor souls have so much evil in their hearts, they are in need of much prayer.
Janie: I will do as You ask of me, for it hurts me very much when people say evil things against Our Lord. Blessed Lord and my Holy Mother, please pray for all my grandchildren. I love all of them in a special way. They are truly a gift from God, but they suffer so much, sometimes, as You well know why.

Protect them always and shelter them in the love of Your Two United Hearts. Keep all evil away from them, for they are all pure and innocent. Provide good spiritual friends and caretakers and educators.

I wish I could always have them by my side, but I place them in the care of Your love and the love of St. Joseph. By the way, give St. Joseph a

big hug for me.
Our Lady: Our sweet angel, have no concern about your grandchildren and family; they are in Our care. We give you Our blessing. I will give St. Joseph a hug for you.

October 3, 1995 *Look at the fruits*

Jesus: Our humble servant, We are here to bless you and your family. Our dear one, We know of your great suffering and how little sleep you had. We are deeply grateful for your tireless efforts to suffer for My Bride and for poor sinners. Know that We are aware of your great pain in your hand as you write what We tell you. This is also a great cross for you, and you embrace all your crosses with love in your heart. This consoles Our Two United Hearts.
Janie: My Beloved Savior and Master and my Most Holy Queen, I abandon myself to the hands of God. May He do with me as He wishes. I am grateful for the little suffering that I can offer Him Who created me, a miserable sinner. I will never be able to show Him my deep gratitude for taking me out of the hell that I had created in my own life. Praised be His Holy Name forever and ever. Amen.
Our Lady: Our precious angel, your beautiful canticle is pleasing to God. You recognize that the heart of God is love and mercy and you respond to His love and mercy with deep gratitude. Know, Our dear angel, that as your suffering continues to increase, you will draw closer to God and to Our Hearts. Many are the great acts of charity that you will perform in your life. Many will be the souls that you will help to draw closer to God.
Janie: My Dear Blessed Mother, right now I feel so much joy in my heart, even though I know that in a few days I won't be visited by you daily. I know you love me, but sometimes I worry that I might be crazy and that perhaps all of this isn't true.

You know that I've had much schooling in the area of psychiatry, therefore I know that the mind is pretty strong and clever. This is why I question myself. Please pray for me and ask God to help me. Tell Him that if I am really not receiving heavenly visitations, to give me the punishment I deserve, but to help me not to separate from His love and mercy.
Our Lady: Our precious angel, be at peace and know for certain that God has chosen you to have these heavenly visitations. God knew that you would have these doubts; this is also part of your cross. Look at the fruits in your own life and your family. Look at the fruits of those many souls who are truly helped through your own witness. Recall what Holy Scripture says, "a tree is known by its fruits." Allow this Scripture to

penetrate your heart.
Know that I shall always be with you in all the things that you do for love of God and neighbor. You will suffer when I am no longer visiting you daily, and your heart will be sorrowful, but you will know my presence in your faith journey. I will come when you are in great distress, on your birthday, your Anniversary with me and when the Church celebrates special feast days in my honor.
Janie: Oh, Blessed Queen of my heart, I promise, though I may be sorrowful, I shall also rejoice in gratitude for having your friendship in a special way in my life. I will do my best to spend my Heaven doing good deeds on earth. I promise I will do my best.
Our Lady: Our precious angel, We know that you will. We love you very much. You are a good person. Continue to embrace your suffering with joy in your heart. We give you Our blessing.
Janie: Thank You both. I love You, my Dear Heavenly Friends.

October 4, 1995 *Feast of St. Francis - Words from St. Francis about love*

St. Francis: My spiritual daughter, always pray to God to plunge you into His love. In this way, you will be able to love all of His creation. Never allow jealousy or envy to enter into your heart, but rejoice and be grateful to God for His goodness, for all the precious gifts that He bestows upon His people. Abandon yourself completely to God and disregard all worldly desires which you love. Deny yourself everything in the world that you may obtain holiness as you continue your faith journey.
Listen to me, my child, the world has nothing to offer you but only death. Desire eternal life and do everything possible to die to yourself, so that Jesus Christ, your Lord and Master may live in your heart. Love and embrace the cross. Pray for poverty of spirit and live in simplicity, giving all your service to God. Everything you do, do it for the sake of love. When you suffer do it with joy in your heart. I bless you, my spiritual child, I bless you.

October 4, 1995 *Songs of thanksgiving and praise to the Holy Spirit*

Jesus: Our humble servant, We are here to bless you and your family.
Janie: Thank You so much for blessing us, please always keep us under Your love and protection. Please protect and watch over my sons and my grandchildren. They are so important to me, and I love them so much.
Our Lady: Our precious angel, know that you and your family are under Our protection, for all your prayers and sacrifices keep your fam-

ily safe. Prayer is so important, for it is only through prayer that you learn to communicate with God. Through prayer you discover God and when you discover God, you have total peace and trust.

Janie: Blessed Mother, please help me to do everything that you have taught me about prayer, love, forgiveness and trust. I want to do everything that you have asked us to do. Please help my family as well. I don't want a day to go by without my attending Holy Mass, praying my Rosary, spending time in the Blessed Sacrament, reading Holy Scripture. I want to be like St. Francis and imitate the Gospel and apply it to my everyday life.

Please Blessed Mother, ask God to please bless me with the spirit and love of St. Francis. He was so much like your Son. I want to love like he did, I want to understand like he did, I want to die to myself so that your Son may truly live in my heart.

Blessed Mother, I want to live Heaven on earth. I want to run from sin like I would from a poisonous snake. I want to have a charitable spirit. I want to love God with all my strength, my mind, my heart and soul. I want to love like St. Francis. Please tell God to grant me this. I want to be transformed by my prayer and my love.

Our Lady: My precious angel, have no worry, God will grant you the desires of your heart, for He is pleased with your request. You must persevere and discipline yourself, so that you may always be open to the works and guidance of the Holy Spirit. Pray unceasingly and trust God with everything. Our sweet angel, always abandon yourself to the Holy Spirit and allow yourself to be led by Him. He will provide all that you need to do the Most Holy Will of God.

Every morning, as you open your eyes give thanks to God and praise Him for sending the Holy Spirit to all of humanity. Pray everyday unceasingly with the Holy Spirit. Throughout the day say silent praises to the Holy Spirit as you go about your daily tasks. Sing songs of thanksgiving to Him for guidance. Invite Him to anoint every prayer that you pray and ask Him to invest you with all the gifts that you need to do the Holy Will of God. My sweet angel, always trust in the Holy Spirit, and you will truly please God.

Janie: Thank you, Blessed Mother, I promise I will continue to abandon myself everyday to your Spouse, the Holy Spirit.

Jesus: Thank you, Our humble one. We give you Our blessing.

Janie: Thank You both, I love You.

Our Lady: We love you.

October 5, 1995 *Last scheduled message from Mary to the prayer group*

Our Lady: Dear children, today, I invite you to continue to live what I came to teach you regarding family prayer, love, compassion and forgiveness. I came for your sake, to help draw you closer to my Son, Jesus. I came to teach you the importance of praying together as a family so that you may discover God together and to grow in His goodness.

Little children, I have been with you for a few years now. I came to you every week as you gathered to pray your Rosary. Many of you have been so dedicated and persevered in meeting once a week to pray with your heavenly Mother. I wish to extend my deep gratitude to all who came to be a part of this beautiful prayer gathering in my honor. Oh, what joy you have brought your heavenly Mother, what joy. I love you all so dearly.

Little children, many of you are sad, for I soon will stop coming to you as Mother of Compassion and Love. I wish to tell you that I will always be with you. I will never leave you as a family. I shall be with you as you pray, as you live my motherly messages and continue to follow the path which leads towards holiness.

My dear children, I invite each one of you to continue to pray together as my prayer group. Do not stop gathering because I will no longer be coming. Know that in my place I have asked God to allow the three Archangels to come, because of my great love and gratitude to you, as my prayer group. St. Michael, St. Gabriel and St. Raphael will help you to live my messages.

My Spouse, the Holy Spirit, will enlighten you as a family everyday. Pray to Him Who is the Spirit of God, the Most High God. The Holy Spirit will lead you as a family and help you to lead good lives. Do not allow one day to go by without asking my Spouse, the Holy Spirit, to guide and to bless all your activities and efforts. He will give you strength, He will comfort you and fill your hearts with joy.

Remember your spiritual tools to help you to grow towards holiness and to lead good lives: **family prayer, fasting, the Holy Eucharist, receiving the sacrament of Reconciliation, reading and living Holy Scripture, family Rosary and Eucharistic Adoration. These are your weapons also to help you to remain under my motherly protection. Remember that you cannot say that you belong to me if you** do not live my messages. **Embrace all that I am telling you and let it penetrate your hearts. I speak to all my children young and old. I speak to my beloved priests and religious that have embraced me under this title of Mother of Compassion and Love.**

To my beloved Son and priest Monsignor. L. R.: To you, my son, I extend my deepest gratitude for the great love that you demonstrated in allowing my children to meet in your church to pray the Rosary with their heavenly Mother. You opened your heart completely to me and permitted many celebrations in my honor to take place in your Church.

My dearest son, I cannot thank you enough. Know that I will always hold all that you did for me and my children close to my Immaculate Heart. Know that I will help you with all that you need to help those entrusted to your care. Again, my son, I wish to thank you and your staff who have helped so much. God will bless you all in great abundance.

My children, I ask that you love all my beloved priests and embrace all of them through your prayers. Pray for the safety of my beloved Pope and for all his good efforts. He is truly special in God's eyes and has been chosen for these times.

Little children, be a joyful and loving family. Forgive one another, always forgive and you will have peace in your hearts, for forgiveness helps to set you free from sin. I love you and I wish to take you all to Heaven with me; that is why I am asking you to do all that I tell you. If you do all that I ask of you as a family, you will enter into eternal glory with your heavenly Mother. I give you my motherly blessing, I love you all. Thank you for listening to my message.

October 7, 1995 *Our Lady's last scheduled visit to Janie*

Our Lady: Dear children, I greet you with God's peace. Today you are honoring your heavenly Mother as the Lady of the Rosary. You, my little ones, have a deep love and devotion to your Rosary; this pleases me so much. Know that I desire that all my children pray their Rosary every day. The Rosary is a powerful weapon and Satan hates it. I, your heavenly Mother am ever so present wherever my children are praying the Rosary. I am so happy to be with you. Thank you, dear children, thank you.

Janie: *Our Lady said that the family Rosary is so important. She said* *that the Rosary is more powerful than any weapon ever created by mankind.*

I saw Our Lady dressed in white as Our Lady of the Rosary. She had roses in her hands and she allowed the roses to fall from her hands. As the roses came down, suddenly it was only the petals of roses that were coming down. The petals were different colors and as they came down on the people it looked like a shower of petals, so beautiful!

Then, Our Lady had a white dove in her hands. The dove flew to my hands and stayed with me for a while. I kissed it and then it flew up into the sky and then disappeared. Our Lady placed a very beautiful Rosary in my hands and I placed it on the life-size statue of Our Lady of Fatima that belongs to my family.

Our Lady was very happy on this day because so many had come to be with us, however she was sad because I was sad as this was her last scheduled visit with me. She comforted me and told me that she would always be with me in a special way. She told me she would come in times of great suffering for me, on my birthday, special feast days and Anniversaries. This was a very difficult day for me, but I am grateful for all the time that Our Lady spent with me. Within a few moments of Our Lady leaving, St. Joseph came to comfort me. Our Lady told me a few days ago that St. Joseph would come to comfort me when she left.
St. Joseph: My little one, know that Most Holy Mary has not left you; she lives in your heart. Do not be sad, she loves you very much and she too is sad. If you could bring a smile to your face, you could put a smile on her face.
Janie: *I made an effort to smile because I didn't want Our Lady to be sad.*
St. Joseph: My little one, know how much you are loved by God. Know how much God loves His people. Remember this and let this be your strength. Never doubt God's love for you. Never doubt Most Holy Mary's love for you. Never doubt my love for you. My little one, if you smile you will make the people smile.
Janie: St. Joseph, these people can see through me. *I tried to smile and I was able to smile. My heart became filled with joy.*
St. Joseph: Share with the people your joy. Now, my little one, I can leave you. Now you are joyful. Now you can begin your work.

October 10, 1995 *Let your heart be a living tabernacle*

Jesus: My humble servant, remain pure in your suffering and you will draw your strength from Me. I have sent angels to encamp around you to protect you in your time of great suffering. I, your Eucharistic Savior, will help you to embrace your suffering with joy in your heart.

Know that through your suffering you will obtain the virtues of endurance, love, faith, hope and joy. Through this suffering you will grow stronger in your filial abandonment to My love and mercy. Know that you are helping many souls draw closer to Me. You are making much reparation for many poor sinners as you embrace your suffering.

Be silent, My humble one, be silent and keep still, listen to My voice. It is My voice that will guide you during this time. Remain by My side and trust in My instructions. You are My delight, for your obedience pleases Me. Your littleness is a joy to My Eucharistic Heart. Always remain like a little child, for it is only in this way that you will learn to trust Me.
My humble servant, My Mother has not abandoned you, she is even closer to you now, she lives in your heart. Continue to keep your heart pure, that I may also live in your heart. We want your heart to be a living tabernacle for Us to always dwell in, and you in Our Hearts. I love you My humble servant. Remain close to Me and I will guide you in your time of suffering.

October 10, 1995 *Smile with Heaven*

Jesus: My humble servant, do not think that you are all alone. I, your Jesus, am here with you. You will not be alone as long as you abandon yourself to Me. Your heart is filled with deep sorrow, for I know that you miss My Mother. She is with you as well. She is with you in your prayers, in your family prayers, as you attend to your husband and children. She is with you in your apostolate work.

Know that We are most pleased with this community prayer gathering where many have come to be healed. Many are the healings that have taken place in their hearts. Rejoice, My humble servant, and know that I am with you. Smile with Heaven as you continue to spend time with Me. Know that you are My delight.
Janie: *Oh Mother most pure, my heart longs to hear your heavenly voice and to gaze upon your holiness. My heart is sorrowful, my heart feels empty, for you no longer come to visit me. Throughout the day I have moments of joy and moments of sadness.*

At times I feel your presence in the beauty of the clear blue sky or at the end of the day in the sunset. Please, my Most Holy Queen, pray for me to be strong and to endure my cross. I want so much to make you happy, but I am much too weak to pretend that I am happy. Please pray for me.

October 20, 1995 *You miss her*

Jesus: My humble servant, I am here to help you in your daily struggles. You have been suffering so much and your faith has been tested, but you have remained strong. I, your Eucharistic Savior, encourage you to remain steadfast in your suffering. Do not allow My adversary's attacks to distract you from following the path in which I am leading you. I know, My humble servant, that his attacks have been strong, but again I tell you truly, you have done well in resisting his attacks.

My humble servant, you have much to accomplish in helping many families to draw closer to My Eucharistic Heart and to the Immaculate Heart of My Mother. I will give you much work, and you will be very much involved in witnessing to and harvesting the hearts of the families. Do not worry about your property which is now consecrated to Me under the title of the Infant Jesus of Prague. All will be accomplished there, abandon everything to Me.

Janie: My Beloved Savior, I feel like I've been so weak lately, and I know that I have been angry. Why is this?

Jesus: My humble servant, you are suffering much and your heart is sorrowful for My Mother. You miss her much and you feel abandoned by her. You have mixed feelings because you want to do the Holy Will of My Father, but your human emotions distract you, so you become angry with yourself. Continue to abandon yourself to the guidance of the Holy Spirit. You are doing well in allowing the Holy Spirit to enlighten your path.

My humble servant, know that as long as you trust in the presence of the Holy Spirit in your prayers, you will follow the path which I traced out for you. Remember all that My Mother told you to do and embrace her every moment that you live. She loves you very much.

Janie: My Dear Lord, I doubt so much and I don't like doubting. I do believe, please help the part of me that struggles with doubt.

Jesus: My humble servant, have no worry. We are indeed speaking to you and teaching you. Be at peace. Pray for My Bride and for families everywhere. There is so much evil in so many hearts. Offer all your suffering in reparation for poor sinners.

Janie: I will, My Lord, I promise.

October 21, 1995 *I delight in you*

Jesus: My humble servant, I, your Eucharistic Savior, ask that you continue to abandon all your concerns to Me. You are in the midst of tremendous suffering, these are very difficult times for you. Know that you are special to My Eucharistic Heart and that I delight in you. Continue to pray for all My special intentions which I entrust to you. I know, My humble servant, that you are experiencing much loneliness. Your heart continues to be sorrowful for My Mother and for St. Joseph as well, for they are dear to your heart, as you are dear to them. Know that you are growing in virtue as you continue in your faith journey.
Janie: My dear Lord, these are most hard times for me, but what I want to do most of all is to do the Most Holy Will of God, my Father. Sometimes I feel like I am in neutral and that I cannot do anything because of my suffering.
Jesus: My humble servant, you are doing well in your abandonment to the Holy Will of My Father. My adversary is busy trying to deceive you with his lies. Remember, you are walking in faith, trusting in the guidance of the Holy Spirit. You will recognize Satan's deceptions.
Janie: Thank You my Most Adorable Savior, for Your love and words of comfort. Thank You also for blessing my grandson on his first birthday. Thank You for all the angels that were present at his birthday party. This made me very happy. Please, I pray, bless him always with all that he needs for his own faith journey. I consecrate him to the Holy Trinity, to your Eucharistic Heart, to the Heart of my Mother and Queen, to St. Joseph, to his guardian angel, to St. Joachim and Ann and all the intercession of Heaven. In doing this, I consecrate my four sons and all my grandchildren and all other children to come in the future generations. I promise to pave the way for my family, for Your Bride and all families with my own suffering. I will live my life praying, fasting and doing penance for all that You have asked of me.
Jesus: My humble servant, your love and dedication to be in Our service touches My Eucharistic Heart. Know that I love you with immense love. It's late now. I give you My blessing. Goodnight.
Janie: Goodnight, My Lord and my Savior.

October 22, 1995 *Pray the Joyful Mysteries after Communion*

Janie: Our Lady came to me while I was praying the joyful mysteries right after I had gotten home from Holy Mass. It was made known to me last night while in prayer, through the prayer of the Holy Spirit, that one should recite the Joyful Mysteries right after receiving Jesus in Holy Communion. He is with us in the same way that He was with Our Lady *when the Archangel Gabriel appeared to her.*

I was offering my intention on the second Joyful Mystery. I was also feeling sad, because the Holy Family came to bless my grandson on his first birthday, and I could only see Our Lord, but not St. Joseph and Our Lady. In my intention I was praying for the intercession of Our Lady to help me to reflect her love for Our Lord and to help me to pray well and to be good. She came to me immediately.

Our Lady: My dear child, know that I love you very much and that I am always with you. You are dear to me. You are in the bosom of my Immaculate Heart. Always remember this, my child.

Janie: *Then she was gone. Praised be Jesus forever and ever. Praised be His Most Holy Name, He Who was in the Immaculate Womb of my Queen and my Mother. Oh, I love You both with all my heart. Amen.*

October 22, 1995 *Make good out of bad situations*

Jesus: My humble servant, I am pleased with all your hard efforts today. My Mother came to visit you while you were in prayer asking for her intercession. You are most dear to Our Hearts. You endure your suffering well, and you try your best to make good out of bad situations. You are always concerned about other souls that suffer because they live in darkness. You have a compassionate and loving heart.

Janie: My Adorable Savior, I do care about other people who do not have Your love in their lives because they choose not to. I remember how it was for me when I was separated from Your love by my own free will. I want to tell everybody that you love all with unconditional love. Your love is my reason for living everyday; this is what I long for people to know.

Jesus: My humble servant, I, too, long for them. My Eucharistic Heart is sorrowful because they choose darkness instead of light. I am the Light of the World, that is why I came, to give light to a world walking in darkness. Pray with Me and keep vigil with Me, so that through Our suffering, souls will open their hearts to My love and mercy.

Janie: My Adorable Savior, please know that I will pray with You for all Your special intentions. I love You as much as I am capable of loving You. Please help me to love You more and more everyday.

Jesus: My humble servant, your love continues to blossom like a beautiful heavenly flower. Continue to love and to pray unceasingly, for your love and prayers bring the light of the Holy Spirit to those suffering souls.

Janie: Oh, My Lord, Your words bring such joy to my heart. My soul melts with Your heavenly words. Thank You for loving me.

Jesus: My humble servant, I will always love you.
Janie: And I will always love You, too!
Jesus: I know this, My humble servant. Goodnight, My dear one. Until tomorrow.
Janie: Goodnight, My Lord and my Love and my All. Until tomorrow. Give my heavenly Mother and St. Joseph and all my heavenly friends a hug and kiss for me.

October 23, 1995 *Adoration: I spend endless hours alone*

Jesus: My humble servant, I, your Eucharistic Savior, come to you to ask you to offer your suffering for My Bride, for She is in need of much prayer. Look at all My brother priests who reject Me. They do not believe in My True Presence in the Holy Eucharist. They do not believe that I am truly present in the Blessed Sacrament.
Right now, you are experiencing My Passion. Your hands and your feet are pierced with pain. You are experiencing the nails that were driven through My flesh before I was put to death. I know, My humble servant, that your suffering is very painful, but endure it a little longer for the purification of My Bride.

I have given you the strength to write in the midst of your pain, so that you may always love Me in the True Presence of the Holy Eucharist. I want you to spend time with Me in the Blessed Sacrament where I spend endless hours alone without anyone going to visit Me. My brother priests put Me to the side where nobody recognizes me in the Blessed Sacrament. I am given no reverence, because My brother priests do not tell the flock entrusted to them about My True Presence in the Blessed Sacrament.

You are suffering alone in your pain. Your family is sleeping, and they have no idea of your great suffering. This is how it is with Me. My brother priests have no idea of My great suffering and how much they offend Me by refusing to believe in My True Presence.
Janie: My Most Wounded and Suffering Lord, thank You for allowing me to share in Your great suffering. I know my suffering is really nothing compared to Your suffering, but thank You. I embrace You, My Lord, and I send my spirit with my love to all the tabernacles in the world where You are not honored and where You are forgotten. I will pray for all priests whose hearts are closed to believing in Your True Presence. Please Lord, forgive our sinfulness and our stupidity.
Jesus: My humble servant, thank you for listening to Your Eucharistic Savior. You have consoled My Eucharistic Heart.

Janie: I love You, My Lord, and I will spend my time praying for Your special intentions for Your Bride.
Jesus: Thank you, My humble servant.

October 26, 1995 *You are afraid of being rejected again*

Janie: *Our Lord came tonight with the three Archangels. St. Michael was right above Our Lord, St. Gabriel to the left of Jesus and St. Raphael to the right of Jesus. Our Lord stood before the prayer group with His hands extended.*
Jesus: Beloved of My Father, come to your Lord and Savior. Give Me all your woundedness. Do not allow all your pain and suffering to turn you away from Me. I am here to mend your broken hearts, I am here to refresh you and bring you My peace.

Beloved of My Father, many of you have been wounded and rejected by your loved ones. You have been abandoned by those that you love so much. You feel alone, unloved and frightened. Your heart has been so wounded, and you are having much difficulty with trusting anyone for fear of being rejected again. Come to Me and give Me everything that is keeping you from responding to My love and mercy.

Beloved of My Father, I love you just as you are with all your problems and in your weakness. Trust Me, little children, and do not think for one moment that I will abandon you or reject you. I will never hurt you. I will take away all your pain and I will refresh your soul.

Hear My words, beloved. I love you. Allow My words to penetrate your hearts, so that you will never feel unloved. I tell you again, I love you, beloved of My Father. Turn to Me and trust Me and you shall know joy like never before. Trust Me, please trust Me.

October 28, 1995 *Mexico City, Mexico* *I shall comfort you*

Janie: *I arrived at the Basilica of Our Lady of Guadalupe. I began to cry because on arriving there I realized how much I missed Our Lady. As I drew near the Basilica, my heart was pounding faster and faster. When we went inside the Basilica, as I gazed upon the Tilma I burst into tears. Fr. M. S. comforted me and prayed over me. Then Our Lady began to speak to me. I will write in English although she spoke to me in Spanish.*
Our Lady: Do not be sad, my little daughter, for I am with you. I have

brought you back to come and visit this region as a token of my deep gratitude.
Janie: *I was shocked to hear her speaking to me.* Blessed Mother, I thought that you wouldn't be speaking to me!

Our Lady: My little daughter, why shouldn't I speak with you when your heart is overcome with sorrow. I want you to know that I love you very much and that I am grateful for the endless hours that you spend praying and suffering in reparation for my Son's special intention. Thank you so much, my little daughter, for everything. I want to tell you that during your stay in Mexico, I shall be most near to you and I shall comfort you. Welcome back, my little daughter.

November 8, 1995 *Rejoice and embrace suffering with great joy*

Jesus: My humble servant, I, your Jesus of Love and Mercy, ask that you abandon yourself to My loving heart. I know, My dear friend, that you are suffering. I want you to know that you are helping many souls through your suffering. Rejoice and embrace your suffering with great joy in your heart. It is late. I give you My blessing. Go to sleep now, My humble one, for tomorrow I shall visit with you before you depart to go on your trip.
Janie: I love You, Jesus, My Love. Take care of my family while I am gone. Please help my husband and sons to take good care of my little grandson.
Jesus: Have no worry, My humble servant. All will go well with your family. I will watch over them. Go in peace on your trip for you will help many souls.

November 23, 1995 *Thanksgiving Day - Abandon yourself to My mercy*

Jesus: My humble servant, I, your Jesus of Love and Mercy, am grateful to you for enduring your physical suffering without complaining.
Janie: Oh, my dear Beloved Savior, I am grateful for Your love and mercy, for this is what helps me during my suffering. My dear Jesus, how long will this suffering last?
Jesus: My humble one, you will have this suffering until My Father calls you to your heavenly home. You will suffer much during your life. At times your suffering will be unbearable as it was with Me during My Passion. As you endure your suffering, abandon yourself to My love and mercy.

November 24, 1995 *My True Presence in the miracle of the Mass*

Jesus: My humble servant, how are you doing today?
Janie: Dear Jesus, I am doing all right. How are You today?
Jesus: I am well, thank You for asking, though My Heart is sad for many of My beloved brother priests do not take their priestly vows seriously. Many are tired of being priests so they engage in many worldly pleasures. They have abandoned their priestly responsibilities. They have lost their focus as priests.

Many are the priests who refer to celebrating Holy Mass as routine. They do not believe in the miracle that takes place during Holy Mass. They no longer believe in My True Presence during Holy Mass. This wounds My Heart so much. My beloved brother priests have become self-centered. They are not centered on me. They have abandoned their flock, for they are no longer living their priestly vows. Pray for My brother priests.

November 25, 1995 *Feast of Christ the King - I am Eternal Life for you*

Jesus: My humble servant, come and allow My love to be your strength, for I know that things are difficult for you as you suffer in reparation for My Bride. Endure your suffering and unite yourself to My Eucharistic and merciful love. Know that many of My brother priests are drawing closer to me through your suffering.
Janie: My Adorable Savior, thank You for being so loving to me. I am so unworthy of Your love and mercy. Only You, My Master, understand My suffering. Please do not allow me to separate from Your love. Sometimes I am concerned about my spiritual well-being, because it's so hard for me to do my daily prayers when I am suffering. Holy Mass for me is what I look forward to. Your Body and Your Blood are eternal life to my being. Only by eating Your Body and drinking Your Blood can I embrace my suffering for love of Your Bride.
Jesus: My humble servant, know that I am eternal life for you. All who believe this and eat of My Body and drink of My Blood will have life and have it more abundantly. I came to give light to a world walking in darkness. Many accepted this light, many rejected the light and chose to remain in darkness.

Continue to eat of My Body and drink of My Blood and you will accomplish all things that I ask of you. You are My little friend, My humble servant. To you I choose to share My many concerns regarding My Bride. Trust Me in everything, for I will never abandon you. I give

you My blessing.
Janie: Thank You, My Jesus, thank You.

November 26, 1995 *Love is the answer*

Janie: Welcome My Lord and Master. How are you doing on this glorious day? Thank You for coming.
Jesus: Peace to you, My humble one. I am doing quite well today. Thank you for preparing for Our visit.
Janie: My Lord and Savior, as you can see, I am cooking lunch while my family is attending Holy Mass. My grandson is resting, so I have free time. Our lunch is cooking in our oven so, I thought that this was a perfect time for Our visit. Is there anything special that I can do for You, My Lord and Savior?
Jesus: My humble servant, I am so pleased with your perseverance to continue to embrace all your crosses without complaining. You are doing well in helping your youngest son with his child. You are truly united as a family and your efforts in working together is most pleasing to My Father. Your family is truly blessed for choosing to do My Father's Holy Will. Know that many graces and blessings are being bestowed on you and your family.

Continue praying together as a family and let your love for one another be your strength. Remember, love is what every family needs to forgive, to lead good lives and to accept one another unconditionally. Love is the answer to heal this wounded world. I give you My blessing so that you may continue to cook for your family.
Janie: I love You, My Lord, I love You. We will continue to persevere to become a holy and loving family.

November 27, 1995 *Gentle concern*

Janie: *I was very sick with my suffering today. Our Lord came to bless me while I was in bed.*
Jesus: My humble servant, do not try to get up, for I know how much you are suffering. I am here to bless you and to tell you that I am with you in your suffering. Sleep now, My humble servant, sleep.

November 28, 1995 *I will comfort you*

Jesus: My humble servant, today has been most difficult for you, but you have done well in embracing your suffering with joy in your heart.
Janie: My Beloved Savior, thank You for being with me. Please for-

give me, but I am having a hard time concentrating on my prayers. These past few months have been very difficult for me. I miss St. Joseph and I miss my Blessed Mother, and soon You will not be coming to visit me on a daily basis.
Jesus: My humble servant, have no worry, I am here with you. Abandon yourself to your Eucharistic Savior. I will comfort you. I will melt away all that is bothering you. Trust Me.

November 30, 1995 *From beginning to end, remain with the Holy Spirit*

Janie: Good morning, my dear Lord.
Jesus: Good morning, My humble servant. How are you doing this morning?
Janie: I am doing well My Lord, how are You doing?
Jesus: I am doing well, thank you for asking. My humble one, today I ask that you offer all your prayers and sacrifices in atonement for the sinfulness of humanity.
Janie: Oh Lord, I know that we are such sinners. Please be merciful to us. We need Your love and mercy to help us to repent.
Jesus: My humble one, true repentance begins in the heart. Pray that My love enters into the hearts of mankind, for a loving heart helps to bring about true repentance. My love does not exist in many souls, that is why there is so much darkness in many hearts.
Janie: Lord, how much can my prayers and sacrifices help others to repent?
Jesus: My humble servant, your prayers and sacrifices help many souls to have a change of heart and to turn away from their sins. Humanity is in a time of extreme sinfulness. So many souls are on the path to perdition and these souls are leading other souls to perdition as well. Those souls who are trying to do the Will of My Father must be on guard against the many false prophets that exist throughout the world. These false prophets are great in number.
My humble servant, remember to invoke the Holy Spirit in every prayer. He is the One Who will enlighten your heart. Abandon yourself to the Holy Spirit everyday. Begin your day with prayers to the Holy Spirit. Remain united to Him throughout the day in everything that you do, and end your day with thanksgiving to the Holy Spirit.

Now, My humble servant, I give you My blessing. Today, listen with your heart to the guidance of the Archangels. As of tomorrow I shall come to visit with you more than once a day, so prepare through your prayers. **Janie:** Thank You, My Lord and Savior. Thank You for this wonderful gift of love of coming more than once.

Editor's Note: At this time Our Lord started to come everyday to pray with Janie. No separate messages were given. These were special personal times of prayer in addition to His daily visits.

December 18, 1995 *Prayer of Consecration for priests*

Editor's Note: Jesus gave to Janie this sacred prayer for the use of His priests. By this prayer, the priests consecrate their priesthood to the Sacred Heart of Jesus. This prayer is found in the Appendix of this book.

Janie: Good morning, My Lord, My Jesus, My All!
Jesus: Good morning, My humble servant. Sit down and let Us visit as two loving friends.
Janie: Yes, My Lord, yes, I would like that very much.
Jesus: My humble servant, I know that it has been most difficult for you and that your suffering is unbearable at times. I am here to console your hurting and suffering soul as you, My little friend, have consoled My aching Heart so many times. Tell Me, My little humble one, what do you wish Me to do for you this morning?
Janie: My Lord and Master, could You give me a prayer of consecration for priests? My Spiritual Director has asked me to request this of You.
Jesus: My most humble servant, with all My love I will honor the request of your Spiritual Director, My beloved little brother. I shall be most present as this prayer is embraced by My beloved brothers. It is most pleasing to Me that My beloved brother would have such a desire to be consecrated to My Eucharistic and Most Sacred Heart.
Janie: Thank You, my Beloved Savior! This will make my Spiritual Director very happy. He loves You very much.
Jesus: I love him with immense love.
Janie: My Lord, if it be Thy Father's Will, could I be freed from the pain that I have had for sometime? I continue to offer it up, but I have much difficulty in writing. I shall bear it as long as I need to. Tell me what to do please, for my only desire is to do God's Most Holy Will.
Jesus: My humble servant, abandon this concern to Me. I shall help you, have no worry.
Janie: Very well, my Master, consider it done. Thank You. My Lord, I wish to thank You for answering my prayer concerning the Chapel in our land. I am so happy that I will have my last scheduled visit with you there. I am forever grateful. Christmas Day will be a great day for me,

although my heart will be sad.

You answered my prayer to have the floor of the Chapel built when we did not have any money for it. This Chapel is Yours My Lord, for you know that I gave You this piece of land that Your Father blessed us with. This Chapel will bear Your Infant Name as the Infant Jesus of Prague.

I will keep vigil with You in this little Chapel, praying for poor sinners like myself. When I die, I shall request my family to leave my remains there beside the Chapel, so that others may always remember to keep vigil with You in the Blessed Sacrament, praying for poor sinners.

Jesus: My most humble servant, I am most honored. I give you My solemn word that this little humble Chapel consecrated to Me will bring a multitude of graces and blessings to you as a family and to all who visit this Chapel, for it is given to Me with all your love. I promise you that many healings will come to those souls who embrace Me under the title of the Infant Jesus of Prague. I am most powerful under this title. Recall My words to My beloved brother priest Fr. Cyril, **"Occupy yourself in Me and I shall occupy Myself in you. The more you honor Me, the more I shall bless you."** These are the very words I gave him. Now I continue to give these words to all who embrace Me under this title.

Janie: Please, My Lord, tell me everything I need to do to get You everything for Your little Chapel where You shall live near our home. I shall visit with You first thing in the morning and last thing before I retire to bed.

Jesus: My humble servant, your love consoles My Eucharistic Heart. Know that My little Chapel will have My Perpetual Presence under its title. You and your family will celebrate your first Eucharistic miracle of Holy Mass on Christmas Day. This is My gift to you, to be able to celebrate Holy Mass there on the humble floor of My little Chapel. You have shown much love for Me under the title of the Infant Jesus of Prague. I am most grateful to you, My suffering servant.

Janie: Oh Jesus, My Lord and my Love, I do love You so, and I want to be at Your side every moment of my life. Help me to be good and never cause Your Heart to be sad. I don't want to offend You, my Most Beautiful Savior.

Jesus: My humble servant, the key to eternal happiness is Divine Love. As long as you pray, I shall pour the flame of My love into every fiber of your being. Love others as I love you, and you shall have eternal happiness, for this is the Holy Will of My Father. Now, My humble one, I give you My blessing, for in a short time your husband will be waking up.

Become Eucharistic

Janie: Thank You, My Lord, thank You. Oh, Infant Jesus of Prague, pray for us. Amen.

December 20, 1995 *Eat of My Body and drink of My Blood*

Janie: Good morning, My Precious Lord.
Jesus: Good morning, My humble servant, how are you this morning?
Janie: I am doing quiet well, and even better now that You are here with me. How are You doing?
Jesus: I am doing quite well and am most happy to be here with you. My humble servant, you are doing well in trying to hide the pain and sorrow in your heart. You know that you cannot hide anything from Me. Do you wish to speak to Me about what you are trying to hide from others.
Janie: Dear Lord, my true Love, You are right, of course. I know that I cannot hide anything from You. I am going to miss You so much even though You will visit on certain days. I feel like I have failed You in some way, perhaps through lack of self dedication. It's hard trying to accomplish all my responsibilities as a wife and mother. My family is precious to me. Am I doing well in this area Lord?
Jesus: My humble servant, you have nothing to be concerned about, for you continue to do well in all that My Father has asked of you. Know that I will always be with you. I will never leave you. We will be united in the sacrifice of Holy Mass. As you eat of My Body and drink of My Blood, you shall live in My love. Do not allow one day to go by when you do not eat of My Body and drink of My Blood.
Janie: My Lord and my Love, I will do the best that I can to follow what You ask of me.
Jesus: I give you My blessing, My dear humble servant. Rest now, for I know that your body is in pain and you are tired. I shall be with you to comfort you as you suffer for My Bride.
Janie: Thank You, Jesus. I love You.

December 21, 1995 *My Body and Blood mingle and run into every vein*

Janie: Good morning, my Beloved Lord and Savior. Welcome to my heart and to our home.
Jesus: Good morning, My most humble servant. Sit down My little friend and let Us enjoy this time together. How are you doing this morning?
Janie: I am quite well. I just returned from Holy Mass, and I am most happy. I feel in my heart and soul that Holy Mass is the very center of my life. Your presence is most profound during Holy Mass, and I am

so grateful for the great love that You continue to demonstrate to all of humanity through the Holy Sacrifice of Holy Mass. Thank You so much Jesus. I do not have words in my heart to express my deep gratitude for the miracle of Holy Mass.

Oh, how blessed are the hands of all the priests who touch Thy Most Precious Body and Blood in the great Sacrifice of Holy Mass. Blessed be Your Most Holy Name, Jesus, King of kings. Through the Holy Sacrifice of Mass, You continue to demonstrate Your humility as You come in the form of bread and wine. Oh, Lord my God and my All, teach me humility and poverty of spirit. Lord, am I talking too much? Please forgive me.

Jesus: My humble servant, you are not talking too much. You are adoring your Lord and Master. Your heart is absorbed by the great love of Holy Mass. My Body and Blood mingle and run into every vein in your body. Because your heart is open to My True Presence in Holy Mass, My Father has given you the grace to truly experience My great love. Know that the Sacrifice of Holy Mass is the greatest miracle in the world. No other miracle or apparition will be greater than the miracle of Holy Mass. Embrace your Beloved Savior in Holy Mass and let this be your daily heavenly food.

Janie: Oh Lord, I love You. Help me and my family and all the world to understand the miracle of Holy Mass.

Jesus: I shall help all who have a deep desire to become one with Me in the Sacrifice of Holy Mass. Now, I give you My blessing.

Janie: Thank You, Jesus, my Love and my All.

December 22, 1995 *Spend one hour with Me everyday*

Janie: Good evening, my Beloved Savior.

Jesus: Good evening, My humble servant. How are you doing this evening?

Janie: I am not doing very well, My Lord. I am feeling a bit anxious about my last scheduled visit with You. I don't wish to be sad, for You have done so much for me. Tell me what to do.

Jesus: My humble servant, you are experiencing your human emotions. Do not worry about being sad, for you will experience a great sorrow in your heart. You will suffer much, but I shall be with you in the very depth of your heart to console you. You will experience great sadness and you will feel abandoned by Me. I ask that you remain in a prayerful attitude during your great suffering for your prayers will bring you strength.

Janie: My Dear Jesus, will I be all right after I go through this suffer-

ing? I am afraid, please help me.
Jesus: My humble servant, do not fear anything, I shall always be with you. **Remember what My Mother asked, that you spend one hour everyday with Me in the Blessed Sacrament where I am present. There I shall comfort your suffering heart. In times when you cannot visit me in the Blessed Sacrament, spend one quiet hour with Me. No matter what happens you are to spend one hour with Me everyday.**

During this hour, the Holy Spirit will reveal to your heart My special intentions for you to pray for. You will not see anything, but the Holy Spirit will put thoughts in your heart. Write these thoughts down and continue to share these experiences with your Spiritual Director. The Holy Spirit will enlighten your heart about many things concerning the world and things to come. The angels will also be speaking to you about things that will happen in the world.
The Holy Spirit will be strong in your life; that is why you must abandon yourself to the Holy Spirit for discernment, wisdom and enlightenment. After My last visitation with you, the Holy Spirit will be with you in a strong way to help you in all the things that you will continue to do to draw souls closer to My Sacred and Eucharistic Heart. I ask that you continue to embrace My Bride through all your suffering and prayers and sacrifices. Never stop praying for My Bride, for She is in much need of prayer.
Janie: Oh Jesus, I will do everything that You ask of me. I promise to spend one hour with You everyday for the rest of my life. I shall continue to be led by the Holy Spirit. Jesus, I love You.
Jesus: I love you with immense love.

December 23, 1995 *Trust Me in everything*

Janie: Good evening, My Lord and my Love.
Jesus: Good evening, My humble servant. How are you doing this evening?
Janie: I am not doing well My Lord. I am beginning to feel more anxious about Our visit. My heart is sad.
Jesus: My humble servant, you will know sadness and this sadness will grip your heart, and you will feel overcome by your sorrow. Recall My words to remain in the spirit of prayer through all this, for your prayers will be your strength.
Janie: Dear Lord, Your little Chapel is so beautiful. Just knowing that You answered my prayer concerning our land makes me joyful. Thank You for everything that You have given us as a family. We are truly

grateful. Lord I will do everything that You tell me. Please give us a beautiful sunny and warm day like today on Christmas.
Jesus: My humble servant, have no concern regarding the weather. Trust Me in everything, and I will help you with all that you ask of Me. I give you My word.
Janie: My Jesus, I shall trust You with all my heart in everything, I promise. Thank You, Jesus. I love You.

December 24, 1995 *Allow My love to console you*

Jesus: Good evening, My humble servant. I am here to console your suffering heart.
Janie: Thank You, my Adorable Jesus. My heart is very sad and I don't even want to look for tomorrow to come. I know that this is most selfish of me since tomorrow the world celebrates Your Birthday. Please forgive me for being so selfish.
Jesus: My humble servant, do not be so hard on yourself, for you know that I truly understand how very sad you are. You are not being selfish. You have had the privilege to receive divine visitations for almost seven years. During this time you looked to Our visitations with joy in your heart. Know, My little friend, that you will suffer much.
Janie: Oh Jesus, I hurt so bad, please help me. I just want to die. I cannot stand the sadness in my heart.
Jesus: My humble servant, allow My love to console you. Think of how much I love you. Think about My Mother and St. Joseph and their immense love that they have for you. Abandon yourself to Our love and be consoled, for We know how much you love Us.
Janie: Oh Jesus, I will try to be strong, but I already feel so alone. I cannot stand the emptiness that I feel in my heart. I don't want my family to see me sad or crying, but yet, I cannot help myself. I guess I have to allow myself to go through this suffering. Jesus, I feel like I'm in mourning. Please cover me with Your Precious Blood, so that I may be strong. Ask Your Father to send me an angel to give me strength. Please help me so that people will not see me too sad.
Tomorrow is a time for opening gifts; it's a time to rejoice, for You are the greatest gift of love to the world. Many Holy Souls will enter Heaven, so I want to rejoice for them as well as for Your Birthday. I shall try very hard to be joyful even if my heart is crying. Please, my Jesus, help me. I do not want to be self-centered. I want to focus only on You.
Jesus: My humble servant, trust Me with everything. I will help you to be strong during your suffering. You are My delight, for you have such love for Me and this pleases Me. Tomorrow you will rejoice, and

you will cry tears of joy, for I have something that I will tell you that will make you happy. Wait for tomorrow with joy in your heart. I give you My blessing now.
Janie: I love You, Jesus. I love You. I love You. I will 'til I die.
Jesus: My humble servant, all who live in My love have eternal life.
Janie: Thank You, thank You.

December 25, 1995 *Last scheduled visit from Jesus*

Jesus: My humble servant, rejoice with all of Heaven, for today is a day filled with My love and My peace. Today the world celebrates My birth. Open your heart and allow your Savior to be born in your heart. I will pour My love into your heart. I will pour My light into your heart. I will array your heart with My love and out of this love will shine forth light. Everyone will know that you belong to Me.
I am the Light of the World, and all who accept Me will live in My light. All who reject Me remain in darkness. Honor your Savior today and be My reflection. Remain pure, holy and simple in everything you do. I shall provide you with all that you need to follow after Me. Honor Me today and I will bless you. Trust Me and I will help you. I will turn your hearts of stone into hearts of gold. Today I bless the world with My immense love.
Janie: *I saw Jesus as the Infant of Prague. He came in brilliant light and the sky was illuminated. There were so many angels of all sizes around Him. He was arrayed in gold and was wearing a gold cape and a gold crown. He blessed all the people there and said that many blessings would be poured out on the people who were there and those who would come there in the future. He told me that He was very grateful for the little Chapel that we had dedicated to Him under this title.*

Then I saw Baby Jesus before me. He was wrapped in what appeared to be somewhat like receiving blankets, but they were all gold. He blessed all the people, and said that all the people who were there would receive a heart of gold to love others with. He wanted us to embrace Him on this day because God demonstrated a great act of love by giving us His Son on this day. He said He came as the Prince of Peace. He asked that as we embraced His peace that we would share it with others. He was grateful to all who united on this day to be with us in honoring Him. He said He loves us all very much and that there's no limit to His love. He smiled and blessed the people.

I shared personal things with Him. He knew that I was sad. He told me that He would be with me on my birthday, on special feast days, on

Anniversaries and especially in times of great suffering. He told me that I was called to a life of suffering and that through my suffering I would experience a great closeness to Him, to His Mother and to St. Joseph. He asked me to embrace the gift of faith and to believe that He would be with me. He said that from time to time I would be overcome with great sorrow and that I would doubt, but that I would be strengthened again and I would overcome my sadness.

He told me that I would continue to suffer for His Bride, especially the Holy Father and for the conversion of the family. Jesus told me that He didn't want me to be sad, but that He understood.

I cried, and I could see that the visit was coming to an end. I begged Him not to go. I told Him that I couldn't make it without Him. He told me that I could and that He had already given me the grace to do so. He told me to offer up my suffering for my own purification and for the hard times to come. He blessed me and then He left. When He left, St. Joseph came to comfort me. He came to give me strength and to tell me that God loved me very much. St. Joseph was so beautiful. This was a gift from Jesus.

December 25, 1995 *I am the Mother of All Humanity*

Our Lady: My child, I come to you on this most holy morning, on the Birthday of my Son, Jesus Christ, Savior of the World. Glory be His Most Holy Name forever and ever. Amen. My dear child, today I come to you under the title of Nuestra Senora de Guadalupe to ask you to help my son, Fr. W., to accomplish that which I have requested of him a few years ago.
Janie: How can I help him? What must I do for him, and why do you ask me? You know that I will gladly with all my heart do anything that you ask of me. I'm just wondering why you would ask this of me, because Fr. W. has many helpers for his work. Please do not be sad with me for asking you this, and if it's disrespectful of me, please forgive me. I did not mean any disrespect, my Most Holy Mother.
Our Lady: Know, my dear child, that I have many of my children who are helping my son, Fr. W. However, I come to you to ask you to convey to all my children involved in this, my work, to persevere in this effort and not to become discouraged. My son, Fr. W., has worked very hard to carry out my request. He has suffered much and has been ridiculed in the process, but he has continued to persevere. He is dear to my Immaculate Heart and I carry him in my motherly bosom.
To you, my child, I have shared with you that I am with Child under the

title of Nuestra Senora de Guadalupe. You had the honor of seeing the Child in my womb this last Christmas as you visited my land in Mexico where my work shall begin.

Help my son, Fr. W. through your prayers, fasting and sacrifices. Tell my children not to give up on this effort.
Janie: Blessed Mother, will the sonogram take place and what will this mean for the world? *Although she did not respond 'yes' to the sonogram, these are the words she continued with.*
Our Lady: Many of those who have rejected me will believe that I am the ever Virgin Mary, Mother of the One True God Who was born of a woman to give light to a world walking in darkness. Many will believe that I am the Mother of all Humanity, and they will embrace me as their heavenly Mother. In doing this, they will repent of the evil that is killing millions of my little babies in the wombs of their mothers. They will turn away from this horrible evil that is most offensive to God. Together we will put an end to this evil.

My son, Fr. W., has been chosen to begin my work, but the work that he is doing now will be continued by another chosen one. For now, my son is in need of much help through your prayers. Pray for him, pray for him.
Janie: Thank you, Blessed Mother, I will carry this out for you and convey this to my Spiritual Director for approval. *Our Lady came with the three Archangels: Michael, Gabriel and Raphael. Their words on this day are located in the Archangel section of this book.*

December 28, 1995 *The Holy Spirit's guidance*

*Editor's Note: Following the last visit of Our Lord, the Holy Spirit began guiding Janie to help her in her suffering.

Holy Spirit: Pray for your persecutors, for they shall increase in number. Do not allow this to weaken your faith, remain steadfast through all forms of tribulations that will come your way. Allow your faith to be the very foundation of your strength. I shall enlighten your path, so that everything that is asked of you will be crystal clear.

Live under God's Commandments and abandon yourself to My guidance. I shall continue to lead you through the narrow path that very few choose. Your suffering will be strong.
From your suffering you will bear good fruit, and you shall become a stronger witness of the truth. Confide in me and I shall teach you more

about the ways of the Divine Love.

Pray for your persecutors and do not be filled with anger or pain, from the evil that is spread about you. Know that it is the work of the evil one, and those who spread this evil are his advocates. Remember, you are God's beloved. If He is for you, who then can be against you? Rejoice and live in His immense love.

Janie: *From what the Holy Spirit reveals to me, I am quite aware that my suffering will increase. I am, however, rejoicing at the words of the Holy Spirit: "If God is for me, who can be against me." He alone is my judge and jury. Thank You, Holy Spirit, for these words.*

December 29, 1995 *Adoration: Remain steadfast under attacks*

Janie: *These thoughts came to my heart from the Holy Spirit.*
Holy Spirit: Again, I tell you, remain steadfast under the attacks of the enemy. You will be put to the test by those you love and that love you.

Do not give into the inclinations that the evil one puts in your mind, for his only goal is to bring division where there is God's peace. Hard will be the days to come, but victory will be yours if you remain obedient and steadfast to what I am giving you - My Divine Light. Abandon any negative thoughts or harsh words which you feel compelled to say to others. Listen to My voice, of My indwelling within your soul, for I am God's Spirit speaking on His behalf.

Janie: *I must admit that I need to pray to truly grasp what the Holy Spirit is speaking to my soul. I feel turmoil in the days to come, and this turmoil will perhaps manifest itself in great suffering caused by others. I will have victory if I remain obedient and steadfast.*

I am finding it most difficult to pray and to concentrate on my prayers. I know by faith that God is with me, but my spirit is dry. I mean that I do not feel God's presence with me since my last scheduled visit with Our Lord on Christmas Day.

I feel empty, and it appears that my soul is suffering with illness. My soul is ill, because it no longer sees or hears the Master's voice. Oh what a longing I have for Him Who is everything to me!

I am being obedient in keeping one hour vigils daily with Our Lord. I was asked by Our Lord and Our Lady to do this on a daily basis. I was asked to keep this hour before Our Lord in Eucharistic Adoration and when I could not go to Our Lord, to keep a holy hour at home. During this time, the Holy Spirit reveals things to me and I write them down. Then I share them with my Spiritual Director. This is a very special time for me.

December 31, 1995 *He becomes poor so we may be rich*

The Holy Spirit: Abandon yourself to the Bread of Life Who remains present for you day and night, keeping vigil out of His great love for you. Though you long to hear His voice, offer this great pain for your own purification. Come to Him in faith. He hides Himself and His glory, because He wants you to love Him for Himself. He becomes poor in appearance so that you become rich in grace!

Believe with your heart My words that Jesus truly conceals His glory from you, so that you may come to Him everyday in faith. As you spend time with Him Who loves you with immense love, He will transform your very soul with His own glory. Believe by faith in His immense love for you.
Tonight, before this new year approaches, pray for world peace. Beg the Eternal One for mercy for the world, so that sinners will embrace His mercy before it's too late! Keep vigil with Jesus, praying for world peace.

December 31, 1995 *Visit with the Holy Family*

Janie: *The Holy Family came and they greeted me, and I was so happy to be with all three of Them.*
Our Lady: Good evening, Our dear one. Rejoice on this, the feast of the Holy Family, for We are blessing families everywhere.
Janie: Good evening. I am so happy to be with You. Beloved Lord, My Lady and St. Joseph, thank You for coming. How are you, beloved St. Joseph? I've missed you.
St. Joseph: My little one, I am doing quite well and I, too, miss you. Are you doing all right?
Janie: With all due respect, I've seen and had better days. My prayers are so dry. My soul is like a plant that wasn't watered and died. I find myself surrounded by so much family activity, that I feel like I don't have time for myself. Sometimes, I want to run away and hide from everyone, including God, but I know that this is not possible. I am like a kite just going wherever the wind pulls me.
Jesus: My humble servant, you are experiencing the absence of Our visits. Recall My words that you would suffer and feel abandoned by Me. I know that you are suffering for the sake of My love, but know that I am with you.

Janie: Oh Lord, Your words are life to my soul! My soul feels alive again and everything feels strong. Oh, that I could have Your voice imprinted in my very soul, so that I could hear You all the time. However, I accept God's Holy Will for me.
Jesus: My humble servant, you are doing quite well. Have no worry, you will recover from this suffering, but you will suffer for a while.
Janie: Oh Jesus, please know that I'll do anything for You. Please help me. My hands feel like they are on fire. It hurts to write anything You tell me.
Jesus: My humble servant, offer your pain for My Bride, who suffers much for many of My beloved brothers have gone astray from My love. Oh how My Heart bleeds for My Bride. My beloved brothers must live Holy Scripture everyday.
Janie: *He gave me this Scripture reading for His Bride, Peter 1: 13-18.* **Oh My Lord, Jesus, please help us all to become holy in every aspect of our conduct, just as You so long for the holiness of Your Bride. May by Your example, we, as a family, decide for holiness. I promise to pray for Your Bride everyday. I will offer all my sorrow and distress that I am enduring these days in the absence of Your visits.**

Jesus, Son of God, sweet Redeemer, pour the flame of Your love into the heart of Thy Bride. Brighten up Her heart with the glory of your Incarnation. Give Her peace, oh Prince of Peace, direct Her according to the holiness of Your Divine Love. May Your Blood purify Her so that She may remain pure like You. Grant Her the spirit of poverty and shower the power of Your gentleness upon Her.

Give Her Your Heart, so that She may be patient, obedient, meek and humble of heart under all circumstances. I ask this in Your sweet and precious Name. Amen.
St. Joseph: My little one, that prayer was inspired by the Holy Spirit for the love that you have in your heart for the Bride of Jesus. Pray this prayer daily for the family of the Bride of Jesus, Her beloved Groom. My little one, pray with Us for all families, so that they will become holy families.
Janie: Beloved St. Joseph, do you have holy instructions to give to the family to help us?
St. Joseph: My little one, write what I tell you. To all families, I, St. Joseph, Protector of the Holy Family, invite you, as a family, to follow and live the order that God gave you to live according to His Divine Will. This is that order: God put the Father as head of the household. He sets the father in honor of his children, the mother is

under the authority of the father, the children are under the authority of their parents.

Wives must be submissive to their husbands, this is their duty in the Lord. Husbands, love your wives. Do not have any bitterness towards them. Children must obey their parents in everything as acceptable to the Lord. Fathers must not nag their children lest they lose heart. This is Holy Scripture for all families.

God wants every family to live according to His Holy Order. In this way His blessings will come upon the family like rain drops. Families who live according to God's order are clothed with compassion, kindness, humility, meekness and patience for one another. Their hearts are filled with God's love. He will help the family to abandon their old ways and live in His justice. His love and mercy will radiate from Heaven into their hearts. These families will come in the company of the saints, for the love of God will dwell in their hearts.

Families who embrace the ways of the Lord will be perfected as a family. The spirit of love and joy will reign in their homes and wherever God leads them. They will have prosperity in all that they do. The husband will be a strong prayer warrior who watches over his own; the wife will be like a fruitful vine and bring joy to her family. The children will be like olive plants who will grow into healthy children of God.

Great will be the virtues of the family who hungers to live like God commanded all of humanity to live. Great will be the joy that comes to families who embrace God's love. The husband and wife will grow old together, and their prayers will be heard immediately. They will be respected and honored by their children. Great will be the love in their hearts for one another.
My little one, to all who have a desire to live according to God's plan, He will give them the graces they need. The Holy Spirit will be strong in these families, and they shall be victorious over all obstacles and temptations. Know that God's love will protect all who accept and live by His ways.

My little one, I, St. Joseph, Most Holy Mary and my foster Son, Jesus, thank you for your patience in embracing all that We tell you. Remain strong in your love for Us, for We are with you with each step that you take. We give you and your family Our Blessings.
Janie: Thank You, Most Holy Family, and pray for us.

Heaven's Messages for The Family

Chapter Eight

THE HOLY SPIRIT AND DIVINE UNION 1996

"These things I have spoken to you, while I am still with you. But the Counselor, the Holy Spirit, whom the Father will send in My name, He will teach you all things, and bring to your remembrance all that I have said to you.

John 14:25-26

January 1, 1996 *Solemnity of Mary, Mother of God*

Our Lady: Good morning, my dear child. How are you doing this morning?
Janie: I am doing well My Lady, how are you?
Our Lady: I am well, and joyful to be with you. Write down my words. My dear child, convey to my children that I am the ever Virgin Mary, Mother of the One true God. I am the compassionate and loving Mother of the Savior of the World. As the heavenly Mother, I intercede before God for all of humanity.

I see to and occupy myself with the well-being of all my children. All who have devotion to me and embrace me as their heavenly Mother, I take them under my motherly mantle and protect them all the time. Those who reject me as their heavenly Mother, I cannot protect them, but I plead to God for His mercy over them, for He is truly a loving and forgiving God. His mercy reaches the darkest area of the souls of all His people. His love is immense.
Janie: Blessed Mother, why is it that those who reject you are not protected by you?
Our Lady: My dear children, know and understand that I cannot protect those who do not trust in my motherly intercession and who do not pray. If only my children would open their hearts, they would understand the importance of prayer and know that only through prayer can one discover God. This is why I beg my children to pray, pray, pray. God in His love and mercy has allowed me to come to many places throughout the world to help my children to be converted and to return back to God. I come under many titles, so that My children may be able to relate to their heavenly Mother.

The world has entered into a new year, a world which continues to live without God in their lives in many parts of the world. I, the Ever Virgin Mary, Mother of the One true God, will continue to walk through this new year with those who embrace me as their heavenly Mother. Together we will offer our prayers to God for the conversion of those souls walking in darkness. I will be with all families throughout the world through all the prayers of the faithful.

I give my motherly blessing to all my sons, the priests, and all religious who have dedicated their lives to live a life of prayer and service to others. I beg the Bride of my Son, Jesus, to be centered in His love and mercy through the Sacrifice of Holy Mass. Prayer will transform their hearts; this prayer is Holy Mass. It is in Holy Mass that all who partake in this rich affair meet with my Son. Let Holy Mass be your daily prayer. I bless all families consecrated to my Immaculate Heart and invite you as a family to let Holy Mass be your daily prayer. Together let us begin this new year with a joyful and prayerful heart.

January 1, 1996 *Adoration*

Holy Spirit: Remain steadfast.

January 3, 1996 *Adoration*

Holy Spirit: Remain steadfast.

January 4, 1996 *Adoration: I will empower you with the gifts you need*

Holy Spirit: Keep thy heart open and yield to My words. God is calling you to be a strong witness of the Gospel and defend your faith. Much persecution will come your way, and the attacks will be strong. Remain steadfast and do not yield to the evil that is said of you. I will enlighten your heart so that you may continue to walk in the narrow path. Pray as a family and I will empower you with the gifts that you need to help draw others closer to God. Allow your love to grow through your prayers. Pray for world peace and pray for your persecutors.

January 5, 1996 *Forgive me in my weakness*

Janie: Today I have been in the garden of Gethsemane and My Lord was not there. It has been hard for me to keep my one hour vigil with Our Lord. Only He knows my pain. May He forgive me in my weakness.

January 6, 1996 *Perseverance*

Janie: *I continue to feel abandoned by Our Lord. I visited the Blessed Sacrament for about five minutes. Again my heart is in deep suffering. My soul is being purified.*
Holy Spirit: Remain truthful to your love for the Lamb.

January 7, 1996 *The grace of the Holy Spirit*

Janie: *Today is the feast of the Epiphany. I had my visit with Our Lord. He was with me in the pit of my very misery. If it wasn't for the grace* *of the Holy Spirit, I think I could become the victim of my doubtfulness. Praised be God for His love and mercy.*

January 7, 1996 *Epiphany - Interior conflict*

Jesus: My humble servant, I am here to comfort you in your deep sorrow. I know that you are going through a most difficult time. You feel abandoned by Me and those who love you. Trust in My love during these difficult times. I will see you through all your suffering.
Janie: My Dear Jesus, I do not want to complain, but I am not doing well. You know everything about what is going on within my heart and soul. Please help me to not separate from You in my weakness. Jesus, lately I am so distracted in everything, please strengthen me in this area.
Jesus: My suffering servant, you will recover from this deep sorrow, but you will suffer a while longer. You have been sad all day, and you have felt all alone. You have experienced anger and confusion. Know that I have been with you all during this time. Do not give in to the temptations that are set before you, but allow your prayers to be your strength.
Janie: My Dear Lord, today I wanted to celebrate the feast of your Epiphany, but there was no one to rejoice with me. I did feel very sad. I have been struggling with myself, and it's hard to do the things that I know that I must do.
Jesus: My humble servant, do all that My Mother has asked of you, no matter how difficult it may be for you. You must not give in to the conflict that you feel inside your soul. Your spirit is battling with your flesh, this is why you are having such a difficult time. You will recover and you will rejoice. For now, trust in My Eucharistic love and allow My Body and Blood to be your daily sustenance. You will overcome your doubt as well.

January 8, 1996 *Today I breathe on you*

Holy Spirit: I am the Spirit of the Father and of the Son. We are One in the Holy Trinity. Recall the words of the Son of God to His disciples, "Receive the Holy Spirit." Then He breathed on them and this gave them strength before His Ascension into Heaven.

Today, I, the Spirit of God, breathe on you to give you strength in your suffering. I have come to fill your heart with light, joy, and the gift of Divine Love to help you in the decision which you are seeking from the Eternal One. Look no farther than your own heart for the truth which you need to know. Do not be moved by your feelings, for these are human emotions. Be moved by divine faith and reason.

You have been wounded deeply because of the love that you have for humanity. You will continue to suffer for the injustice against you and against others. I am the Spirit of the Father and of the Son. I dwell in your heart. Do not be troubled with anything. I will enlighten your path. Remain steadfast under all attacks and you will please the Father.

January 9, 1996 *A beautiful lesson from the Holy Spirit*

Janie: *Today, as I entered the church, it was very cold. Then, as I prayed and began to read Holy Scripture, it became warm where I was sitting. Praised be Our Lord for His kindness and love.*
Holy Spirit: I am the Spirit of God who speaks to your soul. Listen to My words. Be consistent in your thoughts, steadfast be your words. Be swift to hear, but slow to answer. If you have the knowledge, help those who seek your help, if you do not have the knowledge, pray for enlightenment, and I shall give you the knowledge you seek to do the Lord's work.

Test every spirit to know whether it's from God or from the evil one. Be faithful only to God and trust only in His goodness. Do not be deceived by false prophets, but look to God for guidance in all you say and do.

Do not resist the call to Divine Love which God wants to impregnate your soul with. Allow your soul to be consumed with this love. God is calling you to a state of purgation. He wants to consume you with the fire of His love. Much will be the suffering that you endure while your soul is in the state of purgation. Abandon yourself to the shelter of God's love. Allow Him Who created you to have His way with you. Do not resist the fire of purgation. Enter into this consuming fire which is the Heart of the Eternal One.

I shall enlighten your soul everyday. I shall teach you how to pray with your heart. Your soul shall become like a healthy green tree, which is planted near the spring of living water. Great will be the wisdom that comes from your mouth. Great will be your witness of the love of God for humanity.

Be silent, do not talk much, but spend quiet time with Me, for I am the Spirit of the Father and the Son. I shall guide your words and footsteps. Embrace this state of purgation and know that God is calling you to a life of contemplation. Listen to My words carefully, for He is speaking through Me.

Janie: *It is obvious to me that God is calling me to be purified. I recognize all the many distractions in my life which bring much sorrow to my heart. I feel restless at times, and at other times angry at myself for allowing myself to enter into these distractions that weaken the level of my prayers and commitment to My Lord and Master.*

I struggle with the flesh, my spirit wants so much to do God's Holy Will, but my flesh forces me to give in to these distractions. God only knows how I struggle with trying to remain steadfast. I am deeply grateful for the gift of the Sacrifice of Holy Mass, for this I love everyday and look forward to eating of the flesh of my Savior and drinking of His Blood.

This is my strength, for He is life to me. I know that no matter what struggles I may have, I can give them to my Master in Holy Mass. Praised be Jesus in the Holy Sacrifice of Mass forever and ever. Amen.

January 10, 1996 *I am the Spirit of the Father and the Son*

Holy Spirit: Say to the Lord, **"Here I am Lord, I come to do Your Will. Lord, write Your law within my heart that I may know Your Holy Will."** Begin each day with these words to the Eternal One, and He will bless your day.

I am the Spirit of the Father and of the Son. Listen with your heart to all that I say. Humble yourself before the Mighty One and recognize His love and mercy. Humility is pleasing to God. The more you humble yourself the greater you are, and you will find favor with God, for great is His power and by the humble He is glorified.

Be consistent in your abandonment to God and He will give you clear understanding of what He is asking of you, but first you must respond to His call to divine union with Him. Embrace the state of purgation and do not resist it. Enter into this union with God. Darkness will surround you as your soul is in the state of purgation. Your soul will be infused with a life of contemplation.

Your level of understanding God's Holy Will will be infused in your soul. You will learn to die to your very self as your soul is being purified. Again I say, darkness will surround you, but your union with God will increase. Fear nothing during this time and do not resist this way of contemplation, for this is a call to the divine, which all are called to but few embrace. I shall guide you during this time, and no harm will come to you as you enter the chamber of contemplation. I am the Spirit of the Father and of the Son, listen to My words and humble yourself. Accept the call to the divine.

Pray for the souls that are victims of the weather conditions, for there are many poor souls that are truly suffering. Offer your sacrifices for these suffering souls to know that God is in control of everything. The world must recognize that prayer is the answer to the needs of the world.
Janie: *As I prayed my Rosary, I saw many visions where the Holy Spirit took me while I was in prayer.*

January 11, 1996 *Bless me in my illness*

Janie: *To God my Father, to His Son and to the Holy Spirit, bless me in my time of illness and keep me close to You. Amen. I was unable to keep my holy hour with the Holy Spirit and receive My Lord in Holy Mass due to my illness.*

January 12, 1996 *Thankful to suffer*

Janie: *Today I continue to remain ill, unable to do anything. The Lord sent me two special people to take me to Confession and to Holy Mass. What an honor to be able to have a profound encounter with My Lord in Holy Mass and to be able to be released from my misery through the sacrament of Reconciliation. I remain ill today, but I am thankful to have this privilege to suffer for Our Lord and to stay awake at night with this illness. I was unable to keep my holy hour today.*

January 13, 1996 *I received My Lord*

Janie: *Today I continue to be ill, but I received My Lord in Holy Communion. I was unable to keep my holy hour today.*

January 14, 1996 *I am always thinking of Heaven*

Janie: *Today I was unable to attend Holy Mass, but Sr. I. was so kind to bring me Jesus, My Lord, to my home where I continue to be ill. Although I haven't been able to have a holy hour, I think about My Lord, my Blessed Mother and St. Joseph all day. I am always thinking of Heaven. I have been able to pray the Holy Rosary alone and with my family.*

January 15, 1996 *A deeper union with His love*

Janie: *This morning I went to Holy Mass. I felt a little weak, but had the strength to wake up early enough to go to Holy Mass.*

I have begun my holy hour as I write. My hand is very weak and in great pain. I pray that God will give me the grace to be able to write. I have a doctor's appointment in an hour or so. I ask the intercession of Heaven during this most painful time.

Holy Spirit: Bless the Lord with every breath that you take. Say to Him, **"To You I lift up my soul, Oh Lord My God. In You I put all my trust, for You have been my guide since I was first formed in my mother's womb. You are My God and My all. Help me, Oh Lord to live in Your goodness everyday of my life. Amen."**

Humble vessel of God, listen to My words, for I am the Spirit of God the Father and God the Son. Open your heart and soul that I may inscribe My words. The Lord knows your pain and your suffering. Be at peace, for He knows that His Holy Will reigns first in your heart. He is pleased with your desire to do good and to glorify His Holy Name in all your hard efforts. Do not be afraid of the darkness that surrounds you and your lack of understanding of this darkness.

Again I say to you, oh humble vessel of God, be patient in your suffering for the Lord is plunging your soul into deep purgation. He is preparing you for greater works to help His people. You have entered into a life of contemplation where words are not necessary and your only longing is to be in a quiet union with God. You are in total surrender with God. Your spirit is yielding to all the secret wisdom that God is impregnating your soul with.

He is teaching you prayer of the heart, where your soul is being plunged into a deeper union with His love. He wants you to know and understand that being consumed by the fire of His secret wisdom is truly to be in the state of prayer of the heart. Remain steadfast, quiet and obedient to the Lord. Resist not His invitation to deep contemplation. Surrender to God and many will be the miracles that He works through you.

January 16, 1996 *A prayer of the heart*

Janie: *The Holy Spirit speaks to my soul. He teaches me to pray from my heart. He inspired this prayer with His words.*

"Oh God, let Your divine justice reign in my heart, let no evil desire prevail in my heart. Be gracious and bless me, oh God, that I may trust You in all that I do. Open the gate to Your Heart that I may be filled with Your glory.

Oh God, let my spirit surrender to all Your goodness, let the light of Your love shine upon me. Make my soul yearn for Your love day and night. Oh God, inflame my soul with Your goodness that I may exalt Your Holy Name. Make me foolishly in love with You that all who see me will say I am truly a fool for God. Oh yes, my Lord, this is what I desire the most in my soul.

Oh God, let me be your slave. Make me truly Your property. Mark my soul with your brand, let that brand be the mark of Your love. Clothe my soul with the garments of humility and meekness. Clothe my soul with Your glory, and I shall live in Your love forever. Amen."

Holy Spirit: Humble vessel of God, remain steadfast in your faith and in your love for God. Allow nothing or no one to separate you from His love. Great is His love for you, great will be His blessings upon you. Abide always in His love. Let no obstacle come between His love for you. Enter into a life of contemplation and allow the Lord to plunge your soul into the state of purgation. Do not resist, but surrender your all to the Lord. Let His peace reign over you. Let nothing distract you. Keep your eyes, your mind on God always, and He will bless your steps.

February 15, 1996 *I cried with them*

Jesus: Console Me by drinking from the cup of My bitter Passion. Yes, please drink every ounce of My Bitter Passion without complaining. In doing this, you will truly embrace your suffering Master. I suffer for My Bride, for all My beloved brothers that have gone astray. Oh how they wound My Eucharistic Heart! Oh how they offend Me when they disobey My beloved and good Vicar, who suffers so much for love of Me.

My humble servant, I love My beloved brothers, but many have turned against Me. Many have become slaves to the empty promises of the world. So many of My beloved brothers are leading so many souls to perdition, for they have fallen out of relationship with My love. They do not live the Gospel, for they have abandoned the true teachings of My Father's Commandments.

Oh how distant they are from My love. Their hearts are drier than the forsaken desert. Their souls are swollen with pride. There is no light in their souls, only darkness. Yes, My humble servant, there are many of My fallen beloved brothers who have turned against My love.

Have pity on your suffering Master and do not complain about your lack of sleep. Unite your suffering with Mine for the purification of My Bride. Embrace my beloved Vicar who faces much opposition everyday. Pray for him and for all My obedient beloved brothers who love and support My Vicar. Especially keep in mind My beloved brothers that have gone astray, for I suffer greatly for these dear ones.

My humble servant, in just a few hours you will be celebrating your seventh Anniversary with My Beloved Mother. I know that you haven't slept, and you wonder why I would ask you to suffer for My Bride, especially on this happy occasion.

Know, My dear friend, that My Bride is living the terrible time when there is much division among My beloved brothers. The spirit of apostasy is swallowing many of My beloved brothers who are weak in their faith. My humble servant, the suffering of My Bride will intensify. This is why I have come to ask for your prayers. Many of My beloved brothers will abandon their vocation as priests.

Oh if you only knew how great is My suffering, knowing the great tribulation that My Bride will encounter. No one has the ability to comprehend the great suffering that My Bride will undergo. Console Me, My humble servant and suffer with Me for My Bride.

Trust Me, for I shall refresh you, and your heart will know great joy as your visit with My Holy Mother approaches. St. Joseph and I shall accompany My Holy Mother during your visit. Thank you, My dear friend, for giving of your love and time to your Eucharistic Master. I give you My blessing, and I shall come to you again in a few hours.

Janie: *Our Lord and Our Lady came to me later during this hour. They were both weeping at the great pain that pierced Their Hearts because of the great apostasy in the Church. I cried with Them, as I was able to have a clear vision of what Our Lord was sharing with me. Our Lady was quiet, there were no words from her to me. I was able to embrace her in her great sorrow for the Church.*

February 15, 1996 *Seventh Anniversary of Our Lady*

Our Lady: Dear children, rejoice and give thanks to God for allowing me to be with you for such a long time. Today I give you all my motherly blessing. You are so precious to my Immaculate Heart and I, too, am rejoicing with you. I am here to help you to continue to live by faith and to live everything that I have given you.

Little children, you have made me so happy by embracing me as your Mother of Compassion and Love. It is important that you practice these two virtues everyday. The world is so much in need of compassion and love. So, my little children, be compassionate and loving to everyone. Pray your Rosary everyday with your family. Attend Holy Mass and visit with my Son in the Blessed Sacrament.

Dear children, continue to pray for my beloved Pope and all the Church. Offer all your suffering and sacrifices for the Church. Know that Lent is approaching. Prepare well, for God wants to purify your hearts. During Lent allow my Son to help you to suffer well. He will help you to embrace your crosses.

Pray, little children, pray and do not grow tired of prayer, for only through prayer will you discover God. Live my messages! Be living witnesses of the Gospel.

Little children, I want to take you all to Heaven, but you must do all that I ask of you. Love your family and thank God for blessing you as a family. I love you, I love you all. You have brought so much joy to my Heart. Thank you for listening to my message.

February 27, 1996 *Mt. Pleasant, Texas I, Jesus, have heard your cry*

Jesus: Beloved ones, I, Jesus, have heard your cry and your prayers. I ask that you open your hearts truly, so that I may help you. I have not abandoned you, though many of you have abandoned Me and forgotten to ask Me to help you. Abandon yourself to My Eucharistic love and trust in My love and mercy. I will refresh you and give you My peace.

Beloved ones, I know all the suffering that lies deep within your hearts. I know everything about you. You cannot conceal anything from Me. I tell you this, because I want you to learn to trust Me and to return back to My love and mercy. Do not be afraid. Know that My love for you is immense. Do not allow your troubles and worries to separate you from

Me, instead draw closer to My Eucharistic love. I want to help you. Peace, beloved, peace.

Editor's Note: Our Lord came to Janie in Mt. Pleasant and told her that He and His Mother would come to her from time to time during her travels to help those families that she would be witnessing to.

March 22, 1996 *Embrace My Sacred Heart*

Janie: *I arrived in Denver yesterday, as I was invited by D. and B. to come here. Today I went to the top of the mountain at Mother Cabrini's Shrine. While I was there Our Lord came to me twice, once before the big crucifix on the bottom of the steps, then in front of the big statue of the Sacred Heart of Jesus on top of the mountain.*
Jesus: Welcome, My humble servant, to this special place of prayer. Many are the souls that have drawn closer to My Sacred Heart and to the Immaculate Heart of My Mother. Do you like this place?
Janie: Oh yes, My Lord, yes. Thank You for this great honor.

Jesus: My humble servant, embrace the words that Mother Cabrini, My humble vessel, shared with you. Many are the souls that continue to come to Me because of her great love for Me. She was most humble during her life on earth. She entrusted everything to Me, therefore I provided her with everything that she needed for the mission entrusted to her by My Father. Model after her and trust Me in everything, and I will give you everything that you need to accomplish all that My Father has given you.
Janie: *Before I write the second conversation I had with Jesus, I have to write that while I was praying the station where Jesus falls the third time, I had something strange happen to me. As I was half kneeling and half sitting I felt the ground tremble underneath me. I had my eyes closed, and I quickly opened my eyes. It was still trembling. I knelt down to feel the ground, and at the same time I looked around because I thought we were having a small earthquake or something. Then the trembling stopped. I proceeded to the top. I was looking at the statue of the Sacred Heart, and Our Lord talked to me for the second time.*
Jesus: My humble servant, I, your Jesus of Love and Mercy, wish to thank you, for you have a special love for My Sacred Heart. My humble vessel, Mother Cabrini had great love for My Sacred Heart. She helped many souls to have love for My Sacred Heart.

If only souls would understand how much I am consoled when My Sacred Heart is embraced with such love and devotion. I am always

present in the lives of those souls that embrace My Sacred Heart and the Most Immaculate Heart of My Mother. Share with your family and all other souls, that have love and devotion to My Sacred Heart, that they console Me.
Janie: *I was moved to tears to know how much we console Our Lord by having devotion to His Most Sacred Heart.*

March 25, 1996 *Denver, Colorado* *Feast of the Annunciation*

Janie: *This morning when I woke up and while saying my prayers, my angel came and told me to prepare because Our Lady was coming to pray with me.*
Our Lady: Good morning, my child. You are not feeling well this morning.
Janie: No, I am not feeling well, but I don't mind because you are here to help me. Thank you for coming.
Our Lady: My child, I have come so that you and I may pray for my Son's Vicar. He is suffering and our prayers will help him.
Janie: *We prayed one Our Father and one Glory Be.*
Our Lady: My child, always embrace my Son's beloved Vicar through your prayer. Today, offer the suffering of your illness for him. Pray also for all my beloved priests that have gone astray. This causes much sadness to my Immaculate Heart. Pray also for all the Marian Movement of Priests, for these dear ones are the ones that are bringing many souls back to my Son and to my Immaculate Heart. Especially pray for my beloved son, Fr. Gobbi, who spends tireless hours bringing many of my beloved priests back to my Immaculate Heart. Embrace him also dearly in your prayers. My child, I must go now. I give you my motherly blessing.
Janie: *I asked her to touch the first class relic of St. Philomena, and she did. She blessed the other people that were with me as well. Our Lady will come again tonight for her scheduled visit. She came this morning to pray with me for her Church.*

March 25, 1996 *Denver, Colorado* *The world has nothing to offer*

Our Lady: Dear children, today I invite you to rejoice with your heavenly Mother as the Church celebrates the Feast of the Annunciation. This is the day when God sent St. Gabriel to bring me the Good News of our salvation. Let us together, little children, turn to God with deep gratitude for His great love and mercy.

My children, today, I wish to speak to you about the importance of liv-

ing my messages. For a long time now, I have been giving you heavenly messages to help you to convert. Many of you have embraced my messages, but many have ignored them. You must embrace these heavenly messages if you want to draw closer to God.
Little children, remember, I cannot help you if you do not pray and if you do not live my messages. The day is coming when I will no longer be giving you these heavenly messages. That is why I beg you to embrace my heavenly messages, for these messages will help to lead you to Heaven.

Little children, you are precious to me, and I wish to take you all to Heaven with me. Please act on all that I tell you and abandon the ways of the world, for the world has nothing to offer you. My Son, Jesus, offers you eternal life. Now is the time of decision. Now is the time to decide for God and to abandon sin. With God you have everything. He is blessing the areas in the world where I am appearing. As your heavenly Mother, I give special graces to those souls who embrace my heavenly messages.

I desire little children, that you continue to live these messages even after I am no longer appearing in the world. My Heart will always be with you. I love you all. Pray, pray, pray! Thank you for listening to my message.

May 1, 1996 *St. Joseph introduces St. Philomena*

Janie: *I had been visited by a young girl saint a few times. She called me her little sister. I could only see her silhouette. Today, St. Joseph came for his feast day as St. Joseph the worker and this young girl saint was with him. He introduced her to me as St. Philomena and at that moment I was able to see her completely. She is very young and beautiful. St. Joseph said she would be coming to me every day with guidance for the youth and for the family. I am so happy!*

June 4, 1996 *Adoration: My Divine Mercy*

Janie: *I had been praying and asking for guidance for Fr. W. when Our Lord came.*
Jesus: My humble servant, welcome to My Eucharistic Heart and to My love and mercy. My child, I, your Jesus of Love and Mercy, asked that you come to spend time with Me, for I wanted to share how important My Divine Mercy is to those souls who accept and welcome My Divine Mercy. My Holy Mother is also Mother of Divine Mercy. She

The Holy Spirit and Divine Union

was also sent to the world as a merciful Mother to help her sinful children to convert and to bring them to My mercy. My Mother's mercy and My mercy are inseparable. Together we seek to flood every heart with Our mercy.

My beloved little brother, Fr. W., continues to work endless and tireless hours helping souls to realize that when My Mother appeared under the title of Our Lady of Guadalupe, she came with Child. At that time, through her love and mercy many were converted. I, Jesus of Divine Mercy, her Beloved Son, was in her virginal womb as she appeared to the pagan children.

My beloved brother has worked so hard in trying to understand how to help souls to believe that My Mother was with Child under this title. My little brother attempted to prove this by having a sonogram done of My Mother's Image. In doing this, they were able to see My Image of Divine Mercy. My little brother understood what I, Jesus of Divine Mercy, wanted to tell him concerning My mercy. The very reason I, Jesus, ordered my humble servant Sr. Faustina to paint a special image of My Divine Mercy was so that this image would be a reminder of the demands of My mercy, because I wanted souls to know that even the strongest faith means nothing if it is without works of mercy.

As My little brother travels with these two images of My Most Holy Mother and My Image of Divine Mercy, we want the world to understand the great importance of Our Divine Mercy. Souls must understand that if they do not perform works of mercy they will not obtain My mercy on Judgment Day.

When souls practice mercy towards others daily, they gather for themselves eternal treasures. I will remember all the mercy they showed others on Judgment Day. It will go well for these souls. Wherever these images are venerated, My Mother and I will flood hearts with Our Divine Mercy.

My little brother has accomplished so much by his hard efforts and perseverance. We are most pleased with his work, suffering and obedience. His treasures are great in Heaven. Thank you, My humble servant, for listening so patiently to all that I share with you. Go in My peace.

Janie: *I understood that Jesus wanted to remind us that the reason He came as Jesus of Divine Mercy was to teach us about His mercy, and to help us to understand the importance of practicing works of mercy everyday towards everyone. In doing this, we will truly be reflecting*

Jesus' Divine Mercy, but we, too, must follow in His footsteps in being merciful.

June 6, 1996 *Leave all judgment to Me*

Janie: *I was under severe attack and was having very bad thoughts. Jesus came to help me.*
Jesus: My child, do not give in to the anger or the resentment that lurks in your mind. Know that it does not please Me to see you entertaining such thoughts. Do I not know everything that delights you or upsets you? The person which you are distracted with does not deserve any harsh thoughts circulating in your mind. Leave all judgment to Me. Remember, you are called to carry your cross out of love without complaining. You must act as I did in the midst of My cruel suffering when I carried My Cross out of love for you.

You feel like a prisoner for you are surrounded by the obligation of caring for your loved ones. Abandon these feelings quickly, for it only serves as an obstacle and keeps you from trusting in Me. Do not pity yourself or do not allow anyone to show pity or compassion because of your suffering. Abandon yourself to My Divine Will. Embrace all your crosses with joy in your heart, dismiss anything else. I call you to be absorbed only by My goodness, nothing else. I shall manifest My love in you in ways that you cannot imagine.

June 14, 1996 *Feast of the Sacred Heart of Jesus*

Jesus: My dear child and humble servant, welcome to My Eucharistic and Most Sacred Heart. Abandon yourself to My Most Sacred Heart that is filled with My love and mercy.

My humble servant, I am deeply grateful to you and your family for the love and devotion that you have to My Most Sacred Heart and the Immaculate Heart of My Mother. Know that it is the love of Our Two Hearts that is your strength during times of difficulties and times of great suffering. Our love dwells in the hearts of the families where We are loved and honored.

Through your love and devotion to Our Two Hearts, We bless all your daily tasks and activities. Your young children are under Our protection while they are away from you. We bless everything that surrounds you. An army of angels are encamped around the family and souls that love and honor Our Two Hearts.

The Holy Spirit and Divine Union

My child, this is the time of the reign of the Two United Hearts. The world so needs Our love to help souls to convert. Our Hearts are filled with love for all souls. Today, I, your Eucharistic Savior, bless all the world with the love in My Most Sacred Heart. Tomorrow you will honor the Most Immaculate Heart of My Mother. These are two important and blessed days. Continue to honor the Two Hearts. Recall My words to you four years ago concerning Our Two Hearts. There is salvation in the devotion to the Two United Hearts.

Janie: *I saw the Most Sacred Heart of Jesus. Three rays came from it. Red (love), brilliant gold (joy), and white (peace). These are the three blessings that Jesus gave our world, His love, joy and peace.*

June 15, 1996 *Feast of the Immaculate Heart of Mary*

Our Lady: Good morning, my angel, how are you doing this morning?
Janie: I am well, My Lady, thank you. Happy feast day.
Our Lady: Thank you, my angel, thank you.
Janie: My Lady do you have a message for us today?
Our Lady: Yes, my angel, but first I wish to ask you, is there anything that I can do for you today?
Janie: Thank you for asking. Yes, please intercede for me and my husband so that our prayers and fasting will increase. Pray for all my family for their conversion and for our world. Especially remember my Spiritual Director, my Pastor and all the priests that are dear to me. Pray for my special friends and my persecutors.
Our Lady: My angel, I will honor your intentions. This is my message for all my children: Dear children, today I wish to thank you all for living your consecration to my Most Immaculate Heart. Know that all who are consecrated to my Most Immaculate Heart, you are helping the reign of your heavenly Mother, and you are helping to usher in my Most Immaculate Heart to a world that is in need of my love and intercession.

Little children, do not fear all the pestilence and calamities that surround you. I beg you, keep vigilant through your prayers and be aware of false prophets. Satan is deceiving many of my children including my beloved priests through these false prophets. Pray to my Spouse, the Holy Spirit, for divine discernment so that you will not be misled. Be alert and know that God does not cause fear in your heart. God gives you peace and joy through the power of the Holy Spirit.

Little children, know that there is no other refuge than the refuge of the Two United Hearts. Abandon yourselves to the Two United Hearts and live in the garden of Our Paradise. Do not live in fear and do not be anxious about the things that you hear or read. Live my heavenly messages, attend Holy Mass daily if your schedule allows you to, but I beg you to make every effort to do so. Holy Mass will help to keep you spiritually fed and well maintained in your spiritual journey. Read and live the Holy Gospel and pray your Rosary together as a family.

Little children, if you do what I ask of you, you will have God's peace in your heart. Live your consecration to the Two United Hearts and no harm will come to you, for you are under Our protection. Thank you for listening to my message.
Janie: *I saw the Immaculate Heart of Mary and from her heart came three rays. One red, one white and one blue. I knew in my heart that the red meant love, the white purity and the blue holiness.*

June 17, 1996 *Family cooperation is important*

Jesus: My child, I, your loving Jesus, am here to console your suffering heart. Lately you have kept much to yourself. You have not asked for My help. Do you not know by now that you cannot accomplish anything without My grace? Tell Me everything and I shall make your burden lighter.
Janie: *I told Jesus all my troubles and that I was having a hard time getting things done, due to lack of cooperation from my family.*
Jesus: Know, beloved of My Eucharistic Heart that family cooperation is important when trying to accomplish family tasks. When family members put aside their own agendas and enjoyment to give a helping hand, the blessings that they receive from Me are without limit. In return for their charity I see to it that they accomplish all that they had planned. When a family works together, they please Me, and I bless them with My peace. Share this with your family. Be at peace.

June 18, 1996 *Peace, and abandon yourself to Me*

Janie: *I was so frustrated and I cried out,* "Jesus I am so behind in responsibilities and tasks. I feel frustrated." *I heard Jesus speak.*
Jesus: Peace is what's important. Abandon yourself to Me and I will help you.

July 2, 1996 Medjugorje *Apparition Hill*

*Editor's Note: Whenever Janie travels to holy places she has the privilege of being visited by Our Lord and Our Lady.

The Holy Spirit and Divine Union

Our Lady: My dear child, I am happy that you came again to visit this special place.
Janie: I am most happy to be here.
Our Lady: My child, pray for my beloved priests for the spirit of apostasy is strong in the Church. Especially keep in mind the Holy Father, his suffering is immense.
Jesus: My humble servant, look at how he will suffer.
Janie: *I saw a vision and there in the bed our Holy Father was very ill. I felt that maybe he would die. I saw something happen to our Pope that I cannot write about. I saw many priests who were Cardinals planning evil plots against our Pope to do away with him. I saw the apostasy in the behavior of these priests.*
Jesus: My humble servant, My Bride is entering into an era where the division will be much stronger. The apostasy is growing in many hearts of My beloved brothers, therefore keep vigilant with Me in unceasing prayer for My brothers whose hearts are weak.
Our Lady: My child, pray with Us while you are here for Our intentions. My Son will give you much more knowledge concerning the battle within the Church. We give you Our blessing.
Janie: Please, Blessed Mother, help me to embrace and love myself, my family and all whom I meet during my life on earth. Jesus, remember, I am yours, have your way with me. Eternal Father, I submit totally to Your Divine Will. Today and everyday of my life give me only what I require to live Your Divine Will. You are my everything, Oh Fountain of Holiness, let Your holiness absorb my whole being. Take care of my family whom you have given me to love. I shall spend my life loving You in them. Thank You for the gift of my family. I shall embrace them as my heavenly treasures, for I know that they are gifts from Heaven. Amen.

July 2, 1996 *Medjugorje Priests prayers are so powerful*

Jesus: Our humble servant, again, I come to you to thank you for your prayers. I know, My poor little vessel, that this is hard for you, to see the dilemma that exists within the hearts of My brothers.
Janie: *Again, Jesus showed me a vision of the condition of the Church. I saw a war going on inside the Church. Priests were being murdered by other priests. Many priests were being treated with such cruelty because of their obedience to the Holy Father.*

The spirit of fear gripped many of the obedient priests, for they knew that they would suffer. Many good priests joined the disobedient priests for fear that they would be killed. I saw the spirit of homosexuality, the

feminism movement, fornication, abortion, control and hunger for power. Such terrible things occurring within the house of God.
Jesus: Now you understand the need for prayer and fasting. This is what I, your suffering Savior, am asking all My brothers, the remnant of My Heart: To pray and fast for the apostasy that is overshadowing My Bride. Through their prayers and fasting many of My brothers who have fallen out of relationship with Me, they shall return back to Me.

Oh, if only My brother priests would listen to what I am asking of them. Their prayers are so powerful, because I have given them the power to forgive, to heal, to wipe out all evil forces, to convert hearts, to raise the dead, to walk among poisonous snakes and to bring light where there is no light - all of these and much more if they have faith in their hearts.

Through their prayer and fasting many hearts will heal not only with My brother priests, but wounded souls everywhere. It saddens My Heart for many of My brother priests have forgotten the power that I invested them with when they were ordained. Pray for My Bride, My humble servant. Know that I suffer for My Bride like you suffer for your family. We give you Our blessing.

July 3, 1996 *Medjugorje My beloved sons, my special priests*

Our Lady: My dear child, I wish to thank you for the love that you have for my beloved sons. They are special priests, for they are consecrated to my Most Immaculate Heart. These are serious troubled times for my sons who are consecrated to my Most Immaculate Heart. My poor little sons suffer so much persecution, and their persecution comes from many directions and in many forms. They are able to withstand many attacks, for I protect them with my motherly mantle. They live in the garden of my Immaculate Heart. I watch over them as a Mother watches over her children. I nurture their hearts, I pray for them to have good impulses and inspirations. My Holy Spouse infuses their hearts with divine clarity to carry out their priestly tasks.

These priests consecrated to my Immaculate Heart are the instruments that are helping to heal the woundedness in my other sons that are not consecrated to my Most Immaculate Heart. Their prayers and suffering are the remedy that is helping their separated brothers that are caught in the web of apostasy. Pray for my priests, pray for my priests. Thank you, my child, for being so patient in listening. We know you are tired.
Janie: *Our Lord again showed me the vision of the apostasy within the Church. Again I saw such hatred and violence between many priests.*

The Holy Spirit and Divine Union

Our Lord: My humble servant, pray for the protection of My Vicar, you see the violence that surrounds him.
St. Philomena: My little sister, remain prayerful for the Bride of our Master. I shall be praying with you.

July 4, 1996 Medjugorje *The real gift of being set free*

Janie: *I spent the night at Cross Mountain and I was privileged to have heavenly visitations. St. Francis came to ask me to pray with the Queen of Peace for peace in all hearts. Padre Pio, St. Joseph and Jesus also came.*
St. Joseph: My little one, how are you? Know that you have brought joy to Most Holy Mary for bringing her children to visit her. She will bless all who came with her motherly blessing. It is important to remain prayerful, especially when you return back to your country, for Satan will try to take your peace away. Pray for your family as well, and share your blessing with them. My little one, I shall see you on your birthday.
Janie: *When St. Joseph came, K.C. and L.B. heard a loud sound like an explosion which they then realized was Heaven visiting me. I did not hear this, of course, but it was heard by them at the moment that St. Joseph came to me. Padre Pio and St. Francis came to strengthen me and told me to love Jesus with all my heart and soul, to suffer for Him with joy in my heart. Rays from their hands came to my hands as rays of fire. I understood that this was to help me in being strong in my suffering for Jesus.*
Jesus: My humble servant, pray not only for your country, but for all the world. The freedom that humanity celebrates is the freedom that the world teaches. True freedom begins with repentance and forgiveness. Pray for all of humanity, so that they may understand the real gift of being set free.
Janie: *I was praying for my country on July fourth, Independence Day.*

July 4, 1996 *Medjugorje* Love one another

Janie: *I was visited by Our Lord, Our Lady, St. Philomena and the Three Archangels.*
Our Lady: My dear child, share with my children how much I love them. Tell them that I know that many of them are suffering, but to persevere in their hard efforts to pray and to trust in my Son. I am praying for all my children. They must not feel that they are alone in their suffering. We are with them, helping them to remain faithful and prayerful.

I ask my children to share all that they have received here with their

family. They must allow the message of Medjugorje to live in their hearts. In this way they will not forget my message of prayer, fasting, conversion, praying their Rosary and Holy Mass. Satan will try to take their peace away. They must disarm him with the prayer of the Rosary. Everyone will receive from my Son what they need to draw closer to him. I give you my motherly blessing.
Janie: Lord, is there anything we can do for You?
Jesus: Love one another. I give you My peace, My love and My joy. Share it with your family and everyone you meet.
St. Michael: Beloved of God, know that I, St. Michael, protect all who trust in the intercession of the angels.
St. Philomena: I will intercede for all who are here present and their families.
Janie: *St. Gabriel and St. Raphael did not speak.*

July 5, 1996 Medjugorje Souls will never understand

Jesus: My humble servant, welcome to My Eucharistic Heart. Thank you for coming to spend time with Me. Souls will never understand the enormous graces that are received when souls come to visit their Eucharistic Savior. Many come for different reasons and while they are here, I refresh their souls with My love. I heal their wounded souls, and I help them to carry their cross. I hear all their prayers, and I attend to all their needs. While they are here praying for their loved ones, I am also attending to the needs of those souls that they bring Me in prayer.

Every second that you spend adoring your Savior, you receive a multitude of graces to help you in your faith journey. I give you an infusion of My love and mercy, so that you may love and show mercy for others. Know that I shall grant your request that you ask for My brother priests. I will bless the gifts that you will present to them. They will receive the gift of prayer of the heart which will lead them closer to My Heart.

As they recite their Rosary, they will be infused with divine wisdom of knowledge to pray for souls who are suffering much. During their prayers of the Rosary, they will receive holy inspirations and their desire for holiness will increase. They will hunger for holiness and those souls that they are praying for, these souls will receive healing. My humble servant, thank you for praying for and loving My brother priests. I give you My blessing.
Janie: Thank You, My Master. I am Yours to do with as You Will.
Our Lady: My dear child, ponder in your heart all that you are receiving from my Son. He is giving you a multitude of graces to pray for all

His special intentions for His Bride. He loves you, and He is counting on your prayers and sacrifices. Remain obedient and steadfast. Embrace His Bride and all her suffering with your prayers. Thank you for the love in your heart. Thank you for helping my children.
Janie: *Our Lord continues to give me self-knowledge. He is revealing things about myself that will help me to be His reflection. Although this self-knowledge is most painful, I thank God for this purgation. He is purifying my soul. I know I must love and accept myself before I can love and accept others. I cannot put in words what a cleansing of the soul it is for me to journey on this painful path of self-knowledge.*

July 6, 1996 Medjugorje *Suffer for those who reject My Mother*

Jesus: My humble servant, embrace your suffering Savior and console Me as I suffer for love of humanity. Today I ask that you offer your own suffering for those souls who reject My Mother. This hurts Me so much, for she is a model of purity and holiness. She loves all her children, and she suffers for them. Tell her how much you love her through your prayers. Always embrace her as your heavenly Mother and let her be a Mother to you and your family. She will help and protect you through her prayers.

Know that she is unceasingly praying for love and peace in the world. She suffers for all who reject me, she suffers for all unbelievers, and she suffers for all poor sinners. She is your heavenly Mother, please take her love and peace to all who reject her motherly love.
Janie: My Lord, how can I do this?
Jesus: By your prayer, your love for her and by your example. I give you My blessing.
Janie: Your Will, My Lord, is my will also. Amen.

July 6, 1996 *Medjugorje Return to your homes and share*

Our Lady: My dear children, what joy you have brought to your heavenly Mother. I wish to extend my deep gratitude for all your prayers. Know, little children, that the graces and blessings that you have received from God are without limit. These blessings and graces extend to your loved ones back home as well. I love you all. Continue to offer your prayers, especially the prayer of the Rosary, for your conversion and your family's conversion. Little children, God has blessed you in a special way during your stay here. Now, return to your homes and share what God has placed in your hearts. I give you my motherly blessing and I thank you.

Janie: Thank you, my Dear Mother. Lord is there anything You wish me to convey for You?
Jesus: Again I ask that you love one another with My love.
St. Philomena: My little sister, I will intercede for your intentions.
Janie: *I was sad but joyful to know that I would be leaving Medjugorje in a few hours. I have experienced so much peace while I have been here in this Oasis of Peace.*
Our Lady: My child, do not be sad that you are leaving this place. Remember, I live in your heart. This peace that you have comes to you because your prayers have opened your heart. Live this peace and share it with your family and others. It is my Son's peace that dwells in your heart. Pray with your heavenly Mother everyday, so that Our prayers will help souls to open their hearts to this peace that my Son so yearns to give to all the world. I love you, my sweet angel. Thank you for loving my Son.
Janie: Thank you, My Lady, for this heavenly guidance. I promise to follow all that you ask of me. I truly promise from my heart. *She smiled and then she was gone.*

July 7, 1996 *Paris, France* Time alone with my Savior

Janie: *This morning we left Medjugorje, and I thank God for our heavenly Mother. This pilgrimage has been my retreat. God took me into His Mother's Immaculate Heart, and she gave me daily motherly teachings. She helped me to better understand how to handle family problems and how to embrace my family during difficult moments. So much happened to me on a daily basis, and I enjoyed all those precious souls that were with me on this pilgrimage. Most important was the time alone with my Savior during Eucharistic Adoration. For this quiet time I am truly grateful.*

July 7, 1996 *Paris, France* Perpetual Adoration

Janie: *We visited Notre Dame and the Miraculous Medal at Rue de Bac. This was a most holy moment for we were able to receive our Lord in Holy Communion. We were pressed for time and I was sad that so little time was given to spend there, but I was most grateful for the gift of being there. We visited the Church of the Sacred Heart (Sacre Coeur), and this was truly another moment from Heaven. This is a holy place where the Presence of Our Lord in Perpetual Adoration has lived for over a hundred years.*
Jesus: Know that this region (Paris, France) has been spared from many disasters because of My Perpetual Presence in this holy place. It

The Holy Spirit and Divine Union

is holy because I am here and have been here for a very long time. My humble servant, pray so that the Perpetual Eucharistic Adoration will be in every place that believes in My Presence during Holy Mass.

July 16, 1996 *Begin a community of families*

Janie: Good morning, my Blessed Mother.
Our Lady: Good morning, my angel.
Janie: *She smiled, and then we prayed together one Our Father and one Glory Be for peace in the world.* Blessed Mother, I am so happy to be with you.
Our Lady: My angel, it brings me great joy to be able to visit with you on this special day. How are you doing?
Janie: Well, I am very busy these days being a mother to my little grandson. He takes much of my time, but I am very grateful for the opportunity to give of myself and my love to him.
Our Lady: My sweet angel, God is giving you an abundance of special graces to accomplish all your daily responsibilities. Trust Him with all your daily tasks and do not become discouraged when you are tired, but place all at God's disposal.
Janie: Blessed Mother, could you give me guidance on this community of families that was given to me while I was in prayer in Medjugorje? My Spiritual Director suggested that I ask you about it.
Our Lady: My angel, I encourage you to pray and fast much on this effort. I will intercede for you as you pray and discern more. Know that I, too, encourage you to begin such a community of families devoted to my Immaculate Heart. My hand will be in this work. Know that you will be met with great obstacles, this is why I encourage you to pray and fast for this work and effort. My spouse will enlighten you with all that you have to do. Trust in his guidance.
Janie: Thank you for everything!
Our Lady: You are most welcome, my angel. Now I will give you this message for today.

July 16, 1996 *Never be without your Scapular*

Our Lady: Dear children, today I invite you to embrace my Garment of Grace and wear it faithfully everyday. Never be without your scapular. I know at times you are asked about the scapular and why you wear it. Never be embarrassed to wear it. Whenever you are asked about it simply say: "This is the Garment of Grace of the Mother of God and my Mother. It is her habit. To wear it means that I am in her service and that I belong to her. She protects all who believe and wear her Garment of Grace. This is her promise to all who wear her scapular."

Little children, know that I am always praying for you and helping you to obtain purity of heart. Pray with your heavenly Mother, especially pray your family Rosary. Know that the prayer of the Rosary is more powerful than any atomic weapon made by mankind. Your Rosary will dissolve any obstacle and will avert wars and natural disasters.

Your prayers of the Rosary are even more powerful when you are clothed with my Garment of Grace. Recall my words to St. Dominic, "One day through the Rosary and the brown scapular I will save the world." Know, my little ones, that the devil cannot touch you if you wear your brown scapular. He hates my scapular, because he knows that he has no power over my children who wear and believe in my Garment of Grace.

My children, pray your family Rosary and keep in mind to pray for all souls, especially the unbelievers and those who never pray. I give you my motherly blessing. Thank you for listening to my message.

August 15, 1996 *My little stars, my heavenly flowers*

Our Lady: Dear children, rejoice with your heavenly Mother on this day of my Glorious Assumption. Today I am blessing all the world with God's peace. This is indeed a glorious day, when all of Heaven honors their heavenly Queen and Mother.

Little children, I wish to extend my deep gratitude for responding to my request of offering five decades of the Rosary in expiation for the sins of the world. Together, little children, we are helping sinners to convert and to return back to their faith.

Know, little children, that God is sending His blessing to your own family as you unite in prayer with your heavenly Mother. My little ones, be brave in your faith for your heavenly Mother, for it is your faith that will help you in these troubled times. Much evil is being committed against many innocent souls. Pray for God's justice and pray for peace in evil souls. Many do not yet believe that these are evil times, although they are aware of the pestilence and calamities. These souls are the ones that you must pray and fast for their hearts to melt.

My children, I wish to share with you that I am pleased with all your prayers and hard efforts. You, little ones, console your heavenly Mother.

The Holy Spirit and Divine Union

You are my little children, my little stars that twinkle throughout the world through your prayers. You are my heavenly flowers that bring the fragrance of peace to the world through your prayers.

Pray, my children, and continue to bring the light of my Son, Jesus, to those souls that live in darkness. I love you, little children, and I give you my motherly blessing. To you who are experiencing sadness in your heart, rejoice with your heavenly Mother. Fear nothing, but pray. Thank you for listening to my message.

August 25, 1996 *I desire to be known as Mother of Compassion and Love*

Our Lady: My dear child, peace, my child, peace. This morning I have come to visit you to tell you that your suffering is helping many souls throughout the world. Your suffering is especially helping many of my beloved priests whose hearts are closed to the True Presence of my Son in the Holy Eucharist. Your suffering is helping many of my priests whose souls are complacent and who have become self-centered. They have stopped loving my Son.

Many of my beloved priests, whose hearts have no room for my Son, are responsible for leading many souls to perdition. Please, my child, help your heavenly Mother to pray. Do not grow tired of your constant suffering. Know, my child, that the angels are constantly at your side, praying for you to help you during your suffering.

My child, these are evil times. There is very little true love in souls. Many of my children continue to fail to respond to my call to return back to my Son. This is one of the very reasons why I weep tears of blood in many of my statues. Pray, my child, for the upcoming victory of my Immaculate Heart over evil. As this time approaches and is already in your midst, many more miracles will take place throughout the world to draw the attention and to awaken complacent souls. I am employing many different means to help my children to respond to the love and mercy of God.

My child, I have come this morning to ask of you a special favor. I desire that souls know me under the title of Mother of Compassion and Love. I know this is hard, for you for you do not want to draw attention to yourself. My child, do this for your heavenly Mother. Already many souls have been healed by venerating this picture and by touching my image.

Janie: Blessed Mother this is hard for me, but I will share this with my husband and with my Spiritual Director. We will pray and will respond to your request.

Our Lady: My child, again I say to you, I know how hard this is for you. If you respond to my request, many souls will receive the healing that they need to draw closer to the Two United Hearts. I ask of my children to venerate my image with faith in their hearts. My child, do not be concerned about what I am asking of you. Remember that I am employing many means to awaken complacent souls. This image I gave to you is one of those means. I give you my motherly blessing.

September 8, 1996 *To those families who do not pray together*

Our Lady: Dear children, today I bless you as your heavenly Mother, and I rejoice with you as you honor your heavenly Mother through this joyful celebration. You have brought so much joy to my Immaculate Heart, so much joy. I am deeply grateful.

My little ones, I invite you to continue to pray for your family. Many of you are sad because your loved ones do not pray with you. Please, I beg you, do not allow the lack of faith in your loved ones hearts to keep you from praying, but pray more. Prayer and love is the only way that you can help those souls most distant from God.

I know, my little ones, that you struggle much with those in your family who have turned away from God's love. This hurts you very much, but know that it hurts me also, for I love all my children with God's love. My little ones, I beg you, please do not blame God for all the suffering in your family and for the evilness that is happening throughout the world. Understand, dear children, that God does not cause bad things to happen. Only goodness comes from Him. Remain faithful to God in your suffering. He will turn your suffering into joy and fill you with His peace.

Continue to pray as a family, especially pray the Holy Rosary. Oh, little children, if you only understood the power of the Rosary, you would pray it everyday. I invite those who do not pray together as a family to pray each day one Our Father, one Hail Mary and one Glory be. Pray these prayers with your hearts. I promise you that if your respond to my request, you will soon begin to pray the Rosary as a family. This is my promise to you.

My little ones, again I wish to thank each one of you for honoring your heavenly Mother with such a loving celebration. God will bless you, God will bless you. Little children, do one more favor for your heavenly Mother, pray for the Holy Father and all the Church. There is much suffering in the Church. I bless you as your heavenly Mother. Thank you for listening to my message.

September 13, 1996 *New Orleans, Louisiana* *Honor My Mother*

Janie: *While I was praying over the people during the healing service we gathered together in a circle to pray for our children and Our Lord came. These are His words to me to convey to the people there.*
Jesus: My humble servant, I, your Jesus of Love and Mercy, come to bless all My people. Know that I am deeply pleased with all the love that has been demonstrated here to honor My Holy Mother. I especially extend my deep gratitude to your Bishop and priest who left all their programs to come to help honor My Holy Mother. Many graces and blessings are bestowed on you, beloved.

I, your Beloved Savior, love you all with immense love. Fear nothing beloved, for I am with you always helping you to carry out My Father's Commandments and helping you to live the messages that My Holy Mother is giving the world. Blessings to all, beloved.

September 14, 1996 *New Orleans* *Triumph of the Cross*

Janie: *Our Lord came to me and showed me this vision. I saw a huge Cross in the sky that illuminated the whole world. Our Lord was standing by the Cross.*

Jesus: Beloved of My Father, today I bless the world through My death and Resurrection. Know, beloved, that I had to die on the Cross in order that you would have life and to be reconciled back to My Father. Great is the victory that came through My death on the Cross. You must embrace My Cross with joy in your heart. In doing this you proclaim Me as your Lord and Master. I resurrected on the third day and took my place with My Heavenly Father. For all who believe in My death and Resurrection, you will also be with Me in Paradise.

Beloved, live the victory of My Cross and extend My victory to those who do not believe. Never forget the great love that I demonstrated for you beloved through My dying on the Cross, for this love is the greatest love ever demonstrated for humanity throughout eternity. Live this love, beloved, and you will live in Me and I in you. As My Father and

I are One, so will you be one in Us.
Janie: *Then Our Lord showed me another vision of all the blessings that came to all the world when He died on Calvary. When He breathed His last breath and expired, millions of rays of fire went throughout the world. It seemed to me like fire works on the fourth of July. This was the victory of His death on the Cross. Great blessings came to the world. He purchased our rewards for eternal life. Through His Resurrection He demonstrated that there is no death for those who believe in Him, only eternal life. Praised be Jesus our Beloved Savior, for the great victory that He purchased for us on the Cross.*

September 15, 1996 *Feast of Our Lady of Sorrows - My deep sorrow*

Janie: *Our Lady came to me. She was very sad. These are her words.*
Our Lady: My dear angel, thank you for preparing yourself through prayer. You knew in your heart that this visit would be a difficult one for you. God has allowed you to experience some of my deep sorrow far in my Immaculate Heart.
Janie: *She began to weep.*
Our Lady: My angel, console your heavenly Mother by doing all that I ask of you. You, too, have been chosen to suffer for poor sinners. This is hard for you, but God is pleased with your 'yes' to suffer all that He gives you to help save souls. I will tell you, my child, the reason for my tears of sorrow.
The world is in the midst of evil times. Many of my beloved priests have turned their backs on my Son. They are responsible for leading many souls to perdition. Many of my beloved priests do not believe in the True Presence of my Son in the Holy Eucharist. My Son is being desecrated by many of my beloved priests. Many of their actions are too horrific. Pray for holy priests, especially keeping in mind all my priests who love my Son and suffer for Him.

I cry tears of blood because of all the millions of little babies who are being killed throughout the world. This, my angel, is the ultimate child abuse. These are precious little gifts from Heaven and the only reception they receive from their own parents is a horrible death. Console your heavenly Mother, my angel, console your heavenly Mother.
Janie: *At this point Our Lady cried bitterly, and I cried with her. If only we could stop this horrible sin of killing our babies, but I know that only prayer and fasting can help. Our Lady did not speak for a few moments, but wept. It hurt me so much to see her weeping. I understood that she weeps for every baby that suffers some form of abuse, including being aborted.*

Our Lady showed me a vision of Black Masses where her Son was so desecrated. Things that I cannot put into words. I saw all kinds of evil actions in the world. At this point I will hold all this in my heart and offer it up in prayer.

September 29, 1996 **Waco, Texas** *Feast of the Archangels*

Janie: *Our Lady came with the three Archangels.*
Our Lady: My angel, know how honored I am to accompany the three glorious Archangels.
Janie: *This is a perfect demonstration of Our Lady's humility.*
Our Lady: Thank you, my angel, for the love that you have for the Archangels. God is so pleased with this prayerful gathering. I wish to extend my deep gratitude to all my children who responded to this invitation to gather together for prayer.

I bless all my children with my motherly blessing. Convey to my children not to worry about their loved ones. I, their heavenly Mother, am interceding for them and all their family. Convey to my children to abandon all their sufferings and concerns to my Son, Jesus. He will see to their every need.
Janie: *I asked Our Lady to bless this family and their home.*
Our Lady: I not only give my motherly blessing to them and their home, but to all who will visit this family and their land.

October 7, 1996 *Praying the Rosary helps you to forgive*

Our Lady: Dear children, today I invite you to continue to pray as a family. Prayer is so important little children. Without prayer there is no peace in your life.

Today you honor me as Our Lady of the Rosary. This title, little children, is most pleasing to your heavenly Mother. I invite you to pray the Rosary everyday for peace in the world. Little children, you will never comprehend the power of praying the Rosary, especially as a family. Through praying the Rosary as a family, you drive Satan away from your family life.

Know that I am always with you as you gather to pray your family Rosary. Praying the Rosary helps you to forgive, to love and to accept one another. Pray the Rosary, little children, and God will bless you. Thank you for listening to my message.

October 15, 1996 *My brothers' prayers govern the Heart of My Father*

Janie: *I was praying my Rosary in bed. My angel informed me that Our Lord would come to visit me. I quickly got out of bed and came to our prayer room. Our Lord came. Good morning, My Lord. What can I do for You?*
Jesus: My humble servant, write what I, your Lord and Savior, tell you. I, your loving Savior, have such a yearning to help My people. There is so much misery in their souls because they do not know how to love. I want to pour My love into their miserable souls, but they turn away.

I want to give them an infusion of My love to bring about healing in their lives, but their hearts are closed and filled with coldness. I want to help them to be good and gentle people, to live in peace with one another. I want them to know how much I love them.
Janie: Lord, how can I help You?
Jesus: My humble servant, you can help by being an example and a reflection of My love. Share with souls how much they are loved by Me and how much I long to be in relationship with them. I shall teach them how to live in My love. I will teach them how to detach themselves from the things of the world. I will teach them total abandonment. My love will remove anger, pride, selfishness, jealousy, envy, evilness and all vices that separate them from My love.

I will teach them how to love My Cross and how to suffer with joy in their hearts. I will teach them that it is through suffering that they are made pure. They will understand that sufferings are steps that lead to Heaven. My humble servant, I know that you have gone without sleep for love of Me tonight. You have suffered in expiation for the sins of My Bride and of the world. I am deeply moved by your love and commitment to Me. No one except Me knows of your suffering. You have come to understand that I am always at your side. You are learning to trust Me in everything, especially in your suffering.

Know, My poor humble servant, that you are a slave to suffering and your suffering pleases Me, for you embrace your crosses with joy and peace. I have come to you to share My pain for My people, and you welcomed your suffering Savior. My love will be your strength in all that you do. I am grateful to you, My poor tired servant. Pray with your Savior for all that I have shared with you.

Share with My beloved brothers not to grow weary of praying for the salvation of souls. Their prayers storm the heavens and answers come

The Holy Spirit and Divine Union

their way quickly. The prayers of My brothers govern the Heart of My Father. My Father receives their prayers like the morning embraces the morning dew. Prayer is the remedy for poor sinners. Peace, My humble servant, peace.

Janie: I love You, Jesus, my everything.

October 22, 1996 *Jesus teaches about the horror of sin*

Janie: *I had been up all night because I had been very upset with my family. I had really lost my temper with them and I had been crying. Our Lord came to give me guidance.*

Jesus: My humble servant, tonight, I, your Jesus of Love and Mercy, wish to teach you about sin. You have been suffering because you hate sin. When you sin you suffer much, for you wish with all your heart that you could escape sinning. Tonight, I, your loving Savior, will teach you on the horror of sin.

Janie: *Jesus is speaking of mortal sin.*

Jesus: When a souls sins, that soul rebels against My Heavenly Father. By sin you crucify Me all over again. You become the offspring of the devil. By sin you cause Me much injury, and you become My enemy. By sin, you despise My love, and you give your heart to the devil and become deaf to Me. By sin you reject the eternal happiness that My Father offers you, you choose hell instead. By sin you reject My love and mercy and accept the passions of the devil which destroy your soul. You embrace every temptation that he sets before you, knowing that you are deeply wounding My Eucharistic Heart.

By sin you reject all the graces and blessings that My Father is giving you. By sin you allow the devil to keep you blind to the evil which you are doing. By sin the devil makes you turn your back on Heaven. He leads you to indulge in every moment's pleasure which is most offensive to My Heavenly Father. By sin you accept the death of your soul that the devil offers you. You reject true happiness. By sin the devil gets you to commit every evil that he can lure you to.

By sin you reject prayer, the sacraments, good thoughts, and the inspirations of your guardian angel. Sin, my humble servant, leads to death. The only way out of sin is by approaching the tribunal of penance. By sin a soul is destroyed. Implore the clemency of My Father when you sin against the One Who created you out of great love.

Now, My humble servant, you have a better understanding of what a horror sin is against the law of My Father. Pray and offer much sacrifice for the sinfulness in many, many hearts. Sin is what will destroy humanity. True repentance will mend sinful hearts.

November 21, 1996 *Stronger than any atomic weapon*

Janie: *Our Lady came with the three Archangels for the feast of the Presentation of Mary. Greetings Blessed Mother, St. Michael, St. Gabriel and St. Raphael.*
Our Lady: Good morning, my angel, how are you doing this morning?
Janie: I am doing fine. Thank you so much for coming!
Our Lady: My angel, it is good to be here with you once again. You have been up early this morning, suffering and offering up your sleep for the Holy Pope. My daughter do not grow weary of your suffering, but offer all your prayers and sacrifices for peace in the Church. The Holy Vicar of my Son, Jesus, suffers from much opposition from many of my beloved sons and daughters in the Church. This opposition pierces my Immaculate Heart, so please ask God to, through your prayers, strengthen all my beloved sons and daughters who oppose the Holy Vicar of my Son, Jesus. God knows, my angel, that your prayers and sacrifices come from your heart.

My angel, on this feast day that commemorates the day when my parents presented me to the Lord in the temple, present all your children to the Lord that He may bless them. Everyday, give your children to the Lord through your prayers. In doing this, you are demonstrating your trust to God.
Janie: My Blessed Mother, do you have a message for us today?
Our Lady: My angel, convey to my children how much I love them and that I am with them in all their prayers. I wish to tell them that I am protecting their family from my adversary, who is always trying to set traps for them to fall into temptation. I watch over all the families that are living my messages, and their prayers and sacrifices are helping to lead my children that do not pray for conversion. I so enjoy and look forward to being with my children when they are praying as a family. I rejoice in the good that they are doing.
Oh, if only my children could begin to know how their prayers draw them closer to God, they would pray unceasingly. I want all my children to pray their Rosary as a family. Through praying the Rosary, they avert many disasters in their family and throughout the world. The Rosary is stronger than any atomic weapon ever created by mankind.

This is why I beg my children to always pray their Rosary as a family. The Rosary is like a spiritual vacuum that eliminates much evil in the heart and it brings God's peace. Tell my children to pray their Rosary everyday as a family.

Janie: Blessed Mother, people have been asking me when the warning will come. Do you have anything to tell me?

Our Lady: My angel, tell my children to prepare their hearts everyday through prayer and not to allow themselves to be distracted. God wants all His children to lead good and holy lives everyday. In doing this they will be prepared for all things to come. Share with my children that their prayers can avert many oncoming tribulations, this is why the world is receiving so much guidance from Heaven, so that they may turn to God and stop living sinful lives.

Tell my children to abandon themselves to my Most Immaculate Heart. I am the temple of the Lord and the dwelling of the Holy Spirit. My intercession is powerful before God. Therefore, my children are under my motherly protection. Tell them to have no fear or worry, but to pray, pray, pray. Now, my angel, I give you and your family my motherly blessing.

The Three Archangels: Beloved of God, embrace your heavenly Mother and all that she tells you. She is the heavenly Queen and her intercession is powerful. God denies her nothing. Trust in her motherly intercession.

December 8, 1996 *Renew this Consecration often*

Our Lady: Dear children, rejoice, and give thanks to God for His great love and mercy. It is in these troubled times that God continues to bless the world like never before through the prayers and sacrifices of His faithful children.

Today, little children, I, your heavenly Mother, invite you to continue to lead good and simple lives. Live my messages, consecrate yourselves as a family to the Sacred Heart of my Son and to my Most Immaculate Heart. Know, my little children, that the family consecrated to the Two Hearts is under God's protection. I invite you to renew this consecration often. In doing this the blessings from God will be without limit. Pray your Rosary everyday! Make sacrifices; offering them for poor sinners. I love you, little children. Trust in my motherly intercession. Thank you for listening to my message.

Janie: *Our Lady asked us to embrace our crosses with joy in our hearts. She added that our crosses are our spouses, children, relatives, neighbors, Christian brothers and sisters, our employers and all other sufferings that come from people we meet.*

December 12, 1996 *Feast of Our Lady of Guadalupe - Be simple*

Our Lady: Dear children, praise and glory to Jesus Christ forever and ever. Amen. Today, I your heavenly Mother, greet you with God's peace. I am most grateful, my children, for all the prayers and sacrifices that you have offered to end the slaughter the unborn. You have been most diligent in this effort. In doing this, you have brought consolation to my Immaculate Heart.

Today, dear children, you honor me as Nuestra Senora de Guadalupe. Great is the honor given to me throughout the world. I invite you, dear children, as I invited all my children when I appeared to my little son, Juan Diego, to lead good and simple lives, a life of prayer and purity. Do not, little children, hesitate about your conversion, but convert! God is pouring His love and mercy to all souls throughout the world.

Dear children, you are living in troubled times. Many of you are worried about these times that you are living in. Know, my little ones, that what is needed is trust in God and much prayer. Prayer is the remedy that the world needs to convert. So many souls have forgotten God. I have come to tell you that God truly exists. He has sent me to help you to convert through my motherly intercession. I invite you to trust in my motherly intercession, which is powerful before the Throne of the Most High God.

Little children, I invite you to imitate my little son, Juan Diego, who was poor, simple, and uneducated, and who lived a simple life of a peasant. There was little regard given to this poor Indian. He found favor with God. Do not be concerned, little children, if people do not give you recognition. Spend time in prayer and long only to please God. Be simple, be childlike, trusting your heavenly Mother, and your reward will be great in Heaven. Love yourselves, your family and all whom God puts in your path. I give you my motherly blessing.

December 25, 1996 *The Glory of My Father will be revealed*

Janie: *I saw the Baby Jesus in a brilliant light. He was surrounded by a multitude of angels. He did not move His lips, but these were the words spoken to my heart.*
Jesus: Peace to all here. I am here to invite you as a people of God to live in My peace. I am the Light of the World. Today My light is giving light to all people walking in darkness. Beloved of My Father, today the grace of My Father appears in the form of an Infant offering salva-

tion to all nations. Embrace this salvation that comes to the world through the splendor of the Son of God. I will heal all the injustice and bring justice to a world that has grown to be cold to the love and mercy of My Father. Rejoice beloved, for the Glory of My Father will be revealed and all people will see His saving power.

Beloved, today the world celebrates the beginning of My life as an Infant on earth. Open your hearts and allow My love to consume you. Embrace the Son of God and you will be blessed. Beloved, recall the words said through the prophet: "The virgin shall be with Child and give birth to a Son, and they shall call Him Emmanuel, a name which means God is with us." Beloved, I am with all hearts who embrace their beloved Savior. Peace, peace, peace.
Janie: *Our Lord shared many personal things with me. He told me that all prophecies given will be revealed. He mentioned La Salette, Fatima and all other areas where Our Lady has appeared and is appearing. He blessed everyone.*

December 29, 1996 *Feast of the Holy Family - The sanctity of family life*

Janie: *I saw Our Lord, Our Lady and St. Joseph.*
St. Joseph: Greetings, my little one! God's blessings to everyone here. Today God is blessing all families in the world. Rejoice, as God is pleased with all your many efforts to draw souls closer to God.

Today, I, St. Joseph, invite all the families to trust in my intercession before God. I, St. Joseph, will help all who invoke my intercession. I especially invite husbands who find it hard to relate to their wives and children. There are many troubled marriages that suffer from lack of communication. I, St. Joseph, will come to the aid of all spouses who turn to me, St. Joseph, Protector of the Church and Protector of the Family.

God has given me charge over the care of the Church and the family. I will assist the Church to remain pure and holy in all Its' sufferings and persecutions. Through my powerful intercession, the Church will remain strong through those souls who remain faithful to God. Strength will come to their brothers and sisters who are weak in their faith.

The family that trusts in my intercessions will remain strong in the midst of many sufferings. Through my intercession, these families will be the reflection of the Holy Family. Through my intercession

they will be united in love, respect and peace. Through my intercession the family will embrace the sanctity of family life. They will come to understand more clearly the value of family life. Together, families who invoke my intercession will embrace and accept one another with unconditional love. My little one, share this with families everywhere.

Our Lady: My angel, listen to all that St. Joseph teaches you about the family life and let it penetrate your heart.

Jesus: The family is the splendor of My Father's creation. Offer all your prayers and sufferings for the salvation of all the families in the world.

Janie: *They blessed me and all the people who were present here.*

Chapter Nine

TRUST, AND THE SAFE REFUGE OF THE TWO UNITED HEARTS 1997

Then Job answered the Lord: "I know that thou canst do all things, and that no purpose of thine can be thwarted."

Job 42"1-2.

January 1, 1997 *Solemnity of Mary Pray and fast for unbelievers*

Our Lady: My angel, I, your heavenly Mother, am deeply grateful for all your prayers and suffering. Today I wish to thank you with great joy in my Heart. Know, my angel, that today I am here to share with you the great pain in my Immaculate Heart. I am here to invite you to even a greater suffering than what you have already endured. My dear angel, are you ready to accept this invitation?
Janie: My Dear Mother, you know my answer. I am thine own. I embrace your invitation with love in my heart.
Our Lady: The pestilence and calamities will continue to occur throughout the world.
Janie: *At this point I saw a vision of the world. In different parts of the world I saw cities flooded and destroyed by floods. I saw severe cold and hot weather. I saw earthquakes. I saw maybe one third of the world covered with darkness. I understood that many would suffer from illness like viruses and other unknown diseases. The economy will suffer (will decline). Suffering will happen everywhere and the dysfunction in the family will increase.*
Our Lady: My angel, today I ask that you offer all your prayers and suffering for all the unbelievers, for it is the unbelievers that my adversary uses to spread corruption - evil that comes in all forms. My angel, know that God will use all your prayers and sacrifices to help His unconverted children. Prayer and fasting will help these unrepentant souls to convert. Only through prayer and fasting will my Son have victory over poor sinners.
Janie: *Our Lady was sad as she talked to me. She loves her children so much. I also was asked to pray for China.*

January 12, 1997 *Baptism of Our Lord Pray for consecrated souls*

Jesus: My humble servant, welcome to My Eucharistic Heart. Today My dear friend, I, your Jesus of Love and Mercy, ask that you pray for all My brother priests and consecrated souls. Your prayers will help My Bride.
Janie: My Lord, why are you sad?
Jesus: My humble servant, many of My brother priests have taken their eyes off Me and this pierces My Heart. These priests live for themselves and have become materialistic. Many do not take the time to pray and this is the reason for their many problems. They are good souls and have good intentions, but they have forgotten the importance of prayer. Pray for them. I love My brother priests so much. Thank you, My humble servant and My friend. I know that you, too, love My Bride. I bless

you. I bless you.
Janie: *I comforted Our Lord by praying for His intentions for His priests.*

February 2, 1997 *Presentation - Do not give into anger*

Janie: *Our Lady once said to me that after my heavenly visitations would cease that Our Lord and Our Lady would continue to speak to my soul. I did not understand what she meant at that time. Whenever Jesus, Mary or St. Joseph would come to me, I would see them and hear them. Now I can only hear their words (except on special feast days when I see them), but the words have such clarity. I have been doubting about my heavenly visitations and Our Lord spoke these words to me in my soul.*

Jesus: Do not doubt about your heavenly visitations, for it is I, your Jesus of Love and Mercy, who speaks to your soul. My humble one, you do not have the imagination to write all the thoughts that you hear in your soul. As for the simplicity of the things that I say to you, know that I Who am the Lord, The Eternal Wisdom, am more simple than you.

Have I not given you proof that I am with you? Yes, I have given you many proofs, and yet you continue to entertain doubts about My visits with you. I speak of simple things to you that you may clearly understand what I say to you and what I ask of you. I am not complicated. I come to you in a simple way to teach you simplicity. My little servant, know that when you doubt, you confuse yourself, and you can no longer hear My word, but only your doubts. This is when you think complicated thoughts, but these are not My words but your own complicated thoughts. Trust Me and put all doubt aside. If you do this, then you will be at peace with yourself, and My words to you will be as clear as a blue sky. Know that I will never disappoint you or any soul who trusts in Me. It is I Who am disappointed.

Remain silent in the midst of your suffering and do not give in to your anger, otherwise you will say things that you will regret. If you remain quiet in all your suffering, I will tell you and show you what to do in all circumstances. Trust Me and do what I ask of you. Would you deny Me this that I am asking of you? If you trust in all that I say to you, you shall not regret it.

February 2, 1997 *Adoration: Allow Me to speak to your heart*

Jesus: My humble servant, welcome to My Eucharistic Heart. Come

stay with Me and allow Me to refresh you. Trust Me, remain silent and allow Me to speak to your heart.
Janie: *I spent a long time in quiet with Our Lord. I spoke no words but responded to Our Lord's request. He made me understand the need to spend quiet time with God. I felt so refreshed and had such peace.*
Jesus: My humble servant, you have pleased Me in being quiet. You allowed Me to speak to your heart. You received self knowledge and hidden wisdom that will help you in your faith journey. Go in My peace.

February 5, 1997 *Feast of the Epiphany - Devotion to the Infant of Prague*

Janie: *After my prayers to the nine choirs of angels I was praying for some special intentions for myself. I then thought of the story of the Infant of Prague and began to recall its history. I asked the Infant of Prague to help me and I heard these words in my soul.*
Infant of Prague: Little suffering soul, I am always at your side, but you have left My side. For a while you and your family practiced strong devotion to Me before you began your daily work. Your devotion to Me under this title has grown weak.

Draw close to Me, the Infant of Prague, and I shall draw closer to you. Honor Me more daily and I will bless you in thousands of ways. Continue to pray the prayers that you were praying as a family and you will see My power in the midst of your daily lives.

February 15, 1997 *Eight Anniversary of Our Lady - Put God first*

Our Lady: Dear children, I, your heavenly Mother, greet each one of you with all my love. I invite you, little children, to trust in my intercession in everything that you do. I will help you to draw closer to God Who loves you with immense love.

Little children, know that you need God in your lives to help you to live a pure and simple life. You, dear children, are creating your own world - a world without God. Know that a world without God is a world without love. Many of you suffer from lack of joy, lack of peace and lack of love. This is because you do not have God in your lives. Put God first in your lives, little children, and you will know great joy. God has sent me to help you to convert and to embrace one another as a family.

Today, dear children, I am here to bless you and your family. I want, dear children, to be invited into your daily activities, to your prayer and everything that you do. Know, little children, that this is pleasing to God - to embrace your heavenly Mother. Do not have the smallest worry, but bring your heavenly Mother all your problems. I will present them to my Son. I love you, I love you, I love you. Peace, little children, peace. Thank you for listening to my message.

March 3, 1997 *Mt. Pleasant, Texas* *Make a commitment to pray*

Janie: *I was speaking at a parish mission in Mt. Pleasant when my guardian angel announced to me that Our Lady would come to visit with us momentarily. I shared this with the pastor of this parish and with the people present there. We prepared for Our Lady's visit by praying one Our Father, Hail Mary and Glory Be. Then Our Lady came.*
Our Lady: My angel, I have come to give you my motherly blessing and to extend my deep gratitude to my beloved priest and son for all his hard efforts. I want him to be free of even the smallest worry in his heart, for he is under my shadow and protection. I am with him each step of the way.

My angels, you are my treasures and you have brought so much joy to my Immaculate Heart. You have worked so hard and prepared through your prayers to make all this time possible for my Son to bless and help everyone.

You, my angel, did quite well in sharing the importance of prayer with my children. Tonight I invite everyone here to make a commitment to pray everyday and to make prayer the most important part of their day. I bless you all with my motherly blessing. Thank you, my angel, and goodnight.

March 3, 1997 *Mt. Pleasant, Texas* *Like raindrops from Heaven*

Our Lady: Dear children, renew your prayer before the Cross, and renounce those things to which you are attached but which are causing you much pain and are hurting your spiritual life. As you pray before the Cross, reflect on the Passion of my Son, Who loves you so much. I invite you to pray the Rosary together with your family before the Cross.

As you pray, God will enlighten your hearts to understand the importance of family prayer. Know, little children, that I will be praying with you. As you pray before the Cross reflecting on the Passion of my Son,

God will infuse your hearts with His love, His peace and His joy. Open your hearts, little children, to my request, and blessings will be bestowed on you and your family like raindrops from Heaven.

Janie: *Our Lady gave me this message this afternoon as I prepared for the mission talk tonight. It is very clear to me how much Our Lady loves her children and wants to help them.*

March 4, 1997 *Mt. Pleasant, Texas* *God helps those who turn to Him*

Our Lady: Dear children, today I invite you and your family to pray together everyday. Some of you never take the time to pray. You have forgotten that God always helps those who turn to Him in prayer. Turn to God and accept His love and mercy, especially during this time of Lent. Little children, make a commitment to begin praying together as a family. Do not procrastinate any longer.

Little children, only through prayer will you be able to draw closer to God. Look at all the suffering in your family. How much longer will you ignore my invitation to turn to prayer. I cannot help you, little children, if you do not pray. You give yourselves over to Satan when you refuse to pray; he then makes you his slaves. He continues to torment you and your family in ways which you cannot imagine.

Today, I invite you and your family to make the commitment to pray, especially the Rosary. Put on the armor for battle, and with the Rosary in your hands, together, we will defeat Satan. Please, little children, make a decision to begin to pray as a family. I give you my motherly blessing.

Janie: *Our Lady came to me this afternoon shortly after my guardian angel announced that she would come to visit me. After Our Lady gave me this message, she again talked with me about the importance of praying the Rosary together. She asked me to share with her children her words concerning the commitment to pray the Rosary as a family everyday. She asked her children to make a commitment to praying the Rosary and to give a Rosary to those who would make that commitment. Also, along with the Rosary, to give them a picture of her, so that as they pray their Rosary, they would be reminded that she was praying with them.*

She also asked Father G.H. to bless all the sacramental marriages tomorrow night, and that in this way the whole family would receive blessings. She shared with me that during the time when the marriages would be being blessed, the Holy Family would be present in a very intense way. She invited us to pray the Rosary again before the Cross on Wednesday night.

April 7, 1997 Rome, Italy Annunciation of Our Lord

Janie: Our Lord came and visited with me. I am on my way home to the United States today. My visit was very short with Our Lord and there was no public message. I was in Rome with Fr. Henry and others for the Symposium of the Two Hearts

May 8, 1997 *The Ascension - I am pruning your unnecessary attachments*

Jesus: My humble servant, welcome to My Eucharistic Heart. How are you doing today?
Janie: My Adorable Jesus I am here and nothing else matters now that I am with You, visiting with You.
Jesus: My humble servant, know that I am quite aware of your interior and physical suffering. Know, beloved of My Father, that I will not spare you from your suffering. It is through your suffering that I am pruning away all your unnecessary attachments to the world. I am drawing you closer to Me in all your suffering, and your suffering is helping poor sinners to repent. So, how can I spare you from this suffering which is bringing about your sanctification?

No, beloved, I, your Eucharistic Savior, will not spare you from your suffering, but will give you more suffering than you could imagine. With this suffering you will draw so close to Me, for your suffering will be so intense that you will think only of Me. I shall give you special graces to endure this suffering and also you will have short periods of rest. I want you to occupy yourself with only My love, My suffering and My mercy.
Janie: Lord, my Beloved Savior, I trust You. Spare me nothing, but please help me not to separate from Your love. I am Yours. Do with me as You wish.
Jesus: My beloved humble servant, I delight in your response. Have no fear, for I will not test you beyond your strength. All I ask is that you trust Me. I shall always be with you as you go about proclaiming the Kingdom of My Father. I will bless you on this feast of My Glorious Ascension with sound faith, so that all you ask in My Name My Father will grant you. Go therefore, My humble one, take the Good News to all families you meet. Share with families far and near the importance of repentance, love, prayer and forgiveness. Cultivate their hearts with

the message of the Gospel. I send you among believers and unbelievers to proclaim the Gospel. Remember, those who believe will be saved, those who refuse to believe will be condemned.

Know, My humble servant, that in these days, many signs and wonders will continue to happen. These signs and wonders will accompany you and all who believe in My Glorious Ascension. Remember, in My Name you will drive out demons, speak new languages, you will pick up serpents, drink any deadly thing and no harm will come to you. As you lay hands on the sick they will recover. All of this and more will come to those who believe in My Name.

My humble servant, much is given to you, much is expected from you. Remain in My love and allow nothing to distract you and many will be the signs and wonders that will come your way. I give you My love and blessings to share this love and blessing with those you meet. Peace, My humble servant, My peace to you.
Janie: I love You, My Lord and Master, I love You. *St. Philomena came with Our Lord. I saw Our Lord surrounded by great light. A multitude of angels surrounded Him. St. Philomena remained quiet and smiled at me.*

May 18, 1997 *Pentecost - The Holy Spirit is God's gift to us*

Janie: *Today Our Lord shared with me the importance of always praying to the Holy Spirit. The Holy Spirit is God's gift to us, His children. I cannot write what Our Lord shared with me because of the pain in my hands.*

June 6, 1997 *Feast of the Sacred Heart of Jesus - No greater refuge*

Jesus: My humble servant, welcome to My Eucharistic Heart. Today, I, your Jesus, call you to total abandonment to the love of My Sacred Heart. I am here for you. Allow the love in My Sacred Heart to refresh your entire being.

To all My children, I, your Jesus of Love and Mercy, invite all those who have devotion to My Sacred Heart to consecrate yourselves to Me. Give Me your children by consecrating them to My Sacred Heart. Consecrate your homes, your belongings, all your possessions to My Sacred Heart and I will enrich your lives with special graces and blessings.

I invite My beloved brother priests to consecrate themselves to My Sacred Heart and all those entrusted to you. I give you My solemn word that your Church will increase in worship and participation. I invite all religious to have devotion to My Sacred Heart and consecrate your communities to My Most Sacred Heart and your vocations will increase. Trust in My words.

There is no greater love than the love that you find in My Most Sacred Heart and the Immaculate Heart of My Mother. There is no greater refuge or protection. My Sacred Heart and the Immaculate Heart of My Mother are inseparable. One reflects the other. This is the safety for all who love the Two United Hearts.

June 7, 1997 *Feast of the Immaculate Heart - God sent me to help you*

Our Lady: Dear Children, today I invite the family to consecrate yourselves to my Immaculate Heart. Know, my little ones, that God sent me to come to help you to convert. Some of you are struggling and you are having a difficult time abandoning the ways of the world. This is why, my dear ones, I invite you to family consecration. There is so much suffering in your family, but you do not allow your heavenly Mother to help you.

Take refuge in my Immaculate Heart and I will protect you from my adversary. No harm will come to those families who consecrate themselves to my Immaculate Heart. I will dwell in your midst and be with you wherever you go. I will protect and watch over you and your children always. I will help you to have a deeper relationship with my Son.

I am the gate that will lead you to my Son. Come little children, let your heavenly Mother teach you all about prayer, about purity and holiness. Abandon yourselves to my Immaculate Heart and to the Sacred Heart of my Son. You shall not regret it, little children. I give you my motherly blessing. Thank you for listening to my message.

July 16, 1997 *Our Lady of Mt. Carmel - The family of the Mother of God*

Our Lady: Dear children, today I invite you to embrace your heavenly Mother under the title of Our Lady of Mt. Carmel.

Abandon yourselves as a family to my powerful intercession by wearing your brown scapular without being embarrassed. Wear it devoutly and perseveringly, little children, for it is my garment.

Remember, my children, that in order for your heavenly Mother to protect you, you must call upon my intercession. When you wear your brown scapular, you let Satan know that you are members of the family of the Mother of God. He cannot stand it when my children wear their scapular. He knows that his temptations are useless against my children who call upon the protection of their Mother by simply wearing their brown scapular.

Teach your children about the love and devotion of wearing the brown scapular. Young people today are embarrassed by wearing holy medals or any object that will say that they believe in God. For this reason many young people expose themselves to such danger.

Janie: *Our Lady means that we as believers in God should demonstrate our faith by wearing holy sacramentals.*

Our Lady: Little children, wear your brown scapular always. You venerate your heavenly Mother, you tell me how much you love me; you do all these things by simply wearing the scapular. Always share with others the importance of wearing the scapular. The scapular has the approval of the Church. With this comes more graces and blessings to those who wear the scapular. God's blessings to you, my dear children. Thank you for listening to my message.

July 26, 1997 *Live Heaven on earth doing God's Holy Will*

Janie: *On this special day of my birthday I received a visit from Our Lord, Our Lady and St. Joseph. Saints I have devotion to were also present. The Holy Family greeted me.*

Jesus: Our humble servant, We are here to bless you on your birthday. You had a difficult morning as you suffered for Our special intentions. Are you happy, Our little servant?

Janie: Oh, yes! Everything is fine now that You are here. Is there anything that I can do for You, My Lord? I'll do anything You ask of me.

Jesus: Our humble dear one, today I, your Beloved Savior, together with My Mother and St. Joseph, wish to do something special for you. What do You wish today?

Janie: Gee, I wasn't really thinking of anything in particular for myself. I would like a special blessing for my family and all the families here present and all families in the world. For myself, I wish to go be in Heaven with you. *The Holy Family smiled.*

Jesus: Our dear one, it is not your time to be in Heaven with Us. Remember that We are with you wherever you may be.

Janie: I know this, My Lord, but I still wish to be in Heaven. *They smiled again.*

Jesus: Our humble one, continue to do all that We ask of you and you will live Heaven on earth.
Janie: I can do that, My Lord? But how?
Jesus: Our dear one, you live Heaven on earth by simply doing the Will of My Father in all that you do. This is how all the saints in Heaven lived their lives on earth. In all their struggles, persecutions, their sufferings, they remained true to doing the Will of My Father. You are doing the same, so do not let anything disturb your peace.
Janie: Thank You so much, this is truly food for my soul. I will do my best to live Heaven on earth.

Blessed Mother, I miss all three of You so much, but I am truly grateful to God for allowing me to have these heavenly visitations. Blessed Mother, I really need your prayers to continue to love my family with unconditional love. Sometimes this is so hard, especially when my family has a hard time coming together for prayer time. They are dedicated, but sometimes I feel that their hearts are far away from their prayers. How do I handle this?
Our Lady: My precious angel, pray for the grace to remain loving under all circumstances. Do not be concerned with the distractions that your family experiences while in prayer. Be grateful that they agree to pray together as a family. Say nothing to them about how they are praying. Offer your own prayers for you and your family. After prayer, kiss and embrace your family. Thank them for coming together for prayer.

Remember, my angel, that God is pleased when a family prays together. Many blessings and graces are given to families who take the time to pray together. God's peace reigns in their hearts. Be at peace, my angel. You love, you love much and God loves your family much also.
Janie: Beloved St. Joseph, I need your guidance for questions which I am asked by the people whom I speak to on the teachings which I have received from Heaven. Many spouses struggle because one is a believer and the other isn't. One believes in prayer, the other spouse says that he or she believes in God but they believe prayer is not necessary. Many are women who have spouses that don't believe. These wives wonder if God wants them to leave their unbelieving spouses. Many spouses who pray together have a hard time getting their children to pray. Can you help me?
St. Joseph: My little one, spouses who have unbelieving loved ones should remain dedicated to praying for their conversion. To the wives who suffer and struggle because their husbands do not believe in praying together, to them I, St. Joseph, say be patient with your husbands. God's Will is not that you leave your husband because he is an unbe-

liever. Remain loving and obey your husbands. The most certain and sure way to win your husband is through your conduct. Remain peaceful and trust God with the conversion of your husband.

Live a simple and pure life being a loving wife. Allow your prayer and trust in God to be the cause for your joy. Prayer will give you peace and a calm spirit. Your husband will notice your gentle disposition and your non-judgmental attitude. This will help his unbelieving heart. This conduct, beloved wives, is precious in God's eyes. Stop worrying and put your trust in God.

The husband must be loving and considerate toward his wife. The husband must have respect for his wife and love her like Christ loves the Church. This is most important for the husband, for the husband is the head of the family, as Christ is the head of the Church.

If both spouses conduct themselves according to God's Holy Will, nothing will keep their prayers from being answered. Their children too, will draw closer to God. My little one, share this with spouses who are struggling with their marriages.
Janie: Thank you, St. Joseph.
Jesus: Now, our humble one, We give you Our blessing and thank you for all that you do in reparation for poor souls.
Janie: *They blessed everyone present and my visit was over. I thank God from the bottom of my heart for this day. St. Joseph asked that we continue to pray for the completion of our book. He said there would be many obstacles, sufferings and distractions. He said that I would suffer persecution.*

August 15, 1997 *Wimberley, Texas* *You will miss these times*

Janie: *The Holy Family came to bless everyone present. We had our new home enthroned to the Sacred Heart of Jesus and the Immaculate Heart of Mary, and of course to the intercession of St. Joseph. There were many people present. Our land was surrounded with many angels.*
Our Lady: Dear children, today I invite you to rejoice with your heavenly Mother on this glorious feast day. God has sent me, little children, as a gift to you to help you to draw closer to my Son, Jesus. Live all the messages which I have given you, for the time will come when I will no longer be giving you these messages. You will miss these times. That is why I beg you to live every word of all these heavenly messages. You shall not regret it!

Embrace this time of grace. Live your consecration to my Immaculate Heart and pray together as a family, especially pray the Rosary. The Rosary will help you in your conversion as a family. When you pray the Rosary as a family, you allow me to help you to renew your prayer as a family. Little children, I love you and I will help you to love me as you live my messages. Thank you for listening to my message.

August 22, 1997 *Renew your commitment to praying the Rosary*

Our Lady: Dear children, today I invite you to renew your commitment to praying the Rosary as a family. So many of you are suffering because you do not take the time for family prayer. Little children, you do not comprehend the blessings and graces which you receive when you pray as a family.

When you spend time praying your Rosary for the needs in your family, God helps you to find joy in family prayer. Little children, you will have struggles, crosses and sufferings as a family, but when you pray together you endure all your trials with peace in your hearts. Thank you for listening to my message.

August 24, 1997 *St. Joseph's Anniversary Visit*

Janie: *St. Joseph's visit was a private conversation concerning my suffering. Some people were with me and some general guidance was given to them.*

September 8, 1997 *Our Lady's Birthday - Let your lives be transformed*

Our Lady: Dear children, I invite you to renew your prayer time together as a family. Your family and all your concerns are so important to your heavenly Mother. When you suffer I suffer with you and it pierces my Immaculate Heart that in your suffering you forget to call upon my intercession. Pray, my children, pray as a family. It is so important to believe in prayer. I wish that you pray so that your lives may be transformed. I wish that you pray so that I am able to help you. Today I say to you, little children, pray, pray, pray! Thank you for listening to my message.

September 14, 1997 *Triumph of the Cross-At times you will prefer death*

Jesus: My humble servant, embrace your cross with joy in your heart. You will suffer much, and at times you will prefer your death. Remain united to your Eucharistic Savior. I will be your strength.
Janie: *He showed me a vision of my suffering which I cannot share.*

September 15, 1997 *Many are the tears I cry*

Our Lady: My precious angel, come and console your Sorrowful Mother. Deep is the suffering which pierces my Immaculate Heart.

Many are the tears which I cry for many of my unconverted children who ignore my messages of prayer, fasting, conversion and returning back to the Sacraments. Deep and sorrowful is the pain which tears my heart for each little soul that is aborted. Oh how I suffer for these precious and innocent souls. How horrible it will be for these men and women who participate in the slaughtering of the unborn. Oh how they offend God, how they offend God!

My angel, comfort and console your Sorrowful Mother through your prayers and sacrifices. Pray with your heavenly Mother so that God will hear our prayers and be merciful to all who participate in the slaughtering of the unborn.
Janie: *Our Lady was crying tears of blood. She was so very sad. I felt so bad because I couldn't really comfort her, for I knew that the killing of the unborn would continue.*
Our Lady: My precious angel, pray with your heavenly Mother so that parents will stop abusing their poor children. Poor little children, they suffer so much at the abuse and rejection of their parents. Poor little children, they are so innocent and yet many parents treat their children so cruelly. Poor little children, who live in fear of being harmed by their own parents. This fear causes these poor children to suffer many forms of physical and mental illness. Poor little children, who turn to their parents for love, but no love comes from their parents. These parents have no love in their hearts for they have tuned away from God. Many do not believe that God exists. Poor, poor little children. Love all children, my angel, all children, and pray for them.

Today I pour out the concerns in my sorrowful heart to you, my angel, and ask you to embrace all that I share with you. I wish that you remember all that I share with you and pray for my concerns in your daily prayers. Another concern which causes me to cry copious tears is the abuse which my Son receives by many of my beloved priests and religious. My angel, this is a serious problem within the Bride of my Son. You will suffer persecutions when my beloved priests and religious read what I share with you. Fear nothing, but remain obedient to God. He will protect you.

My angel, the spirit of homosexuality is increasing within the Church, but many discount this most serious lifestyle. This lifestyle is so offensive to God, for it is not what God intended for the many who take religious vows and are living this lifestyle. This is a very serious situation and must not be allowed to continue for those souls who have given their lives to God. These poor souls need much prayer, love and redirection in having a deeper understanding of God.

My angel, I know that you are concerned about what I am telling you. Do not worry, but pray for these intentions. Pray for all my unconverted children, all my unconverted children. I give you my motherly blessing.
Janie: *St. Philomena was with Our Lady.*

October 2, 1997 *Feast of the Guardian Angels-Conversion comes easier*

Janie: *Our Lady came on this day. It was also the first Thursday of the month when I receive a visit from the Archangels.*
Our Lady: Good morning, my angel, how are you?
Janie: Blessed Mother, I am quite well and grateful that you came on this special day. Tell me what do you want me to do for you? Everybody is so happy that you came.
Our Lady: My dear angel, I came on this day to comfort all my children who came to pray together. It is their suffering that has called out to their heavenly Mother. My angel, convey what I say to you to my children. I am here to comfort them in their suffering, for many of them are going through difficult times. I am here to remind them how much I love them, and that I am always at their side praying with them and for all their special intentions. I am here to remind them not to be fearful, but to have courage in their suffering, for God will take care of all their needs.

I want to remind my children how much God loves and cares for them and their loved ones. God has provided a guardian angel for each one of His children. The guardian angels never leave the side of those souls entrusted to them. The role of these heavenly spirits is to help God's children to lead good and simple lives by doing the Will of God. The guardian angels are ever so busy helping and praying for those souls whom they have been assigned to.

It is so important that my children pray to God to help them to have devotion to their guardian angels. In this way my children will become friends with their guardian angels and conversion will come easier for those who embrace their guardian angels. The guardian angels provide good inspirations and good impulses to those souls assigned to them. Together, a beautiful heavenly friendship develops and my children become better people and make such a difference in this world.

I invite my children to trust in the powerful intercession of the Archangels: St. Michael, St. Gabriel and St. Raphael. I had asked the Father to allow the three Archangels to come in my place, for I knew that my regular visits would cease. That is why the three Archangels came in my place, to remind my children of how I love them. I did not want them to feel abandoned by their heavenly Mother.

This prayer group is especially dear to me for so much good comes to those who join. The obedience of meeting together continues to bear so much fruit, so much fruit. I know that at times, many of my children stop coming, but those of you who have been with me for so long remain dedicated to coming together to pray the Rosary. Know that all who come will receive special blessings and graces.

I requested to you, my angel, to begin a prayer group after your trip to Medjugorje and you were obedient.
Janie: *Our Lady requested this of me in Medjugorje in 1990.*
Our Lady: My angel, you have been so patient in listening to your heavenly Mother. All my children have brought much joy to my Immaculate Heart. I give you all my motherly blessing.
Janie: The Archangels did not give a message on this day, but stood by Our Lady as she spoke to me. Our Lady was surrounded by a multitude of angels.

October 7, 1997 *You can stop wars and natural disasters through prayer*

Our Lady: Dear children, today I invite you to continue to pray your Rosary for peace in the world and for the conversion of poor sinners.

Know that as you pray your Rosary for these intentions, many souls are being converted. The Rosary, dear children, is a powerful prayer, a prayer which is so dear to my Immaculate Heart.

Dear children, you are living in troubled times when sin is spreading like a plague in every part of the world, infecting millions of souls. Evil is everywhere. Do not allow the evil in the world to frighten you, rather allow the evil in the world to draw you to pray more, especially praying the Rosary.

Little children, the Rosary is the weapon which I give you to disarm all the attacks of my adversary, whose only goal is to separate you from God. Through praying the Rosary, you can stop wars, change natural disasters from occurring, and bring poor sinners to true repentance. Always have the Rosary in your hands as a sign of your readiness to do spiritual warfare against my adversary. You are not alone, little children. Your heavenly Mother is with you whenever you pray your Rosary.

Today I especially wish to remind families everywhere to pray the Rosary together. Be aware that my adversary will put many obstacles in your way to keep you from praying the Rosary as a family. He that knows the power of the Rosary can drive him and all his demons out of your lives and away from your homes.

I most especially invite all my beloved priests and religious to pray the Rosary together to help them to live their vocations according to God's Holy Will. I invite my beloved priests and religious to encourage others to pray the Rosary everyday. Praying the Rosary, little children, will help you to desire purity and holiness of heart. Pray your Rosary as a family everyday and God's love and peace will reign in your hearts. Happiness will exist in your family. Thank you for listening to my message.

Janie: *Our Lady said to me that beginning on the eighth of October until the thirteenth she would come every morning at 5:00 a.m. to pray the Rosary with me. Her intentions would be to end the horrible evil of abortion and to help convert those souls who believe and promote this horrible evil. She said the following words to me.*

Our Lady: My angel, I know that you are ill and what I am asking of you will be a great and most difficult sacrifice. I would not ask this of you, but your sacrifice is so needed to put an end to the slaughtering of the unborn.

Janie: *I have pneumonia.*

Our Lady: For six days you will suffer more intensely as you offer your suffering for the intentions of your heavenly Mother. Remember my words. This will be a most difficult task for you, but God will give you the grace and strength to carry out this request. I will come promptly at 5:00 a.m.. I will come as Our Lady of Guadalupe during these six days. The 13th of October will be my last visit for this special request. Thank you, my angel. Thank you so much.

December 8, 1997 *Feast of the Immaculate Conception - Do not judge*

Our Lady: Dear children, today I invite you to continue to follow the path of purity which my Son has paved for you. It is the path which leads towards Heaven where your heavenly treasure awaits you.

Little children, I know that many of you are suffering for those members in your family who do not believe in God. I urge you, little children, to pray more for the members in your family who are in need of conversion. Do not judge them, do not alienate them from you. Love them and accept them just like God loves and accepts you.

Little children, you are living in a time of grace so please do not waste precious time, but prepare your hearts through prayer and sacrifices. Know that God will help all those souls that you offer your prayers and sacrifices for. Have faith in your prayer and do not submit to the spirit of doubt.

Little children, allow your heavenly Mother to help you prepare your hearts for the birth of my Son. He loves you with immense love. He yearns to be welcomed by you, simply by opening your heart to His love. He will remove all fear, all worry, all anxiety. He will set you free from all your troubles. He will fill your heart with His love and peace.

Little children, listen to my words. This is a time of preparation and of great rejoicing. Pray for yourselves and for all your family, so that the joy and peace of my Son will be yours during this Holy Season. Remember to love all your family and pray for them. Your prayers, little children, will help their unconverted hearts. I love you, my little ones, I love you. Thank you for listening to my message.

December 12, 1997 *Feast of Our Lady of Guadalupe - Trust me*

Our Lady: Dear children, you bring great joy to my Immaculate Heart as you honor me as Our Lady of Guadalupe. I am honored under this title in many parts of the world. For this I am deeply grateful. Thank you, dear children, thank you.

Dear children, I invite you to build a little place in your heart for your heavenly Mother. Through my son, Juan Diego, I asked for a temple to be built on the hill of Teypeyac, the site where I appeared to him. I ask you, dear children, to let your hearts be the hill of Tepeyac. I want to be embraced by all my children; in this way I can help you.

Little children, I invite you to embrace the words that I spoke to my son, Juan Diego, when I said to him, "Am I not here, I who am your Mother? Are you not in my arms, and are you not under my charge and protection? What else do you need?"

Little children, God has sent me to help you to convert. Trust in my motherly intercession. I will help you to become a more prayerful and loving family. I will help the husbands, wives and children, my beloved priests and religious. I will help each one of you in a personal way to embrace God's Holy Will for you.

To all who trust in my intercession and seek my assistance, I will show forth my loving kindness, my compassion. I will be your companion in all things. I will help you in your labors and in all your afflictions. All I invite you to do is to trust in my intercession; in this way you will truly have recourse to me. I invite all to take refuge in my Immaculate Heart. I will truly draw you closer to my Son, Jesus. Trust me, dear children, trust me.

Dear children, you are living in a period of great grace. Embrace this time. Hear me and let my words penetrate your hearts. Thank you for listening to my message.

December 25, 1997 *Christmas Day - Pride, money, power, TV*

Janie: *The Lord came accompanied by Our Lady, St. Joseph, The Three Archangels, St. Philomena, Padre Pio, St. Francis and a multitude of angels. Our Lord came as the Infant Child. All were arrayed in brilliant light and dressed in gold and other brilliant colors.*
Jesus: My humble servant and dear friend, I, your loving and merciful Savior, greet you with My love and all the love in Heaven.
Janie: Greetings, My Love and my All. Happy Birthday, my Beloved Savior. I give you my love as your birthday gift. Greetings my heavenly Mother, Most Glorious St. Joseph, and greetings to all my heavenly companions and helpers. Thank you all for coming.
Jesus: My humble servant, today, I, Jesus, bless all people in the world. I will pour My love into every heart. Not one soul will be without My blessing. I invite all who believe that I am the Savior of the World to come to Me. I will flood their hearts with My peace. I will turn no one

away. I gave My life so that all who believe will have life and have life in great abundance. I came as the Prince of Peace to bring My peace to a world walking in darkness. I am the Truth, the Light and the Way. No one can go to My Father unless they come to Me. All who believe in My words and put My words into practice will have eternal life.

Today, I, Jesus, Savior of the World, invite all to rejoice and to embrace My peace, which I extend to all who believe. I desire that all who believe in Me, to reflect in My peace and to carry My peace in their hearts, extending it to others. I invite all who believe to embrace My love, My peace and My goodness. I yearn to be friends with everyone who will accept Me as their Savior.

My humble servant, as you and your family celebrate My birth, remember that you are carriers of My love, My mercy and My peace. Remain small, humble, and poor in spirit, trusting in the loving goodness of your Savior.

I give you My solemn word that you will have all that you need to follow in My path. My peace I leave you, My peace I give to you, not as the world gives, but as I, your Jesus, give. This peace which I give you no one can take it away. Peace, peace, peace.

Janie: *Our Lord showed me the world and all the areas where there was no faith. Our Lord then poured His light into every heart. He told me that for those who believe that He is the Savior of the World, both physical and spiritual healing would take place. He said that many victims with AIDS have turned to His love and mercy and He healed them. He asked me to pray for the obstacles which keep people from being in relationship with Him.*

The first obstacle was pride - which kept people away from having faith, from loving and from praying. The second obstacle was money - which in many cases leads people away from Our Lord. Money takes the place of God. The third was power - from power comes control, and when people control they enslave many innocent souls. Another great obstacle was television and the rise in technology. Many souls are addicted to these obstacles and have no time for God, because they have no time for people. He showed me many other obstacles such as fear, worry, anger, unforgiveness, etc. He asked me to offer my prayers and sacrifices for these obstacles which keep souls from being converted.

Our Lord was very happy in spite of all the rejection He receives from many of us. No one spoke except Our Lord. Our Lord allowed me to see all the souls that were released from Purgatory. All these souls were rejoicing. I heard many of them thanking me for my prayers. Our Lord said to me, "Always pray for the Holy Souls in Purgatory."

December 28, 1997 *Feast of the Holy Family-Guidance of the Holy Spirit*

Janie: *The Holy Family came in heavenly splendor and greeted me. There was some personal suffering in my heart.*
St. Joseph: My little one, We greet you with God's holy peace. You are suffering for the continual conversion of your family and for families throughout the world. My poor little one, how great is the cross which you endure. You do not complain and you keep your suffering hidden from your family and from others.
Janie: Greetings Oh Most Holy Family! I am so happy that You are here. I guess I cannot conceal my suffering from You, but my suffering becomes so insignificant now that You are here. I must say that Satan's attacks are so strong against me and my family that at times I feel like I will fall apart!
St. Joseph: My little one, you are protected because of your perpetual prayers and sacrifices. You will not fall apart. Satan lies to you in times of suffering to keep you from prayer. He hates you because he knows that your prayers are strong. He knows that you pray with love, faith and trust in your heart. Have no worry.
Janie: Please, Oh Most Holy Family, I wish to take this time to recommend all those dear souls who asked me to entrust their special intentions to Your loving care. I recommend the Holy Mother Church, our dear Pope and all his flock, my Spiritual Director and all priests who are dear to my heart. I recommend all the world and my dear friends - the Holy Souls in Purgatory, and all whom I have promised to pray for.
St. Joseph: My little one, all your petitions will be honored.
Janie: St. Joseph, we are about to finish this year of 1997. I implore you, please give families throughout the world heavenly guidance for the new year of 1998.
St. Joseph: My little one, in order to embrace the new year with all its many blessings and sufferings, the Universal Church and families everywhere must turn to the guidance of the Holy Spirit in everything. The Holy Spirit will guide all who turn to Him through every day of the new year. The Holy Spirit will bestow on those who turn to His guidance, extraordinary graces to embrace their daily crosses. He will pour His wisdom and discernment into all who turn to His guidance.

I, St. Joseph, encourage all families to continue to pray together as a family. Through family prayer the Holy Spirit will help the family to put God first in their daily lives.

As the family continues to pray together, they will reflect God's peace to others around them. Through their prayers, the family will become peace makers and carry the message of God's love wherever they may be. My little one, God desires the good of all His children, for God Himself is good. Prayer dissolves all darkness in the heart, then goodness settles in the heart. From this goodness comes a desire for holiness and purity. The family that prays together will obtain goodness, peace, joy, holiness and purity.

My little one, many trials and sufferings will take place throughout the new year. Calamities will be strong.
Janie: *I saw world disasters, earthquakes, bad weather (chaotic weather).*
St. Joseph: Pestilence will also prevail. The spirit of apostasy will be most evident. The tribulation and purification will be strong also. The faithful will be put to much testing through the attacks of the evil one. The Holy Spirit will help them through everything. This is why family prayer is so important.

I, St. Joseph, encourage God's children to remain sincere of heart and steadfast undisturbed in times of adversity accepting whatever befalls them and during misfortune to be patient, and God will send His Holy Spirit to help His children in everything. Their faith and trust in God will be their strength.

My little one, I share all this with you so that you may prepare with strong prayer, for you, yourself, will suffer much. Reflect on everything that We, the Holy Family, share with you and ponder everything in your heart.
Jesus: Humble servant, prepare to suffer in reparation for the purification of My Bride and for poor sinners. As you suffer I will flood your heart with My mercy. Do not fear your suffering. I give you My solemn word, you will not be tested beyond your limits. I tell you this, that you may remember My words in times of great suffering. Your suffering will be most redemptive. Rejoice, My humble servant, you are a delight to the Holy Family. Rejoice!
Our Lady: My angel, how dear you are to Us. Remain small and humble. Fear nothing, only trust in God in everything. You will suffer much

for your family and families everywhere. You will suffer physical infirmity; this will also be part of your redemptive suffering.

Our little victim soul, you are precious to Us. You are a vessel of Our love. You consider yourself nothing and wretched, and your humility is most pleasing to Us. Pray, Our dear Janie and my angel, pray for poor sinners everywhere. Heaven is at your disposal.

Janie: *The Holy Family blessed me and then They left.*

HOLY FAMILY PRINTS AVAILABLE

For prints of the Holy Family painting on the cover of this book, call or write for sizes available and prices to:

Signs and Wonders for OurTimes
P.O. Box 345
Herndon, Virginia
20172-0345

Phone: (703) 327-2277
Fax: (703) 327-2888

APPENDIX

A Compilation of Beautiful Prayers

Prayer given by Jesus to be said upon waking every morning

My Father, Who are in Heaven, I, a miserable sinner, abandon myself to your mercy. I come in the Name of Your beloved Son, Who is One with You as You are One with Him. My Eternal Father, listen to the cry of this miserable sinner and send me Your Holy Spirit, so that this very day, I may walk in Your light. Pour Your love into my miserable heart so that I may be transformed into Your likeness.

My Eternal Father, only You know the many crosses that await me. Only You know all the temptations that will come my way. My Father, no harm may come to me if only Your love enfolds me. I recognize that without You I can do nothing, but with You I will accomplish all things. Take this poor miserable sinner into Your loving arms and let Your love dissolve all my misery. Breathe Your breath into my sinful heart, that I may be strong in You. Let me walk with You, not behind You or in front of You so that I may not separate from Your love.

Take my hand, Eternal Father, today and everyday of my life, so that I may know Your Will, be Your Will and live Your Will. I ask this, My Eternal Father, in the Name of Your Son, who is King and reigns forever and ever. Amen.

Family Consecration to the Sacred Heart of Jesus given by Jesus

Oh Most Sacred Heart of Jesus, we come to You as a family and consecrate ourselves to Your Sacred Heart. Protect us through Your Most Precious Blood and keep us pure and holy.

Oh dear Jesus, we are so far away from Your most pure and Sacred Heart. As a family we need Your help. Heal all the quarrels that exist in our family due to our unforgiveness and lack of love for You. Heal our unbelieving and unconverted hearts and lead us to Your Sacred Heart with love. Unite us as a family and remove all stain of sinfulness from our souls. Help us to be a prayerful and loving family, so that through our example we may lead other souls to Your Most Sacred Heart.

We give You our hearts, dearest Jesus, and consecrate our family through the fourth generation. Through the prayers of our dearest Mother, Mary, may we live this consecration everyday of our lives. Amen. Most Sacred Heart of Jesus, have mercy on us.

Family Consecration to the Immaculate Heart of Mary given by Mary

Oh Mother Most Pure, we come to you as a family and consecrate ourselves to your Most Immaculate Heart. We come to you as a family and place our trust in your powerful intercession. Oh dearest Mother, Mary, teach us as a mother teaches her children, for our souls are soiled, and our prayers are weak because of our sinful hearts. Here we are, dearest Mother, ready to respond to you and follow your way, for your way leads to the Heart of your Son, Jesus. We are ready to be cleansed and purified.

Come, then, Virgin Most Pure, and embrace us with you motherly mantle. Make our hearts whiter than snow and as pure as a spring of fresh water. Teach us to pray, so that our prayers may become more beautiful than the singing of the birds at the break of dawn. Dear Mother, Mary, we entrust to your Immaculate Heart, our hearts, our family and our entire future. Lead us all to our homeland which is Heaven. Amen. Immaculate Heart of Mary, pray for us.

Family Consecration to the Holy Spirit given by Jesus

Come, Holy Spirit, our Creator, come to hear us and to prepare our sinful hearts, as we consecrate ourselves, as a family, to You. Oh Divine Light, You, Who knows and searches all hearts, receive our family consecration. Unite our hearts with Your flame of love and guide us to live our family consecration, that all we do may be pleasing to God.

Come, Holy Spirit, and inscribe Your love and light in our hearts. Write in our hearts the Commandments and the love of God, that we may live in Your light. Holy Spirit, knit our souls to You and draw us closer to You. Send the flame of Your love and give us the gift of prayer, that we may pray with our hearts, "Abba, Father, we love You and we praise Your Holy Name."

Come, Holy Spirit, Love of God, and accept our family offering, and receive our prayers, which we give to You today. Come, Holy Light of God, come and make Your dwelling in our family. You, Who are the giver of many gifts, renew our love for You and for one another. Renew our understanding and heal the conflicts that exist in our family, which create distance between us and God.

Come, Holy Fire, and enlighten our hearts with wisdom and discernment, that we may have only one desire: to please God. Holy Fire, renew in our hearts the wonders of Pentecost and enlighten each family member both present and absent. Let Your love possess our whole being, and with Your love heal our marriages, our addictions, our unforgiveness and the many problems that exist in our family. Enlighten us and help us detach from all worldly desires and to make Heaven our goal.

Holy Spirit, be our comforter and consoler. Rule our lives and with Your love; burn away all our faults. Bring unity to our family. Give us new hearts that are loving and patient, hearts that are generous and charitable, and hearts that have no room for jealousy or evil, loving hearts that desire only God's love and truth. Come, Holy Spirit, come. Come, Holy Spirit, come, now and forever, come. Amen.

Invocation to the Holy Spirit for the Family

Oh Holy Spirit, come into every fiber of our being and inflame our hearts with the fire of Thy love. Oh breath of God, come help us to be meek and humble of heart. Oh Holy Spirit, come into our life and be the every breath that we take.

In the morning, when we open our eyes, come Holy Spirit.
When we offer our morning prayer, come Holy Spirit.
As we begin our daily responsibilities, come Holy Spirit.
As we prepare for Holy Mass, come Holy Spirit.
When we are weak in our prayers, come Holy Spirit.
When we have family quarrels, come Holy Spirit.
In the midst of great turmoil, come Holy Spirit.
In our work, our play and throughout the day, come Holy Spirit.
When our day is finished and we retire to bed, come Holy Spirit.
When our hearts are wounded, come Holy Spirit.
During our family prayer and activities, come Holy Spirit.
When we despise and ridicule one another, come Holy Spirit.
During our studies and quiet time, come Holy Spirit.
When we are fearful and feel unloved, come Holy Spirit.
When the evil one attacks us, come Holy Spirit.
When we fall into temptation, come Holy Spirit.
When we are disobedient to the teaching of the Church, come Holy Spirit. When we humiliate one another, come Holy Spirit.
When we are not truthful to one another, come Holy Spirit.
When we criticize one another, come Holy Spirit.
When we abandon our children and abuse them, come Holy Spirit.
When we are not living our marriage vows and our marriage suffers, come Holy Spirit.
When our hearts are prideful and we lack in charity, come Holy Spirit.
When we are angry and refuse to forgive, come Holy Spirit.
When we are jealous and envy the gifts that others have, not recognizing our own gifts, come Holy Spirit.
When our faith is weak and we are nervous and restless, come Holy Spirit. When we have addictions and are codependent on those things that destroy our relationship with God, come Holy Spirit.
When there is no love in our family and our children turn away from God, come Holy Spirit.
When the spirit of fornication, adultery and divorce dwells in our hearts, come Holy Spirit.

When we need financial guidance, come Holy Spirit.
When we prepare to receive the sacrament of Reconciliation, come Holy Spirit.
In our poverty, our illness and when we are homeless, come Holy Spirit.
When our loved ones leave this world and when tragedy happens, come Holy Spirit.
When we are without family, come Holy Spirit.
When we lack wisdom and discernment, come Holy Spirit.
At the moment of our death, come Holy Spirit.
Now and forever and in every need that we have, come Holy Spirit.

Oh Holy Spirit, God speaks through You. He gave You to us, therefore, You are our Helper, our Consoler, our Comforter. You are our everything and You know our every need. Come and bless this humble prayer that we offer you as a family. Come Holy Spirit, please accept and hear our payer. Come Holy Spirit, come to us as a family. Amen.

Prayer to Our Mother of Compassion and Love

Mary, my sweet Mother, help me to embrace my suffering and daily crosses like you did when you witnessed the Passion and Death of your Son. My sweet and suffering Mother, your soul was pierced by the terrible sword as you united in your Son's suffering. Except for the Father, no one knows of your suffering, but even in your deepest suffering you rejoiced, for you knew that the suffering and death of your Son would glorify the Father.

In your deepest suffering you remained compassionate and loving to those who killed your Son. You were united with the words of your Son when He said, "Father, forgive them, for they know not what they do." Teach me to be your reflection so that I, too, will remain compassionate and loving when others pierce my own soul. Fortify my soul so that no pain or sorrow may ever break it.

Oh sweet and Holy Mother, I place everything in your hands. Protect me and cover my soul with your motherly mantle. Help me to live by the Father's love and power. Defend me with your prayers against all enemies. Unite my soul to your Son, Jesus. Let no obstacle separate me from your love and the love of your Son. Mary, Mother of Compassion and Love, I trust in your intercession. Pray for me. Amen.

Prayer to St. Joseph

Oh most chaste pure spouse of Most Holy Mary, Holy Guardian of the Most Holy Family and Guardian of All Families, pray for us. Most Holy St. Joseph, I come to you and beseech you with all the ardor of my heart and soul, to listen to my prayer. I commend myself, my family and all families in the world to you. Hear my prayer, oh most pure and humble foster father of our Savior, and intercede for all families in the world.

Most pure St. Joseph, God entrusted you with complete charge over the Savior of the World and the Queen of Heaven. You provided for them with tender, loving care, until you were called by God. I, your daughter (son), ask that you take complete charge over me and my family. Intercede for us before the throne of the Most High God, for I know in my heart, that God will hear your prayer as you intercede for us. He will not deny you anything, for you never said 'no' to God, but you responded with your heart and soul with a total 'yes'. I love you, my beloved St. Joseph, I love you. Help us to be pure, humble and obedient. Amen.

Act of Consecration to the Sacred Heart for Priests given by Jesus

My Jesus of Love and Mercy, Splendor of the Father, today, I, _____, consecrate myself to Your Most Sacred Heart. Jesus, my beloved Brother, help me to be a holy priest, so that You may engrave in my heart Your wisdom, that I may teach those souls entrusted to my care. Oh my sweet Jesus, by this act of consecration, help me to have an ardent desire for Heaven so that I may advance more toward Your Divine Love, to be more detached from worldly desires and to be empty of everything that separates me from You.

Oh my Jesus, I give You my heart, make it pure and humble like Your Heart. Never allow me to separate from You. Let Your wisdom penetrate my heart so that I may truly be Your voice on earth. Give me a childlike faith so that I may not look for you in the big things, but in the small things in life.

Oh Most High Priest, enflame my heart with the fire of Your love. Lace my heart to Your Heart so that I may always be united with You. Help me to live my daily consecration by abandoning myself to Your care. My adorable Jesus, give me the grace everyday to give You my memory, my liberty, my understanding, my entire will, so that everything I do will be for Your glory. Whatever I have belongs to You, for You have given it to me. I place it in charge of Your Will and offer You everything I have.

Through this act of consecration, deliver me from all evil temptations and surround my heart, mind and body with the glory of Your love, that I may be totally under Your protection. Anoint my entire being with Your holiness so that I may be Your holy priest in this world. Bless me as I walk in Your footsteps, planting the seeds of salvation into every heart that lies open to You.

Oh Jesus, may every Holy Mass that I celebrate become a deeper encounter with You, where no obstacle stands between us. As I embrace Your adorable Body and Blood in Holy Communion, let Your Flesh truly be mingled with mine and Your Blood truly flow in my veins. Oh Jesus, may every holy Mass that I celebrate transform me, a worthless sinner, into a humble servant, that I may look to Holy Mass as my heavenly food.

Oh Jesus, my beloved Brother, may every holy Mass unite Us so close together. Let Your divinity dwell in me and fill my soul with holy inspirations and good impulses. I, _____, consecrate myself to Your Eucharistic and Most Sacred Heart. May my love for You become like a spring whose water never runs dry. May I, _____, live in the garden of Your paradise now and for all eternity. Amen.

Prayer for the Ordination of a Priest

Oh Most Sacred Heart of Jesus, Eternal Priest, keep Thy beloved brother within the shelter of Thy Divine Love. Bless this day in which he is ordained as a beloved priest. Bless and anoint his hands which daily will touch Thy Sacred Body during the celebration of Holy Mass. Keep unstained his thoughts, words and deeds. Bless all his labors with abundant fruit. Keep most holy and pure his heart, and seal it with the sublime holy marks of Thy Glorious Priesthood. Shelter him from the world's darkness through Thy Precious Blood.

May all the souls to whom he ministers be converted and find their way to Your Sacred Heart. Oh Jesus, may Your holy teaching be his light here on earth and the path that he follows. Amen. Oh Most Holy Mary, Mother of all priests, pray for them.

Prayer for Priests

Oh Lord, tonight I pray that you protect every priest under your Heavens. Keep them pure and let them reflect the light of your Son. Console Your lonely priests. Enlighten those priests who have lost their way. Heal your priests who suffer from woundedness of mind, body and spirit. Oh Lord, give Your Divine Light to all Your beloved priests who live in darkness. Bring joy to those priests who are sad and who suffer from depression. Bring Your love and peace to the hearts of all priests.

Oh Lord, God, please do not allow my prayer to go unheard, for Your priests are Your voice on earth. They are Your representatives. Be merciful and loving toward all Your priests, especially those who have abandoned You. Through Your love and mercy help them to be pure and holy. Lord, so many of Your priests have helped and guided me. I thank You for these priests. Lord, this is my prayer for Your priests. Help them and bless them. Let not one of them escape Your love and mercy. Bring them all to Your Eternal Glory. Amen.

Inspired on the Feast of the Precious Blood

Dear Jesus, I thank you for all you have done for me. Take me, Jesus. I offer myself to You all over again. Let me remain with You forever. Make me an instrument of Your peace. Teach me obedience, so that I may do God's Will. Give me an open heart, that I may always be at prayer. Touch my mind Jesus, bless me with the gift of comprehension, so that I may always understand what you teach me. Bless and touch my eyes that I may only see You, my ears that I may only hear Your words, my nose that I may always smell the fragrance of Your Divine Will, my mouth that all I say may be pure and holy. Bless my hands so I may help others, my feet that I may walk towards the path of holiness. Amen.

Prayer in Times of Suffering

Oh Lord, help me to suffer everything with joy, patience and perseverance for the sake of love. Oh Lord, help me to love my crosses, to wish for them, to take pleasure in them, and to be happy to be able to suffer for the love that you, my God, demonstrated by dying on the Cross for love of me.

Oh Lord, help me to find consolation in my suffering. Let me feel the sweetness and happiness in suffering. Help me to know that it is easy to suffer when I suffer with love in my soul. Oh Lord, help me not to fear my crosses, give me the courage to carry my cross. Help me not to escape my crosses, but to make use of them, that they may lead me to Heaven.

Oh Lord, receive me into Your arms. Withdraw me from this world and restore my soul through Your Cross, which I embrace with my all. Let all crosses in my life be the ladder which leads me to Heaven. Amen.

Letter from Vicka

Letter from Vicka

Since 1981, Our Lady has been appearing to several individuals on a daily basis in a small village in the south-western Croatian area of former Yugoslavia (now Bosnia). While in Medjugorje for the Thirteenth Anniversary of the apparitions, Janie met with Vicka Ivankovic, (one of the original apparitionists) who continues to visit with Our Lady. After praying together in Vicka's prayer room, Vicka wrote these words for Janie's book.

Bijakovici, June 27, 1994

Our Lady, is, in a special way concerned about young people, families and peace. The young people are in a very, very difficult situation. We can help them with our love and prayers from our hearts.

This is the time of great graces. She wishes that we come back to her messages and that we begin to live them with our whole heart. Our Lady is praying for peace and she is inviting us to pray for her own intentions and that we help her with our own prayers.

Vicka

IN MEMORIAM

*In Memory of Enereo Aguilera
September 25, 1996*

Janie: Today my brother in Christ, Enereo Aguilera went to Heaven to meet our Creator. His time on earth came to an end. He went to his heavenly home where we will all go when Our Lord calls us. I am happy for him, but I feel much sadness and emptiness in my soul. He was dear to me, and we loved each other very much. I am so used to seeing him and his beloved wife. The two were inseparable, they were together everywhere they went. They were always there for us for our prayer meeting and special celebrations. I will miss him dearly. He was loving and kind and filled with the Holy Spirit. He had his wife call me every week to see how I was. They were both very close to my family. We were like family.

Oh Lord, please give me the grace to comfort his wife, daughter and grandson. Bless them in this time of need and be their strength. Cruz will need you dear Lord. She will need you. Blessed Mother, he loved you very much, and he loved your Spouse, the Holy Spirit, so much. Be a Mother to his family in their time of need. Help me, too.

Additional Information

FOR COPIES OF THIS BOOK
CALL OR WRITE TO
ST. DOMINIC MEDIA
P.O. BOX 345
HERNDON, VIRGINIA 20172-0345
Phone: (703) 327-2277
Fax: (703) 327-2888

VISITATION OF THE ARCHANGELS
AND PRAYER MEETING EVERY
FIRST AND LAST THURSDAY OF THE MONTH
AT ST. JULIA'S CATHOLIC CHURCH
900 TILLERY
AUSTIN, TEXAS 78702

Painting of Janie's vision from
Jesus of the Two Hearts. Jesus asked Janie
to have this vision painted. She saw the vision
three times. These words appeared in the vision
each time :
*"There is salvation in this devotion -
to the Two United Hearts."*

Painted by a homeless artist from Austin TX.

Heaven's Messages for The Family Vol. I

How to become the family God wants you to be.

"The future of humanity passes by way of the family" — Pope John Paul II

Families are under attack by the forces of evil. The rise in divorce, spousal violence and child abuse - all point to a situation which makes supernatural intervention appropriate and credible.

Mrs. Janie Garza of Austin, Texas, wife, mother and mystic was chosen by the Lord to be a vessel of simple and holy messages for the family of today. She has been receiving messages and visions since February 15, 1989.

Read and learn about:

- ✞ What the main spiritual attacks are against the family today.
- ✞ The spiritual tools given by Heaven to combat the attacks against the family.
- ✞ What the roles of the husband, wife and children are according to God's divine order.
- ✞ What you can do to protect your marriage and family members.
- ✞ The seven visions about the state of the world and families today.
- ✞ How prayer in each family is the spiritual pre-condition for world peace and the renewal of the universal Church.

Order Form

❑ **Yes**, Please send me ___ copies of *Heaven's Messages for The Family - Volume 1* for $14.95, plus $3.95 shipping and handling within the U.S. Please call for exact foreign shipping rates.

Check or Money Order enclosed. U.S. funds only.

❑ MasterCard ❑ VISA ❑ Discover Expiration Date _____

Card# ☐☐☐☐☐☐☐☐☐☐☐☐☐☐☐☐ (Include all 13 or 16 digits)

Signature (required for credit card orders) _____

Name/Recipient _____

Address _____

City _____ State _____ Zip _____

Work (___) _____ Home (___) _____

Please make checks to **SIGNS AND WONDERS for Our Times**
PO Box 345, Herndon, VA 20172-0345.
For immediate attention, call our Order Department at (703) 327-2277 or
FAX (703) 327-2888
Thank you for your love and support.

THE GREAT SIGN
Messages and Visions of Final Warnings

A Powerful book on God's warnings and great mercy to prepare us, His children for a new Era of Peace. His greatest act of mercy will be a universal warning or illumination of souls, accompanied by a miraculous luminous cross in a dark sky.

This is a book you must read if you want to learn how:

- ✞ The Mother of All Humanity warns her children.
- ✞ Priests must inform and prepare God's people, with faith, hope, love, prayer and sacrifice.
- ✞ The thunder of God's justice will resound and nature will mirror the fury of God's anger, bringing mankind to its knees.
- ✞ Worldwide economic and financial collapse will far surpass anything that has ever happened.
- ✞ The Church and the Pope will be attacked.
- ✞ **The GREAT SIGN, a miraculous, luminous cross in the sky,** will accompany **the warning or illumination of souls**
- ✞ Forces of Antichrist will impose worldwide order and the sign of the beast.
- ✞ The Holy Rosary is a most powerful weapon to strengthen and protect.
- ✞ Christ will end the rebellion and bring a glorious, new Era of Peace for His Father's remnant which remains true.

Order Form

❏ **Yes**, I would like to receive **THE GREAT SIGN!** Please send me ___ copies for $14.95, plus $3.95 shipping and handling within the U.S.
Please call for exact foreign shipping rates.

Check or Money Order enclosed. U.S. funds only.

❏ MasterCard ❏ VISA ❏ Discover Expiration Date _____

Card# ☐☐☐☐☐☐☐☐☐☐☐☐☐☐☐☐ (Include all 13 or 16 digits)

Signature (required for credit card orders) _____

Name/Recipient _____

Address _____

City _____ State _____ Zip _____

Work (____) _____ Home (____) _____

Please make checks to **SIGNS AND WONDERS** for Our Times
PO Box 345, Herndon, VA 20172-0345.
For immediate attention, call our Order Department at (703) 327-2277 or FAX (703) 327-2888
Thank you for your love and support.

Read Tomorrow's News TODAY!

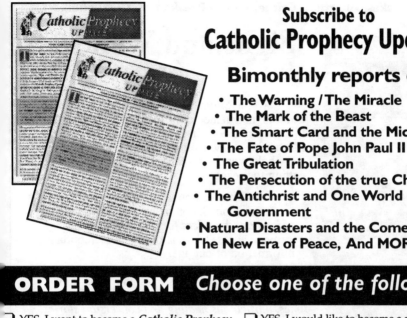

Subscribe to
Catholic Prophecy Update!

Bimonthly reports on:
- The Warning / The Miracle
- The Mark of the Beast
- The Smart Card and the Microchip
- The Fate of Pope John Paul II
- The Great Tribulation
- The Persecution of the true Church
- The Antichrist and One World Government
- Natural Disasters and the Comets
- The New Era of Peace, And MORE!

ORDER FORM *Choose one of the following:*

❑ YES, I want to become a *Catholic Prophecy Partner*. Here is my annual membership of $50.00 and I will receive the *Catholic Prophecy Update* bimonthly. My donation is included in this.

❑ YES, please give a GIFT SUBSCRIPTION to *Catholic Prophecy Update*.
  ❑ U.S.-$50 ❑ Canada-$70 ❑ Foreign-$100

Please send the name, address, telephone, (if applicable) of both sender and recipient.

❑ YES, I would like to become a monthly partner for the *Triumph of the Two Hearts*. Here is my monthly donation:
  ❑ $10 ❑ $20 ❑ $25 ❑ $50 ❑ $100
  ❑ other

❑ YES, I would like the 1997 *Catholic Prophecy Update* Binder - 6 issues in one place for **$49.95** including shipping and handling.

Topics include: the Warning, the Miracle, the Mark of the Beast, the SMART card, the Great Apostasy, the Antichrist and the Triumph.

❑ Check or Money Order. U.S. funds only   Signature _____

❑ MasterCard ❑ VISA ❑ Discover   Expiration Date _____

Card # ❑❑❑❑❑❑❑❑❑❑❑❑❑❑❑❑   (Include entire number, 13 or 16 digits)

My Name/Donor _____

Address _____

City _____ State _____ Zip _____

Work ( ) _____ Home ( ) _____

FAX # ( ) _____ (if this subscription will be received by fax)

Earthquakes. Abortion. Crime. Family Breakdown. Corruption. War.

Signs and Wonders
for our Times

We, at *Signs and Wonders for Our Times* Catholic magazine, know that heaven is intervening in a powerful way. In these end times, our Blessed Mother has come from Heaven with messages for the whole world—revealing secrets of the future and calling for peace.

With the dramatic increase in apparitions occurring on all continents like never before, **Signs and Wonders for Our Times** exists to provide access to some of the most important information of our age.

With the latest messages and visits from heaven, timely features inter-preting the *signs of our times, miraculous healing and conversion stories, church history and devotions,* the all-new children's corner—each issue promises to enrich you spiritually and prepare you for what lies ahead. Be part of Our Lady's army and equip yourself with this powerful evangelization tool!

Subscription Request Form

❏ Yes, sign me up now for a 1 year subscription (four quarterly issues) to *Signs and Wonders for Our Times*. I understand the price is $30 per year for U.S. subscriptions; $40 to Canada; $70 to all other foreign countries.
U.S. Funds Only.

❏ Check or Money Order enclosed. U.S. funds only
❏ MasterCard ❏ VISA ❏ Discover   Expiration Date _____
Card # ☐☐☐☐☐☐☐☐☐☐☐☐☐☐☐☐ (Include all 13 or 16 digits)
Signature *(required for credit card orders)* _____

My Name/Recipient _____
Address _____
City_____ State_____ Zip_____
Work ( )_____Home ( ) _____
Phone number is required to process order.

Please make checks to SIGNS AND WONDERS for Our Times • P.O. Box 345, Herndon, VA 20172-0345. For immediate attention, call our Order Department at (703) 327-2277 or FAX (703) 327-2888 Thank you for your love and support.

Tribulations and Triumph

The End of An Evil Era and the Dawn of a New Glorious Time...

Now, a new voice from the American Midwest is added to the Chorus. The Lord is giving an American housewife, Joanne Kriva, words of warning and pleas for peace—and imparting details of events that will soon overtake the world. Joanne's new volume focuses on the messages she received from Our Lord and Lady between February 1995 to August 1996.

Read and Learn:
- why the apparitions of Our Lady are about to close;
- the dangers that threaten Pope John Paul II—and his place-within the Divine Providence;
- how the Antichrist is alive and plotting to fully exert his power in the world;
- how destruction will be unleashed on a scale never before witnessed in human history;
- what glorious era awaits those who remain faithful during these troubled times.

Book Order Form

☐ Yes, I would like to receive *Tribulations and Triumph*! Please send me _____ copies of Volume 1 for $11.95 and _____ copies of Volume 2 for $4.95, plus $2.95 shipping and handling for the first copy and $1.00 for each additional copy sent within the US. Please call for exact foreign shipping rates..

☐ Check or Money Order enclosed. U.S. funds only

☐ MasterCard ☐ VISA ☐ Discover   Expiration Date _____

Card # ☐☐☐☐☐☐☐☐☐☐☐☐☐☐☐☐ (Include all 13 or 16 digits)

Signature *(required for credit card orders)* _____

My Name/Recipient _____

Address _____

City_____ State_____ Zip_____

Work ( ) _____ Home ( ) _____

Please make checks to SIGNS AND WONDERS for Our Times • P.O. Box 345, Herndon, VA 20172-0345. For immediate attention, call our Order Department at (703) 327-2277 or FAX (703) 327-2888 Thank you for your love and support.

Warnings, Visions & Messages

Father Hebert has written another
BLOCKBUSTER!

A comprehensive overview of the visions, messages and warnings given to various Irish visionaries today about the times we are in; warnings, visions, and messages for the entire world.

Our Lord and his Blessed Mother are warning Mankind before Chastisement disasters strike.

The famous "Our Lady of Knock" silent apparitions of 1879 that opened the Apocalyptic Times blend today with new apparitions, urgent messages and merciful warnings of a Great Chastisement, if the warnings are not heeded.

READ AND LEARN ABOUT:
- *Miraculous phenomena and movements of statues documented on video.*
- *Irish children witnessing biblical visions and warnings of impending judgment if Mankind does not repent.*
- *Christine Gallagher, one of the greatest mystics, stigmatists and visionaries of our times; visionaries Beulah Lynch and Mark Trainer from Bessbrook, Ireland receive Apocalyptic visions and messages of great disasters.*
- *Visions of the Great Era of Peace*

Book Order Form

☐ Yes, I would like to receive *Warnings, Visions & Messages*! Please send me _____ copies for $9.95, plus $2.95 shipping and handling within the US. Please call for exact foreign shipping rates.

☐ Check or Money Order enclosed. U.S. funds only

☐ MasterCard ☐ VISA ☐ Discover   Expiration Date _____

Card # ☐☐☐☐☐☐☐☐☐☐☐☐☐☐☐☐   (Include all 13 or 16 digits)

Signature *(required for credit card orders)* _____

Name/Recipient _____
Address _____
City _____ State _____ Zip _____
Work ( ) _____ Home ( ) _____

Please make checks to SIGNS AND WONDERS for Our Times • P.O. Box 345, Herndon, VA 20172-0345. For immediate attention, call our Order Department at (703) 327-2277 or FAX (703) 327-2888 Thank you for your love and support.